THE TWO HORIZONS OLD TESTAM

J. GORDON MCCONVILLE and CRAIG BARTHOLOMEW, *General Editors*

Two features distinguish THE TWO HORIZONS OLD TESTAMENT COMMENTARY series: theological exegesis and theological reflection.

Exegesis since the Reformation era and especially in the past two hundred years emphasized careful attention to philology, grammar, syntax, and concerns of a historical nature. More recently, commentary has expanded to include social-scientific, political, or canonical questions and more.

Without slighting the significance of those sorts of questions, scholars in THE TWO HORIZONS OLD TESTAMENT COMMENTARY locate their primary interests on theological readings of texts, past and present. The result is a paragraph-by-paragraph engagement with the text that is deliberately theological in focus.

Theological reflection in THE TWO HORIZONS OLD TESTAMENT COMMENTARY takes many forms, including locating each Old Testament book in relation to the whole of Scripture — asking what the biblical book contributes to biblical theology — and in conversation with constructive theology of today. How commentators engage in the work of theological reflection will differ from book to book, depending on their particular theological tradition and how they perceive the work of biblical theology and theological hermeneutics. This heterogeneity derives as well from the relative infancy of the project of theological interpretation of Scripture in modern times and from the challenge of grappling with a book's message in Greco-Roman antiquity, in the canon of Scripture and history of interpretation, and for life in the admittedly diverse Western world at the beginning of the twenty-first century.

THE TWO HORIZONS OLD TESTAMENT COMMENTARY is written primarily for students, pastors, and other Christian leaders seeking to engage in theological interpretation of Scripture.

Hosea

Bo H. Lim and Daniel Castelo

WILLIAM B. EERDMANS PUBLISHING COMPANY
GRAND RAPIDS, MICHIGAN / CAMBRIDGE, U.K.

Published 2015 by
Wm. B. Eerdmans Publishing Co.
2140 Oak Industrial Drive N.E., Grand Rapids, Michigan 49505 /
P.O. Box 163, Cambridge CB3 9PU U.K.

Printed in the United States of America

21 20 19 18 17 16 15   7 6 5 4 3 2 1

Library of Congress Cataloging-in-Publication Data

Lim, Bo H.
    Hosea / Bo H. Lim and Daniel Castelo.
        pages   cm.   — (The two horizons Old Testament commentary)
    Includes bibliographical references.
    ISBN 978-0-8028-2700-5 (pbk.: alk. paper)
    1. Bible Hosea — Commentaries.   2. Bible Hosea — Theology.
    I. Castelo, Daniel, 1978-   II. Title.

    BS1561.53.L56   2015
    224′.607 — dc23

                                                                2015020472

www.eerdmans.com

To Robert W. Wall

Contents

Contents

Abbreviations

AB	Anchor Bible
ABD	*Anchor Bible Dictionary.* Edited by David Noel Freedman. 6 vols. New York, 1992
ACCS OT	Ancient Christian Commentary on Scripture Old Testament
ANE	Ancient Near East
ANF	*Ante-Nicene Fathers*
AOAT	Alter Orient und Altes Testament
ArBib	The Aramaic Bible
ARS	*The Art of Reading Scripture.* Edited by Ellen F. Davis and Richard B. Hays. Grand Rapids, 2003
BibInt	*Biblical Interpretation*
BibOr	Biblica et orientalia
BR	*Biblical Research*
BTH	*Between Two Horizons.* Edited by Joel B. Green and Max Turner. Grand Rapids, 2000
BZAW	Beihefte zur Zeitschrift für die alttestamentliche Wissenschaft
CBQ	*Catholic Biblical Quarterly*
CCSL	Corpus Christianorum: Series latina. Turnhout, 1953-
ConBOT	Coniectanea biblica: Old Testament Series
COS	*The Content of Scripture.* Edited by W. W. Hallo. 3 vols. Leiden, 1997-
CurBR	*Currents in Biblical Research*
DTIB	*Dictionary of Theological Interpretation of the Bible.* Edited by Kevin J. Vanhoozer. Grand Rapids, 2005
FAT	Forschungen zum Alten Testament
FCB	Feminist Companion to the Bible
FOTL	Forms of the Old Testament Literature

HBM	Hebrew Bible Monographs
HBT	*Horizons in Biblical Theology*
HSM	Harvard Semitic Monographs
HTS	Harvard Theological Studies
ICC	International Critical Commentary
Int	*Interpretation*
JBL	*Journal of Biblical Literature*
JNSL	*Journal of Northwest Semitic Languages*
JSOT	*Journal for the Study of the Old Testament*
JSOTSup	*Journal for the Study of the Old Testament: Supplement Series*
JTI	*Journal of Theological Interpretation*
LHBOTS	Library of Hebrew Bible/Old Testament Studies
LNTS	Library of New Testament Studies
NCBC	New Century Bible Commentary
NETS	*New English Translation of the Septuagint.* Edited by Albert Pietersma and Benjamin G. Wright. New York, 2007
NICOT	New International Commentary on the Old Testament
NPNF¹	*Nicene and Post-Nicene Fathers,* Series 1
OBO	Orbis biblicus et orientalis
OBT	Overtures to Biblical Theology
OTG	Old Testament Guides
OTL	Old Testament Library
OTS	Old Testament Studies
SBLDS	Society of Biblical Literature Dissertation Series
SBLSymS	Society of Biblical Literature Symposium Series
Scr	*Scriptura*
TA	*Tel Aviv*
TIS	*The Theological Interpretation of Scripture: Classic and Contemporary Readings.* Edited by Stephen E. Fowl. Oxford, 1997
TOTC	Tyndale Old Testament Commentaries
VT	*Vetus Testamentum*
VTSup	Supplements to *Vetus Testamentum*
WBC	Word Biblical Commentary
ZAW	*Zeitschrift für die alttestamentliche Wissenschaft*

Preface

On more than one occasion in the writing of this commentary, we have asked ourselves what we'd gotten ourselves into by agreeing to do it. Writing on Hosea has been immensely challenging for the both of us, but we are more than happy to thank those who supported us throughout this process.

Both Lim and Castelo wish to thank our institutional home for two grants that helped us tremendously. The first was administered by Seattle Pacific's Center for Biblical and Theological Education in 2011. Celeste Cranston and Kelsey Rorem were instrumental in helping us gain this grant, which in turn helped us develop a sense of some of the issues prevalent in the popular reception of Hosea. The second grant was given to us through the Center for Scholarship and Faculty Development, led by Dr. Margaret Diddams. This grant helped us allocate much-needed research time during the summer of 2012. Finally, Lim wishes to thank the Wabash Center for Teaching and Learning in Theology and Religion for a summer research grant in 2012 that further helped him in the research and writing process.

Thanks are due to our families and students as well. Castelo's wife, Kim, had to hear more about Hosea than she cared to at times, but their deeply-shared commitment to the enduring witness of the Old Testament for Christian worship and reflection contributed to some very enjoyable conversations; she was also instrumental in sharing her expertise in marriage and family therapy with him. He also wishes to extend thanks to the Samaritan Class at First Free Methodist Church for allowing him to test ideas about Hosea with them.

Lim wishes to thank his wife, Sarah, for her support and enthusiasm for this project, and her willingness to make family sacrifices for the sake of its success and completion. Also, Lim was very much stimulated and aided in his work by students in his courses on Hosea at Seattle Pacific Seminary in 2011 and 2013. He is grateful for Kelsie Job's assistance in transliterating the Hebrew, and he and Castelo want to thank the School of Theology's librarian extraordinaire, Steve Perisho, for his assistance in research.

We dedicate this volume to Robert W. Wall, a colleague who has been for us more than simply a coworker. Through his influence and under his tutelage, we have learned to appreciate and extend the practice of theological interpretation. In this sense, we are his students. But he has also managed to treat us as his equals, something remarkable given his seniority in relation to us and his own professional accomplishments. Therefore, he has proven to us to be a worthy mentor. In fact, on countless occasions, he has seen more in us than we saw in ourselves. He championed our gifts and made it known to others and to us that our future was promising, thereby engendering in us profound gratitude, not only for the pedigree of scholar he is, but also for the kind of supportive person and faithful disciple he demonstrates himself to be. Vocationally, he has modeled what a teacher-scholar can look like: A doctor of and for the church who does not give way to a soft piety at the expense of probative and deliberate reasoning since (as he would say) God is a hard rationalist (at least — we would add — in qualified form). We count him not only a dear friend but a holy and devoted brother in Christ. Thank you, Rob, for your life, ministry, and work. You will always be a significant influence upon us for what we think as scholars, how we believe as Christians, and who we are as Jesus' disciples.

BHL and DC
Seattle, Washington
2015

1. Theological Interpretation and the Book of Hosea

Daniel Castelo

Many have welcomed the momentum associated with the theological interpretation of Scripture; others have not. On the one side, students of Scripture have found a disciplinary orientation that can account for the role the Bible plays in their piety and devotion; for others, this approach is the weakening of a resilience forged over centuries to give some legitimacy to biblical studies as a valid discipline in the academy. The conflict is largely an "in-house" affair, and as with all family disputes, this one can occasion mistrust and a fair degree of antipathy and pain. After all, the two camps are in a sense fighting over the same turf: the proper way to approach the reading of the Bible. Both sides are vying for the hermeneutical privilege of determining the way Scripture is fittingly read and understood.

This division — between those who are favorable to theological interpretation, and those who are not — is far from the only point of conflict within the discipline of biblical studies today, yet it is that division which the present volume, as a contribution to the Two Horizons Old Testament Commentary Series, seeks to address. As an endeavor within the field of theological interpretation, and given this strife-laden context of academic biblical interpretation, this commentary ought to demonstrate to some degree what it aims to accomplish and how it intends to do so. Part of this process involves taking inventory of the many ways this volume could be pursued, and giving a rationale for why it will proceed in the way that it does.

Theological Interpretation

Part of the difficulty with writing a commentary that aims to be an exercise in "theological interpretation" is getting a hold of what that phrase actually means. "Theological interpretation" could signify any number of possibilities, since the approach focuses more on exegetical goals than exegetical methods.[1] Presumably, these goals could be achieved by any number of means, so the phrase retains some level of methodological ambiguity.

"Interpretation"

Take for instance the notion of "interpretation." Interpretation is tied to the apprehension of meaning, yet how one goes about demarcating meaning in the hermeneutical process is a complicated affair. Stephen Fowl mentions the possibilities of determinate, anti-determinate, and underdeterminate strategies in biblical interpretation.[2] The first negotiates a text's meaning as requiring unsheathing and excavation, the second operates out of a sensibility of resisting predetermined meanings, and the third seeks to locate meaning in the motives behind the way texts are used, rather than attributing one meaning to the text itself. Within each of these approaches, the notion of "meaning" is up for grabs, and one could easily say that efforts that pursue a "theological interpretation" of the Bible could employ each of these possibilities and still be considered as properly meriting the designation. Nevertheless, as one can see, each possibility represents a very different hermeneutical strategy, and the results of such varied approaches would themselves be manifold.

The determinate approach is fascinating in that it enjoys wide appeal among self-identified "conservatives" and "liberals" alike. This view's proponents find meaning to be rooted in a text, yet always contingent on its authorial, historical, and linguistic embeddedness. In short, this hermeneutical strategy is largely a contextualizing endeavor, one that emphasizes the historical "otherness" of a text. Such a method attempts to counteract the destabilization of interpretation owing to factors such as cultural and reader-related contingencies. Linguistics, anthropology, archaeology, and a host of other fields can be jointly employed to depict the historical situatedness of the text, allowing it in turn to speak for itself in what is hoped is an unobstructed and pure way. The field of biblical studies under this guise becomes methodologically subsumed under the pursuit of history. Within these concerns, meaning is understood to be something empirically available to all so that facts are understood to exist and bias, it is fideistically assumed, can be overcome.[3]

1. See Michael J. Gorman, *Elements of Biblical Exegesis* (rev. and exp. ed.; Peabody: Hendrickson, 2009), pp. 145-46.

2. *Engaging Scripture* (Malden: Blackwell, 1998), chapter 2.

3. For a helpful summary, see Joel B. Green, *Practicing Theological Interpretation* (Grand Rapids: Baker Academic, 2011), p. 46.

These tendencies associated with the historical task are largely constitutive of a modernist and foundationalist epistemological framework, particularly an Enlightenment one.[4] From its own modernist commitments, the determinate approach purports to arrive at a stable meaning of a text via historical excavation and reconstruction stemming from "a peculiarly modern understanding of what historical reality is."[5] Essentially, this perspective understands meaning through a "container" approach;[6] that is, the meaning is contained within the text itself in an empirically discernible, self-regulated form. Such are the epistemological commitments of historical-critical methodologies: They tend to assume that texts should be read as historical artifacts, and the hard work of immersing oneself as much as possible into conditions and contexts in which a text was written is the key to establishing the text's meaning.[7] This process, as Brian Daley notes, is conducted

> as far as possible under the same standards of evidence and verifiability as those used in the laboratory; historical reality — like physical reality — is assumed to be in itself something objective, at least in the sense that it consists in *events* independent of interests and preconceptions of the scholar or narrator, accessible through the disciplined, methodologically rigorous analysis of present evidence such as texts, artifacts, and human remains. For this reason, the establishment and interpretation of texts from earlier ages, like the study of material archaeological evidence, is understood to be an inductive process governed by the rules of logic, the recognition of natural cause and effect, the assignment of probability based on common human experience. As a result, modern historical

4. We realize that, with sweeping narrations of this kind, nuance has a way of dwindling to dangerous registers of near-nonexistence. Alternative possibilities exist, for instance, in terms of the origins of historical-critical methodologies, including the Protestant Reformation and the Renaissance. Our focus on the Enlightenment partially stems from the affinity one senses between the Enlightenment project and various approaches to biblical studies that have proliferated since this period in the academy. For surveys of such developments, see Michael C. Legaspi, *The Death of Scripture and the Rise of Biblical Studies* (Oxford Studies in Historical Theology; Oxford: Oxford University Press, 2010) and Jonathan Sheehan, *The Enlightenment Bible* (Princeton: Princeton University Press, 2005).

5. Brian E. Daley, SJ, "Is Patristic Exegesis Still Usable?" in *ARS*, p. 71.

6. Green, *Practicing Theological Interpretation*, p. 77.

7. This strategy, however, can buckle under its own assumptions since whatever is said at this juncture is often determined by limited evidence and presumed judgments, which in turn collectively serve as an evaluative mechanism for other data; in other words, whereas objectivity is striven for, oftentimes a vicious circularity is at play in this approach. See Green, *Practicing Theological Interpretation*, p. 50.

criticism — including the criticism of biblical texts — is *methodologically* atheistic.[8]

In this regard, the Bible should be read "like any other book."[9] It should be exposed to scrutiny of the highest standards, for it is a text that for far too long has been given a place of privilege. This in turn has perpetuated both ignorance and bias, both of which facilitate the employment of the Bible for self-interested, power-laden ends. In this sense, historical-critical methods aim to make the Bible a "strange" text, allowing for "interpretation" to have some relative independence outside of the aims and agendas of interpreters.

These commitments to the determinate meaning are held not only by those thinking that the Bible is primarily a collection of ancient texts and that interpretation is largely a historical affair, but also by those who seek to establish the Bible as God's — and by implication, many would say, "universal" — truth. In order to safeguard authoritative legitimacy (usually through the language of "inspiration," "infallibility," or "inerrancy"), many scholars on this side of the debates 1) pursue historical verification of figures, 2) sustain word studies so as to find linguistic similarities and connections across ancient Near Eastern cultures, and 3) maintain a commitment to the original manuscripts or autographs. They see Scripture as an epistemic foundation from which doctrines and practices can be drawn.[10] Despite affirming the authority of these texts as "the Word of God," these scholars and believers assume this particular paradigm of meaning-generation so as to create theological space for their commitments regarding Scripture. Therefore, the appeals that are made by these more conservative scholars are similar to the ones made by those on the liberal side; in both cases, history and modernist approaches to knowledge suggest the way forward in establishing the Bible's meaning and Scripture's authority overall.

This privileging of the historical for the meaning of texts implicitly contributes to a "muddy ditch" between "what the text meant" and "what it can mean today." This division has reigned supreme within the academy of biblical studies, and it is still very much detectable on the contemporary scene. Through this bifurcation, "what the text meant" is the proper domain of biblical scholars

8. Daley, "Is Patristic Exegesis Still Usable?" p. 72.

9. Usually this phrase is associated with Benjamin Jowett. For a recent historical and critical analysis of the claim, see R. W. L. Moberly, "'Interpret the Bible Like Any Other Book'?" *JTI* 4 (2010): 91-110.

10. Unfortunately, the movement is unidirectional — from Scripture to doctrines and practices, and not vice versa; see Fowl, *Engaging Scripture*, p. 34. This foundationalist account of Scripture could not exist apart from modernist sensibilities and commitments.

trained in historical-critical methodologies, and they in turn create the baseline that subsequent readers of the text have to observe in order for their reading to avoid randomness and bias and truly be intellectually respectable in nature. This presentation of the matter, however, naturally contributes to the text's contemporary marginalization, given that the "application" or appropriation is considered artificial with respect to its true meaning because it involves an additional, subsequent step in relation to primordial historical investigation. Within such conditions, the text's relevance is cast as idiosyncratic to the reader's experience and purposes. The bias here is that Scripture meant something determinate in the past, and only in meaning something in the past can it mean something (if anything) today.

What is often missing from this commitment to the determinate meaning approach is a sense of how tentative was the Enlightenment project that brought about such a pursuit of meaning in the first place.[11] Far too often, those who pursue a text's contextual localization fail to question not only the degree to which one can know "what it meant" but, more pertinently, why that pursuit is legitimate in the first place as a way of securing meaning. In this shared neglect, historical-critical methodologies, as well as those pursuits that require complex and foundationalist accounts of Scripture's inspiration or inerrancy, are simply mirror images of one another or nonidentical offspring of the modern spirit. The way these traditions of investigation and interpretation establish the legitimacy of their pursuits is through an assumed intellectual tradition that has its roots in the modern era.

Especially worrisome about the determinate approach generally is the neglect of a self-awareness that recognizes its own dependence on a particular intellectual formulation. Through such refusal, proponents often employ such modifiers as "scientific,"[12] "scholarly," and "academic" as suitable self-descriptors. In other words, the tendency by these academicians is to assume that their approach is a pedigreed one within the scholarly project. To take one prominent example, Michael Fox has repeatedly been quoted by theological interpreters for claiming that faith-based study has no "place" in academic scholarship because it is, at the end of the day, not scholarly at all.[13] Historical-critical

11. We realize that we ourselves make this critique in an "Enlightenment spirit," one that recognizes the self-interest of those with power or influence; for this reason, we hold to the commitment that one cannot thoroughly return to a pre-modern, pre-critical situation, as advantageous as it was in certain aspects.

12. Here we mean the typical way of understanding this term in English and not the wide range of meanings that the German term *wissenschaftlich* and its various renderings and mutations suggest.

13. See Green (*Practicing Theological Interpretation*, p. 7) for one such instance. Michael V. Fox,

methodologies are still preferred within the academy[14] as a way to secure the autonomy of biblical studies and so avoid the "bias" of theological readings. Scholars, in other words, often see this privileging as a way to secure their methodological independence as academics. The troublesome feature of such privileging, however, is precisely its presumption. Such accounts often assume that theirs is the only way to establish a non-biased reading of ancient texts. But the assumption of non-bias is not only unsustainable; it is itself one of the worst kinds of biases because of its resistance and denial of its own particularity and contingency.[15]

For this reason, the "critical turn" in biblical interpretation is to be welcomed, in that it allows for an ongoing assessment of the reader's location and aims within the interpretive task. This critical awareness marks the other two approaches outlined by Fowl — the anti-determinate and underdeterminate perspectives — in varying degrees because both resist the totalizing closures associated with determinate readings. This kind of critical localization of the interpreter — not simply vis-à-vis his or her historical and cultural embeddedness, but also in terms of the reader's aims, goals, and purposes — has in turn enabled the gesture toward theological interpretation of Scripture to have intellectual merit despite the prominence of historical-critical methodologies. Once the process of interpretation (and not simply the text to be interpreted) has been particularized, multiple readings can be permitted and deemed as significant in the hermeneutical process.

At this point, it is important to register a basic claim that many theological interpreters have made regarding the "whence" of theological interpretation. Essentially, reading the Bible theologically — that is to say, looking to it as Scripture — is a churchly exercise, practice, and art. This particular localization is simply nonnegotiable for theological interpreters: Confessing Christians look to the Bible as sacred text; as such, for them the Bible is Holy Writ or Holy Scripture. Robert Jenson has made the claim as strongly as one

---

"Bible Scholarship and Faith-Based Study: My View," *SBL Forum* (2006), at http://www.sbl-site.org/publications/article.aspx?articleId=490.

14. As John Barton opines in *The Nature of Biblical Criticism* (Louisville: Westminster John Knox, 2007), p. 31. It should be noted that this position is not Barton's per se as his is a nuanced account (note his preference for the term "biblical criticism").

15. One should be cautious here. It could very well be the case that "few biblical critics have ever claimed the degree of objectivity they are being accused of" (Barton, *The Nature of Biblical Criticism*, p. 49). Importantly, a distinction between the terms "objectivity" and "neutrality" is worth making: The former is a requirement of any serious study, whereas the latter is simply a human impossibility. Nevertheless, it has been our experience far too often that historical-critical biblical scholars assume a superiority for themselves based on their preferred methods, ones that are labeled "historical" as opposed to "theological."

could: "The question, after all, is not whether churchly reading of Scripture is justified; the question is, what could possibly justify any other?"[16] Serious attention to the way the church has used this book and its engagement from an ecclesial location can both be forms of scholarship that depend on the critical turn of localizing the whence of interpretation as a whole. To deem an ecclesial reading of the Bible illegitimate on scholarly grounds is to offer a caricature of a deeply rich process that has merit in the field of hermeneutics. The continued privileging of historical-critical methodologies one readily finds within the guild of biblical studies should be esteemed for what it is: a distinct gesture of alignment with one hermeneutical approach, one that has been challenged and itself particularized as an extension of a modernist intellectual agenda; it is one option within the panoply of possibilities available currently within the field of hermeneutics. As Joel Green remarks, "As important as historical investigation and linguistic inquiry are for critical biblical study, they do not exhaust the subject matter of the Bible or the ways in which the biblical materials might be engaged critically or the role of Scripture among God's people."[17]

Once the suggestion is made that multiple kinds of interpretive strategies exist and that the privileging of historical-critical methodologies is a kind of "bias" itself, the matter becomes much more complex. As with so many things in the academy specifically and life generally, one always finds it easier to specify what something is not rather than what it is. And here is where a number of options are available for those claiming to be doing theological interpretation, including allegorical, typological, figurative, and other methods. The range of possibilities can become burdensome since what could emerge are very different outcomes all under the umbrella of theological interpretation. In this sense, the assumed simplicity associated with historical-critical methodologies gains some appeal in light of the overwhelming options that come with the critical turn. After all, the identities of readers, and their interpretive goals, can vary significantly, and this admission in turn destabilizes the pursuit of meaning in the eyes of many, thereby creating the apparent need for a methodology that presumably stabilizes the interpretive task across contextual particularities.

---

16. "Scripture's Authority in the Church" in *ARS*, p. 29. This claim makes sense on the basis that the Bible as a singular entity exists because "the church gathered these documents for her specific purpose: to aid in preserving her peculiar message, to aid in maintaining across time, from the apostles to the End, the self-identity of her message that the God of Israel has raised his servant Jesus from the dead" (p. 27).

17. "The (Re)Turn to Theology," *JTI* 1 (2007): 3.

How Do We Pursue "Interpretation"?

Given this state of affairs and the many possibilities that exist for the term, how do we, the authors of this commentary, pursue "interpretation"? As is clear from what has been said so far, we tend to privilege the critical turn in hermeneutics, and this for a number of reasons. One reason is that we are members of ethnic minority groups that stand in tension with the status quo of the context in which we currently live and work. Given that we continually recognize that dominant narratives tend to collude with power arrangements, we worry about the prevalence of historical-critical methodologies and the totalizing way they are employed in order to render determinate meanings. We recognize that these approaches are highly specialized academic discourses that only a privileged few can engage and sustain. Given how foreign these discourses can be for the communities that claim us, we know all too well that these approaches and their outcomes are limited in their ability to speak and be relevant to various populations, including those on the fringes of a given society.[18] To recall Fowl's typology, we are inclined in some fashion to participate in a species of anti-determinate or deconstructive readings simply because, as a Korean-American (Lim) and a Mexican-American (Castelo), we know first-hand the dangers and occlusions of dominant narratives. These sensibilities in turn contribute to our felt need to hear other voices, voices we may not understand fully but with which we sympathize because of similarities that exist among those who experience marginalization and systemic oppression.[19]

Furthermore, we are both academicians, teaching at this time at the same Christian university. We make our living by nuancing, debate, and argumentation because we are part of a guild that fosters such activities. For this reason, we do not wish to dismiss entirely what we believe to be the achievements of historical-critical scholarship of the Bible. Quite the contrary, one of us in particular (Lim) will use these to make cases for certain readings and approaches to Hosea particularly and the prophets generally. We believe that it is impossible

18. For a treatment of these challenges, see Miguel De La Torre, *Reading the Bible from the Margins* (Maryknoll: Orbis, 2002).

19. Through this admission, we do not presume to understand all marginalized voices and the contexts and particularities in which they emerge. One deficiency that we are highly cognizant of when speaking of Hosea is that of gender. We realize as males that we are oftentimes unbeknownst beneficiaries and perpetuators of patriarchal arrangements. What we wish to express at this point is that we have some sensitivity to the marginalization of the few by the many given our own location, and we wish to honor such complexities to the degree that we can as we comment on a biblical book that has been marked significantly in the current literature by concerns surrounding gender, trauma, and violence.

to return to a pre-critical situation for Bible study, as "superior" as this approach may have been in some ways when compared to contemporary approaches.[20] But we also realize that the era that succeeded it — modernity — is increasingly becoming particularized and so it too cannot claim unquestionable predominance any longer. In this regard, we hope to employ a variety of strategies since we realize that any single one on its own can only do so much.

As academicians, we also have an abiding appreciation for interdisciplinarity. This posture is partly reflected in our friendship. One of us is an Old Testament scholar (Lim); the other is a theologian (Castelo). We recognize the gifts of the other *and* the legitimacy of the other's place at the table when reading Scripture. We are not proprietary when it comes to our areas of specialization and the consequences these would have for our work in biblical interpretation. Lim does not approach Bible study in such a way as to create a foundationalist account upon which Castelo must rely. Neither does Castelo see his expertise as the only disciplinary outlook by which to make these texts do theological work within the contemporary scene. We see our scholarly undertakings as complementary, and we can do so partly because of the friendship we have forged through many years, but also because of the intellectual culture that exists at our institutional home.

We come from ethnic minority backgrounds, we are academicians, we are friends and colleagues, but we are also churchmen. Our parents are ministers, we grew up in the church, and we in turn have attended, been members of, and even worked on the pastoral staffs of local churches. Through such experiences, we recognize that the church can be part of the problem of marginalizing foreign or unaccepted voices and of perpetuating oppression, injustice, and class distinctions. However, the church can also, by the grace of God, be a source of healing and redemption so as to demonstrate another way of sustaining a communal form of life. For this reason, our churchmanship is vitally constitutive of our approach to biblical interpretation in this commentary.[21] In fact, of the three descriptors mentioned above, we especially value our churchmanship for the task before us because of the understanding we perpetuate for our vocation as scholars who produce material evidences (such as this volume) of our collective reasoning. Simply put, we consider ourselves doctors of the church catholic, called by God to serve God's people and to

20. The allusion is to David C. Steinmetz's piece, "The Superiority of Pre-Critical Exegesis," which can be found in a number of venues, including *TIS*, pp. 26-38.

21. This approach is also in keeping with the guiding aims of the Two Horizons Commentary series, one that "seeks to reintegrate biblical exegesis with contemporary theology in the service of the church" (Joel B. Green and Max Turner, "New Testament Commentary and Systematic Theology" in *BTH*, p. 2).

hallow God's name.[22] Our first allegiance is not to our ethnic/minority communities, nor to the academic guild per se, but to the people of God. This is a group that can and does include minority and academic voices, but does so in a way that re-narrates their significance so that the barriers and violence that these human localities often carry need not be hindrances to the perpetuation of the life-giving gospel. We are convinced of the power of the triune God to re-narrate and heal personal identities, thought forms, and group dynamics, because we are witnesses to its transformative potential.

Because of this self-understanding we share, our work here mostly falls into Fowl's third category, the underdetermined approach. This outlook actively and explicitly foregrounds the interpretive aims, interests, and practices of the interpreters themselves so that clarity and transparency are involved in the hermeneutical task. In this sense, when we come to the reading of the Bible, we — in all of the dynamics of our embeddedness shared above — see it as Sacred Scripture, as "the Word of God for the people of God." To quote one of our colleagues, "Scripture's legal address is the worshiping community, where biblical interpretation helps to determine what Christians should believe and to enrich their relations with God and neighbor."[23] Under the prompting of the Spirit, the people of God wrote these texts, collected them, recited them, and preserved them since they were seen as "useful for teaching, for reproof, for correction, and for training in righteousness" (2 Tim 3:16). Holy Scripture emerges within and is directed back to the church as a means of grace to lead God's people into all righteousness. For this reason, we operate out of a hermeneutic of trust rather than one of suspicion or indifference,[24] for these texts can and do contribute to the sanctification and healing both of the church and the world. Our reading of Hosea is pursued with precisely these aims and commitments at the forefront of our consciousness.

Our admission of these claims from the start sets up a trajectory that has specific hermeneutical implications. As we have noted, interpretation is significantly conditioned by "interested readers," but it also involves the text or object in question as something distinct from the reader's gaze. We are "critical realists" in this sense since we pursue understanding as "the event of the interpenetration of horizons."[25] Given what we have remarked of Scripture's identity and role within the life of the church in the preceding paragraph, the

22. To use Stanley Fish's terminology, this is our primary "interpretive community" (*Is There a Text in This Class?* [Cambridge: Harvard University, 1982]).

23. Robert W. Wall, "Reading the Bible from within Our Traditions," in *BTH*, p. 90.

24. For a helpful taxonomy of possible interpretive postures, see Gorman, *Elements of Biblical Exegesis*, pp. 140-43.

25. Daley, "Is Patristic Exegesis Still Usable?" p. 73.

interpretive process can subsequently be cast with some degree of specification as an aim emerging from this interpenetration of horizons. As "the Word of God for the people of God," this text cannot be approached simply like any other text. To a certain degree it has to be approached as a text *qua* text to be sure, but that orientation is not all-determinative given Scripture's character and role within the church. Speaking to these matters, Joel Green offers a useful definition for the kind of interpretation we are seeking to foster: "A theological hermeneutics of Christian Scripture concerns the role of Scripture in the faith and formation of persons and ecclesial communities. Theological interpretation emphasizes the potentially mutual influence of Scripture and doctrine in theological discourse and, then, the role of Scripture in the self-understanding of the church and in critical reflection on the church's practices."[26] These reflections highlight strongly the "whence" of theological interpretation, namely the church. As such, theological interpretation stems from, and is directed to, confessional communities. It is a kind of practice that involves "those habits, dispositions, and practices that Christians bring to their varied engagements with Scripture so they can interpret, debate, and embody Scripture in ways that will enhance their journey toward their proper end in God."[27]

"Theological"

If "interpretation" is a complicated matter to consider, the qualifier "theological" is equally challenging. As with hermeneutics, a bevy of methodological concerns also occupies those who engage in theological studies. Following the lead of one of its most distinguished current-day practitioners, one can say that "systematic theology occupies itself more generally with Christian claims about reality."[28] These claims in turn constitute Christian teaching. Staying true to its etymological roots, theology should have as its focus Christian teaching about God and all else there is, but often, as the term is instantiated and embedded in intellectual pursuits, it can mean any number of more particular concerns and agendas. Part of this diversity is due to "judgments reached about the sources, norms, and ends of systematic theology, and about its relation to other spheres of intellectual activity."[29] Different practitioners of theology privilege different

26. "The (Re)Turn to Theology," 2.

27. Stephen Fowl, *Theological Interpretation of Scripture* (Eugene: Cascade, 2009), p. 14.

28. John Webster, "Introduction: Systematic Theology," in *The Oxford Handbook of Systematic Theology* (ed. John Webster, Kathryn Tanner, and Iain Torrance; Oxford: Oxford University Press, 2007), p. 1.

29. Webster, "Introduction: Systematic Theology," p. 2.

features of the "source-norm-end" triad, and once one feature is privileged in a certain way and direction, the others follow quite naturally along such paths, leading to a splintering of the theological task as it is pursued and negotiated publicly today. Some might privilege a particular document or collection of documents, others a particular group's experience. As these emphases and judgments are pursued and over time retain a certain level of inviolability, they give rise to a number of subfields that become areas of specialization in their own right. For this reason, various schools of theological thought and reflection have emerged, and often they appear and sound more like different worlds or languages than aspects of a single pursuit. A Thomist, liberationist, Barthian, and Tillichian may in their own minds be pursuing a single task that can be called "theology," but one wonders if a single term can accommodate the wide diversity that exists within the field today.

Among those who advocate theological interpretation, certain theological commitments are often sustained and assumed, but rarely are these brought to light for what they are. For instance, the consultation that worked on "The Scripture Project" and yielded the generative volume *The Art of Reading Scripture* distilled their work into nine theological theses that in turn introduce the volume. The first thesis runs, "Scripture truthfully tells the story of God's action of creating, judging, and saving the world," with a further elaborative sentence suggesting that "God is the primary agent revealed in the biblical narrative."[30] As compelling as these claims may be to certain readers, they are specific ones that are readily available in certain theological orientations more so than others.[31] To say that "God is the primary agent revealed in the biblical narrative" implies that God presents Godself as an object to be known within the pages of the Bible. In other words, God is active, God is knowable, and God does things. All these claims are legitimated by particular faith commitments related to the veracity of the biblical witness and its function as a revelatory set of texts.

For some, this kind of characterization of God's role within biblical interpretation is dangerous. Issues of projection, anthropomorphism, philosophical and cultural dependence, and a host of others easily come to mind. One need not look further than the book of Hosea for warrants related to these concerns. For instance, if one were to say that God really proclaimed and commanded the things that God is portrayed as saying and doing in this book, how can a coherent picture of God be maintained across the two testaments? We raise such

---

30. "Nine Theses on the Interpretation of Scripture: The Scripture Project," in *ARS*, p. 1.

31. The claims in this volume show, *inter alia,* an occasional Barthian sensibility. Daniel J. Treier explores the Barthian connection to theological interpretation in *Introducing Theological Interpretation of Scripture* (Grand Rapids: Baker Academic, 2008), pp. 14-19. Of course, Roman Catholics have their own twentieth-century influences, most notably the *ressourcement* approach.

a concern simply to point out that theological readings of Scripture do carry assumptions about the theological task that may not be conducive or amenable to certain ways that theology is pursued today. This situation alone contributes significantly to why certain theological orientations have been slow to adopt this hermeneutical strategy.

Assumptions related to God and God's role and availability within the text are not the only ones that typically make theological interpretation so distinctive. Another consideration is at play, and this one we will label the "whither" of theological interpretation. We have already alluded to the "whence" of theological readings of the Bible, but now we must point to the other "end" of the matter: Why, after all, do Christians read Scripture? What is the point of periodically reading this ancient text that, at the end of the day, is difficult to understand and that is removed from us in so many ways? In light of this concern, another major voice in these discussions is worth citing: Kevin Vanhoozer, in his introduction to the *Dictionary for Theological Interpretation of the Bible*, offers that theological interpretation is "biblical interpretation oriented to the knowledge of God."[32] At play with this definition is more than meets the eye. If theological interpretation takes place among the community of Christ followers and within the modality of their common life together — a modality we refer to as "worship" — and if this collective life includes the recitation and reading of a text in which God is the primarily-disclosed agent, then interpreting Scripture is an act of reading unlike any other. Moreover, this reading community is called to be unlike any other community, its worshipful activity is meant to foster an ethos unlike any other, and its end or object is unlike any other. Simply put, if the church and Scripture have as their ultimate source and end the triune God of Christian confession, then their interplay leads to a certain species of knowledge.

God-knowledge is not simply factual or propositional, but is, in some sense, relational, transformational, participatory, and reconstituting for the knower because its object is the source and end of all things. This sensibility is in part an Augustinian one; for example, it is on display as the Latin father deals with hermeneutics in *On Christian Teaching*. For Augustine, the reading of Scripture should promote the love of God, the one who is to be truly and solely loved for one's own sake. As Matthew Levering puts it, "Gaining knowledge of the texts of Scripture means primarily, according to Augustine, gaining a transformative participation in the divine Persons."[33] Therefore, the

32. Kevin J. Vanhoozer, "What Is Theological Interpretation of the Bible?" in *DTIB*, p. 24.
33. *Participatory Biblical Exegesis* (Notre Dame: University of Notre Dame Press, 2008), pp. 69-70.

species of God-knowledge pursued in theological interpretation is of a kind that involves the reordering of the reader's love. Such knowledge cannot be approached "objectively" and from a distance, for it is self-involving and thus self-destabilizing, all toward the goal of the knower loving from a pure heart, a good conscience, and a genuine faith.[34] The whither of theological interpretation is the face of God.

How Are We Inclined "Theologically"?

Rarely in matters related to theological interpretation are its advocates forthcoming regarding their theological commitments, but we find it appropriate to be so here, at least to some degree. Following the lead of the definition and aims of theological interpretation mentioned above, we do believe that, through Scripture, the triune God of Christian confession can be apprehended and heard. From this commitment, several subclaims follow.

First, we believe that the Trinity presents itself within the biblical witness of both the Old and New Testaments. We do not subscribe to supersessionist or dispensationalist approaches to divine revelation, nor do we find it anachronistic to search for the triune God in the Bible, even in the Old Testament or Tanakh. We are of this opinion because "trinitarian faith is predicated not of an otherwise unknown subject, but of the God of Israel."[35] Trinitarianism is not a "new Christian doctrine" that allows the Christian community to dispense with God's self-presentation in the Old Testament, but rather a mechanism of coherence aiming to account for all that Christians wish to say of their God, including that this One is the God of Israel.[36] In this sense, "the doctrine of the Trinity is not and does not seek to be anything but an explanatory confirmation of this name [Yahweh-Kyrios]. This name is the name of a single being, of the one and only Willer and Doer whom the Bible calls God."[37] This move is counterintuitive on a number of levels, not the least of which is the historicist sensibility that would pose such a gesture as an interpretive imposition on the Hebrew Scriptures. But at this point we take exception to such a classification

---

34. This phrasing is an echo of 1 Tim 1:5, to which Augustine alludes at the end of Book One of *On Christian Teaching*; see Augustine, *On Christian Teaching* (trans. R. P. H. Green; New York: Oxford, 1999), p. 29.

35. R. Kendall Soulen, "Theses on YHWH the Triune God," *Modern Theology* 15 (1999): 26.

36. For more on this point, see Daniel Castelo, *Confessing the Triune God* (Eugene: Cascade, forthcoming), chapter 2.

37. Karl Barth, *Church Dogmatics*, I/1 (trans. G. W. Bromiley; Edinburgh: T & T Clark, 1975), p. 348.

of this body of materials: This collection is Tanakh for Jews, and it is the Old Testament for Christians. As such, Christians have retained this collection as Holy Scripture because they believe it bears witness to the God 1) proclaimed by Jesus (as his Father), 2) made visible and exegeted through Jesus (the incarnate Son),[38] and 3) sent by Jesus and his Father as God's ongoing, abiding presence among Jesus' disciples (the Holy Spirit). The thrust of all these commitments is the subsequent, counterintuitive claim we believe to be at the heart of Christian dogmatics: *YHWH is Trinity, and Trinity is YHWH.*

The challenge of such a conviction points to two matters in particular. Through this claim, we hope to preserve insights that Soulen mentions in light of the possibilities inherent to Barth's construct "Yahweh-Kyrios"[39]:

> First, Christian theology is concerned with a God whose revealed name is sufficiently attested only by the "simultaneous" witness of the canon *as a whole*. Second, God's revealed name is attested in a differentiated way that corresponds to the canon's two parts, both of which are, in some sense, equally weighted. Third, God's revealed name as attested by the canon's first part is encapsulated in the name of Israel's covenant God, *Yahweh.*[40]

The value of these insights is that they acknowledge the divine self-presentation in Tanakh as constitutive of what one says about the Christian conception of God. In this way, we can exclude a latent supersessionism that assumes the dispensability of the Old Testament's depiction of YHWH for Christian theology proper.[41] At the same time, Christians come to confess the Trinity through

38. This point is one of the most important features of David Yeago's running argument in "The New Testament and the Nicene Dogma" which can be found in *TIS*, pp. 87-100. Christian trinitarianism works because the Christian claim is not just that YHWH and Jesus' Father are the same entity; rather, trinitarianism receives much of its dynamism by the additional recognition that YHWH and Jesus — as the incarnate Son — are closely aligned as well, a point noticed by Barth in terms of the language of "lordship." To establish the point, Barth remarks, "Jesus is Lord . . . . Now the Christ who reveals the Father is also a creature and His work is a creaturely work. But if He were only a creature He could not reveal God, for the creature certainly cannot take God's place and work in His place. If He reveals God, then irrespective of His creaturehood He Himself has to be God" (*Church Dogmatics*, I/1, p. 406). Richard Bauckham makes a similar point in *Jesus and the God of Israel* (Grand Rapids: Eerdmans, 2008), pp. 24-25.

39. For an elaboration of this Barthian formulation, see R. Kendall Soulen, *The Divine Name(s) and the Holy Trinity* (Louisville: Westminster John Knox, 2011), pp. 95-100.

40. Soulen, "YHWH the Triune God," 37.

41. This neglect was most likely not the case in early Christian practice, since the first Christians probably continued the tradition of avoiding direct use of the Tetragrammaton, yet retained some consciousness of its presence through the use of surrogates (Soulen, *The Divine Name(s) and the Holy Trinity*, p. 11). Of course with time matters changed so that this consciousness waned.

Jesus: As the revelation of God, Christ shapes the dogmatic imagination of believers for their understanding of who God is and what God is like. In this sense, Christ represents a character grid for interpreting the speech and acts of YHWH because Christ is a gloss on that testimony,[42] not as a definitive enactment that makes that witness dispensable (as Soulen fears in terms of an economic supersessionism), but as a "second narrative" that functions as a "disclosure of the architectonic structure of the whole story."[43]

The trajectory of the preceding paragraph extends in such a manner as to give some workable sense of the difficulties laypeople face when reading the Bible "cover to cover." In short, the Jesus of the NT oftentimes appears very different from — maybe even scandalously morally contrasted to — YHWH's presentation in the OT. With the former, one often sees a renunciation of violence and the offering of grace; with the latter, one can see a figure who inflicts judgment and vengeance both on the elect and on the elect's neighbors and enemies. What to make of these discrepancies? First, one has to take into account whether the ways the discrepancies have been constructed are true to the entire witness of the biblical materials. After all, Jesus speaks of hell more than any other voice within the NT, and the great love commandments have their source in the Law of Moses. It is a profane reduction to say that the Old Testament's portrayal of God is one of judgment and that the New Testament's is one of love. Second, and to push the critical angle one degree further, what is problematic to the contemporary reader may not have been problematic for ancient readers of these texts. As a simple case in point: If one were to ask today if a certain text is "patriarchal," the intelligibility of that line of inquiry is more reflective of the one raising the question than the literary or historical features of the text itself since the way "patriarchy" is defined and determined will be largely reader-dependent.

But what is ultimately at issue in these discrepancies between the OT and NT is a theological concern: How can the same God who suffers the cross

---

42. This predominance of Jesus' example is partly due to his own hermeneutical moves. Take for instance the implications of his reply to the lawyer's question regarding the greatest of the commandments for consideration of Jesus' identity and role: Jesus answers with the two love commandments, followed by the interpretatively authoritative phrase, "On these two commandments hang all the law and the prophets" (Matt 22:40).

43. David C. Steinmetz, "Uncovering a Second Narrative," in *ARS*, p. 55. Steinmetz continues: "Therefore, the second narrative quickly overpowers the first in the mind of the reader, who can no longer read the story as though ignorant of its plot and form. *The second narrative is identical in substance to the first* and therefore replaces it, not as an extraneous addition superimposed on the story or read back into it, but as a compelling and persuasive disclosure of what the story was about all along" (p. 55, emphasis added).

be the one who urges Israel to exact violence in certain situations? Christians, particularly in pre-modern forms of biblical interpretation, have repeatedly found themselves "cleaving to Christ" at such moments. "Cleaving to Christ" requires a particular commitment to salvation history in which history is envisioned "not only as a linear unfolding of individual moments, but also as an ongoing participation in God's active providence, both metaphysically and Christologically-pneumatologically."[44] If the incarnation of the Son is a kind of culminating moment of God's healing work, then this event represents a guiding framework through which readers interpret all that preceded and all that has followed in terms of God's self-disclosure and activity. We find this claim to be scriptural itself, as noted in the Emmaus Road encounter in which the resurrected Jesus, "beginning with Moses and all the prophets . . . interpreted to them the things about himself in all the scriptures" (Luke 24:27). This kind of reading strategy, one that is found in a number of places throughout the NT, requires something other than the historicist variety.

Interpreting Scripture this way requires forms of "spiritual reading" (allegory, typology, figuration, and the like) so that chronicity and subsequence give way to providence and having one's eyes opened by Jesus himself.[45] Because of the centrality of Jesus and the challenges this privileging presents for understanding the OT, Robert Louis Wilken can observe that, "over time allegory achieved almost universal acceptance as a way to give the Old Testament a Christian interpretation."[46] These kinds of determinations led Augustine to say that Scripture should lead to the promotion of the love of God and neighbor, and, when it apparently does not, it requires another reading strategy, namely a figurative one.[47] To conclude the point, we believe that Christians cannot read Numbers, Joshua, or Hosea apart from the one they proclaim as Lord,[48] and we hold that the OT offers its own unique witness to Christ, so that "it is not possible to speak of Christ without speaking of him 'in accordance with

44. Levering, *Participatory Biblical Exegesis*, p. 1.

45. See R. W. L. Moberly's masterful elaboration of Luke 24 in *The Bible, Theology, and Faith* (Cambridge: Cambridge University Press, 2000), chapter 2.

46. *The Spirit of Early Christian Thought* (New Haven: Yale University Press, 2003), pp. 70-71.

47. See *On Christian Teaching*, pp. 75-76. We do not endorse this extreme but are highly sympathetic with the Augustinian notion. Of course, reading figuratively has to be a taught and learned practice, and because this kind of formation rarely takes place in the church, we realize that certain ill-advised interpretive traditions of difficult passages take a life all their own. We believe such is the case with Hosea, a point we will pursue in what follows.

48. We find that this strategy is often downplayed because of the regnant historicism that plagues biblical studies, but this issue precisely stresses the need for Christian readings of the OT to be "spiritual" at some points and in varying ways.

the Scriptures.'"[49] The significance of a Christian two-testament Bible cannot be explained away, and its shape is non-reducible. Looking for Jesus in all of the scriptures, therefore, is a practice and a hermeneutical outlook stemming from certain primary theological commitments and forged through centuries of Christian commentary on Scripture. Obviously, this orientation was thoroughly disqualified in modernity, and such a move had deeply destructive implications for theological coherence across the testaments. We are committed to answering the "Who is God?" question by attending to the canon as a whole in a way that is christologically normed and pneumatologically vivified.[50]

Moving to a third point regarding our theological outlook, we wish to point out that the memory of Jesus was maintained during the first couple of centuries of the early church through the apostolic testimony, but this kerygma became embedded not simply in what was emerging as the collection of NT books, but also in formulae and constructs often denominated through the notion of the "rule of faith." Rather than being a simple relationship of antecedence-consequence or cause-effect, both the NT canon and the *regula fidei* ("rule of faith") were simultaneously-emerging and mutually-influencing phenomena.[51] Essentially, each deeply influenced the final shape of the other. The *regula fidei* was in many ways brought to formal expression through the creeds that emerged within Christianity, meaning that these not only helped to influence the historical developments of Scripture's canonization, but also "ruled" or guided the church's reading of Scripture by functioning as a "grammar of theological agreements which Christians confess to be true."[52] Therefore, it is important to note that the "second narrative," that is, the Christ-event, is

---

49. Christopher R. Seitz, *The Character of Christian Scripture* (Studies in Theological Interpretation; Grand Rapids: Baker Academic, 2011), p. 18. This last commitment opens the door for canonical approaches to the text in its final form, and these play an important role in Lim's readings of Hosea in this volume.

50. Soulen's "Theses on YHWH the Triune God" are very helpful, as we just echoed 1.1.1 and 2.4 ("YHWH the Triune God," 44, 46). A helpful reminder Soulen makes with Thesis 2.4.1 is the etymology of Jesus (Y'shua), which is "YHWH saves" (46); this point represents a further connection between YHWH and the Trinity. We take Soulen's point not to be an outright dismissal of the privileging of Jesus, but rather a dismissal of the problematic assumption of the dispensability of the testimony of YHWH — Israel's God — for Christian God-talk, however it be justified.

51. Green, *Practicing Theological Interpretation*, p. 73. The relationship is quite complex, but interestingly enough, as Paul Gavrilyuk points out, for some early Christians (such as Tertullian and Origen), the *regula fidei* was "even more foundational than the words of scripture themselves" since it provided the baseline upon which Scripture could build; see "Scripture and the *Regula Fidei*" in *Canonical Theism* (ed. William J. Abraham, Jason E. Vickers, and Natalie B. Van Kirk; Grand Rapids: Eerdmans, 2008), p. 32.

52. Wall, "Reading the Bible from within Our Traditions," p. 88.

in many ways summarized and brought to a pivotal focus in the proto-creeds or *regulae fidei* that emerged during the church's early history.[53] We acknowledge this development and continue to work within this determined heritage as a way of recognizing "theological boundary markers for Christian identity" and identifying "criteria for assessing the coherence" of our interpretation of Scripture.[54] Nevertheless, within this ruled form of reading we believe that the *regula* "grants us true freedom by guiding us to pursue particular directions of interpretation" in their sundry and rich ways.[55]

Finally, we find the reading of Scripture to be a theological practice because of the person and work of the Holy Spirit, who both inspires and illuminates the reading of these texts.[56] The divine self-presentation is not simply a matter of historical record, so to speak, but very much an ongoing reality experienced through the church's worshipful practice of reading and being addressed by these hallowed texts. Therefore, as important as sundry disciplinary perspectives are to the interpretive process, we hold that what keeps these together and what influences their fitting interpretive sensibilities is the ongoing work of the Spirit's illumination within doxological space. We prayerfully and worshipfully approach these texts because seeing the face of God is not a human achievement; it is a miracle of divine grace. We firmly believe that we need God's help in order to see God in Scripture. For this reason, we hold that the theological reading of Scripture is not simply something one does in order to create a basis for the theological; rather, and more primordially, the act is properly theological to its very core.

The Book of Hosea as Holy Scripture

We have painstakingly taken the trouble to explain what we mean by "theological interpretation" in part because of the difficulty associated with reading the book of Hosea. It is no secret that Hosea poses considerable challenges for its reading and appropriation by the contemporary faithful. Often when scholars evaluate the book, moments and reflections arise that occasion awkwardness

---

53. And, simultaneously, Scripture is needed to substantiate the claims made by these proto-creeds, since their theological communicability and coherence are unavailable when they are considered all-sufficient and isolated from other canonical materials in catechesis. On this score, once again, we are indebted to conversations with our colleague Robert Wall.

54. Wall, "Reading the Bible from within Our Traditions," p. 89.

55. Treier, *Introducing Theological Interpretation of Scripture,* p. 63.

56. This claim is in keeping with Gorman's "charismatic" principle of theological interpretation (*Elements of Biblical Exegesis,* p. 153).

and downright embarrassment. How can Christians today read a book like Hosea that appears so ready-made for misconstrual and misappropriation?

One possible way to answer such concerns is by the realization of just how important and difficult the task is before us. Ellen Davis's claim rings true especially in the case of Hosea: "Interpretation of symbols is the church's most serious and most consequential business."[57] As a book, Hosea is rich with imagery and metaphor,[58] and these are of a species that is difficult to accommodate, much less understand. Prophetic texts generally, and Hosea specifically, are ones brimming with a particular kind of language and style, a type of symbolism that is meant not only to communicate and illustrate, but also to shock, startle, and confuse. A constant with Hosea is that it causes a visceral reaction among its readers. We are inclined to believe that it has always done so, but if so, then the hard work of specification is required: What is a proper or fitting reaction to reading Hosea? To what are readers supposed to be reacting? What are the purposes at play in the use of such symbolism? In short, how is Hosea to be read as Holy Scripture?

We believe that the only way to answer these questions satisfactorily for contemporary readers is via a theological interpretation of Hosea. Without this possibility, other strategies — be they historical, literary, reader-centered, or otherwise — are not enough to make Hosea available as a relevant and compelling text for Christians today. The obstacles are simply that formidable in the case of this book. One of the aims of this volume, then, is the cultivation of certain intuitive registers and intellective sensibilities so that first impressions of this book are not misleading.

In terms of preliminaries, we have structured this volume in the following way: a running commentary on the text (by Lim) with theological essays (by Castelo) interspersed throughout. We are subdividing Hosea into three sections: chapters 1–3, 4:1–11:11, and 11:12–14:19.[59] Each of these sections will be followed by a theological essay that is largely catechetical in nature; as a whole, these catechetical chapters aim to help the reader learn not only about Hosea, but of the God who speaks and works through the testimony of Hosea. Theologically, we have opted to subdivide Hosea in this way partly because we see within each of the sections a movement typically associated with prophetic texts, one that centers on rebellion, judgment, and hope in some sustained way. As a collection of oracles, Hosea is difficult to gauge in terms of streams

57. "Teaching the Bible Confessionally in the Church," in *ARS*, p. 13.

58. In fact, Hosea is understood to express more similes than any other Old Testament writer; see Ernest W. Nicholson, *God and His People* (Oxford: Clarendon Press, 1986), p. 187.

59. Lim will justify this subdivision further in the following chapter on the basis of canonical considerations.

of development, but these three motifs taken collectively are as central as any other set of concerns within the work.

Theologically Situating Hosea

The reader is not given much at the beginning of Hosea to understand the context of the book, but this much is clear early on: The reader is stumbling upon a situation of tension between YHWH and Israel. These two parties have a long history with one another, and it is a relationship marred by unfaithfulness on Israel's side, contrasting with steadfast love on YHWH's. The best way to describe this relationship is that it is one of covenant. Although more will be said of the topic below, we will say now that YHWH fashioned "a (grant) covenant [with Abraham], in which God *obligates himself* to Abraham and his descendants as Lord, Savior, and Protector in promising them a place (land, temple), people (Israel), and blessing (spiritual and material)."[60] Important to note is that YHWH initiates and sustains this covenant, while Israel is to respond in faithfulness in light of it. Time and time again, however, Scripture portrays Israel as failing in its own covenant obligations, a situation which requires some kind of reaction from YHWH. At such crisis moments, YHWH has the choice of either ending the covenant or providing a way forward, and if the latter, the path includes both judgment and restoration. Because of YHWH's own faithfulness to the covenant bond, YHWH repeatedly chooses the latter course of action, but such a move is not to be taken for granted. Given the people's offenses, YHWH is not obligated to continue repairing the covenant bond through YHWH's superabundant mercy and love. Quite the contrary, given that the covenant requires faithfulness from both covenant partners, Israel's defiance and unfaithfulness repeatedly put the covenant — and so Israel's existence — in an exceedingly precarious state.

For this reason, the threefold motif cycle is important to observe and should be felt and imbibed by readers in each of the respective theological moments. In other words, the reader cannot rush through these, assuming that "it will all end well" simply because hope is extended at the end of the cycle. Quite the contrary, YHWH repeatedly and markedly emphasizes each of these conditions throughout Hosea's oracles. As readers, we are to "sit and dwell" in

---

60. Scot McKnight, "Covenant" in *DTIB*, p. 142. McKnight specifies and privileges a grant type of covenant; one should note that other types exist and that this privileging is not without its difficulties. See Scott Hahn, *Kinship by Covenant* (New Haven: Yale University Press, 2009), pp. 29-31.

each of the themes so as to live into their correspondences with our own lives. A certain kind of readerly *naiveté* is in order as one moves through the cycle.

a. Rebellion

The first of the themes, that of rebellion, is to be taken seriously and acknowledged; if this first move is not granted and accepted, then nothing generative can follow. Hosea makes it clear that YHWH finds Israel's behavior intolerable. What, precisely, is the behavior in question? What possibly could excite the ire of God and jeopardize the covenant bond as a result?

Theologians often make the distinction between personal/individual sin and corporate/structural sin. Given the predominance of liberal democratic states, people in the trans-Atlantic North understand, find logical, and are compelled by the idea of personal/individual sin. These are acts undertaken by individual agents for which they are subsequently responsible.[61] For instance, if a person steals an item of merchandise and in turn is caught in the act, that person bears the guilt and burden of making restitution in whatever way the legal processes render fit. That person, and solely that person (unless accomplices were directly involved), is responsible for the grievance. Analogously, when believers sin, the predominant understanding for many Western Christians is of an individual's own moral failure. Undoubtedly, this understanding has to be in the mix with the themes sounded in Hosea, but interestingly enough, this view of sin and unfaithfulness is startlingly de-emphasized. Hosea does not call out particular individuals for their rebellion; rather YHWH's prophet warns and chastises *a people*. The focus of Hosea is corporate/structural sin.

At one level, it is true that individual choices and acts are at the heart of corporate/structural sin, but the matter is further complicated by issues of power, collective force, and time. Corporate sin becomes increasingly tolerated by a culture over time; soon, it constitutes features of socialization that influence subsequent generations. A vicious cycle ensues, in which people are trapped and burdened by collective systems that are implicitly endorsed by both powerbrokers and an increasingly desensitized public. These claims are all

---

61. Michael O. Emerson and Christian Smith highlight this tradition in terms of American evangelicalism and race: "White conservative Protestants are accountable freewill individualists. Unlike progressives, for them individuals exist independent of structures and institutions, have freewill, and are individually accountable for their own actions" (*Divided by Race* [Oxford: Oxford University Press, 2000], pp. 76-77). They go on to make a startling evaluation: "Contemporary white American evangelicalism is perhaps the strongest carrier of this freewill-individualist tradition" (p. 77) in part because the understanding derives from a particular theological outlook.

counterintuitive to those socialized in liberal democracy, but that "unnatural" feel is itself a reflection of the desensitization being mentioned: Our society colludes to make it difficult for an individual to see corporate or institutional sin because of its formative influence upon all of us. Furthermore, we are not inclined to think collectively in the first place, so it is difficult for us to think of collective guilt, responsibility, or sin as a result.[62]

And yet, Hosea's focus is on collective sin and rebellion. Contemporary readers are thus at a significant disadvantage in appreciating the outcry of YHWH against the collective unfaithfulness of the people of Israel. Perhaps a way forward in the midst of this debilitating reality is for one to take inventory of how one's nation, one's city, one's race, one's gender, and one's family have collectively affected — both positively but also (especially for the sake of understanding Hosea) negatively — the surrounding world. Once these sensibilities have been honed to some degree by the active practice of narrating particular cases and circumstances in a sustained and honest way, perhaps one can come to the text with a greater sensitivity to the crises that Hosea highlights. This strategy and others are needed if the reader is to appreciate (to the greatest degree possible) the rebellion that occasions YHWH's judgment in this text.

b. Judgment

Through Hosea, YHWH is judging the people for their collective misdeeds. God's act of judgment is another matter that is difficult for us on the contemporary scene to understand. Often when Western Christians think of judgment today, they think of eternal developments and consequences. The "Final Judgment" inspires a level of apocalyptic fear for some believers, but more broadly, the tendency by many is to think in terms of eternal destinations: Because of God's judgment, we will be eternally blessed in heaven or eternally punished in hell. What is conveniently lacking in this particular depiction is the "here and now." By associating judgment with future events and circumstances, many Christians absolve themselves from the worry that God's judgment can be at work in their everyday affairs. If people intuitively believe that God does not judge now but only later, then the urgency of Hosea's message for Israel is devastatingly muted for contemporary hearers.

Why are so many Christians inclined to think of judgment in such futuristic — and so, to some degree, reductive and innocuous — ways? Once again,

---

62. A work that explores this condition is Hugh Heclo, *On Thinking Institutionally* (Boulder: Paradigm, 2008).

processes of socialization and cultural formation may come into play. For those who are products of late capitalism, rising secularism, and liberal democracy, the tendency is to think that Christianity is an option that people choose because "it does something" for them; people are "consumers" of religion. Of course, followers of a religion like Christianity have to be compelled by it at some level such that this worldview and spirituality grant meaning to one's life. But is that meaning "consumed," so to speak? What is meant by that phrasing is the tendency we have, forged through practices and influences of late capitalism, to consider our allegiances and adherences as commodities we obtain and keep.[63] Faith, in this sense, is not something that has us but something that we come to have at some point in our lives because "it works" or "it makes us feel good."[64] And given that we obtain it, we are inclined to think (most likely subconsciously) that we can constrain and shape it in ways that best suit us, our desires, and our aspirations.

To put the matter poignantly, a God who judges now is not only inconvenient to Westerners today but in some deeper sense highly illogical. God's judgment does not fit well with the idea of modern progress and therapeutic affirmation, and we may find it easier to dispense with or avoid this notion than to grant it space in our lives somehow so that it in turn calls for an alteration — dare we say, a transformation — of our very selves.[65] We would much rather have a god who is love, who is endlessly merciful and forgiving and ultimately the guarantor of everything we deem sacrosanct, than a god who "gets in the way" of our lives and aspirations and who judges us for the sake of growth and truth.[66]

63. Daniel M. Bell Jr. remarks of this tendency: "Thus we are conditioned to approach religion as a commodity, as just another consumer good alongside toothpaste and vacation homes" (*The Economy of Desire* [Grand Rapids: Baker Academic, 2012], p. 21). For a work that extends the point, see Vincent J. Miller, *Consuming Religion* (New York: Continuum, 2003).

64. This assessment finds support in the study, by Christian Smith and Melinda Lundquist Denton, of American teenage perspectives on faith. Their summary interpretation, "Moralistic Therapeutic Deism," has five points, one of which relates to the idea that religious life should be "about providing therapeutic benefits to its adherents. This is not a religion of repentance of sin. . . . What appears to be the actual dominant religion among U.S. teenagers is centrally about feeling good, happy, secure, at peace" (*Soul Searching* [Oxford: Oxford University Press, 2005], pp. 163-64). The authors often say this view reflects the teenagers' parents' beliefs.

65. In this regard, the material and socializing forces those of us in the modern West experience in turn complicate our vision of the gospel and feed into modern forms of supersessionism and Marcionism that we contemporary Christians know all too well. Put bluntly, the mantra we often hear from our students, that the God of the OT is mean and judgmental and the God of the NT is merciful and loving, is not simply a product of bad catechesis but of particular cultural formations.

66. On the subject of the God of Moralistic Therapeutic Deism Smith and Denton add: "This God is not demanding. He actually can't be, because his job is to solve our problems and

Particularly on the American scene, the chief culprit in these tendencies is the individualism already alluded to above. Robert Bellah and his associates speak from the American context and point out: "Individualism lies at the very core of American culture. . . . We believe in the dignity, indeed the sacredness, of the individual. Anything that would violate our right to think for ourselves, judge for ourselves, make our own decisions, live our lives as we see fit, is not only morally wrong, it is sacrilegious."[67] In such an environment, can God's judgment make sense? Maybe it could make sense to us if it were relevant only to other contexts separated from us by centuries, but is the idea workable if it brushes against that which we hold to be unquestionably holy and good?

These concerns relate to the matter at hand: What to do with the theme of judgment as one reads Hosea? Part of a salutary approach to this particular theme of the text is the cultivation of a love of truth, so that the ways we have been conditioned and shaped can be recognized for what they are and exposed to scrutiny. These are tasks of a lifetime that relate in part to the first theme, that of rebellion. If people are antithetical or apathetic to the truth about themselves and their conditioning, then this disposition is a form of covenant unfaithfulness. But part of these acts of retrieval, reassessment, and exposure relates not only to matters of political, economic, and cultural consequence, but to matters of theological gravity as well. The conscientization of our collusion, antipathies, and cultural pathologies is part of the life of faithfulness.

c. Return/Hope

Given where late modern Christians are situated, they would benefit from sitting in the first two movements so that a healing of desire, thought, imagination, and affectivity can take place because of, and in the presence of, the Holy Spirit. Only through this *via dolorosa* can hope truly be apprehended as genuine hope.

Once again, we are obliged to point out that ours is a pessimistic and jaded age. As one indication of this sentiment, one need only look at the many depictions of an apocalyptic wasteland in popular media to show that this is the case. One of the most distressing consequences of 9/11 for our culture has been the recognition that humans ultimately are not in control of their lives

---

make people feel good. In short, God is something like a combination Divine Butler and Cosmic Therapist: he is always on call, takes care of any problems that arise, professionally helps his people to feel better about themselves, and does not become too personally involved in the process" (*Soul Searching*, p. 165).

67. Robert N. Bellah et al., *Habits of the Heart* (Berkeley: University of California Press, 1996), p. 142.

and futures; all deleterious contingencies cannot be accounted for; all threats and dangers to our well-being cannot be quelled and held at bay.

A future brought about by human innovation and means is not equivalent to Christian hope.[68] The latter is a God-enabled and God-promised possibility, one hinging once again on YHWH's covenant bond, now understood to include all nations because of the life and faithfulness of Christ. Christians can only learn to be hopeful once they learn to live within a modality of covenant-conditionedness in which God's grounding reality and their responsive obedience touch and vitally interact. If YHWH does make our entire lives possible from beginning to end, then Christian hope is possible as a result of participation in God's triune life. This gaze is not instantaneously achieved, but rather shaped and refined over time in those who cleave to Christ. As Christian Scripture, Hosea can feature in such a process of spurring a hopeful imagination. By God's grace, we aspire to illustrate one way it can.

---

68. For a sustained treatment, see Margaret A. B. Adam, "The Perfect Hope" (PhD diss., Duke University, 2011).

2. Introduction to the Theological Exegesis of the Book of Hosea

Bo H. Lim

In Brevard Childs' groundbreaking commentary on Exodus, he engaged in theological and critical interpretation that treated the biblical text as canonical scripture for the church. Rather than viewing Scripture as a static deposit, he proposed, "It is incumbent upon each new generation to study its meaning afresh, to have the contemporary situation of the church addressed by the word, and to anticipate appropriation of its message through the work of God's spirit."[1] As already highlighted by Castelo, it is the aim of this commentary to interpret the prophecy of Hosea afresh in light of both current research on the book and contemporary challenges facing the church.

Text & Canon

Since Hosea is embedded within the collection of the Twelve Prophets, which is more broadly embedded within the prophetic literature, its canonical role must be ascertained in order to understand its theological message. In the past three decades, scholars began to consider seriously the canonical ordering of the individual books and to explore the literary relationships between them.[2] Emphasis has been on the final form of the Twelve as a unity, with the view that redactors intentionally shaped the collection for theological purposes and that authors of individual books wrote with the larger collection in mind. Arguments for unity are based on the following types of intertextuality within the Twelve:

---

1. Brevard S. Childs, *The Book of Exodus: A Critical, Theological Commentary* (OTL; Philadelphia: Westminster, 1974), p. ix.
2. What follows is a summation of my article "Which Version of the Twelve Prophets Should Christians Read?: A Case for Reading the LXX Twelve Prophets," *JTI* 7 (2013): 21-36.

quotations, allusions, catchwords, motifs, and framing devices. Furthermore, the Twelve possess common themes or motifs such as the "Day of the LORD." Lastly, framing devices provide structure to the Twelve, as demonstrated in how the superscriptions to Hosea, Amos, Micah, Zephaniah, Haggai, and Zechariah all possess chronological indicators that match their literary order.

The designation of the name "the Twelve" for a collection finds warrant from second temple Jewish and early Christian sources. The earliest Jewish and Christian canon lists refer to the Twelve as both a collection and one book. Ben Sira (ca. 190 BCE) offers the first mention of the Twelve as a collection: "May the bones of the Twelve Prophets send forth new life from where they lie, for they comforted the people of Jacob and delivered them with confident hope" (Sir 49:10). Some have argued that the manuscript evidence from Qumran confirms that the order of the Twelve according to the Masoretic Text goes back to at least 150 BCE.[3] The designation of the Twelve preceded "Minor Prophets," since the latter title appears in Latin Christian sources such as Augustine's writings[4] (for example, *City of God,* 18:29). Even though the Christian tradition has by and large referred to these books as "minor prophets," the earliest Christians received the Twelve as a collection from the Jews. Jerome observes a thematic unity and narrative development in the Book of the Twelve and considers its literary and theological contribution on par with the Major Prophets. He reads the Twelve as the story of the illness and healing of Israel:

> In the Twelve Prophets we have the description as it were of a sick person who has refused to care for his illness right up to the point of death, and then the story of his healing after death by Christ, who is the true physician. So what the Twelve Prophets do each in part — not without themselves briefly letting understand that they include the same purport — the greater prophets did in a general way.[5]

Hosea and the Twelve function, literarily and theologically, in a manner similar to the way the composite, multi-authored prophecy of Isaiah addresses the healing of wounded Israel (cf. Isa 1:5-6). It appears Jerome learned to read the Twelve as a unified collection from the Jews, and when he did so, he read it theologically and christologically.

Karen Jobes argues that the author of James reads the Twelve as a unity.

---

3. Russell Fuller, "The Form and Formation of the Book of the Twelve: The Evidence from the Judean Desert," in *Forming Prophetic Literature: Essays on Isaiah and the Twelve in Honor of John D. W. Watts* (ed. J. W. Watts and P. R. House; JSOTSup 235; Sheffield: JSOT Press, 1996), pp. 86-101.

4. For example, see *City of God* in NPNF[1], 2:376.

5. Jerome, *In Esaia parvula adbreviatio;* CCSL 73A: 803, lines 1-9.

She believes that the feminine plural vocative in 4:4: "Adulteresses!" (μοιχαλίδες/ *moichalides*) is a deliberate reference to the Twelve, where the same word appears in Hos 3:1 and Mal 3:5. Love, marriage, and adultery serve as unifying themes within the Twelve[6] and appear prominently within its bookends, Hosea and Malachi. Jobes believes that the translator of LXX Mal 3:5 deliberately translated the masculine plural participle "adulterers" (מנאפים/*měnā'ăpîm*) with a feminine plural accusative "adulteresses" (μοιχαλίδας/*moichalidas*) in order to strengthen the literary ties between Malachi and Hosea. Jobes argues that James intentionally cites this use in order to evoke the message of the Twelve regarding adultery. Given the many parallel themes in the Twelve and James, she argues that this reference demonstrates that James was reading the Twelve as a unity.[7] If Jobes is correct, James' reading is dependent on the Septuagint, since the reference to "adulteresses" appears only in the Greek text.

Reading Hosea within the Book of the Twelve is complicated by the fact that more than one order of the Twelve exists:

MT	LXX
Hosea	Hosea
Joel	Amos
Amos	Micah
Obadiah	**Joel**
Jonah	**Obadiah**
Micah	**Jonah**
Nahum	Nahum
Habakkuk	Habakkuk
Zephaniah	Zephaniah
Haggai	Haggai
Zechariah	Zechariah
Malachi	Malachi

The order of the first and seventh-through-twelfth books is the same, but the two versions differ with regard to the second-through-sixth books. When read-

6. Gerlinde Baumann, *Love and Violence: Marriage as Metaphor for the Relationship Between Yhwh and Israel in the Prophetic Books* (Collegeville, MN: Liturgical Press, 2003); John D. W. Watts, "A Frame for the Book of the Twelve: Hosea 1–3 and Malachi," in *Reading and Hearing the Book of the Twelve* (ed. J. D. Nogalski and M. A. Sweeney; SBLSymS 15; Atlanta: Society of Biblical Literature, 2000), pp. 209-17.

7. Karen H. Jobes, "The Minor Prophets in James, 1 and 2 Peter and Jude," in *The Minor Prophets in the New Testament* (ed. M. J. J. Menken and S. Moyise; LNTS 377; London: T. & T. Clark, 2009), pp. 135-53.

ing the Twelve as a collection, meaning lies not at the level of individual books, but in how the books function within the collection. The question remains, Which version ought to be authoritative for the church?[8]

It is the position of this commentary not to canonize a particular version but rather to "affirm that a multiplicity of texts witnessed to the Scriptures in the first century and that the authors were influenced by and may have drawn upon *any* of them without distinction."[9] Norton argues that first-century exegetes such as Paul would have been aware of textual diversity within the prophets but viewed it as "different expressions of a single prophetic tradition."[10] I follow the compromise and conclusion of Augustine, who accepted both the Hebrew and Greek texts as inspired and authoritative for the church.[11] There is not one final canonical form to the Twelve, but rather two final canonical forms: the Hebrew MT and the Greek LXX. The point is evident in the NT since it appropriates both the Hebrew and Greek Old Testament. For example, Mark 1:2-3 conflates three passages: LXX Isa 40:3, the Hebrew form of Mal 3:1, and LXX Exod 23:20. Whereas Matthew is clearly dependent upon the particular nuances of LXX Isa 7:14 in Matt 1:23, the fulfillment text of 2:15 is dependent upon the Hebrew version of Hos 11:1. A rigid separation ought not to be created between the two versions since oftentimes tradents of the Greek versions of OT books harmonized or reshaped the Greek text based upon the Hebrew, and vice versa by scribes of the Hebrew text. The result of this decision is to appreciate the theological contributions of both versions of the text, including their different order of books.

Even though I have made an argument for interpreting the Greek text of Hosea and the Twelve, I have chosen to use the Hebrew as the primary text for this commentary with occasional explorations into the Greek text. In addition to the fact that a critical examination of both versions is beyond the scope of this commentary,[12] part of my decision to primarily use the Hebrew text is based on the nature of the extant manuscripts. It is widely known that

---

8. See Lim, "Which Version of the Twelve Prophets Should Christians Read?" for a more extensive discussion.

9. R. Timothy McLay, "The Use of the Septuagint in the New Testament," in *The Biblical Canon: Its Origin, Transmission, and Authority* (ed. L. M. McDonald; Peabody: Hendrickson, 2007), p. 240.

10. Jonathan D. H. Norton, *Contours in the Text: Textual Variation in the Writings of Paul, Josephus and the Yaḥad* (LNTS 430; London: T & T Clark International, 2011), p. 44.

11. Martin Hengel, *The Septuagint as Christian Scripture: Its Prehistory and the Problem of Its Canon* (trans. M. E. Biddle; London: T & T Clark, 2002), pp. 51-54.

12. For a recent commentary on LXX Hosea, see W. Edward Glenny, *Hosea: A Commentary Based on Hosea in Codex Vaticanus* (Leiden: Brill, 2013).

not all ancient biblical manuscripts are created equal. Scholars are divided over whether the LXX of the Twelve is the product of a single translator or multiple translators.[13] What is clear is that LXX Hosea diverges quite significantly from MT Hosea in several instances. While such variance from the Hebrew suggests a different *Vorlage*, in this case the differences are likely due to the Greek translator's difficulty with the Hebrew dialect of Hosea. The Hebrew of Hosea has been considered second only to Job in difficulty. Not only does Hosea contain numerous *hapax legomena*, but many words from standard biblical Hebrew are used differently. While scholars have traditionally argued that the Hebrew text was corrupt, recent studies have suggested the possibility of a different dialect of Hebrew given the text's origins in the Northern Kingdom. Seow and Yoo have argued that Hosea is written in a regional dialect of "Israelian Hebrew" and that this accounts for the unique character of the language.[14] With its numerous examples of aphorism, asyndeton, repetition, alliteration, assonance, and wordplay, Hosea's language is highly stylized and its content is oftentimes extremely emotive. According to Muraoka, the Greek translator on occasion disregards the poetic structure, fails to account for how words may be vocalized differently, and mistranslates *hapax* or rare words. LXX Hosea may not necessarily possess a different *Vorlage* than the MT nor represent a reinterpretation or free rendering but instead reveals the translator's difficulty to understand the Hebrew text. Certainly, a theological commentary on LXX Hosea is completely in order; however, I have chosen to focus primarily on the Hebrew text due to practical concerns.[15]

Composition & Genre

The superscription, the anti-Assyrian perspective, the Northern Kingdom references, and the close relationship with Amos — all point to an 8th century date for Hosea. Yet based upon the fourteen references to Judah and the numerous promises of restoration, scholars in the twentieth century have asserted that large amounts of material postdated the 8th century prophet. Hans Wolff's influential commentary argued that chapters 4–11 contained the earliest material,

---

13. George Howard, "To the Reader," in *NETS*, pp. 777-81.

14. C. L. Seow, "Hosea, Book of," ABD, 3:292; Yoon Jong Yoo, "Israelian Hebrew in the Book of Hosea" (PhD diss., Cornell University, 1999).

15. Unless noted otherwise, all biblical references will be from the *New Revised Standard Version* and all quotations from the LXX in English will be from the *New English Translation of the Septuagint*. The verses will be displayed in the English followed by the Hebrew versification in brackets.

which was later joined to the other, independent "transmission complexes" (1–3 and 12–14). Looking at both sentence structure and contents, Grace Emmerson suggests a Judean reworking of the book in the time of Josiah.[16] Gale Yee similarly proposes a Josianic redaction to the book, but in keeping with critical views regarding the deuteronomistic history, she argues for an additional exilic redaction to Hosea.[17] What Emmerson and Yee propose is that these redactions were not simply additions to the book; rather, they introduced fundamental changes to the content of the material such that with each additional redaction a new literary work was produced.

Ehud Ben Zvi argues that Hosea ought to be classified as an "Authoritative, Ancient Israelite Prophetic Book" that is the product of an elite group of literati in the Persian period. According to him, individual texts have to be de-historicized, reorganized, and read and reread within the literary context of the entire book. He acknowledges that the book possesses a pre-history that extends back to the eighth century, but in his view, the past is constructed in a manner that serves the interests of a fifth-century audience.[18]

The view taken in this commentary is that much of Hosea was written by Hosea the prophet, yet significant redactional additions were made to the book in the Persian period. The Israelian Hebrew and the fact that Jeremiah is familiar with Hosea's message suggest that much of the book was written before or during the seventh century. It appears that the text of Hosea was conjoined with Amos early on, and by the time of the exile, it introduced a collection that included Amos, Micah, and possibly Zephaniah. The Wisdom-inflected postscript to the book (14:9 [10]) does appear to be postexilic, since this period saw the sapientialization of other sacred Israelite literature. Since this commentary's aims are not to reconstruct the composition of the book, the dating of texts will play a limited role in interpretation.

Structure

If Hosea is a composite prophetic book intended to be read and reread, then it is no surprise that it contains multiple structures. Texts possess multiple points of connection with each other; therefore, literary units overlap such that they

16. Grace I. Emmerson, *Hosea: An Israelite Prophet in Judean Perspective* (JSOTSup 28; Sheffield: JSOT Press, 1984).

17. Gale A. Yee, *Composition and Tradition in the Book of Hosea: A Redactional Critical Investigation* (SBLDS 102; Atlanta: Scholars Press, 1987).

18. See also James M. Trotter, *Reading Hosea in Achaemenid Yehud* (JSOTSup 328; Sheffield: Sheffield Academic Press, 2001), pp. 167-78.

cannot be defined solely in a linear fashion. Nevertheless, positing structures is important since it provides a necessary amount of coherence for a preliminary reading of the text. Certainly, subsequent readings of the text may challenge initial structural proposals and cause them to be reevaluated and modified. It ought to be noted that structures are heuristic devices that aid reading,[19] but they also reflect one's interpretation of the text. Structures inevitably highlight certain features of the text and minimize others, and these inevitably reflect the priorities of the reader. Given that this commentary will focus on the theological message of the final form of the book, texts will be evaluated based upon their function within the last stage of the writing process.

Whereas some commentators suggest that chapters 1–3 have a loose connection to chapters 4–14 at best, it appears that these sections were conjoined so as to complement each other and contribute to the book's overall message. The message of Hos 1–3 need not be harmonized with 4–14, but given the following intertexts, it seems the final authors of Hosea intended for readers to read texts in light of others.

- 2:1-23 [2:3-25] and 11:1-6 possess numerous connections, particularly 2:6 [2:8] and 11:3
- The language of "knowing YHWH" in 2:20 [2:22] appears again in 5:4 and 6:3
- The exodus theme appears in 2:15 [2:17] and also 11:1, 11; 12:9 [12:10], 13 [14]; 13:4
- Egypt appears in 2:15 [2:17] but also in 7:11; 8:13; 9:3, 6; 11:5
- References to "Baal" occur in 2:8 [2:10], 13 [15]; 11:2; 13:1
- "Love" is mentioned in 3:1; 9:15; 11:1; 14:4 [14:5]

Chapter 4 clearly initiates a new section in the book. Ancient writers appear to have read chapters 1–3 and 4ff. as distinct units, since a break between 3:5 and 4:1 occurs in the MT as well as 4QXII^g. Calls to hear (שמעו/*šimʿû*, 4:1; 5:1) are common introductory formulae in the OT, and these also support this reading. The question remains whether Hos 4:1-3 serves as an introduction to 4:1–11:11 or 4:1–14:9 [4:1–14:10] and whether Hosea 4–14 should be treated as one literary unit or two. Hosea 11:12–14:9 [12:1–14:10] appears to function as a separate section since 11:11 ends with the concluding expression, "says the LORD" (נאם-יהוה/*nĕum-yhwh*, cf. 2:13 [2:15], 16 [18], 21 [23]), and 12:2 [12:3] repeats the introductory formulae, "The LORD has an indictment" (וריב ליהוה/*wĕrîb lyhwh*, cf. 2:2 [2:4]; 4:1, 4). In a tripartite structure to the book of

---

19. Ehud Ben Zvi, *Hosea* (FOTL 21A; Grand Rapids: Eerdmans, 2005), p. 124.

Hosea — 1:1–3:5; 4:1–11:11; and 11:12–14:9 [12:1–14:10] — each major section contains a movement from Israel's present apostasy to a future return to the land and a renewed relationship between Israel and YHWH. Each of these units concludes with a statement regarding God's love for the people (3:1; 11:1; 14:4 [14:5]). Whereas each section begins with extensive judgment speeches against Israel, God relents from utterly destroying God's people, and the book concludes with a message of hope. Individual pericopes are not to be read in isolation, but rather as contributions to a dialogical text that possesses a movement from judgment to salvation.

Hermeneutical Implications

This commentary approaches Hosea as a prophetic book whose message was written initially to address the Northern Kingdom, and which was later incorporated into the collection of the Twelve. This collection, along with the rest of the Old Testament, was inherited by the church as Holy Scripture. Viewed in this manner, exegesis will require examination of diachronic and synchronic issues. Unlike Joel, which lacks a chronological superscription, Hosea situates the ministry of the son of Beeri during the reigns of "Uzziah, Jotham, Ahaz, and Hezekiah of Judah, and in the days of King Jeroboam son of Joash of Israel" (Hos 1:1). This book likely came into its final form in the postexilic period, yet by this time it was already part of a collection of prophetic books that consisted of Hosea-Amos-Micah-Zephaniah. In the vast majority of ancient manuscripts or booklists of the Twelve, Hosea consistently appears first, as in the case of both the MT and LXX versions. As such, Hosea functions hermeneutically and theologically as an introduction to the Twelve Prophets.

History is essential for properly interpreting the text, but historical reconstruction of the events behind the text is not necessary. Brevard Childs' comments regarding Isaiah also apply to the study of the Twelve since their compositions are similar: "The hermeneutic point to emphasize is that for Isaiah history is understood in the light of prophecy, not prophecy in the light of history."[20] Historical references ought not to be understood as merely ciphers for events, places, and persons for the final editors of the book, nor should one historically reconstruct ancient Israel through its prophetic literature. With that said, if "the prophetic books want Israel to look outward in order to learn about right conduct by comparing themselves to others and in order to see the

---

20. Brevard S. Childs, "Retrospective Reading of the Old Testament Prophets," *ZAW* 108 (1996): 373.

power of YHWH at work,"[21] then the historical references to these "others" within the text must be properly identified. That is, historical markers must be understood in regard to their function as they relate to the theological message of the prophetic book.

Prophetic books were designed to be reread since they possess a complex interplay of unity and depth, double *entendre*, ambiguity, and multidirectional intertextuality. The following attributes characterize prophetic books:[22] (1) Prophetic books call their readers to ascribe the book's divine authority to the image of the prophet mentioned in the book; (2) Individual pericopes have been "dehistoricized" through the process of being incorporated into the logic of the final form of the book; (3) The final form of the prophetic book within a fixed canon would be considered a theological norm by the community. Christian exegesis takes seriously the fact that redactors were constrained by the tradition they *received*. Prophetic editors were foremost preservationists and interpreters of tradition and only lastly creative originators.[23] Therefore, Ben Zvi's characterization that "only the literati can have direct access to YHWH's word, and by implication to YHWH's mind"[24] ought to be rejected. He believes that meaning is bound to the textual imaginations of the literati of the postmonarchic period, so for him, "The question of whether actual authors had in mind all these meanings is not only unanswerable but also immaterial."[25] From our end, a theological reading not only assumes divine action in the production of the text, but also in its rhetorical performance. In addition, Christian exegesis focuses on the received tradition of the church, so the text need not be bound to a particular moment in Israel's past, whether it be in the eighth century or the fifth. A Christian canonical reading of Hosea ultimately finds meaning not in the original oral speeches of the prophets nor the redactional moves by the editors, but in the final form(s) of Hosea embedded within a wider canonical conversation.

If Hosea is a prophetic book, then interpretation involves what can be

---

21. Megan Bishop Moore, "Writing Israel's History Using the Prophetic Books," in *Israel's Prophets and Israel's Past: Essays on the Relationship of Prophetic Texts and Israelite History in Honor of John H. Hayes* (ed. B. E. Kelle and M. B. Moore; LHBOTS 446; New York: T & T Clark, 2006), p. 31.

22. Ehud Ben Zvi, "The Prophetic Book: A Key Form of Prophetic Literature," in *The Changing Face of Form Criticism for the Twenty-First Century* (ed. M. A. Sweeney and E. Ben Zvi; Grand Rapids: Eerdmans, 2003), pp. 276-97.

23. Ronald E. Clements, *Old Testament Prophecy: From Oracles to Canon* (Louisville: Westminster John Knox, 1996), pp. 217-29.

24. Ben Zvi, *Hosea*, p. 19.

25. Ben Zvi, *Hosea*, p. 255.

termed a dialogical process. In this regard, many scholars have noted the contributions of the philosopher and literary critic Mikhail Bakhtin to theological interpretation.[26] Bakhtin defines "monologic" truth as propositions or abstractions decontextualized from the particular realities of individual persons. This kind of discourse has dominated philosophical, theological, and literary scholarship. Unfortunately, such speech is removed from the complexities and specifics of everyday life that operate on different systems of coherence. Bakhtin describes the phenomenon in this way:

> Life by its very nature is dialogue. To live means to participate in dialogue: to ask questions, to heed, to respond, to agree, and so forth. In this dialogue, a person participates wholly and throughout his whole life: with his eyes, lips, hands, soul, spirit, and with his whole body and deeds. He invests his entire self in discourse, and this discourse enters into the dialogic fabric of human life, into the world symposium.[27]

In contrast to the artificiality of monologism, life for most occurs on a dialogic level, where truth is inescapably tied to particularities, resists abstract systems, and requires the participation of two or more parties in order to be realized. Monological literature fails to capture the thoughts of human consciousness and the dialogical sphere of the mind's existence in all its depth and specificity. Dialogism does not reject monologization, but it recognizes the latter's provisionality until it is engaged on a dialogical level. In addition, Bahktin recognized that literature could function on a polyphonic level where, within the course of a text, changes occur in the position of the author, the role of the reader, the state of the plot, and the nature of the outcome. In a polyphonic work, the text functions to create an event where the reader participates within the dialogues of the text.

Hosea operates on a dialogical level, and therefore individual pericopes express provisional truths until the completion of the dialogue. In the case of Hosea, its dialogue is concluded only with the final form of the book, its function within the canon, and its reception by God's people. The propensity of interpreters is to read individual sections within Hosea as if they express monological truths. Doing so inevitably results in straining the limits of the text and theology, and it has resulted in scholars rejecting the book because of

26. Carol A. Newsom, "Bakhtin, the Bible, and Dialogic Truth," *Journal of Religion* 76 (1996): 290-306.

27. Bakhtin, "Toward a Reworking of the Dostoevsky Book," in *The Dialogic Imagination: Four Essays; Problems of Dostoevsky's Poetics* (ed. C. Emerson; Minneapolis: University of Minnesota Press, 1984), p. 293.

its inability to "render itself plausible or to achieve any real level of coherence."[28] By separating the book into a series of monologizations, the book inevitably implodes upon itself. But if a dialogical coherence is assumed from the outset — and for the community of faith, such a belief is warranted — then, should dissonant readings arise, the solution lies in reading further. As Castelo will develop later, the prophetic books assume a stance of faith on the part of readers, so although the dialogue may push the boundaries of the reader's commitment to God, it never reaches a breaking point.

Since the full significance of the prophetic word is not limited to original authorship, Hosea's ethical and theological vision ought not to be understood solely in an eighth-century context. Wellhausen famously asserted that the Decalogue and much of the Pentateuch were unknown to the eighth-century prophets since they were written much later.[29] This evolutionary scheme runs counter to the canonical progression of Law followed by Prophets and instead reads the OT canon in the order of Prophets then Law, both in terms of chronology as well as importance. Yet an alternative reading views the canonical sub-collections of Law and Prophets developing alongside each other so that each maintains its distinct priorities and characteristics, yet both are always working within a coordinated and dialogical relationship. The "Law and Prophets" served as a theological grammar that preceded the final formation of these collections and therefore should continue to serve as a hermeneutical principle by which individual books should be read.[30] When Hosea is read as part of a canon in which the Prophets accompany the Law, the reader cannot help but read Hosea in light of the Pentateuch. In fact, the Hebrew version of the Prophetic collection emphasizes the importance of Mosaic Torah at the beginning and end of the collection (Josh 1:7-8; Mal 4:4), and among the Twelve, the word תורה/*tôrah* appears more than once only in the first and last books. In its final form, the Old Testament is not to be read as "First Prophets, then Law" or "Prophets vs. Law," but rather as "Law *and* Prophets." Hosea, then, works in conjunction with the testimony of Mosaic Torah and complements its theological and ethical instruction.

---

28. David Jobling, "A Deconstructive Reading of Hosea 1–3," in *Relating to the Text: Interdisciplinary and Form-Critical Insights on the Bible* (ed. T. J. Sandoval and C. Mandolfo; JSOTSup 384; London: T & T Clark, 2003), p. 206.

29. Speaking about the relationship between the Law and Prophets, he writes, "Dimly I began to perceive that there was between them all the difference that separates two wholly distinct worlds" (Julius Wellhausen, *Prolegomena to the History of Ancient Israel* [trans. M. Menzies; New York: Meridian Books, 1957], p. 3). Later he writes, "It is a vain imagination to suppose that the prophets expounded and applied the law" (p. 399).

30. Stephen B. Chapman, *The Law and the Prophets* (FAT 27; Tübingen: Mohr Siebeck, 2000), pp. 71-110.

Themes and Hermeneutical Foci in Hosea and the Twelve

When read within the context of the Twelve, it is apparent that Hosea contributes a number of theological themes and hermeneutical foci to the collection. Some of these will be developed by Castelo in his contributions; I will make mention of the following here:

1. **Hosea as prophecy for Israel, Judah, and the church.**

   The Twelve in rough form address the crises facing preexilic Israel, preexilic Judah, exilic Judah, and postexilic Yehud. Placed first, Hosea serves as an introduction to this prophetic collection. Even though Hosea does not explicitly mention the "Day of YHWH," it does speak of a future "day" or "days" of vindication and renewal (1:5; 1:11 [2:2]; 2:16 [2:18]; 2:18 [2:20]; 2:21 [2:23]; 3:5). Given Hosea's close proximity in the MT to Joel — which serves as the programmatic "Day of YHWH" book within the Twelve — the message of Hosea is inextricably linked to this futuristic hope. Upon reading Acts 3:24 ("And all the prophets, as many as have spoken, from Samuel and those after him, also predicted these days") and other NT texts (Acts 3:18; 1 Pet 1:10-12), Ronald Clements concludes that the "unity of the prophetic message and its concern with the age of salvation provide a basic pattern of interpretation for the NT understanding of prophecy."[31] Following the Babylonian exile, prophecies of hope were given an additional eschatological dimension when placed in new literary arrangements. Clements believes these patterns are embedded within the OT prophetic literature itself rather than imposed externally by NT interpreters. As Christian Scripture, Hosea is received as prophecy that culminates in the revelation of Jesus Christ, the inauguration of the church, and the blessed hope of a new creation.

2. **Hosea and Amos as an interrelated message.**

   Jörg Jeremias argues that Amos was intentionally written to supplement the book of Hosea; therefore, "they are to be seen as two messengers with one common message."[32] They are the only two prophets to minister primarily to the Northern Kingdom, their superscriptions possess synchronistic royal dates, and in the LXX version they successively introduce the

---

31. Ronald E. Clements, "Patterns in the Prophetic Canon," in *Canon and Authority: Essays in Old Testament Religion and Theology* (ed. G. W. Coats and B. O. Long; Philadelphia: Fortress, 1977), p. 43.

32. Jörg Jeremias, "The Interrelationship between Amos and Hosea," in *Forming Prophetic Literature*, pp. 171-86.

Twelve since they fall in the first and second position. One hermeneutical implication of this close tie is that eighth-century Israel must be given proper attention, since both Hosea and Amos direct their prophecies to this setting. Additionally, the canonical message of Hosea is to be found in its intertextual dialogue with Amos.

3. **Return to YHWH and return to the land as a central theme of Hosea and the Twelve.**

To "return" serves as a major theme in these texts since 1) the exact wording of Hos 14:1-3 [14:2-4] reappears in Joel 2:12-14, and 2) the topic of land and people joined to YHWH appears in Hos 9:3; Joel 1:14-20; Amos 4:6-10; Mic 2:4; Hag 1:5-11; Mal 4:1 [3:19]. On a related note, Laurie Braaten has demonstrated that "God sows" is a major theme running through Hosea and the Twelve.[33] The Twelve begins with an emphasis on the land: "Go, take for yourself a wife of whoredom and have children of whoredom, for the *land* commits great whoredom by forsaking the LORD" (Hos 1:2), and it ends with God's warning, "so that [God] will not come and strike the *land* with a curse" (Mal 4:6 [3:24]). Agricultural images abound throughout Hosea, reaffirming God's commitment to restoring the land as well as God's people.

4. **Love and the marriage motif as a frame for not only Hosea but also the Twelve.**

Baumann observes that the story of Israel as a woman continues into Amos with the fall of the virgin in 5:2 and appears for the final time in the Twelve in Mic 1:7.[34] Within the Twelve Prophets, the theme of love of God for Israel portrayed through the motif of familial relations appears only in Hosea and Malachi. John Watts observes that the word love (אהב/'āhab) speaks of God's love for his people only in Hos 3:1; 9:15; 11:1, 4; 14:4 [14:5]; and Mal 3:1 within the Twelve.[35] Both Hosea and Malachi address the crises of broken relationships between husband and wife and parent and children, and the domestic issues of adultery, divorce, and abandonment. The marital metaphor in Hosea ought to be understood as representative of Israel's covenant relationship to YHWH since Malachi interprets it as such (Mal 2:10, 14). A proper understanding of the topics of love and

33. Laurie J. Braaten, "God Sows: Hosea's Land Theme in the Book of the Twelve," in *Thematic Threads in the Book of the Twelve* (ed. P. L. Redditt and A. Schart; BZAW 325; Berlin: Walter de Gruyter, 2003), pp. 104-32.

34. Baumann, *Love and Violence*, p. 208.

35. Watts, "A Frame for the Book of the Twelve," pp. 209-17.

sexuality within Hosea will then require an engagement with the rest of the Twelve since the theme re-emerges later.

5. Hosea and the Twelve as Scribal Wisdom and Theodicy.

Gerald Sheppard set forth the thesis that, at a late stage in the development of OT literature, wisdom became a major theological and hermeneutical category for Israel through which to interpret Torah and the Prophets.[36] This phenomena occurs in Eccl 12:13-14; Ps 1–2; 2 Sam 23:1-7; and Hos 14:9 [14:10]. Even though Hos 14:8 [14:9] seems like a perfectly logical ending to the book, Hosea ends with the insertion of a wisdom saying: "Those who are wise understand these things; those who are discerning know them. For the ways of the LORD are right, and the upright walk in them, but transgressors stumble in them" (Hos 14:9 [14:10]). Raymond Van Leeuwen argues that this sapiential redaction employs Exod 34:6-7 as a base text for developing an overarching theodicy within the Twelve.[37] Exodus 34:6-7 captures the seemingly conflicting attributes of love and wrath that function dialectically throughout Hosea and the Twelve. The question that ends Hosea — "Who is wise . . . [who is] discerning?" (14:9 [14:10]) — is taken up in Joel 2:14 — "Who knows whether he [YHWH] will not turn and relent?" The question posed in Jonah 3:9 — "Who knows, God may relent and change his mind (נחם/*niham*)?" — recalls the actions of YHWH in Exod 32:14 — "And the LORD changed his mind (נחם/*niham*) about the disaster that he planned to bring on his people" — prior to the theophany of Exod 34:6-7. Micah answers these questions by his very name, which is a pun on "Who is like YHWH?" In 7:18, Micah asks, "Who is a God like you?" and goes on to praise God for pardoning sin (עון נשא/*nōśē' 'āwôn*), passing over transgression (פשע/*peša'*), withholding anger (אף/*āp*), and extending steadfast love (חסד/*hesed*). These attributes of the covenant God are highlighted in the theophany of Exod 34:6-7:

> The LORD passed before him, and proclaimed, "The LORD, the LORD, a God merciful and gracious, slow to anger (אף/*āp*), and abounding in steadfast love (חסד/*hesed*) and faithfulness, keeping steadfast love for the thousandth generation, forgiving iniquity (עון נשא/*nōśē' 'āwôn*) and

36. Gerald T. Sheppard, *Wisdom as a Hermeneutical Construct: A Study in the Sapientializing of the Old Testament* (BZAW 151; Berlin: Walter de Gruyter, 1980), p. 13.

37. Raymond C. Van Leeuwen, "Scribal Wisdom and Theodicy in the Book of the Twelve," in *In Search of Wisdom: Essays in Memory of John G. Gammie* (ed. L. G. Perdue, B. Scott, and W. J. Wiseman; Louisville: Westminster John Knox, 1993), pp. 31-49.

transgression (פשע/*pešaʿ*) and sin, yet by no means clearing the guilty, but visiting the iniquity of the parents upon the children and the children's children, to the third and the fourth generation."

If "prophetic books were not intended to be read only once, but to be read, reread, and meditated upon,"[38] then the wisdom conclusion serves as the hermeneutical introduction to the rereading of Hosea. In addition, if the Twelve are to be read intertextually, then the ending of Hosea indicates that the Twelve are to be read as a theodicy in response to the catastrophes of 722 and 586 BCE, since these events feature so prominently within the collection.

38. Ehud Ben Zvi, *Micah* (FOTL 21B; Grand Rapids: Eerdmans, 2000), pp. 187-88.

3. Hosea 1:1–2:1 [1:1–2:3]

Bo H. Lim

Hosea 1:1 as a Hermeneutical Key to Hosea and the Twelve Prophets

The prophecy of Hosea begins with the superscription, "The word of the LORD that came to Hosea son of Beeri, in the days of Kings Uzziah, Jotham, Ahaz, and Hezekiah of Judah, and in the days of King Jeroboam son of Joash of Israel" (Hos 1:1). Traditionally, scholars used the prophetic superscriptions to date the prophet's ministry. In the case of Hosea, the kings mentioned span roughly a hundred years. The lone Northern king mentioned, Jeroboam son of Joash, reigned from 786 to 746 BCE. The dates of the Judean kings are as follows: Uzziah, 783-742 BCE; Jotham, 742-735 BCE; Ahaz, 735-715 BCE; and Hezekiah 715-687 BCE. It is noteworthy that the six northern kings that overlap this period of Judean kings (Zechariah, 745-738 BCE; Shallum, 745 BCE; Menahem 745-738 BCE; Pekahiah 738-737 BCE; Pekah, 737-732 BCE; and Hoshea 732-722/1 BCE) are unmentioned, since they play such an important role in the political intrigue of this period. It is unnecessary to argue that the author failed to mention these kings because he considered them illegitimate or confused the chronology of the kings.[1] The argument that Hosea migrated to Judah following the death of Jeroboam II and therefore listed only the Southern Kingdom's kings does not merit consideration either.[2] The author possesses only a distant memory of the reigns mentioned in the superscription and therefore it ought not be used to date oracles with precision or reconstruct the life of the prophet. The mention of son of Beeri with regard to Hosea and son of Joash with Jeroboam are to ensure

---

1. James L. Mays, *Hosea: A Commentary* (OTL; Louisville: Westminster John Knox, 1969), p. 21.

2. Francis I. Andersen and David Noel Freedman, *Hosea: A New Translation with Introduction and Commentary* (AB 24; New York: Doubleday, 1980), p. 18.

that the reader, who is at a significant historical distance, does not confuse these individuals with Hoshea, son of Elah, and Jeroboam, son of Nebat. The form of the name Hezekiah in the superscription (יחזקיה/*yĕḥizqiyyāh*), cf. Mic 1:1), is dated to the mid-sixth to mid-fourth century BCE. This form differs from the other three forms (חזקיהו/*ḥizqiyyāhû*, חזקיה/*ḥizqiyyāh*, יחזקיהו/*yĕḥizqiyyāhû*), and, according to Kutscher, it represents a transitional form between preexilic writers and the Chronicler.[3]

Scholars have postulated an exilic Book of the Four (Hosea, Amos, Micah, Zephaniah) based on the following evidence.[4] These books all begin with the phrase, "the word of the LORD which came to" (דבר־יהוה אשר היה אל/*dĕbar yhwh ăšer hāyāh ʾel*), and in the case of Amos, "the words of Amos" (דברי עמוס/*dibrê ʿāmôs*). In this collection, two prophets to the Northern Kingdom are followed by two prophets to the Southern Kingdom. Micah, the first Judean prophet of the four, addresses his message to Samaria and Jerusalem (Mic 1:1). These books view the exile of both kingdoms as an act of purification and oppose false prophecy, kingship, and a return to a preexilic state.[5] The following table demonstrates how the kings mentioned in Hosea 1:1 (with the exception of Josiah) align with the kings mentioned in the superscriptions of the other three books:

Hosea 1:1	Amos 1:1	Micah 1:1	Zephaniah 1:1
Uzziah	Uzziah		
Jotham		Jotham	
Ahaz		Ahaz	
Hezekiah		Hezekiah	(Hezekiah)
Jeroboam	Jeroboam		
			Josiah

The superscription in 1:1 appears to be an editorial comment since 1:2 provides an introduction to the prophecy itself: "the beginning of the word of the LORD

3. Eduard Yechezkel Kutscher, *The Language and Linguistic Background of the Isaiah Scroll* (Leiden: Brill, 1974), p. 104ff.

4. James D. Nogalski, *Literary Precursors to the Book of the Twelve* (BZAW 217; Berlin: Walter de Gruyter, 1993), pp. 278-80; James D. Nogalski, *Redactional Processes in the Book of the Twelve* (BZAW 218; Berlin: Walter de Gruyter, 1993), pp. 274-75; Aaron Schart, *Die Entstehung des Zwölfprophetenbuchs: Neubearbeitungen von Amos im Rahmen schriftenübergreifender Redaktionsprozesse* (BZAW 260; Berlin: Walter de Gruyter, 1998).

5. Rainer Albertz, "Exile as Purification: Reconstructing the 'Book of the Four,'" in *Thematic Threads in the Book of the Twelve* (ed. P. L. Redditt and A. Schart; BZAW 325; Berlin: Walter de Gruyter, 2003), pp. 232-51; Jakob Wöhrle, "'No Future for the Proud Exultant Ones': The Exilic Book of the Four Prophets (Hos., Am., Mic., Zeph.) as a Concept Opposed to the Deuteronomistic History," *VT* 58 (2008): 608-27.

to Hosea." In this case, 1:1 serves as an introduction to the Book of the Four and represents one stage in the canonical process. It functions in a similar manner to Ps 72:20 ("The prayers of David son of Jesse are ended") in the production of the Psalter. Both comments summarize the contents of their respective collections at one point, yet later material was added to both collections. The mention of Jeroboam serves to tie Hosea and Amos together and reinforces the complementary nature of these two prophetic books.

Even if the superscription was originally intended to introduce the Book of the Four, with the addition of the other books of the Twelve, it now serves as an introduction to the Twelve Prophets. With the exception of the mention of Jeroboam, Hos 1:1 mirrors the superscription to the vision of Isaiah: "The vision of Isaiah son of Amoz, which he saw concerning Judah and Jerusalem in the days of Uzziah, Jotham, Ahaz, and Hezekiah, kings of Judah" (Isa 1:1). Given that the Twelve and the Book of Isaiah both function as prophetic collections that possess a preexilic, exilic, and postexilic scope, the similar superscriptions indicate to readers that the prophetic books ought to be read in a complementary way. Tucker points out that the superscription "no longer refers to a particular revelation or a specific oral address, but to the words of the prophet as a whole, *as committed to writing.*"[6] Viewed in this manner, the entire text of Hosea — including narratives about the prophet in chs 1 and 3 as well as the rest of the books of the Twelve — constitutes the "word of the LORD" (1:1) to Israel and the church. Individual pericopes ought not be prioritized nor minimized but rather read conjointly. Ben Zvi observes that the mention of the Judean kings along with Jeroboam in the superscription provides a "double vision" for the book:

> If read with an eye to the (northern) Israelite temporal clause, the book becomes anchored in the last period of strength of the northern kingdom; but if it is read from a viewpoint that is informed by the Judahite temporal clause, it might be understood as anchored in a period in which (northern) Israel moves from a political position of strength to its demise in the days of Hezekiah.[7]

While historicists may be interested in deciphering strands of Judean redaction, the final editors of the book were simply interested in communicating to readers that its message applies to both kingdoms. In addition, since Hosea is to be read

6. Gene M. Tucker, "Prophetic Superscriptions and the Growth of the Canon," in *Canon and Authority: Essays in Old Testament Religion and Theology* (ed. G. W. Coats and B. O. Long; Philadelphia: Fortress, 1977), pp. 63-64, emphasis mine.

7. Ehud Ben Zvi, *Hosea* (FOTL 21A; Grand Rapids: Eerdmans, 2005), p. 31.

as a book consisting of multiple interwoven texts and perspectives, one ought not to expect a singular structure since it coheres on various planes. So while an outline to the book has been proposed, it is admittedly one of many heuristic devices to interpret the text. Dogmatism over matters of form and structure will be eschewed, both because modern readers lack the means to determine the parameters of purported original prophetic sayings, and because the text in its final form has been revised to be read as a multiplex, literary whole.

Scholars have uniformly argued that Amos chronologically precedes Hosea, yet in every canonical list Hosea appears first. Hosea's name (הוֹשֵׁע/*hôšēaʿ*) appears to be a derivation of הוֹשַׁעְיָה/*hôšaʿyāh* (Neh 12:32; Jer 42:1; 43:2), which means "YHWH saves." Hosea contains all the important topics of the Book of the Four: the evil of idolatry; sinful trust in arms and foreign allies; criticism of kingship, officials, and prophets; and social injustice. One can argue, based on its sheer comprehensiveness, that Hosea was placed first. But more importantly, "Hosea has the most developed perspective of salvation of all four books."[8] While all the books of the Twelve will speak extensively on judgment, the final editors of the Book of the Four as well as the Twelve wanted to make clear that the word of the LORD contained in these texts is ultimately a message of salvation. Ben Zvi observes that, whether by accident or design, the names of the prophets that begin the collections of the "former prophets" (Joshua), "latter prophets" (Isaiah), and the Twelve Prophets (Hosea), are all derivatives of the root יָשַׁע/*yāšaʿ* ("salvation").[9] Early on in the reading of Hosea, the audience will hear of God's eschatological salvation for Israel, Judah, and all creation in chapters 1–3. This will serve as a hermeneutical lens by which the rest of the message is to be understood.

The Literary Relationship of Chapters 1–3

Although most translations treat the odd phrase "the beginning of YHWH spoke through Hosea"[10] (1:2a) as a subordinate clause ("when the LORD began to speak through Hosea" [NIV]), the Hebrew lacks a temporal particle for it to be treated as such. The question to be asked is, The beginning of what? Certainly, the phrase marks the beginning of Hosea's prophetic ministry, but since the word "beginning" (תְּחִלַּת/*tĕḥillat*) often marks the first in a series, Hosea 1:2a identifies the first of YHWH's many messages to Hosea. Hosea's prophetic

---

8. Rainer Albertz, "Exile as Purification," p. 246.

9. Ben Zvi, *Hosea*, p. 25.

10. The LXX reads similarly, "the beginning of the word of the LORD in Hosea."

ministry begins with the shocking instruction to "take for yourself a wife of whoredom and have children of whoredom" (Hos 1:2). YHWH's word through Hosea to Israel begins not with Hosea's preaching, but rather the embodiment of it in Hosea's actions. God speaks through both word and deed, and the prophetic books contain both the narrative concerning the prophet's life as well as his oracles. Scholars have tended to read chapters 1–3 as distinct from chapters 4–14,[11] but in this case both prophetic speech and deed are considered the word of God. Just as the Gospel writers view both Christ's teachings and acts as proclamation of the kingdom, so too both the words and actions of Hosea recorded in Scripture comprise the prophetic word. Hosea 1–3 is preparatory for the oracles to follow in 4–13. YHWH will repeatedly speak to Hosea ("the LORD said to me *again*" [3:1a, emphasis mine]) and implicitly through Hosea ("Hear the word of the LORD" [4:1a]); therefore, Hos 1.2a functions to introduce the rest of the prophetic book.

We can be certain that the text is inconclusive as to the actual events of chapters 1–3. Macintosh provides a survey of the numerous options, gives a substantive defense of his own historical reconstruction, and yet concludes, "The fact remains, however, that we do not certainly know the answers to these questions *and it is likely that we never will.*"[12] Rather than end with this point, it appears that interpreters ought to begin here and acknowledge from the outset the impossibility of reconstructing the events of Hosea's marriage. Given that Hosea displays a considerable amount of literary artistry in the book, we can conclude that this ambiguity regarding historical events was not unintentional. For the final author, chapters 1–3 were never intended to communicate the actual events of Hosea's life, for he did not deem such knowledge necessary to receive the text's instruction. So instead of historical accuracy or detail, it seems that the author's prime concerns were the meaning and significance of the prophetic acts. Moughtin-Mumby wisely suggests, "It is time to abandon this 'quest for the historical Hosea.'"[13] Ultimately, the book of Hosea is "about learning about YHWH, Israel's past and future, and the relations between the two."[14] Rather than attempt to reconstruct the events of chapters 1 and 3 and

---

11. Kelle observes that scholars have focused on the marriage metaphor in Hosea 1–3 to the exclusion of serious engagement with the rest of the book, and treated chapters 1–3 and chapters 4–14 as the words of different prophets. Brad E. Kelle, "Hosea 1–3 in Twentieth-Century Scholarship," *CurBR* 7 (2009): 180.

12. A. A. Macintosh, *A Critical and Exegetical Commentary on Hosea* (ICC; Edinburgh: T & T Clark, 1997), p. 126, emphasis mine.

13. Sharon Moughtin-Mumby, *Sexual and Marital Metaphors in Hosea, Jeremiah, Isaiah and Ezekiel* (Oxford Theological Monographs; Oxford: Oxford University Press, 2008), p. 213.

14. Ben Zvi, *Hosea*, p. 6.

those that supposedly underlie chapter 2, the focus of this commentary will be on understanding the instructive value of the events and oracles.

Just as the historical reconstructions of the events of Hosea's marriage to Gomer are exegetically dubious, so are the conjectures into the so-called "poor, dejected, spurned and broken-hearted"[15] psychological state of Hosea. Scholars have even blamed the difficult Hebrew of the book on Hosea's inability "to unfold his thoughts in calm and long sentences, and to arrange his words in firm and strong order. The thought is too full, the sentence rapid and abrupt, the whole discourse breaking itself up as it were in sobs."[16] Virtually all modern commentators claim that the text ought not to be used to reconstruct the life of the prophet, but they seem unable to resist the temptation to do so. Some of this exegetical speculation results from the romanticization of the prophet as poet begun by Lowth[17] and Gunkel's focus on "the prophet's mysterious experience of oneness with God and the identification with his purposes in history."[18] For the most part, the penchant to overinterpret the text is simply due to the gripping human drama of Hosea's sexual, marital, and familial life, and its corresponding absence of historical detail. Since the history of interpretation has proven that Hosea is prone to interpretive speculation,[19] it would be prudent in this case to restrain the use of imagination in exegesis rather than encourage it, since its use may lead to harmful results.

What seems clear is that 1:2–2:1 [1:2–2:3] comprise one unit, 2:2-23 [2:4-25] a second, and 3:1-5 a third. Hosea 1:2–2:1 [1:2–2:3] narrates three prophetic sign-acts of bearing children, followed by an explanation of each of the signs, and ends with a salvation oracle. Hosea 2:2-23 [2:4-25] serves as a discrete prophetic oracle that finds its basis in the first prophetic sign-act narrative in 1:2–2:1 [1:2–2:3]; both culminate with the mention of Ammi/Lo-ammi and Ruhamah/Lo-ruhamah (2:1 [2:3], 2:23 [2:25]). The basic narrative of 1:2–2:1 [1:2–2:3] is assumed by the author of 2:2-23 [2:4-25] since this passage mentions children (2:4 [2:6]; cf. 1:3, 8, 10 [2:1]) and harlotry (2:2 [2:4], 4 [2:6]; cf. 1:2). Yet Hos 2:2-23 [2:4-25] is a theological, poetic reflection that follows from the prophetic sign-

15. George A. F. Knight, *Hosea: Introduction and Commentary* (London: SCM Press, 1960), p. 60.

16. Heinrich Ewald, *Commentary on the Prophets of the Old Testament* (trans. J. F. Smith; London: Williams and Norgate, 1875), I: 218.

17. Michael C. Legaspi, *The Death of Scripture and the Rise of Biblical Studies* (Oxford Studies in Historical Theology; New York: Oxford University Press, 2010), p. 115.

18. Joseph Blenkinsopp, *A History of Prophecy in Israel* (rev. and enl. ed.; Louisville: Westminster John Knox, 1996), p. 20.

19. Yvonne Sherwood, *The Prostitute and the Prophet: Hosea's Marriage in Literary-Theoretical Perspective* (JSOTSup 212; Sheffield: Sheffield Academic Press, 1996), pp. 40-66.

acts of 1:2–2:1 [1:2–2:3] and as such it does not "portray the actual situation of the prophet and his family."[20] The prophetic oracles of 2:2-23 [2:4-25] are related to the narrative of 1:2–2:1 [1:2–2:3] as literature but not as historical event. This section begins with an address to Ammi and Ruhamah, not Lo-Ammi and Lo-Ruhamah, and therefore follows upon the promise of restoration mentioned in 1:10-11 [2:1-2] rather than the judgment speech of 1:6-7, 9. In summary, chapters 1–3 do not provide a continuous narrative of the marriage or family life of Hosea, but rather are comprised of two distinct prophetic sign-acts interrupted by a prophetic oracle.

Rather than privilege one of the units over the others because it is written in the first person or in either prose or poetry, the best option appears to be to read them as three discrete literary units rather than a continual narrative. As will be argued below, the narratives describe prophetic sign-acts, which typically do not possess a consistent symbolic function. For example, the numerous sign-acts performed by Jeremiah and Ezekiel have little to do with one another, and in some cases the prophet plays inconsistent roles.[21] Certainly Hosea's sign-acts are to be read in conjunction, given all their textual links and the unifying household and marital metaphor. So a "web of meanings"[22] binds these chapters together, and they contribute to the overall message of the prophetic book, but their relationship need not be one of continuous narrative.

The prophetic sign-acts of 1:2-9 serve as a means for Israel to understand the prophetic speech contained in 2:2-23 [2:4-25] as regarding not Gomer's relationship to her family, but rather Israel's relationship to its God. Biographical details of Hosea's relationship to Gomer, his children, and the adulteress of chapter 3 are not to be inferred from this chapter. The very function of prophetic sign-acts is to aid the preaching of the prophet, so the narratives of chapters 1 and 3 ought not be used as sources to reconstruct the life of the prophet and his family. Sweeney categorizes Hos 1 and 3 as a "Report of a Symbolic Action." This genre is defined as:

> A first or third person narrative that describes the prophet's performance of an act intended to symbolize YHWH's intentions or actions toward the people. The symbolic action frequently accompanies a prophetic word or vision, and it functions as a sign to confirm the efficacy of that word or vision. . . . The form contains three elements: (1) an instruction to perform a

20. Andersen and Freedman, *Hosea*, p. 117.
21. In Ezekiel 12:1-16, the prophet plays the role of the Jerusalemites going into exile as well as the Babylonian invaders.
22. Ben Zvi, *Hosea*, p. 35.

symbolic act; (2) the report that the act was performed; and (3) a statement that interprets the significance of the act.[23]

According to this definition, the actions are not to be interpreted beyond that of the interpretive word or vision. Prophetic oracles which lack direct ties to prophetic sign-acts are not to serve as the means of reconstructing prophetic actions.

Comparisons can be drawn between the sign-acts of Hos 1:2-9 and 3:1-5 and those of Isaiah in Isa 7:14-17 and 8:1-4, since in both books children and the naming of them are considered signs. In Isa 7–8 the historical details of these events are remarkably sparse, and while it makes good sense to read Isa 8:1-4 as a fulfillment of Isa 7:14-17,[24] the connection between these two narratives is loose enough that they need not be read as a continuous narrative. In fact, if one interprets Isa 7–8 in the way that many have interpreted Hos 1–3 as a tale of Hosea and Gomer, one would have to argue that the prophetess of Isa 8:3-4 must be the maiden Isaiah sees in Isa 7:14. However, if prophecy carries multiple fulfillments, then one prophetic sign-act can signify more than one person or event, as in the case of the Immanuel prophecy. If Hosea 1 and 3 find their closest counterpart in Isa 7–8, then the prophetic sign-acts in the former need not refer solely to Gomer. According to this understanding, the woman of Hos 3 may not be Gomer, yet she continues to function as a legitimate participant or fulfillment of the prophecies of chapters 1 and 3. Chapter 3 is a separate prophetic sign-act from chapter 1, yet in some sense it is a continuation of the sign-act of chapter 1 in the same way that Isa 8:1-4 is *a* fulfillment (although not the final fulfillment; see Matt 1:22-23) of Isa 7:14.

Hosea 3:1-5 is an independent prophetic sign-act narrative that follows after the first, as indicated by the words, "The Lord said to me *again*" (3:1, emphasis mine). This second sign-act narrative introduces a different prophetic message than the first. As such, there is no need to harmonize this second prophetic sign-act with the ones mentioned in 1:2-11 [1:2–2:2] or with the prophetic oracle of 2:2-23 [2:4-25]. Davies provides a sensible reading of the relationship between the two sign-acts:

> There are therefore two separate symbolic actions, involving different promiscuous women. They represent two entirely different situations: the first,

23. Marvin A. Sweeney, *Isaiah 1–39 with an Introduction to Prophetic Literature* (FOTL 16; Grand Rapids: Eerdmans, 1996), p. 19.

24. Joseph Blenkinsopp, *Isaiah 1–39: A New Translation with Introduction and Commentary* (AB 19; New York: Doubleday, 2000), pp. 238-39.

introduced by 'take' (1.2), stands for the improper association of Israel with Baal, while the second, introduced by 'love,' stands for YHWH's seeking out of faithless Israel. *On the level of what is symbolized there is continuity, on the biographical level there is not.*[25]

This commentary will examine Hos 1:2–2:1 [1:2–2:3]; 2:2-23 [2:4-25]; and 3:1-5 as individual prophetic sign-act narratives or discourses, rather than as one continuous story. Ultimately, the text is to be understood as a prophetic "word of the LORD" (1:1) to Israel and the church that contains no information about the life of Hosea except these two events. Inquiries into the psychological state of Hosea or Gomer are pure conjecture. We cannot reconstruct, as Heschel suggests, "what manner of man is the prophet"[26] merely from two prophetic sign-acts and his written oracles; nor are we to equate the prophet's life with the life of God. While some may argue that an injection of speculation is necessary, harmless, or even warranted, the history of interpretation demonstrates that, by and large, it will only distract readers from the main emphases of the text. With regard to these issues, the exegetical imagination ought to be restrained.

The Household Metaphor

Hosea seems unable to remain out of the spotlight of interpretive controversy. For centuries, Hosea's marriage to Gomer scandalized and puzzled interpreters. Questions surrounded 1) the literary and historical relationship between chapters 1, 2, and 3; 2) the timing and nature of Gomer's infidelity; 3) the nature of Hosea's relationship with Gomer; 4) the identity of the adulteress in chapter 3; and 5) whether the narratives in chapters 1 and 3 ought to be read allegorically.[27] In the past thirty years, Hosea has been challenged on different grounds, resulting in a trail of publications equally or more voluminous than what had previously been written. Hosea has been accused of legitimizing oppressive patriarchal structures and violence against women, since the book relies on a metaphor where the husband punishes his wife who is deemed a whore. Some even go so far as to suggest that the book employs pornography to objectify women through its salacious details of the woman's nakedness in chapter 2.[28] Others

25. Graham I. Davies, *Hosea* (OTG; Sheffield: JSOT Press, 1993), p. 90, emphasis mine.

26. Abraham J. Heschel, *The Prophets* (2 vols.; New York: HarperCollins, 1962), 1:3-26.

27. Here Rowley's article continues to be the best summation of these issues. H. H. Rowley, *Men of God: Studies in Old Testament History and Prophecy* (London: Nelson, 1963), pp. 66-97.

28. T. Deborah Setel, "Prophets and Pornography: Female Sexual Imagery in Hosea," in *Feminist Interpretation of the Bible* (ed. L. M. Russell; Philadelphia: Westminster, 1985), pp. 86-95.

assert that chapter 2 describes the behavioral patterns of battered women and conclude that the book depicts YHWH as perpetuating divine spousal abuse.[29]

It cannot be denied that the challenges to reading Hosea today abound. Yet contemporary challenges ought not obscure the fact that Hosea was intended to function as an "Authoritative, Ancient Israelite Prophetic Book." Ben Zvi defines this genre as "one that communicates an explicit or implicit claim for social and theological/ideological authoritativeness."[30] Early Christians inherited this view of Hosea and added the expectation that the book would serve as a witness to Christ. Rather than decide early on whether Hosea 1–3 can continue to function authoritatively today, I would urge readers to defer their decisions until they have read Hosea in its entirety.[31] For the church, the question is not whether Hosea is authoritative, but *how* Hosea functions authoritatively as Scripture for God's people.

The word זנה/*zānāh* "whore" appears in Hos. 1:2 (2x); 2:5 [2:7]; 3:3; 4:10, 12, 13, 14 (2x), 15, 18 (2x); 5:3; 9:1. In addition, the word זנונים/*zĕnûnîm* "whoredom" appears in Hos 1:2 (2x); 2:2 [2:4]; 2:4 [2:6]; 4:12; 5:4. The basic meaning is "to fornicate," that is, to engage in sexual relations outside of, or apart from, marriage. This word is more general than the term נאף/*nā'ap* "to commit adultery," which appears in Hos 3:1; 4:2, 13, 14; 7:4, and its derivative נאפופים/*na'ăpûpîm* "adultery" in Hos 2:2 [2:4]. Phyllis Bird has provided the most comprehensive analysis of these terms in her article "To Play the Harlot."[32] She argues that Israel's legal codes regarding sexual activity are rooted in persons' social and legal status. A woman's sexuality was understood to be reserved for her husband alone or in anticipation of marriage. Female sexual activity, then, is judged according to the marital status of the woman involved. Consensual sex between a man and a married woman who is not his wife would violate the sexual rights of the woman's husband and therefore be the worst of all sexual offenses, warranting capital punishment for both parties (Deut 22:22). Such actions are described by the term נאף/*nā'ap* "to commit adultery," yet all other acts of sexual intercourse outside of marriage are deemed זנה/*zānāh* "to fornicate." So a woman who is

29. Naomi Graetz, "God Is to Israel as Husband Is to Wife: The Metaphoric Battering of Hosea's Wife," in *A Feminist Companion to the Latter Prophets* (ed. A. Brenner; FCB 8; Sheffield: Sheffield Academic Press, 1995), pp. 126-45.

30. Ben Zvi, *Hosea*, p. 11.

31. For readers such as Sharon Moughtin-Mumby and Julia M. O'Brien (*Challenging Prophetic Metaphor: Theology and Ideology in the Prophets* [Louisville: Westminster John Knox, 2008]), Hosea can no longer function in this same capacity and must be declassified as authoritative Scripture in order to remain relevant.

32. As found in Phyllis A. Bird, *Missing Persons and Mistaken Identities: Women and Gender in Ancient Israel* (OBT; Minneapolis: Fortress, 1997), pp. 219-36.

not obligated to another male can only commit זנה/*zānāh*. It is not surprising that this term often designates a prostitute, since by profession she habitually engages in sex with men to whom she is not married. One observes the inequity between the sexes in the patriarchal culture described in the biblical texts. In this case, the very terms used to describe female sexual activity assume such social standards. Bird writes, "The prostitute is that 'other woman,' tolerated but stigmatized, desired but ostracized."[33] To conclude, the term זנה/*zānāh* refers strictly to fornication; therefore, its context will determine how the description of illicit sexual activity is employed.

While commentators in the mid to late 20th century[34] popularized the view that זנה/*zānāh* can refer to cult prostitution and postulated that Gomer was a Baal cult prostitute who would engage in sexual fertility rites, this interpretation has fallen out of favor due to its lack of evidence. The word זנה/*zānāh* lacks cultic connotations, and the theory relies on classical sources for information, which are far removed from ancient Israel and Mesopotamia in provenance.[35] The words זנות/*zōnôt* and קדשות/*qĕdēšôt* (feminine plural form of קדש/*qādēš* "holy ones") appear in 4:14 ("I will not punish your daughters when they play the whore, nor your daughters-in-law when they commit adultery; for the men themselves go aside with whores, and sacrifice with temple prostitutes; thus a people without understanding comes to ruin"), and some have argued that they function interchangeably here to refer to temple prostitutes. But rather than read these words synonymously, we see them as describing two different sinful acts: one sexual in nature and the other cultic.

Brad Kelle argues that the Baal cult was nonexistent in eighth-century Israel. He observes that the Baal cult was popular only for one brief period during the reigns of Ahab and Jezebel (868-854). None of the kings or prophets before or after this period are described as having to combat the cult of Baal. Second Kings 10:28 speaks of Jehu exterminating the Baal cult, and Hos 1–3 does not reflect a deep concern with Baal cultic worship.[36] It seems that the references to Baal in chapter 2 are not the proper name of the Phoenician deity but simply to be understood as "overlord" or "paramour." If an allusion to the cult of Baal is to be made, it is on the basis of the references to the house of Jehu in 1:4 and Jezreel in 1:4-5, 11; 2:22. Yet these references ought to be understood as a rhetorical device aimed at calling Israel to repent through a recollection of its sinful past, rather

33. Bird, *Missing Persons and Mistaken Identities*, p. 225.

34. Mays, *Hosea*; Hans Walter Wolff, *Hosea* (Hermeneia; trans. G. Stansell; Philadelphia: Fortress, 1974).

35. Robert A. Oden Jr., *The Bible Without Theology: The Theological Tradition and Alternatives to It* (San Francisco: Harper & Row, 1987), pp. 131-53.

36. Kelle, "Hosea 1–3," pp. 139-41.

than as indicative of a contemporary Baal cult. Given that these verses are quite removed from 2:2-13[2:4-15], the Baal cult is only a faint echo in this section.

Hosea 1:2–2:1 [1:2–2:3]: Covenant Dissolution and Renewal

Hosea 1:2–2:1 [1:2–2:3] contains 4 interrelated prophetic sign-acts. In this case, the sign-acts are connected since from the outset YHWH announces to Hosea that in addition to taking a wife of promiscuity, he is to have children of promiscuity as well. Rather than use the term זונה/*zō(ô)nāh* for a professional prostitute, or מנאפת/*měno'āpet* for an adulteress, the uncommon term זנונים/*zěnûnîm* is used to describe both the women and the children. Half of the uses of this word in the Old Testament appear in Hosea 1–5. While the terms "woman/wife of promiscuity" and "children of promiscuity" are ambiguous as to their meaning and reference, the last line of 1:2 clarifies their significance: They are signs of the land's utter promiscuity. Hosea's description of the land as the subject and actor makes sense because of the agrarian outlook of the prophet. Davis clarifies, "agrarians know the land, not as an inert object, but as a fellow creature that can justly expect something from us whose lives depend on it."[37] She goes on to describe the basic tenets of agrarianism: 1) Fertile soil is a gift and trust from God; 2) our relationship to the soil, demonstrated in food production and consumption, is fundamental to every other aspect of life; and 3) misuse of the land, including maltreatment of those who work the soil, will ultimately undo every political structure.[38] It is fitting that sin against the land results in the collapse of Israel's most fundamental institution — the family — since they both represent the most basic elements of life.

The verbal form "commits great whoredom" (זנה תזנה/*zānōh tizneh*) indicates frequent and continual action as well as the intensity or comprehensiveness of the sin. The action to "take a woman" in 1:2 is understood in the OT to refer to marriage (Gen 4:19; 24:3, 67; 34:4; Jer 29:6), as well as to extramarital sex (Lev. 20:14, 17, 21). While the message of the prophetic sign-act is fairly clear, it is difficult to determine the exact events of the sign-act itself. From the vantage point of the prophetic book, the narrative indicates that Hosea understood from the outset that Gomer would be promiscuous and that their children would come from infidelity; nevertheless, he was to have sex with her and likely marry her. As noted above, a prophetic sign-act typically progresses

---

37. Ellen F. Davis, *Scripture, Culture, and Agriculture: An Agrarian Reading of the Bible* (New York: Cambridge University Press, 2009), p. 29.

38. Davis, *Scripture, Culture, and Agriculture*, p. 121.

from 1) an instruction to perform a symbolic act; to 2) the report that the act was performed; to 3) a statement that interprets the significance of the act, rather than the reverse. Interpretations that posit that Hos 1 was written in retrospect completely disregard the tenor of the narrative.

Although Gomer has captured the attention of most readers, chapter 1 is primarily focused on the children of promiscuity, not the promiscuous woman. In fact, if the adulterous woman of chapter 3 is not Gomer and chapter 2 does not describe Hosea and Gomer's marriage, then we have close to no information on Hosea's purported marriage to Gomer. Gomer functions only as a vehicle to bear three children, and it is they who take center stage to serve as prophetic signs in Hos 1, in a manner similar to Isa 7–8. The signs are filled with irony. They will signify both blessing and curse, and serve as signs of God's judgment upon Israel in the near future as well as salvation in the distant future. As mentioned above, while Hosea makes many references to "Baals," there is little evidence of an institutional Baal cult in the 8th century. Instead, Israel's cultic practices in Hosea match the traditional family religion described in Genesis, Judges, and Samuel.[39] Perhaps Hosea employs the household metaphor, which includes both the wife/mother and children, because it accords with Israel's social and religious situation.

Children are normally understood to be a blessing from the LORD (cf. Gen 1:28; 12:1-3; Ps 127), but in Hos 1 they are ominous signs of God's judgment upon his people. The name Jezreel should signify blessing since it means "God sows," yet immediately Hosea discovers that this name indicates God's judgment upon the house of Jehu, resulting in the breaking of the bow of Israel in the valley of Jezreel. In the OT, "Jezreel" can refer to four different geographical locations, two of them being quite insignificant.[40] The Jezreel valley is a broad plain that rests south of Galilee and north of the hill country of Ephraim or Samaria. It constituted the "bread basket" of ancient Israel and served as a major trading route between Egypt, Asia Minor, and Mesopotamia. Because of its strategic locale, the Assyrian Tiglath Pileser attacked King Rezin of Aram and King Pekah of Israel (735-32 BCE) and gained dominance in this region. With this action, Assyria controlled a trade route to Egypt that allowed it to dominate commerce in the Eastern Mediterranean, and that eventuated in their conquest of Egypt. It also debilitated Israel's economic and political interest in the region and allowed Assyria to reduce the Northern Kingdom to an Assyrian vassal territory.[41]

39. Karel van der Toorn, *Family Religion in Babylonia, Syria, and Israel: Continuity and Changes in the Forms of Religious Life* (Leiden: Brill, 1996), p. 296.

40. H. G. M. Williamson, "Jezreel in the Biblical Texts," *TA* 18 (1991): 72-92.

41. Marvin A. Sweeney, *The Twelve Prophets* (2 vols.; Collegeville: Liturgical Press, 2000), 1:19-20.

The other significant location associated with the name "Jezreel" is the town that bears its name. Hosea associates this location with great violence. Scholars have repeatedly attempted to pinpoint the historical reference to the "blood of Jezreel" and the "end to the kingdom of the house of Israel" (1:4) with mixed results.[42] Some suggest that the "blood of Jezreel" refers to Ahab's murder of Naboth (cf. 1 Kgs 21), to Jehu's massacre of the house of Ahab as narrated in 2 Kgs 9–10, or to the widespread regicide in Hosea's late period (731-724 BCE), which saw the assassinations of Zechariah, Shallum, Pekahiah, and Pekah. These commentators believe that the phrase "an end to the kingdom of the house of Israel" suggests an end to Jehu's dynasty or, more generally, to the Northern Kingdom of Israel.

Marvin Sweeney suggests that Hos 1:4 is a condemnation of pro-Assyrian alliances initiated by Jehu. Although Ahab is condemned for his unjust and idolatrous activity in the Deuteronomistic History (DtrH), Assyrian records indicate that he played an important role in resisting Assyrian encroachment into western territory. At the Battle of Qarqar in 853 BCE, Ahab joined a coalition that included Hadad-ever of Damascus, defeated Shalmaneser III's armies, and stymied Assyrian expansion for a time. However, Israel under Jehu's rule reversed course and allied itself to Shalmaneser III by paying tribute. Jehu is depicted as prostrating himself to the Assyrian king on the "Black Obelisk." Assyrian records continued to list Israel as a tributary following Jehu's reign, and throughout the book of Hosea, Israel's allegiance to Assyria is anticipated by the prophet and labeled as whoredom.

The difficulty with these historical interpretations is that, while Jehu is condemned for the blood of Jezreel in 1:4, 2 Kgs 9–10 describes him as a religious reformer who purged Israel of the house of Ahab and Baals at the command of the LORD (cf. 2 Kgs 10:11, 30). Some suggest that Hosea was unaware of the Deuteronomistic traditions regarding Jehu or that he held to a higher standard of morality, yet one need not attempt to harmonize these texts historically. Repeatedly, the prophet understands Israel's past to bear typologically upon the present (e.g., the references to the exodus and Jacob narratives in chapters 11–12), so there is no need to make a precise historical correlation between the "blood of Jezreel" and the "end to the kingdom of the house of Israel" in Hos 1:4. In this case, Hosea transfers the guilt associated with the town of Jezreel to a separate location, the valley of Jezreel.

Hosea 1:4 ought to be translated, "I will visit the blood of Jezreel on the house of Jehu," rather than "I will punish the house of Jehu for the blood of Jezreel," as in most translations. The verbal phrase "I will punish" (פקד על/*pāqad*

---

42. Stuart A. Irvine, "The Threat of Jezreel (Hosea 1:4-5)," *CBQ* 57 (1995): 494-503.

'al) does not carry the sense of reciprocal punitive action and therefore does not specify which blood shed at Jezreel will visit the house of Jehu.[43] In this case it can be argued that the singular phrase "blood of Jezreel" subsumes the bloodshed of both Ahab and Jehu. Rather than associate the present Jehudite rulers with the religious reforms of Jehu, Hosea associates them with Jehu's political compromises.

Yet even if the author of Hosea did not associate "Jezreel" with the activity of Ahab, it is possible to connect this text to the immoral and idolatrous activity of Ahab when reading within the context of the canon. In addition to Jezreel resembling the name "Israel," it may also be a word play on "Jezebel." What develops in Israel's traditions is a strong link between Jezebel, bloodshed, Jezreel, whoredom, and Samaria. Jezreel plays a significant role in the Elijah-Ahab narratives in 1 Kgs 18–22 and Jehu's violent purge of the Omride dynasty and Baalism in 2 Kgs 8:25–10:31. As noted above, it was Ahab and Jezebel who promulgated widespread Baalism in Israel, and Jezebel is described as guilty of "whoredoms" (זנונים/*zĕnûnîm*) in 2 Kgs 9:22, for which she is killed. The word "whoredoms" occurs only 12 times in the OT, with half of them in Hosea; therefore, readers may make the connection between these two books.

Jezreel becomes synonymous with bloodshed (דם/*dam*, 1 Kgs 21:19; 2 Kgs 9:26, 33; cf. Hos 1:4). Coincidentally, it is murder for land — precisely a vineyard (1 Kgs 21:1-17) — that initiates a cycle of bloodshed in Jezreel; as Elijah reports to Ahab, "Thus says the LORD: In the place where dogs licked up the blood of Naboth, dogs will also lick up your blood" (1 Kgs 21:19). Naboth would continue to be associated with Jezreel since he is repeatedly identified as a "Jezreelite" (1 Kgs 21:1, 4, 6, 7, 15, 16; 2 Kgs 9:21, 25). Although Ahab dies by blood loss (1 Kgs 22:35), he perishes not in Jezreel but in Samaria, signifying that the term Jezreel ought not to be understood to refer strictly to one geographical locale, and it could possibly be associated with Samaria. Interestingly, 1 Kgs 22:38 includes the enigmatic detail that, following Ahab's death, prostitutes (זנות/*zōnôt*) — a word oft-repeated in Hosea — bathed in Ahab's spilt blood.

While Hos 1:4 may have served initially as a condemnation of pro-Assyrian policies by the Northern Kingdom, in the final form of the book it serves as a condemnation of the house of Israel for continuing in the religious and moral sins of Ahab and in the political compromises of Jehu. Ahab's seizure of Naboth's vineyard initiates a pattern of covenant disobedience wherein the "land commits great whoredom by forsaking the LORD" (1:2). The Septuagint version of Hosea fails to mention Jehu altogether and instead replaces "Jehu"

---

43. Thomas Edward McComiskey, "Prophetic Irony in Hosea 1.4: A Study in the Collocation פקד על and Its Implications for the Fall of Jehu's Dynasty," *JSOT* 58 (1993): 93-101.

with "Judah": "Call his name Iezrael, for in yet a little while I will also avenge the blood of Iezrael on the house of Ieou, and I will turn away the kingdom of the house of Israel" (1:4). This change likely reflects a later Judean reading of the book where tradents in the Southern Kingdom reinterpreted the prophecies first addressed to the Northern Kingdom and applied them to Judah. The pro-Judean passage of 1:7 may also have influenced such a reading. Such a view supports the fact that the book is not meant to be read solely within its original historical context.

Israel's initial judgment will include breaking its bow in the valley of Jezreel (1:5), an action which signified military defeat in the ANE. In addition, threats of bow breaking in the ANE played on masculine fears of being feminized; bow removal would signify the sexual humiliation of a male soldier by transforming him into a woman. Chapman writes, "The soldier who heard the military curse involving bow breaking did not fear literal castration; he feared the humiliation of metaphorical castration."[44] The threat of bow breaking in 1:5 metaphorically castrates Israel from the Abrahamic promise to sow numerous descendants. Yet on the future salvific day of Jezreel in Hos 2:16-23 [2:18-25], YHWH promises once again to break the bow, along with the sword and war itself. With this promised future, breaking the bow no longer serves as threat of emasculation or impotence, since YHWH will sow fertility and virility for Israel (Hos 2:22-23 [2:24-25]). Israel's understanding of sexuality will be transformed such that symbols of fear will be demythologized. While the prophet's judgment oracles assumed commonly-held fears regarding sexuality, Hosea's salvation oracles reject and transform such notions. Jezreel now signifies the renewal of the earth, the cessation of warfare, and the nation's betrothal to YHWH.

What follows in Hos 1 are prophetic sign-acts that together demonstrate a father's rejection of his children. As mentioned above, the focus of chapter 1 is not the woman of promiscuity but rather the children of promiscuity. Following the birth of Jezreel, Gomer gives birth to a daughter. Hosea is not explicitly named as the father for this child or the one to follow, so it is possible that they are fathered by another man. Whereas the first child serves as a prophetic sign for the end of the Northern Kingdom, the latter two children signify the dissolution of YHWH's covenant with Israel in 1:6-9. Hosea will go on to describe in vivid detail and at length the annihilation of Israel's children, whether it be in the form of miscarriage, infertility, starvation, infanticide, or feticide (cf. 9:11-16; 10:14; 13:16). In order to understand the collapse of Hosea's family and the prophet's rhetorical assault on children, it is necessary to eschew romantic

---

44. Cynthia R. Chapman, *The Gendered Language of Warfare in the Israelite-Assyrian Encounter* (HSM 62; Winona Lake: Eisenbrauns, 2004), p. 54.

idealizations of the family and grasp the weighty vocation of marriage and parenting. On this point, Hauerwas remarks:

> [T]he family is morally crucial for our existence as the only means we have to bind time. Without the family, and the intergenerational ties involved, we have no way to know what it means to be historic beings. As a result we become determined by, rather than determining, our histories. Set out in the world with no family, without story of and for the self, we will simply be captured by the reigning ideologies of the day.[45]

In the book of Hosea, the loss of children is much more than a personal or domestic tragedy. Without children, Israel's history will come to a grinding halt; they will no longer be a people nor have any hope. At stake in Hosea's children are the very identity and future of Israel. Without children, Israel will forget who they are and where they are to go. It is unsurprising that throughout the Scriptures God's people and prophet are repeatedly threatened with infanticide, and conversely, God's mighty acts of redemption often begin with the birth of children and a genealogical record. Each year, as the church resets its calendar so that it can recall its past and anticipate its future, it fittingly begins with a season that anticipates the birth of an infant.

In Hos 1:6, God explains the significance of the name of the second child, Lo-Ruhamah, "For I will no longer have pity on the house of Israel or forgive them." Pity (רחם/*rāḥam*) and forgiveness (נשׂא/*nāśā'*) represent an integral part of YHWH's self-disclosure in Exod 34:6-7: "The Lord, the Lord, a God merciful (רחום/*raḥûm*) and gracious, slow to anger, and abounding in steadfast love and faithfulness, keeping steadfast love for the thousandth generation, forgiving (נשׂא/*nāśā'*) iniquity and transgression and sin, yet by no means clearing the guilty, but visiting the iniquity of the parents upon the children and the children's children, to the third and the fourth generation." The verb "to forgive" in v. 6 includes the infinitive absolute form, signifying emphatically that YHWH will never forgive them again.

Prior to Exod 34, YHWH had summarized God's self-revelation as, "I will make all my goodness pass before you, and will proclaim before you the name, 'The Lord'; and I will be gracious to whom I will be gracious, and will show mercy (רחם/*rāḥam*) on whom I will show mercy (רחם/*rāḥam*)" (Exod

---

45. Stanley Hauerwas, *A Community of Character: Toward a Constructive Christian Social Ethic* (Notre Dame: University of Notre Dame Press, 1981), p. 165. See also Stanley Hauerwas, "The Radical Hope in the Annunciation: Why Both Single and Married Christians Welcome Children," in *The Hauerwas Reader* (ed. J. Berkman and M. Cartwright; Durham: Duke University Press, 2001), pp. 505-18.

33:19). While Exod 34:6-7 serves as a unifying feature of the Twelve Prophets (cf. Joel 2:13; Jon 4:2; Mic 7:18-20; Nah 1:3), it is striking that this prophetic collection begins with the prophet *voiding* this statement. In Exodus, this passage addresses the crisis of covenant breaking following the golden calf incident. This text appropriately unifies and introduces the Twelve, since at the very outset of Hosea the validity of the covenant is in question. Bosman assesses every use of Exod 34:6-7 in the Twelve and concludes, "What does seem to be central to all the texts in question is the *ambiguity of YHWH's presence*."[46] Van Leeuwen believes the appeal to Exod 34:6-7 preserves the justice of YHWH even though God's people are riddled with evil. He writes, "By using the full bipolar contrast of mercy and justice from Exodus 34:6-7, the redactor [of the Twelve Prophets] affirms, on the one hand, that YHWH is free to exercise his forgiveness and mercy toward *any* who repent, and, on the other, that he will not be held hostage to the evil of the wicked."[47] The collection opens by answering the question, "Is God with us?" with an emphatic, "No." Going forward, readers of the Twelve cannot assume that Israel is guaranteed its favored status as YHWH's elect people.

The revelation of God's covenant name, YHWH, is integrally related to the election of Israel as God's covenant people. When God first reveals the covenant name "I am" (אהיה/*'ehyeh*) and "YHWH" (יהוה/*yhwh*) to Moses in Exod 3:14-15, God does so for the sake of "my/the people" (Exod 3:10; 12). Later, when God elaborates on the covenant name to Moses, God once again stresses the bond between the name and the people, "I will take you as my people, and I will be your God. You shall know that I am the LORD your God" (Exod 6:7). The revelation of God's name at Horeb initiates a process of redemption that culminates in Israel entering into covenant with YHWH at Sinai (Exod 19–24). Therefore, when YHWH states in Hosea 1:9 that Israel is no longer God's people and declares, "I am no longer 'I am' for you" (ואנכי לא־אהיה לכם/*we'ānōkî lō'-'ehyeh lākem*), in effect God is saying, "I am no longer YHWH to you." Rendtorff observes that the stock expression that signifies a covenant between God and Israel comes in the form of three formulas in the OT: 1) the phrase "I will be God for you"; 2) the phrase "You shall be a people for me"; and 3) instances where the two statements are combined into a single formula.[48] Hosea 1:9, "For

46. J. P. Bosman, "The Paradoxical Presence of Exodus 34:6-7 in the Book of the Twelve," *Scr* 87 (2004): 242, emphasis his.

47. Raymond C. Van Leeuwen, "Scribal Wisdom and Theodicy in the Book of the Twelve," in *In Search of Wisdom: Essays in Memory of John G. Gammie* (ed. L. G. Perdue, B. Scott, and W. J. Wiseman; Louisville: Westminster John Knox, 1993), p. 49, emphasis his.

48. Rolf Rendtorff, *The Covenant Formula: An Exegetical and Theological Investigation* (trans. M. Kohl; OTS; Edinburgh: T&T Clark, 1998), p. 13. Rendtorff notes that the covenant

you are not my people and I am no longer 'I am' to you," is an example of this third formula and communicates that the covenant is nullified.

Moberly observes that the revelation of the divine name is bound up with Moses' prophetic ministry to Israel: "Specifically, it is only in and through Moses being sent to Israel that Israel knows God as YHWH; the revelation of God to Israel is linked to a particular human figure who is the agent and mediator of that revelation."[49] If the divine name is lost, then the covenant relationship with God is void and null, and Moses is no longer Israel's prophet. If this is the case, by the end of v. 9 all elements of a covenant relationship — compassion, forgiveness, the divine name, and Mosaic mediation — have been revoked from Israel.

In a surprising reversal, the prophet announces in 1:10–2:1 [2:1-3] a future — deemed the day of Jezreel — where the prophetic signs of judgment in 1:4-9 will be transformed into signs of salvation. From the outset of the book, the initial prophetic signs signify both judgment and salvation, demonstrating to the reader that Hosea is ultimately a book about salvation. The promise that "the number of the people of Israel shall be like the sand of the sea" (1:10 [2:1]) recalls the Abrahamic promises of "seed/descendants" (זרע/*zeraʿ*) in Genesis,[50] where they will be numerous "as the sand that is on the seashore." Sweeney observes that both references to this promise to the patriarchs occur in narratives where the promise of descendants is jeopardized (Gen 22:17; 32:13).[51] The title "children of the living God" (1:10) is unique in all of the OT, and appears to reverse not only the declaration "you are not my people" in 1:9, but also the collective judgment of all three children as "children of whoredom" in 1:2. Even though the covenantal references up to this point have primarily been Mosaic, they are not at odds with Abrahamic promises because, in the final canonical form of the Old Testament, God's covenant with Abraham is the same as the covenant through Moses. On this point Rendtorff writes:

> In the canonical context of the Hebrew Bible, therefore, it must be said that God laid the foundation for his relationship to Israel in his covenant with Abraham (Genesis 17) and then, with the Exodus generation, extended it

---

formula "expresses in an extremely pregnant way God's relationship to Israel and Israel's to God. At the same time it combines with other terms, above all 'covenant' and 'choose.' . . . In this way the covenant formula contributes essentially to the expression and differentiation in the thematic field which may be summarily termed 'covenant theology'" (p. 92).

49. R. W. L. Moberly, *The Old Testament of the Old Testament: Patriarchal Narratives and Mosaic Yahwism* (OBT; Minneapolis: Augsburg Fortress, 1992), p. 23.

50. זרע/*zeraʿ* occurs in Gen 12:7; 13:15, 16; 15:3, 5, 13, 18; 16:10; 17:7, 8, 9, 10, 12, 19; 19:32, 34; 21:12, 13; 22:17, 18.

51. Sweeney, *Twelve Prophets*, 1:23.

to the people of Israel (Exodus 6). . . . From this point of departure, there can in fact really be no other, further covenant. The covenant has been made once for all, and at its very foundation God had already called it an 'everlasting covenant' (Gen 17:7, 19).[52]

At a canonical level, sharp distinctions between covenants ought not to be made, even though various texts may highlight different features within particular covenants. Neither is it necessary to prove or disprove whether Pentateuchal covenantal traditions preceded eighth-century prophets such as Hosea.[53] Not every reference to covenant in Hosea holds to a Deuteronomistic vision of covenant; rather, each instance possesses its distinct perspective on covenant and is read as part of the canon's witness on covenants. So while Hosea's message originally may have focused on a particular social-historical context, in its final form Hosea was read as part of a larger collection of Israel's sacred Scripture, which began with the Torah. Rather than a strictly biblical/theological or historical category, covenant ought to be understood as an organizing principle within the canon, one that in turn allows for the kind of exploration Castelo will pursue later in this volume.

Jezreel means "God sows," and while "sowing" may imply the scattering of seed and thus signify exile, it also suggests survival of progeny and the hope of return as illustrated in Zech 10:9: "Though I scattered them among the nations, yet in far countries they shall remember me, and they shall rear their children and return." In 1:11 [2:2], Jezreel signifies a future day of salvation when the people of both Judah and Israel — who have been dispersed among the nations — will be regathered, repossess the land, and be united under one ruler. In Hosea, Israel's hope rests in a reunited kingdom under Judean rule; yet there is no corresponding future for any of the Northern Kingdom's dynasties.

Numerous translations and interpretations of וְעָלוּ מִן־הָאָרֶץ/wĕ'ālû min-hā'āreṣ in 1:11 [2:2] have been suggested: 1) "they shall go up from the land" (of captivity); 2) "they shall ascend over the land," possibly signifying resurrection if one understands the land as the underworld; and 3) "they shall flourish on the land."[54] Returning to the land is a dominant theme of the book and collection. עלה מן/'ālāh min is widely used as an expression for leaving a land for Canaan, and motifs of exodus and a return to the land appear in the next two chapters

52. Rendtorff, *The Covenant Formula*, p. 83.

53. According to Wellhausen, the Prophets preceded the Law such that concepts of covenant from Deuteronomistic and Priestly traditions were unknown to eighth-century prophets such as Hosea. For a differing view, see Douglas K. Stuart, *Hosea-Jonah* (WBC 31; Dallas: Word, 1989), pp. xxxi-xlii.

54. See Macintosh, *Hosea*, pp. 31-33.

(2:14-15 [2:16-17]; 3:5). For these reasons, it appears that the author left the land unspecified so as to shape Israel's future restoration in Exodus form.[55] Rather than mention a king, Hosea speaks more generally of one "head" who will lead this united kingdom. This language certainly leaves open the possibility of a Messianic ruler, yet, in its immediate context, the passage suggests a Mosaic figure who will lead Israel out of a land of captivity and into a land of promise.

Whereas "no" (לֹא/*lōʾ*) dominates the prophet's speech in Hos 1:4-9, the word is deleted from the prophet's vocabulary in 1:10–2:1 [2:1-3]. The future day is an age of "yes," which climaxes in the revelation of Jesus Christ (cf. 2 Cor 1:18-20), where the very expressions of covenant relationship that are revoked in Hos 1:4-9 are once again extended, this time to include Gentiles among the people of God. In Romans 9:25-27, Paul designates Gentiles as those who were considered "not my people" (cf. 1 Pet 2:10), and Eph 2:12 specifies that this status meant that they were "aliens from the commonwealth of Israel, and strangers to the covenants of promise, having no hope and without God in the world." Through Christ, Gentiles are grafted into Israel's family tree and now possess a history and a hope.

---

55. Ben Zvi, *Hosea*, pp. 50-51.

4. Hosea 2:2-23 [2:4-25]

Bo H. Lim

The Marital Metaphor and the Rhetoric of Sexual Violence in Hosea 2

Although the majority of commentators interpret the woman of Hos 2 as representative of the people of Israel, the woman ought to be understood primarily as signifying the city of Samaria. The Old Testament frequently uses the terms "daughter" and "virgin/maiden" for cities (Isa 1:8; 16:1; Jer 4:31; Mic 4:8; Lam 2:13). Isaiah chapters 40, 49, 50, 51, 60 and 66, more than any other text, depict Jerusalem as a mother bearing children. John Schmitt observes "that the Hebrew Bible does not know a feminine Israel,"[1] and, where Israel is described as "whoring" (זנה/*zānāh*), the verb is in the masculine form (cf. Judg 2:17; 8:27, 33). In all the other passages in the Prophets where the prophet employs the rhetoric of sexual violence and humiliation against a whore or adulteress, the object is always a city. In Jer 13:22-27, it is Jerusalem who suffers violence, whose skirts will be lifted up over her face, and her shame exposed. Ezekiel 16:39 warns Jerusalem (cf. 16:2) that she will be stripped of her clothes and beautiful jewelry to be left naked and bare. The sister whores of Ezekiel 23, Oholah and Oholibah, receive the same treatment as described in Hos 1, and are identified as Samaria and Jerusalem, respectively. The canonical Prophets extend oracles of judgment against foreign nations, and when they do, they specifically target capital cities. In Nahum, the prophet's warning that YHWH "will lift up your skirts over your face; and I will let nations look on your nakedness and kingdoms on your shame" (3:5) is directed towards Nineveh, and in Isaiah 47:1-3, Babylon will be stripped of her robe, her nakedness will be uncovered, and her shame will be exposed.

---

1. John J. Schmitt, "The Gender of Ancient Israel," *JSOT* 26 (1983): 124; "The Wife of God in Hosea 2," *BR* 34 (1989): 5-18.

The city in Hosea 2 is likely Samaria since Hosea directs his speech against this city (7:1; 8:5-6; 10:5, 7; 13:16 [14:1]) in the manner of other preexilic prophets (Amos 3:9, 12; 4:1; 6:1; 8:14; Mic 1:1-7). Even speech that seems to suggest that the woman refers to the people of Israel prior to the establishment of Samaria (for example, "There she shall respond as in the days of her youth, as at the time when she came out of the land of Egypt" [2:15; Heb 2:17]) can be understood as referring to a city, since Ezekiel similarly situates Samaria and Jerusalem in Egypt in their youth (Ezek 23:3-4). The Targum for Hos 1–3 seems to have understood the woman as a city, as demonstrated in its reading of Hos 1:2: "and the Lord said to Hosea, 'Go (and) *speak a prophecy against the inhabitants of the idolatrous city, who continue to sin.*' "[2]

The rhetoric of violence in this chapter was intended to warn the city of Samaria, not women or individual Israelites, of its impending destruction should it continue in its political treachery. Such rhetoric was a common feature of ANE treaty curses and Assyrian royal inscriptions. Hillers lists the following parallels between these writings and biblical literature: the dwelling-place of animals, devouring animals, removal of joyful sounds, removal of the sound of millstones, to become a prostitute, to be stripped like a prostitute, breaking of weapons, breaking the scepter, dry breasts, to eat the flesh of sons and daughters, ravishing of wives, contaminated water, the incurable wound, warriors become women, no burial, like a bird in a trap, flood, lack of men, Sodom and Gomorrah, and passers-by will shudder.[3] This lengthy list demonstrates that the depictions of sexual violence and humiliation function as part of the larger discourse of treaty curses and ought to be understood in such terms. While aspects of the depiction of sexual violence in Hos 2 may correspond to contemporary forms of domestic violence or pornography, Ancient Israel understood these texts as warnings of the political and military catastrophe that would befall a capital city in the case of a treaty breach. Of the treaty curse motifs listed above by Hillers, Hosea 2 contains the themes of devouring animals (2:12 [2:14]), of being stripped like a prostitute (2:3 [2:5], 2:10 [2:12]), and of the breaking of weapons (2:18 [2:20]).

The language of Hos 2 is undoubtedly ideological and not naturalistic. Cynthia Chapman argues, "Biblical and Assyrian writers drew from a shared set of literary conventions regarding the use of gender in the recording of warfare,"[4] where idealized masculine virtues are associated with military victory.

2. Kevin J. Cathcart and Robert P. Gordon, *The Targum of the Minor Prophets* (ArBib 14; Wilmington: Michael Glazier, 1989), p. 29, emphasis theirs.

3. Delbert R. Hillers, *Treaty-Curses and the Old Testament Prophets* (BibOr 16; Rome: Pontifical Biblical Institute, 1964), pp. 43-79.

4. Cynthia R. Chapman, *The Gendered Language of Warfare in the Israelite-Assyrian Encounter* (HSM 62; Winona Lake: Eisenbrauns, 2004), p. 14.

Assyrian kings assumed a masculine system of signs in which they portrayed themselves as the protector of women and children, successful on the battlefield, and provider of food, oil, and clothing for their subjects. In contrast, opponents of the king were depicted as failures in war and unable to protect one's family or provide for their needs. Foreign women captured in war were depicted as unmolested, clothed, and well cared for by Assyrian kings. Historically, the rhetoric of sexual violence was not directed toward females but rather to males, and revolved around the topic of warfare. Speech depicting a man becoming a woman or a prostitute, forfeiting his land, failing to secure an heir, or losing his bow — all functioned as gendered and sexualized language to humiliate and intimidate opponents, as evidenced in the following excerpt:

> If Mati'-ilu sins against this treaty with Aššur-nerari, king of Assyria, may Mati'-ilu become a prostitute, his soldiers women, may they receive [a *gift*] in the square of their cities like a prostitute, may one country *push* them to the next; may Mati'-ilu's (sex) life be that of a mule, his wives extremely old; may Ištar, the goddess of men, the lady of women, take away their bow, bring them to shame, and make them bitterly weep: "Woe, we have sinned against the treaty of Aššur-nerari, king of Assyira.[5]

Much of the rhetoric employed negative notions of femininity in order to reinforce the power and reach of the king.

In Hosea 2, the prophet employs similar literary and rhetorical conventions to communicate to the people of Samaria that YHWH's kingship triumphs over that of any foreign ruler. In the manner of the Treaty of Aššur-nerari with Mati'-ilu, Hosea 2 depicts the woman practicing prostitution (7 [9]), the removal of bows (18 [20]), the public humiliation of the woman (10 [12]), and the eradication of mirth (11 [13]). While Hos 2 does not fall under the genre classification of a treaty, these shared conventions suggest that the text may function rhetorically in a similar manner. In this case, both texts function as a warning not to sin against their current covenant arrangements. From this vantage point, the rhetoric is primarily directed toward a male audience and attempts to exploit their fears of foreign domination in accordance with their cultural notions of masculinity.

Admittedly both Assyrian and Israelite writers "used wit and literary finesse to play with known categories of gender in order to recast the mili-

---

5. "Treaty of Aššur-nerari V with Mati'-ilu, King of Arpad," in Simo Parpola and Kazuko Watanabe, *Neo-Assyrian Treaties and Loyalty Oaths* (Helsinki: Helsinki University Press, 1988), SAA 2, 12, Ins. 8-15.

tary battle in such a way that their side appeared as the absolute victor."[6] Yet it is important to observe that in the power relation, Assyria was clearly the aggressive and more powerful party. Because of incessant Assyrian imperial western expansion, Israel as the weaker party constantly had to respond to its rhetoric of warfare (cf. Isa 36–37). So while Israel may have espoused rhetoric similar to its ANE counterparts, Chapman observes, "The writings of the biblical prophets concerning Assyria *are necessarily a reaction* to this military, diplomatic, and ideological imposition."[7] It is likely Hosea's audience was already well versed in the language of sexualized violence from Assyrian propaganda when the prophet employed similar rhetoric to describe the actions of YHWH.

It is worth noting that the prophetic rhetoric of sexual violence against Samaria and Jerusalem ceases following the exile and is replaced by the promise of everlasting love (Isa 54:1-8), although the warnings to foreign powers do continue. Following the tradition of the Prophets, the author of the Apocalypse employs the metaphor of whoredom and language of sexualized violence against Babylon because it is she who is intoxicated with the blood of the saints and martyrs (Rev. 17:6). The canonical trajectory for prophecies such as Hos 2 does not focus on individuals per se, but rather addresses human institutions that have forsaken their allegiance to God in exchange for material luxury and political gain. God warns the whore Babylon — in this case Rome — in Rev. 17–18 that it will face the violence and humiliation that it has enacted on the people of God. Barbara Rossing observes that the charge of prostitution (*porneia*, Rev. 14:8; 18:3) serves as a critique of Rome's economic exploitation and militaristic imperialism. Passages such as Rev. 17:16 ("And the ten horns that you saw, they and the beast will hate the whore; they will make her desolate and naked; they will devour her flesh and burn her up with fire") ought to be "read not primarily as assault on and exposure of a woman's body, but as the exposé and destruction of the city and its landscape through siege and warfare."[8] She is well aware of the accusations that the Bible is misogynistic and goes on to comment on its references to nakedness:

> If echoes of voyeuristic Hebrew texts that strip female cities' bodies naked for sexual exposure are present in Revelation, such echoes have been muted. It is striking that Revelation's sole reference to Babylon's nakedness

---

6. Chapman, *The Gendered Language of Warfare*, p. 166.

7. Chapman, *The Gendered Language of Warfare*, p. 19, emphasis mine.

8. Barbara R. Rossing, *The Choice Between Two Cities: Whore, Bride, and Empire in the Apocalypse* (HTS 48; Harrisburg: Trinity Press International, 1999), p. 88.

in Rev. 17:16 is terse and restrained. There is no repetition of the imagery, no listing of specific body parts that are uncovered. The author gives significantly less attention to disrobing the harlot than he did to elaborating the visual description of her expensive dress and adornment in Rev. 17:4. This suggests that the primary aim in portraying Rome as a woman is not to expose or undress her sexually, but to furnish an exposé of the empire's seductive powers and evil wiles to an audience that apparently includes some members who do not yet see them as evil.[9]

The canonical trajectory of the function of the whore metaphor is not one of pornoprophetic titillation but rather resistance literature against empires. As Rossing observes, the author of Revelation censors these images rather than exploits them. Rather than promote violence, Revelation encourages non-violent resistance in the manner exemplified by the slain lamb, even if such a course should result in martyrdom for the saints. Rather than dwell on female nakedness, the Scriptures elaborate on the threat of evil empires. Given that this language was poetic and ideological and never naturalistic, it is unsurprising that it reappears in the Bible only within apocalyptic literature. Ancient audiences knew that this language was not to be taken literally and that its exaggerated rhetoric carried a political message. The full canonical scope of these metaphors ought to be considered before scholars call for the rejection of OT prophetic texts that contain such language. The metaphor may be crude, insensitive, and degrading to women according to modern sensibilities. Nevertheless, its purpose among ancient audiences was to persuade the people of God to reject the seduction of powerful empires.

Even though the woman of Hos 2 functions primarily as a metaphor for the city of Samaria, she also represents the people of Israel within the broader framework of chapters 1–3 and the book of Hosea.[10] Although Israel is consistently described in masculine grammatical terms in the OT, Israel can take on metaphorical feminine forms. More importantly, in Hos 1 Gomer and her children represent Israel, and readers are to associate them with the woman of chapter 2. Both Hos 1:9 ("You are not my people and I am not your God") and 2:2 ("For she is not my wife and I am not her husband") share the language of rejection. So while the woman may serve as a metaphor for the city of Samaria in Hos 2, within the broader context of the book, readers associate her with the people of Israel as well.

9. Rossing, *The Choice Between Two Cities*, p. 97.
10. J. Andrew Dearman, "YHWH's House: Gender Roles and Metaphors for Israel in Hosea," *JNSL* 25 (1999): 97-108.

Hosea 2:2-13 [2:4-15]

In chapter 2 the marital metaphor comes to the fore and the role of the children is diminished. The children appear to be innocent of wrongdoing, yet they are the recipients of punishment due to the crimes of their mother (2:4 [2:6]). They play the role of accuser (2:2 [2:4]), and their fate is bound up with the fate of their mother (2:22-23 [2:24-25]). Like chapter 1, chapter 2 begins with judgment speech, extends the judgment of the mother on to the children (2:4 [2:6]), and concludes with salvation pronouncements (2:21-23 [2:23-25]) in language similar to the conclusion to 1:10–2:1 [2:1-3]. Chapters 1-2 ought to be read in conjunction, and the prophecies of chapter 2 ought to be understood as an elaboration of the message of chapter 1. Yet in chapter 2 the marital metaphor takes center stage rather than the children as representing YHWH's covenant with Israel. As noted earlier in the commentary on Hos 1, the numerous Baal references are a rhetorical device intended to cast Israel's present sins in religious terms. In chapter 2 Samaria is described as promiscuous and adulterous, yet one ought not to assume that this language signifies sexual sin or cultic prostitution. It is first necessary to identify the overarching metaphors and then understand how individual texts contribute to the rhetorical aims.

The children participate as prophetic agents within the drama of Hosea by bringing an accusation (רִיב/*rîb*, 2:2 [2:4]) against their mother. Although this term does not open chapters 1–3, the first unit of Hosea's prophecy, the term will serve as a strategic catchword in introducing the latter two literary units in the book (see 4:1, 4 for 4:1–11:11; and 12:2 [12:3] for 11:12–14:9 [12:1–14:10]). In view of the household metaphor of chapters 1–2, the image here is not of a law court, nor do the prophet and children serve as covenant prosecutors.[11] The image is of a domestic dispute in the manner of Gen 31:36, where the verb רִיב/ *rîb* describes Jacob's contention with his uncle Laban.[12] Later, Hosea extensively draws upon the Jacob traditions (12:2-12 [12:3-13]), and for this reason, Gale Yee suggests that the woman figure in chapter 2 is none other than Rachel. In Jer 31:15, it is Rachel who weeps for her children, the Northern tribes, and as such she becomes a symbol of the moral corruption of the Northern Kingdom.[13] The reader is drawn into a conversation where the participants are covenant partners who speak in covenantal terms, as witnessed already in chapter 1. Many

---

11. Contra Douglas K. Stuart, *Hosea-Jonah* (WBC 31; Dallas: Word, 1989), pp. 45-46. Here Stuart assumes too much Deuteronomistic influence on the author.

12. A. A. Macintosh, *A Critical and Exegetical Commentary on Hosea* (ICC; Edinburgh: T & T Clark, 1997), p. 41.

13. Gale A. Yee, *Composition and Tradition in the Book of Hosea: A Redactional Critical Investigation* (SBLDS 102; Atlanta: Scholars Press, 1987), pp. 124-25.

suggest that the various metaphors of Hosea are incommensurable and therefore negate any hope of theologizing from the text.[14] Perhaps the metaphors in Hosea may not withstand the test of consistency according to modern literary criticism; nevertheless, this speech has continued to shape the manner in which the people of God relate covenantally to YHWH.

YHWH begins the discourse with an assessment of the relationship between God and the children's mother: "for she is not my wife and I am not her husband" (2:2 [2:4]). While this expression may not serve as a divorce-enacting verbal oath, it did function in this manner within Old Babylonian marriage laws,[15] and at minimum, it communicates the threat of divorce. The woman's speech in 2:7 [2:9] ("I will go and return to my first husband, for it was better with me then than now") suggests a divorce or separation has taken place. In the OT a marriage that began "in the days of her youth" (2:15 [2:17]) is regarded as the most important among one's wives (cf. Isa 54:6; Jer 2:2; Joel 1:8; Prov. 2:17; 5:18; Mal 2:14-15), and a marriage to a wife from youth is associated with a covenant (Prov. 2:17; Mal 2:14). Since chapters 1–2 mirror each other in content and form, chapter 2 may communicate a similar message as chapter 1. Given that God employs formulaic speech in 1:9, nullifying YHWH's covenant with Israel, it is likely that chapter 2 announces God's divorce from the woman. Chapters 1–2 both announce God's abrogation of covenant, with Hos 2:23 [2:25] signifying the reversal of both of the judgment oracles of chapters 1 and 2.

The first description of the woman's promiscuity in vv. 5-7 [7-9] is her pursuit of bread, water, wool, flax, oil, wine, and grain from other lovers (2:5 [2:7]). These items ought not to be understood as elements of Baal cult prostitution, but rather the provisions necessary to sustain a marriage. ANE marriage contracts often stipulated that the husband was responsible for providing his wife with food, clothing, and personal supplies, and if he failed to, the wife was warranted in seeking divorce. A Middle Assyrian law states:

> If a woman is residing in her father's house, or her husband settles her in a house elsewhere, and her husband then travels abroad but does not leave her any oil, wool, clothing, or provisions, or anything else, and sends her no provisions from abroad — that woman shall still remain (the exclusive

14. Francis Landy, "In the Wilderness of Speech: Problems of Metaphor in Hosea," *BibInt* 3 (1995): 35-59; David Jobling, "A Deconstructive Reading of Hosea 1–3," in *Relating to the Text* (ed. Timothy J. Sandoval and Carleen Mandolfo; JSOTSup 384; London: T & T Clark, 2003), pp. 206-15.

15. Victor H. Matthews, "Marriage and Family in the Ancient Near East," in *Marriage and Family in the Biblical World* (ed. K. M. Campbell; Downers Grove: InterVarsity, 2003), p. 25. Also Gordon P. Hugenberger, *Marriage as a Covenant: Biblical Law and Ethics as Developed from Malachi* (VTSup 52; Leiden: Brill, 1994), pp. 231-34.

object of rights) for her husband for five years, she shall not reside with another husband. . . . [A]t the onset of(?) six years, she shall reside with the husband of her choice; her (first) husband, upon returning, shall have no valid claim to her; she is clear for her second husband.[16]

Exodus 21:10 legislates that a husband is obligated to provide food, clothing, and oil[17] to all his wives, in the pattern of other ANE maintenance clauses. So the mother's pursuit of these items from lovers suggests willing marital unfaithfulness, since YHWH had not failed to provide these very provisions for her (v. 8 [10]).

As indicated in my introduction, the theme of return serves as a unifying feature of the Twelve Prophets. By featuring this theme from the outset of the collection, Hosea "stands as a programmatic introduction to a major issue posed by the Twelve, the restoration of Israel and its relationship with YHWH following punishment at the hands of various nations."[18] The word turn/return (שׁוב/*šûb*) occurs 24 times in Hosea, and according to LeCureux, each use falls into one of three categories: 1) שׁוב/*šûb* as punishment; 2) שׁוב/*šûb* as restoration (3:5; 6:11b; 11:9; 14:4 [5], 7 [8]); 3) שׁוב/*šûb* as repentance. The category of punishment can be grouped into the following subsections: recompense (4:9; 12:2 [3], 14 [15]), exile (8:13; 9:3; 11:5), and miscellaneous punishment (2:9 [11]; 5:15). שׁוב/*šûb* as repentance can be subdivided into the refusal to repent (5:4; 7:10, 16; 11:5), reluctant repentance (2:7 [2:9]), and call to repentance (6:1; 12:6 [7]; 14:1 [14:2], 2 [3], 4 [5]).[19] Although it is contested, several commentators believe that the woman's speech in Hos 2:7 [2:9] ("I will go and return שׁוב/*šûb* to my first husband") is only a semblance of repentance since it reflects selfish and superficial motives, and that YHWH's actions in the verses to follow are punishments. In fact, the second use of שׁוב/*šûb* in Hosea appears two verses later, in 2:9 [2:11], and describes YHWH's act of judgment against the woman. This verse suggests that the woman's confession of supposed repentance in 2:7 [2:9] was unacceptable and insincere. It seems appropriate that the very first instance

16. "The Middle Assyrian Laws (Tablet A)," trans. Martha Roth (*COS* 2.132.A 36: 357).

17. While most translations interpret the last word as "conjugal rights" (ענה/*ônāh*), several scholars have argued that this *hapax* ought to be translated "oil," in the manner of other maintenance clauses in the ANE. See the discussion in Daniel I. Block, "Marriage and Family in Ancient Israel," in *Marriage and Family in the Biblical World*, p. 48.

18. Marvin A. Sweeney, "Sequence and Interpretation in the Book of the Twelve," in *Reading and Hearing the Book of the Twelve* (ed. J. D. Nogalski and M. A. Sweeney; SBLSymS 15; Atlanta: Society of Biblical Literature, 2000), p. 56.

19. Jason T. LeCureux, *The Thematic Unity of the Book of the Twelve* (HBM 41; Sheffield: Sheffield Phoenix Press, 2012), p. 64.

of שׁוּב/*šûb* in Hosea describes reluctant repentance, since throughout the course of the book YHWH will attempt to correct Israel's penchant for this behavior.

What follows in vv. 8-13 [10-15] is not a description of participation in Baal cult prostitution, but rather the mother's participation in cultic activity through means received from YHWH and her other lovers. In v. 8 [10] the woman uses the very gifts of silver and gold, lavished upon her by YHWH as a bridal gift, for the sake of her lover. Rather than acknowledge YHWH for the gifts of silver and gold, she uses them for Baal (2:8 [2:10]). Kelle observes, "The speech thus suggests a rhetorical horizon in which the leaders of the capital city Samaria have sought out illicit political relationships with foreign allies that constitute an abandonment of YHWH and work to their detriment (2:7, 10) [Eng. 2:5, 8]."[20] The mention of both a singular Baal (2:8 [2:10]) and plural Baalim (2:13 [2:15]) suggests that this term is synonymous with "lovers" (2:5 [2:7], 7 [9], 10 [12], 12 [14], 13 [15]) and ought to be understood as a political overlord or overlords. They are the fundamental competitors for sole allegiance to YHWH because they provide the woman with food, clothing, oil, and fertility. Ackerman observes that the term for love (אהב/*'āhab*) in the OT assumes hierarchical relationships, whether they be familial bonds, romantic love, or political loyalty. Therefore books like Hosea that speak extensively of love can fluidly describe both interpersonal and political relationships with this term. Assumed in this chapter is the woman's dependence upon the male figure, whether he be a paramour according to the logic of the metaphor or a foreign nation or ruler according to the meaning of the metaphor. Given that this key word functions in a dual sense, this chapter ought to be understood at multiple levels and readers ought not to fixate on one particular understanding of the imagery, whether it be the personal or the political.

A more accurate translation for "which were to cover her nakedness" (2:9 [2:11]) is "in order to reckon her indiscretion,"[21] and it describes the financial and property arrangements involved in a divorce. In Hos 2:9 [2:11], YHWH threatens to withdraw spousal support because of the woman's indiscretions. The mention of incense burning in 2:13 [2:15] is part and parcel of the cultic activity associated with political treaties, and the passage lacks the typical vocabulary associated with Baal worship. If the sin of Israel is primarily political in nature, her punishment will also come in political form.

Hosea 2:2-13 [2:4-15] contains gendered language of covenant breaking and warfare and signifies the military destruction of Samaria due to her political

---

20. Brad E. Kelle, *Hosea 2: Metaphor and Rhetoric in Historical Perspective* (Atlanta: Society of Biblical Literature, 2005), p. 181.

21. Kelle, *Hosea 2*, p. 254.

treachery. The exposure and judgment of the woman's sexual misconduct function as a metaphor for the destruction of capital cities. Hosea 2:3 [2:5] essentially voids God's covenant with the people by returning them to their condition prior to the redemptive events of the exodus. The woman will be made into a wilderness, her fertility will be removed, she will be transformed into a parched land, and she will die of thirst. Rather than view 2:6 [2:8] as actions intended to manipulate the psychological state of an individual through enforced seclusion, one should read the passage as describing the limitation of the woman's cultic practices or her prostituting activity. The language of "finding" and "seeking" in 2:6-7 [2:8-9] is erotic speech suggestive of cultic fertility rituals. The language of "going after" (הלך אחר/*hālak 'ahar*) in 2:5 [2:7] can describe political disloyalty, as it does in 5:11: "Ephraim is oppressed, crushed in judgment, because he was determined to go after vanity."

The language of Hos 2:6 [2:8] describes the woman's cultic restrictions, but also serves as a metaphor for the siege of a city. Lamentations 3:7-9, where Daughter Zion personifies the lament of Jerusalem, uses the same vocabulary to describe the actions of the Babylonians against Jerusalem: "He has walled (גדר/*gādar*, Hos 2:6 [2:8]) me about so that I cannot escape; he has put heavy chains on me; though I call and cry for help, he shuts out my prayer; he has blocked (גדר/*gādar*, Hos 2:6 [2:8]) my ways with hewn stones, he has made my paths crooked." The numerous references to land suggest that the woman of Hos 2 represents not only the people but also the land of Israel (cf. Hos 1:2), since the reckoning of her indiscretions involves grain, wine, wool, and flax. The *hapax* in 2:10 [2:12], "shame" (נבלות/*nablôt*), describes sexual misconduct, and within this context it refers to both the woman's nakedness (2:3 [2:5]) and her indiscretion (2:9 [2:11]). This understanding is consistent with other passages that describe the destruction of capital cities in the language of stripping women (Ezek 16; 23; Nah 3:4-6) and the desiccation of the landscape (Jer 50:12; 51:43).

Hosea 2:14-23 [2:16-25]

Chapter 2's structure can be discerned in the threefold use of the conjunctive "therefore" (לכן/*lākēn*) found in 2:6 [2:8], 2:9 [2:11], and 2:14 [2:16]. The chapter opens with a plea in 2:2 [2:4] followed by a series of threats. Given that the threats are introduced with the word "lest" (פן/*pen*, 2:3 [2:5]), they ought to be viewed as genuine possibilities for Samaria, particularly since 2:13 [2:15] concludes the first two "therefore" sections with the phrase, "declares the Lord" (נאם־יהוה/*ně'ūm-yhwh*). The reader is surprised to find that 2:14-23 [2:16-25] breaks from this pattern with a sudden reversal of all the threats of punishment announced in 2:2-13 [2:4-15]. Rather than kill the woman in the wilderness (2:3 [2:5]), YHWH will speak to her with tenderness in that place (2:14 [2:16]). Whereas the land will be stripped of grain, wine, wool, and flax in 2:9 [2:11], in 2:14-23 [2:16-25] a covenant is made such that the land will flourish with wildlife (2:18 [2:20]), grain, wine, and oil (2:22 [2:24]). YHWH rejects the mother as his wife in 2:2-13 [2:4-15], yet in 2:20 [2:22] YHWH promises to betroth her.

The wilderness serves as the state and the site of the remarriage between God and the woman. The grammar is unclear as to whether 2:14 [2:16] ought to be translated, "I will lead her into the wilderness" (NRSV) or "I will lead her through the wilderness" (NJPS), but the context makes clear that both senses are in mind. As a city, she is *made into* a wilderness (2:3 [2:5]), she is then *led to* the wilderness (2:14 [2:16]), and finally she is *brought out* of the wilderness, in this case referring to Egypt (2:15 [2:17]). This pattern is consistent with Hosea's message that exile will be the means of both judgment and redemption. Commentators have long been puzzled over the use of the term "persuade" (פתה/*pātah*) in 2:14 [2:16], which is translated "entice, lure, deceive, coax, seduce." In Exod 22:16 it is used to describe the seduction and rape of a virgin. Here the word has positive connotations, and it may suggest erotic speech, since Song of Songs similarly speaks of the wilderness as the place of birth (Song 8:5). So while "persuade" may have negative connotations, the verse goes on to describe how God will "speak tenderly to her," which can literally be translated as "(I) speak to her heart" (ודברתי על־לבה/*wĕdibbartî ʿal-libbāh*). While some have suggested that these actions resemble the manipulative tactics of domestic violence and the exploitative abuses of pornography, the canonical intertexts suggest the contrary.

After a double announcement of comfort, Isa 40:2 proclaims, "Speak tenderly (דברו על־לב/*dābbĕrû ʿal-lēb*) to Jerusalem, and cry to her that she has served her term, that her penalty is paid, that she has received from the LORD's hand double for all her sins." Like Hos 2:14-23 [2:16-25], Isaiah 40–54 announces salvation oracles to a capital city in the wilderness by addressing it as a bride, virgin daughter, and mother. In Isaiah, God's speech is certainly intimate and impassioned, yet no eroticism is implied. In Isaiah and Hosea, the prophetic announcement that God will "speak tenderly" signifies that judgment has come to an end and the era of salvation has begun. Hosea uses the wilderness — a motif that is typically associated with deprivation, death, and covenant rejection — and reinterprets it as a place of love, renewal, and hope. It is not surprising that movement into and out of the wilderness requires God's coaxing through persuasive, yet tender, speech.

Jeremiah 2:1-3 will later draw upon both this text and Hos 11:1-4 and, in a similar fashion, depict the wilderness as the place of birth and betrothal.

Jeremiah 2:2 in particular shares much of the key vocabulary of these texts, "I remember the devotion (חסד/*ḥesed*, Hos 2:19 [2:21]) of your youth (נעורים/ *nĕ'ûrîm*, Hos 2:15 [2:17]), your love (אהבה/*'ahăbāh*, Hos 11:4) as a bride, how you followed (הלך/*hālak*) me in the wilderness (מדבר/*midbār*, Hos 2:14 [2:16]), in a land (ארץ/*'ereṣ*, Hos. 1:2; 1:11 [2:2]; 2:3 [2:5], 15 [17], 18 [20], 21 [23], 22 [24], 23 [25]) not sown (זרע/*zāra'*, Hos 2:23 [2:25])." Hosea 2:15 [2:17] announces that, unlike the first exodus and conquest, God's people will not stumble as Israel did in the Valley of Achor because of Achan (Josh 7:24-26). The word for "hope" (תקוה/*tiqwāh*) is a pun on "thread" (תקוה/*tiqwāh*, Josh 2:18, 21), the scarlet cord the prostitute Rahab placed on the window of her house during the conquest of Jericho, in hopes of being spared. Hosea draws upon Israel's traditions regarding Abraham, exodus, and conquest in its description of judgment and renewal. With each of these traditions Hosea envisages a great reversal, and in this case the former place of trouble (עכר/*'ākar*, Josh 7:25) will now be a doorway to hope.

The eschatological term "on that day" in 2:16 [2:18] evokes the theme of the Day(s) of the LORD within the collection of the Twelve Prophets. While the more technical term "Day of the LORD" is not present here or elsewhere in Hosea, it is fair to say that the reader is expected to make the connection between these terms given that the formula "on that day" appears in 1:5; 2:16 [2:18], 18 [20], and 21 [23]; and Joel 2:19 goes on to cite Hos 2:22 [2:24].[22] Thirteen of the fifteen references to the term "Day of the LORD" in the OT appear within the Twelve, and the term "on that day" appears 40 times within the collection. Hosea establishes the eschatological expectation for a future act of divine intervention where judgment will extend to the political, religious, and ecological realm, to be followed by a corresponding comprehensive restoration.

Throughout Hos 2:16-20 [2:18-22], YHWH addresses his bride in the second person. Naming and renaming play a vital role in the OT and especially in Hos 1–2; therefore, the change from "my Baal" to "my husband" in Hos 2:16 [2:18] is highly significant. "Baal" means "owner, husband, master, lord" and the verbal form can mean "to rule over" or "to marry." The term can also refer to Canaanite gods who were often associated with rain and fertility. When attached to another name such as Baal-Peor (Num 25:3, 5), Baal-Zebub (2 Kgs 1:6), or Baal-Hadad, the term names a specific deity. In the literature of Ugarit, Baal defeats the sea monster Yamm and claims supremacy over the pantheon of gods. In Hosea, the term appears six times, and half of the occurrences are in the plural form. None of the references carry an additional name; therefore, it is

22. James D. Nogalski, "The Day(s) of YHWH in the Book of the Twelve," in *Thematic Threads in the Book of the Twelve* (ed. P. L. Redditt and A. Schart; BZAW 325; Berlin: Walter de Gruyter, 2003), p. 198.

difficult to identify their historical referents. While "Baal" may have originally referred to political overlords, in the final form of the book the term describes unspecified idolatry and political disloyalty.

In the Twelve Prophets as a whole, the word "baal" occurs infrequently and the final two uses of the word suggest idolatry. According to Zephaniah, Judah continues to be plagued by "every remnant of Baal" (Zeph 1:4), and the prophet goes on to name the deity Milcom explicitly (1:5). The word appears again at the bookend of the Twelve: "Judah has been faithless, and abomination has been committed in Israel and in Jerusalem; for Judah has profaned the sanctuary of the LORD, which he loves, and has married (בעל/*bāʿal*) the daughter of a foreign god" (Mal 2:11). Of the 10 occurrences of the word בעל/*bāʿal* in the Twelve Prophets, only three of them appear outside Hosea and Malachi. In addition, Mal 2:11 also mentions "love" (אהב/*ʾāhab*), another word that appears predominantly in Hosea and Malachi within the Twelve Prophets. When the Twelve are read as a unity, the interpersonal relationships of mixed marriages are viewed as cultic desecration and idolatry. As indicated in my introduction, Hosea and Malachi share similar themes and vocabulary as evidenced in Mal 2:11. When read within the collection, the Baal references in Hosea signify idolatry, but this idolatry may take the form of religious, political, and social sin. Therefore, even though the term "baal" could be a general reference to "husband," in the context of Hosea and the Twelve, calling out to YHWH as "my Baal" is understood as unacceptable syncretistic behavior that demonstrates that the peoples' allegiance lies elsewhere. Although in the present Israel is continually plagued by various suitors, on that future day all competitors to YHWH will be removed (2:17 [2:19]). Instead of judgment, YHWH extends the opportunity to relate to God with the intimacy exclusive to the marital union. The term "my husband" can mean both man and husband, and it recalls God's creative act to bring together man and woman as one flesh in Gen 2:24.

In Hos 2:18 [2:20], YHWH bypasses the traditional parties involved in God's covenants with Israel and instead appeals directly to the animals. The creatures listed in 2:18 [2:20] are commensurate with the categories of animals listed in the creation accounts of Gen 1–2, as well as the post-flood re-creation account of Gen 9:1-17. As in the case of the Noah story, humans are the beneficiaries of God's commitment to non-human creation. In Gen 9:8-17, God establishes an everlasting covenant with Noah and his descendants, but also "with every living creature that is with [him], the birds, the domestic animals, and every animal of the earth with [him]" (Gen 9:10). The salvation oracle of Hos 2:18 [2:20] is consistent with YHWH's charge that the land commits great whoredom by forsaking the LORD (1:2), and with the indictment in 4:1-3. In that passage, Israel's unfaithfulness and injustice lead to the disintegration of creation: "Therefore the land mourns, and all who live in it languish; together with the wild animals and the birds of the air, even the fish of the sea are perishing" (Hos 4:3). Hosea 2:18 [2:20] demonstrates the inseparable tie between creation and redemption and nullifies attempts to categorize God's covenant with Noah as separate from redemptive covenants.

Additionally, in Hos 2:18 [2:20], God's eschatological vision for humanity involves the establishment of safety without the use of violence. In Hosea, true security consistently comes through the abolition of weaponry, not increased armament. Earlier in the book, God announced that salvation does not come through militarization (1:7), and later Hosea rebukes Samaria for seeking security through the means of force: "You have plowed wickedness, you have reaped injustice, you have eaten the fruit of lies. Because you have trusted in your power and in the multitude of your warriors . . ." (Hos 10:13). If the church considers that the promises of 2:14-23 [2:16-25] have been inaugurated in some form through the advent of Christ, then it need embrace not only God's invitation to an intimate love relationship, but also God's ecological and non-militaristic political vision for the world.

Unlike chapters 1 and 3, chapter 2 does not contain prophetic sign-acts; all of it is prophetic rhetoric. The speech of the woman in vv. 5 [7], 7 [9] and 12 [14] is reported by YHWH, and therefore it represents God's assessment of Israel's sentiments. As argued above, Hos 2 provides a theological interpretation of the fall of Samaria, so in this case any "rhetorical violence" on behalf of God translates into national catastrophe for Israel at the hands of the Assyrians. The question remains, What does this text communicate about God? Commentators have often concluded, as Kelle does, that "In this first-person speech by the deity, Hosea purports to give his audience a glimpse into the thoughts and feelings of YHWH himself."[23] Or, in the words of Abraham Heschel, Hosea teaches readers about the pathos of God.[24] Given that the knowledge of God is an important theme in the book (4:1, 6; 6:1) and the end result of God's actions in chapter 2 is so that "you shall know the LORD" (2:20 [2:22]), this text does not merely describe ancient Israel's political predicament in the 8th century, but it also provides instruction about God. "To know" (ידע/*yāda*ʿ) functioned as a technical term in Hittite and Akkadian texts signifying mutual legal acknowledgement between a suzerain and a vassal,[25] so this word communicates the kind of covenant relationship Israel was to have with God. The woman fails

---

23. Kelle, *Hosea 2*, p. 243.

24. Abraham J. Heschel, *The Prophets* (2 vols.; New York: HarperCollins, 1962), 1:39-60, 2:1-11.

25. Kelle, *Hosea 2*, p. 244.

to "know/acknowledge" (ידע/*yāda'*) God in 2:8 [2:10], and in 2:13 [2:15], she is guilty of forgetting YHWH. Hosea makes it clear that Israel's future rests not in political strategizing, but first and foremost in loyalty to YHWH. No longer will God's people prostitute themselves to other powers; they will give their undivided loyalty to YHWH, who in turn will extend mercy and love.

While certainly the rhetoric of 2:2-13 [2:4-15] describes a fierceness in the actions of YHWH toward the woman, no explicit claims about the character of God are made in this section. In contrast, in 2:19-20 [2:21-22], YHWH describes the renewed marriage with the woman as characterized by righteousness, justice, steadfast love, mercy, and faithfulness. These are attributes often ascribed to YHWH (e.g., Ps 89:14), and in this case, they are extended also to the people of God. What is transferred to the people is not the violence that characterizes the actions of God in 2:2-13 [2:4-15], but the righteousness, justice, steadfast love, mercy, and faithfulness demonstrated in 2:14-23 [2:16-25]. Knowing God, being betrothed to YHWH, and being God's covenant people ultimately mean to imitate God, to mirror God's attitudes and actions of righteousness, justice, steadfast love, and mercy. It is precisely these qualities that Israel lacks in the present and which Hosea calls them to pursue (4:1; 6:6; 10:12-13).

Israel's role in its salvation is to willingly accept remarriage. YHWH is clearly the initiator and Israel is to reciprocate God's loving actions toward the people, and Hosea's language suggests a sealing of marriage covenant. The word "betroth" (ארש/*'āraś*) occurs three times in 2:19-20 [2:21-22], and is typically used to describe the bride price paid by husbands (cf. 2 Sam 3:14). The term "answer" (ענה/*'ānāh*) appears five times within Hos 2:21-22 [2:23-24], and earlier in 2:15 [2:17] it describes the woman's response to God's initiative to woo and eventually wed her. In 2:21-22 [2:23-24], the word describes YHWH's response to the heavens, the heaven's response to the earth, and the earth's response to both. The term can be variously translated, including in the sense of conferring legal testimony (e.g., Exod 20:16), and the invocation of the heavens and earth in 2:21 [2:23] is suggestive of witnesses to covenant treaties (Deut 32:1). In addition, much of the language in 2:14-23 [2:16-25] carries sexual connotations. Hosea 2:14 [2:16] opens this section with language of seduction ("I will allure her"), "to know" (2:20 [2:22]) is suggestive of sexual relations (e.g. Gen 4:1), and "to sow" (2:23 [2:25]) in the land carries the imagery of impregnation. The language suggests a relationship that is intimate and legally binding.

The scandal of these texts is the manner in which so many of YHWH's actions mirror those of the baals. The gifts of fertility in 2:22 [2:24] — grain, wine, oil, and the mention of rain later in 6:2-3 — are consonant with expectations from Canaanite deities. Similar goods were identified earlier in 2:5 [2:7] and 8-9 [10-11] as the basic provisions to women in ANE marriages. There is no need to jump to the conclusion that, in Hosea, "YHWH religion becomes indistinguishable from Baal religion."[26] Such is an example of illegitimate totality transfer. One noticeable difference between Hosea and Canaanite religion is that goddesses are absent in Hosea's narrative world. One must remember that this text is an eschatological vision, so the promises of earthly abundance are reflective of a new ecological and political order. Yahwistic faith deeply values creation, so it is no surprise that it shares commonalities with Canaanite fertility religions.

This section closes with a reversal of the prophetic sign-acts of judgment in chapter 1, signifying to the reader that chapters 1–2 are to be read in conjunction. Chapter 2 recalls the judgment pronouncements on Gomer's children in chapter 1 and announces their reversal. Hosea 1:2 indicates that the family of whoredom serves as a prophetic sign for the land committing great whoredom, and 1:4-5 identifies the first child, Jezreel, as a sign of judgment. Thus it is fitting that chapter 2 concludes with a response to Jezreel in v. 22 [24], and v. 23 [25] contains a wordplay on Jezreel (יזרעאל/*yizrĕ'e'l*) with the announcement that YHWH will sow (זרע/*zāra'*) in the land. Hosea 2:23 [2:25] reverses the judgment of 1:9, and in this case, rather than YHWH declaring, "I am your God," Lo-ammi — representative of Israel — responds with the confession, "You are my God." The covenant was never meant to be unilateral; it was always intended to facilitate a reciprocal relationship. In the eschaton, Israel will be characterized as a responsive people, demonstrating fidelity and exhibiting the knowledge of God.

---

26. Jobling, "A Deconstructive Reading of Hosea 1–3," p. 212.

5. Hosea 3:1-5

Bo H. Lim

As argued earlier in the commentary to chapter 1, Hosea 3 provides a second prophetic sign-act narrative that shares symbolic (but not biographical) continuity with the first prophetic sign-act narrative of 1:2-11. The narrative is clearly to be read in conjunction with the preceding text given that Hosea states, "The LORD said to me *again.*" The word "again" signals to the reader that this text is to be read following a previous episode, so while it is separate from the first, it is not independent. Commentators have tended to grant greater authenticity to first-person narrative accounts and have suggested that chapter 3 describes Hosea's first encounter with Gomer, and that the events of chapter 1 were secondary but were then reversed in the redaction of the work.[1] These kinds of speculative reconstructions seem to be motivated out of a desire to fit the prophetic book into a particular version of Hosea and Gomer's love story. Unfortunately, the book of Hosea does not provide such a story and in fact provides very little data as to the historical prophet's marriage. In fact, if one interprets chapter 2 as biographical, one could plausibly argue that "Hosea does not seem to have been an easy man to live with, and the woman mentioned in Hos 3:1-5 might very well be someone different."[2] Attempts at reconstructing the biography of Hosea can lead to very different conclusions regarding culpability for Hosea's failed marriage.[3] Rather than first person indicating historical priority, it functions on

1. A. A. Macintosh, *Critical and Exegetical Commentary on Hosea* (ICC; Edinburgh: T & T Clark, 1997), p. 118.

2. Marvin A. Sweeney, *The Twelve Prophets* (2 vols.; Berit Olam; Collegeville: Liturgical Press, 2000), 1:39.

3. See Gillian Cooper and John Goldingay, "Hosea and Gomer Visit the Marriage Counsellor," in *First Person: Essays in Biblical Autobiography* (ed. P. R. Davies; London: Sheffield Academic Press, 2002), pp. 119-36, and Jonathan Magonet, "Gomer's Revenge," in *First Person,* pp. 115-18. Both works are self-described modern pseudepigrapha.

a literary level. This first-person autobiographical account is embedded within a prophetic book that is prefaced with "the word of the LORD" (1:1). Thus, the use of the first person emphasizes the participatory nature of the prophet in the prophetic message. In this case sacred Scripture is a dialogue between the prophet and God, including Hosea's own retelling of his obedience to YHWH's commands.

Certainly, the woman of chapter 3 may be Gomer, but the text does not definitively demonstrate that to be the case. In this case she is explicitly called an adulteress (3:1), and the payment in v. 2 does not suggest the services of a prostitute[4] but rather a bride price. Such actions indicate that Hosea did not merely cohabit with the woman, as could possibly be the case with Gomer, but did indeed marry her. If this is a different woman from Gomer, some suggest that these events took place in the aftermath of Hosea's failed marriage with her. As we have mentioned throughout this commentary, the text is inconclusive as to the events of Hosea's marriage(s).

What is clear is the significance of the prophetic sign-act. Parallel comparisons are described in v. 1:

Go, love a woman	who has a lover and is an adulteress,
the LORD loves the people of Israel,	though they turn to other gods and love raisin cakes

YHWH makes clear what was implied in the prophetic act of chapter 1. Hosea's love for the woman mirrors God's love for Israel, and the woman's adultery with a lover represents Israel's love for other deities and raisin cakes. YHWH inflicts upon Hosea God's own experience of unrequited love through an unfaithful marriage partner. Whereas in chapter 1 the children primarily served as the prophetic sign-acts, in chapter 3 Hosea himself functions in this role. The reference to raisin cakes is a fairly obscure phrase in the OT, such that rabbinic commentators understood it as "flagons of wine."[5] In any case this food is associated with idolatry. The action of "turning to other gods" occurs in various forms in Deut 29:18; 30:17; 31:18, 20; and Lev. 19:4, and it describes apostasy and the breaking of covenant. A homer is a substantial measure of grain, and to the Hebrew text's description of a lethech of barley, the Greek text adds "a measure of wine" (NRSV). Some scholars calculated the additional grain to be equal to 15 shekels, thus totaling the woman's purchase price to 30, the worth of a slave

4. Contra NJPS, "Then I *hired* her for fifteen *shekels of* silver, a homer of barley, and a lethech of barley."

5. Macintosh, *Hosea*, p. 95.

according to Exod 21:32. Yet there is little evidence to demonstrate the value of the grain at the time of writing. As to whether the woman had incurred debt such that she was a slave or the price represented the value of her prostituting services, the text is ambiguous on such matters. What is clear is that Hosea secured proprietary rights over the woman so that he could control her activities.

A second parallel comparison is described in vv. 3-4. Just as the woman will remain as Hosea's wife for many days without having sexual intercourse with any man, so too Israel will remain many days without royal leadership and cultic worship. Both verses share the vocabulary of "many days" and "to remain," and in both cases activities vital to the welfare of each party are withheld. The woman is to experience a sort of sexual detox; her promiscuity (זנה/ *zānāh,* 3:3) is to be denied as well as access to any lover, including Hosea. It is possible to translate the last phrase of 3:3 as "and I will live with you" (NIV), but the context suggests that the negative particle from the previous clauses ought to carry over to the last phrase so that it reads, "even I shall not cohabit with you" (NJPS). In this case, the act of love (אהב/ *'āhab,* 3:1) is one of discipline and restraint. In this case, to love is to temporarily deny people the ability to carry out behaviors that they have been unable to control. In Hosea, love is not foremost an emotional experience or romantic notion, but instead a commitment, an act of loyalty to another person. Whereas chapter 2 possesses an erotic quality to it, such is not the case in chapter 3.

In the parallel relationship in vv. 3-4, Israel's attachment to human rulers and cultic worship is considered promiscuity and adultery to YHWH. Like the imposed sexual abstinence for the woman in v. 3, Israel will forfeit royal leadership in the form of a king or prince, which is suggestive of military defeat. Sacrifice was a common form of worship in Israelite temples, and pillars symbolized a sacred site and were common in early forms of Israelite worship (Gen 28:18), but were later banned according to Deuteronomy (16:22). The ephod is the garment worn by the priest containing objects for use in consulting YHWH's will (Exod 28:1-43), and the teraphim are either statuettes or masks for the purposes of divination (1 Sam 15:23). Of all these cultic objects only the last, the teraphim, are consistently repudiated in the OT, and in Hosea all other mentions of sacrifices (3:4; 4:13; 4:14; 4:19; 6:6; 8:13 (2x); 9:4; 11:2; 12:11; 13:2) and pillars (10:1, 2) are viewed negatively. Israel's promiscuity and adultery are understood as cultic abuse and political corruption, and the prophetic book will go on to address these forms of Israel's unfaithfulness in chapters 4–14. These religious and political institutions are not inherently corrupt, but, according to Hosea, they played pivotal roles in the spiritual decline of the nation.

The absence of king and cult will be finite, since v. 5 makes clear that after the "many days" have passed, the people will return to seek YHWH and David their king. "Many days" are understood as spanning more than a generation, and while "in the latter days" (באחרית הימים/*bĕʾaḥărît hayyāmîm*, v. 5) may refer to an eschatological future (e.g., Isa 2:2), the phrase merely suggests an unspecified future. What is clear is that only after a distinct period of "many days," during which the people lack a monarchy and a temple, will the events of v. 5 take place.

Hosea 3:5 contains the 3rd mention of the word "return" (שוב/*šûb*) in the book of Hosea, a word that suggests a very significant theme in the Twelve, as described in the commentary on 2:7 [2:9]. In this case, "return" communicates restoration that involves a return from exile as well as the renewal of agricultural blessings. Throughout the Twelve, and in Hosea, restoration is always preceded by a cleansing judgment. LeCureux observes, "Hosea's/The Twelve's first use of שוב/*šûb* as restoration conveys both a physical return from implied exile (cf. Deut 30:3-5), and a spiritual return to a faithful covenant relationship with Yhwh (e.g., Deut 4:30), and in doing so sets the parameters for the use of שוב/*šûb* and for the rest of the Twelve."[6] Israel's eschatological hope is not merely the restoration of covenant relationship but also the renewal of creation; therefore, a true "return" involves the fulfillment of both. The word "seek" (בקש/*bāqaš*) in v. 5 is synonymous with "return," and in Hosea they appear together four times (2:7 [2:9]; 3:5; 5:15; 7:10). The book of Hosea sets forth a four-stage set of events in regard to "seeking" or "returning": 1) in the present, Israel refuses to seek or return to the LORD (2:7 [2:9]; 7:10); 2) in the near future, YHWH will withdraw from Israel such that they are unable to seek YHWH (5:6); 3) Israel will eventually admit its guilt and seek God (5:15), and finally 4) Israel will return to the land and seek the LORD (3:5).

Scholars have long assigned the phrase "David their king"[7] to a Judean editor or even all of 3:1-5 to the final stages of the book's redaction,[8] since a pro-Davidic message would not fit an eighth-century Israelite setting. The phrase, "the LORD their God and David their king" occurs in Jer 30:9 and similarly reflects the hope of freedom from foreign domination through the restoration of the Davidic monarchy. At the level of the book, this passage provides greater specification to the identity of the "one head" who is to gather and reunite Israel and Judah to reclaim possession of the land (1:11 [2:2]). While Israel's eschatological leader will share Mosaic qualities, ultimately he is to come in Davidic form.

6. Jason T. LeCureux, *The Thematic Unity of the Book of the Twelve* (HBM 41; Sheffield: Sheffield Phoenix Press, 2012), pp. 79-80.

7. Hans Walter Wolff, *Hosea* (Hermeneia; Philadelphia: Fortress, 1974), p. 57.

8. Gale A. Yee, *Composition and Tradition in the Book of Hosea* (SBLDS 102; Atlanta: Scholars Press, 1987), pp. 90-91.

The posture of the people in the eschaton will be one of "awe" (פחד/*pāḥad*, 3:5). This word is typically associated with an attitude of fear, but in some cases it is used to describe joy (Isa 60:5). In Jer 33:9 this word appears alongside the word "good" (טובה/*ṭôbāh*) and similarly points to an eschatological future: "And this city shall be to me a name of joy, a praise and a glory before all the nations of the earth who shall hear of all the good that I do for them; they shall fear and tremble because of all the good and all the prosperity I provide for it." In Exod 33:19, YHWH makes clear that God's own self-revelation (which takes place in Exod 34:6-7, a key intertext in Hosea and the Twelve) is to be summarized as God's "goodness."[9] Exodus 33:19 reads, "And he said, 'I will make all my goodness (טוב/*ṭôb*) pass before you, and will proclaim before you the name, 'The LORD'; and I will be gracious to whom I will be gracious, and will show mercy on whom I will show mercy.'" God's covenantal name, YHWH, is also mentioned in Hos 3:5, reaffirming that the restoration of covenant, described earlier in 1:10–2:1 [2:1-3] and 2:14-23 [2:16-25], will take place following the exile and in conjunction with the reestablishment of the Davidic monarchy. Later, in Hos 8:3, the prophet will indict Israel for rejecting "goodness," which in this case refers to knowing YHWH and obeying covenant Law, and the prophecy will close with an invitation to return to YHWH and accept God's forgiveness and goodness (14:2 [14:3]). Later on in the Twelve, Micah will ask, "O mortal, what is good (טוב/*ṭôb*); and what does the LORD require of you?" (Mic 6:8). Goodness here is defined as "to do justice, and to love kindness, and to walk humbly with your God." Even though it is not until the last days that Israel will be betrothed to God "in righteousness and in justice, in steadfast love, and in mercy" (Hos 2:19 [2:21]), Micah calls for Israel to live into this covenantal and eschatological reality in the present. For Hosea and the Twelve, "good" is to be equated with "God" in a manner similar to the words of Jesus: "Why do you call me good? No one is good but God alone" (Mark 10:18; Luke 18:19).

---

9. See the Excursus, "YHWH's Goodness," in J. Andrew Dearman, *The Book of Hosea* (NICOT; Grand Rapids: Eerdmans, 2010), pp. 141-42.

6. The Covenant Conditions for God-talk and God-knowledge

Daniel Castelo

Of Hosea's fourteen chapters, the first three have spurred the scholarly and pop-ular imagination, which in turn has shaped the general outlook people harbor regarding the whole of Hosea. Naturally, Hosea consists of more than these open-ing chapters, but the sheer strangeness of this portion of the book often makes it difficult for readers to see much of anything else in the text. People have repeat-edly wondered why God would command Hosea to marry a "wife of whoredom," to bear children with her, and to name them with such names as "not pitied" and "not my people." These are simply bizarre developments, largely because their significance is obscure to the reading faithful on a "plain sense" reading.

Take for instance the phrase in 1:2, already commented on by Lim: "For the land commits great whoredom by forsaking the LORD." With this one phrase, the reader captures not only a glimpse into another world, but a demand to consider this text in a way other than a typical, contemporary register. What is the significance of "whoredom" in the text, given that its meaning primarily suggests "fornication," the act of engaging "in sexual relations outside of, or apart from, marriage" (Lim)? Understanding this phrase, and Hosea as a whole, requires a sensibility comfortable with the analysis of language and symbolism. In other words, the theological interpretation of Hosea requires a working ac-count of the possibilities surrounding God-talk (including theological speech/ imagery) and its implications for fostering God-knowledge.

The History and Relationship between YHWH and Israel

Beginning with the first verse of Hosea, the reader stumbles upon a very specific set of circumstances, many of which have already been touched upon by Lim. The clues one can garner from 1:1, and their significance for the book as a whole, are obviously important, but their significance is not just historical. In fact, the first verse suggests plenty in terms of a theological localization of this text.

Immediately, one is struck with the phrasing "The word of the LORD" that begins Hosea. For readers of the prophetic literature, this way of introducing a prophetic book is not that unusual: Joel, Jonah, Micah, Zephaniah, Haggai, Zechariah, and Malachi are other instances within the Book of the Twelve that begin similarly. But notice the importance of such a beginning: These words, the text claims, come from YHWH. Earlier in this volume the name YHWH was highlighted with the aim of suggesting that the Tetragrammaton is the true personal proper name for the Christian God. As a personal proper name, the Tetragrammaton "acquires its meaning not from an inherent sense of the word, but from the being and action of its bearer."[1] In this sense, the self-disclosure of the One in question is required, and the testimony of Scripture points to a particular instantiating moment when this One's Name is revealed: the call of Moses in Exodus 3 to lead Israel out of Egyptian bondage. The importance of this divinely-disclosed Name cannot be overstated. With this Name, the people of Israel can call upon One who has declared: "I am the God of your father, the God of Abraham, the God of Isaac, and the God of Jacob," and who at that time remarked, "I have observed the misery of my people who are in Egypt; I have heard their cry on account of their taskmasters. Indeed I know their sufferings, and I have come down to deliver them from the Egyptians" (Exod 3:6-8). The subsequent disclosure of the Divine Name in Exod 3:14-15 is one of permanence: "This is my name forever, and this my title for all generations" (3:15).

In sum, the reference to "the LORD" or YHWH at the beginning of Hosea not only emphasizes the particular identity of the deity speaking in this text, but also serves to situate the speech itself within a shared history, a history in which the One speaking already has a "track record," so to speak, of activity by which to recall and understand this One's character and disposition toward Israel. This "character history" must inform how one interprets what follows in Hosea's oracles; by themselves, and apart from this history, the prophecies do not render a working sense of the identity of the One speaking through the prophet Hosea. Theologically, then, the reading community cannot proceed to interpret the words given to Hosea without an appreciation of the personal history this One shares with the chosen people.

From this shared history, one should ask: What are the salient features of God's character? How could one describe the ways YHWH is depicted in the OT? One of the most focused and suggestive ways to gauge YHWH's character

1. R. Kendall Soulen, *The Divine Name(s) and the Holy Trinity* (Louisville: Westminster John Knox, 2011), p. 13.

in the biblical testimony is through the narrative-theological construct that is the covenant bond this One established with the people of Israel. This construct is especially apropos when considering Hosea, since it is mentioned explicitly in terms of the YHWH-Israel bond (see 6:7 and 8:1) and is echoed throughout the work. Focusing on this term, however, does carry its own set of challenges.[2] Theologically, the language of covenant has been used in Christian circles for specific ends, particularly in Protestant camps where the mechanism sometimes has served as a way to organize salvation history in a manner that recognizes a providential, ordered unfolding.[3] What follows does not aim to rival such works. Rather, the elaboration below is intended to probe an interrelational and interpersonal logic — or, to use Walther Eichrodt's turn of phrase, a "living process"[4] — one that not only describes the interactions between YHWH and Israel as witnessed in Scripture (including Hosea; see Hos 6:7 and 8:1[5]), but also suggests an existential dynamic that is presently relevant and available to the reader and the reading community.

1) This Name is disclosed within covenant arrangements. As mentioned above, this Name is disclosed to Moses at the time of his call to lead the people of Israel from bondage in Egypt, and, as such, covenant arrangements inflect the meaning and significance of the Divine Name.[6] The Exodus narrative functions as an ongoing refrain within the prophetic literature (including in the Book of the Twelve[7]) as a way of identifying the character of this One.

2. I do not feel particularly capable of elaborating covenant logic diachronically within ancient Israel. However, Walter Brueggemann has noted that Hosea is "a child of the covenantal tradition of Deuteronomy," a tradition that allows "enormous latitude for imaginative interpretation" of legal and emotional features of that tradition (see "The Recovering God of Hosea," *Horizons in Biblical Theology* 30 [2008]: 8). I wish to honor the fact that YHWH and covenant-logic are intertwined within Hosea without necessarily explicating some of the technicalities of that mechanism, yet I seek to substantiate that logic through a specific theological reading of covenant as found in various moments of the Torah.

3. This tradition seems to have begun in earnest in the Reformation period with the work of Johannes Cocceius (1603-1669). For a recent survey of some options in this vein, see Peter J. Gentry and Stephen J. Wellum, *Kingdom through Covenant* (Wheaton: Crossway, 2012).

4. *Theology of the Old Testament* (trans. J. A. Baker; vol. 1; Philadelphia: Westminster, 1961), p. 18.

5. I follow Ernest Nicholson's reading that these two texts do in fact relate to the YHWH-Israel bond; see *God and His People* (Oxford: Clarendon Press, 1986), chapter 9.

6. In terms of the exodus, R. W. L. Moberly remarks, "The general point is that what is said about the name of God is only meaningful in the context of Israel's awareness of itself as addressed by God through the mediation of Moses" (*Old Testament of the Old Testament* [OBT; Minneapolis: Fortress, 1992], p. 23).

7. Outside of Hosea, examples include Amos 3:1 and Micah 6:4, as well as Haggai 2:4-5 (cited below). As for Hosea, the applicable examples will be addressed throughout this discussion.

At the time of the exodus, YHWH self-identifies with the God of the ancestors but admits that this Name was not revealed to them at the time[8] (Exod 6:3). The disclosure of the Name here accompanies a double movement: YHWH is responsive to the people's groans and sufferings, and YHWH remembers the covenant made with the patriarchs. In terms of the first point, God demonstrates Godself to be compassionate, responsive, and disposed to free the people, since YHWH knows their suffering. These forms of availability and engagement pivot on the basis of the second point: God made promises to the patriarchs and God intends to uphold them at the time of Moses' calling: "'I will take you as my people, and I will be your God.[9] You shall know that I am the LORD your God, who has freed you from the burdens of the Egyptians. I will bring you into the land that I swore to give to Abraham, Isaac, and Jacob'" (Exod 6:7-8).

Covenant arrangements vary and are multiple,[10] but they suggest at least this much in the Mosaic episode in which the Name is disclosed: YHWH made promises to Israel, and YHWH intends to uphold them in YHWH's own timing and way. As Micah remarks: "You will show faithfulness to Jacob and unswerving loyalty to Abraham, as you have sworn to our ancestors from the days of old" (Mic 7:20). Within this dynamic of the divine initiative and blessing, such matters as human responsiveness, obedience, and faithfulness are required for consummation.[11] These dynamics are seen in the person of Moses himself, for he is charged with the task of leading his people out of Egypt (Exod 3:10) and bringing them back to the mountain so that they can worship God upon their deliverance (Exod 3:12).

Covenant arrangements thus introduce promissory and interrelational dynamics, but these should be differentiated from contractual understandings,[12]

---

8. I am aware that a vast history of critical consideration — particularly in terms of source criticism — has been at play at this point, for whereas these passages of Exodus highlight initiatory moments for the divine name's disclosure, the Name is nevertheless present previously in the Torah (beginning at Genesis 2:5 and distributed throughout). See the treatment of this topic in Moberly, *The Old Testament of the Old Testament,* particularly chapter 2.

9. This is a covenantal oath that has resonances with Lev. 26:12 and Deut 29:13.

10. For a brief survey, see Joel Kaminsky, *Yet I Loved Jacob* (Nashville: Abingdon, 2007), pp. 85-91. A more extensive treatment can be found in Scott Hahn, *Kingship by Covenant* (New Haven: Yale University Press, 2009). Hosea itself shows variety of the term's applicability, using it to refer to the YHWH-Israel bond (6:7; 8:1) as well as agreements between Israel and others (10:4; 12:1). The focus here will be on the distinctive nature of the YHWH-Israel covenant for an understanding of YHWH's character as well as Israel's vocation.

11. In this regard, I am siding with those who understand covenants bilaterally rather than unilaterally; see Hahn (*Kingship by Covenant,* p. 28) for a brief survey of some of the OT scholars who fall into each camp.

12. This move is partially legitimated by the strictly legal connotations that the English

especially as the YHWH-Israel covenant becomes an enactment of a very particular and unique relationship. People enter contracts when they mutually agree to work together in such a fashion that each party benefits from the contractual stipulations and terms. Typically, when one party fails in its contractual obligations or comes to find them disagreeable, the terms of the contract might be nullified, possibly reworked, or upheld through litigation. Given the complexity of contractual arrangements and dynamics, circumstances often require the intervention of legal processes and third parties to settle disputes. In both contracts and covenants, promises and benefits have their role. In the case of contracts, parties pledge to fulfill their contractual obligations for the benefits that can accrue for all involved. But covenant arrangements are different from contractual ones, particularly in the biblical narrative's depiction of the YHWH-Israel bond. In that domain, the promissory features of covenants overshadow the benefits-related emphases of contracts. At the risk of overgeneralizing, one can say that people often enter contractual obligations looking to make sure that they are treated justly and fairly in the process so that they "get what they deserve," and that the terms of the contracts reflect that belief. But covenant partners — particularly YHWH, in YHWH's dealings with Israel — tend to look not inwardly but outwardly, not so much for the benefits to one's own self or party but to goods and benefits for the other parties involved.

Obviously, people can enter and dissolve contracts and covenants with one another, but the suggestion of a covenant between God and a people both transforms and breaks down the idea of covenant itself. That YHWH enters and lives into covenant with Israel suggests something about the importance of covenants for the fostering of meaningful relationships that endure throughout the vicissitudes of lived history. This gesture also indicates something of the divine disposition, namely that God must be a certain way by entering into a kind of relationship in which one looks to the benefit and good of the other more than the good of one's own self. In both senses, there is transformative potential for YHWH's covenant partner. At the same time, classifying the God-Israel bond as one of covenant begins to break down when one recognizes that YHWH is not a typical covenant partner. Yes, obviously God is looking to the goodness of creation, but when one throws into the mix that this One is the *summum bonum* (the "ultimate good"), the "God of heaven, who made the sea and the dry land" (Jonah 1:9), one can begin to sense with both awe

---

word "contract" carries; for this reason, in the following contrast I will assume the delimitations associated with the word in English so as to show the generative theological possibilities for the word "covenant." For a more extensive treatment of these and other matters related to the topic, see *Covenant Marriage in Comparative Perspective* (ed. John Witte Jr. and Eliza Ellison; Grand Rapids: Eerdmans, 2005).

and dread the possibility of an unfathomable, non-circumscribable form of hospitality at play in God's enactment of the covenant-partnership role. The gap between the partners in this particular covenant arrangement is so vast that in some sense it judges all other forms of covenant bonds, particularly in light of YHWH's beauty, elegance, devotion, and longsuffering in the working out of this relationship across time and space. In this sense, one cannot simply apply the concept of covenant bonds to the God-Israel dynamic and maintain a predetermined definition of the idea of covenant throughout, for the concept itself is in some sense narratively redefined when one of the covenant partners is none other than YHWH.

One indicator of the uniqueness and primacy of the God-Israel bond for covenant thinking is the disclosure of God's name precisely at a time in which the promises made in the past are remembered and taken up once more. The revelation of the Tetragrammaton is prompted by Moses' questioning how he should communicate this One's identity to the people of Israel. By revealing this particular name, God not only demonstrates once more God's unfathomable hospitality, but goes on to make Godself available in a particular way to God's covenant partner, a way that will last generations (Exod 3:15). This steadfastness on God's part is a theme that continues in the Twelve: "For I am with you, says the LORD of hosts, according to the promise that I made you when you came out of Egypt. My spirit abides among you; do not fear" (Hag 2:4-5).

2) This Name signifies continuity with a people's ancestry. During the Exodus calling of Moses, God is mindful of the covenant made with the ancestors (Exod 2:24), and YHWH self-identifies as the God of Abraham, Isaac, and Jacob (Exod 3:15). This self-identification in turn recalls the originating circumstances of the covenant made between YHWH and Abraham. It began with a charge to Abraham (then Abram) to leave his father's house, and a promise that YHWH would bless him, make him into a great nation, and, through him, bless all the families of the earth (Gen 12:1-3). Therefore, the promise and commitment God made to Abraham is not only for Abraham himself, but also for the wider world. In contrast to the humanly fabricated form of hegemony and totalization on display at the Tower of Babel (Gen 11), YHWH decides to bless all the peoples of the earth through a particular person and his lineage (Gen 12).

These developments culminate in the visions and appearances granted to Abram as recorded in Gen 15 and 17.[13] In the former, Abram is promised

---

13. Past commentators have often wished to conflate these two biblical moments, but I believe these are distinct covenant-related moments; for more on their differences, see the work of Paul R. Williamson, including *Abraham, Israel and the Nations* (Sheffield: Sheffield Academic Press, 2000), and *Sealed with an Oath* (Downers Grove: InterVarsity Press, 2007), pp. 86-90.

posterity as countless as the stars of the sky; the land is promised once again to Abram's descendants; and the Egyptian bondage of his people is foretold. In the latter passage, YHWH changes Abram's name to Abraham, as he is to be a father of a multitude of peoples. Furthermore, God explicitly makes additional promises and commitments in this passage: God will multiply Abraham's seed and give to his family the land of Canaan; this covenant will be everlasting, since YHWH promises to be the god of Abraham and his offspring. Abraham's covenant obligations entail the ongoing maintenance of the practice of circumcision so that the covenant would continue in him and his line's flesh. These requirements are extended further in Gen 18, when Abraham is visited by the mysterious entities who are in some places equivocated with YHWH. At this juncture, Abraham and his children are commanded "'to keep the way of the LORD by doing righteousness and justice; so that the LORD [would] bring about for Abraham what he [had] promised him'" (Gen 18:19). The LORD therefore acts mercifully and generously with Abraham, granting him promises of vast importance; yet these promises are granted alongside commands related to ongoing covenant maintenance, which include the practice of righteousness and justice.

To conclude, this covenant history suggests that YHWH is the name of a God who makes promises to prior generations, and who in turn fulfills them with the passing of time. In these scenes, God appears to be merciful and steadfast in God's commitment to Abraham and his lineage (for instance, rescuing Lot and his family at Abraham's request). YHWH is also a God of surprises (such as when Abraham and Sarah are promised and given Isaac despite their advanced age), but these surprises work in terms of contributing to the unfolding of God's plans, as well as reaffirming the point that what God promises indeed comes to pass. YHWH also commands the ancestors and their posterity to be faithful to the covenant through their practices and communal life. The people's activity, responsiveness, and obedience are not incidental to the ongoing state and quality of the covenant bond. Despite construals to the contrary, covenants are "essentially two-sided" relationships within the biblical testimony.[14]

3) This Name gains a character description as the covenant relationship unfolds. The institution of the covenant with the patriarchs takes time, and so exhibits a number of twists and turns in biblical history. On the one hand, YHWH on occasion tasks, tests, and requires a great deal from God's covenant people, but these demands, by One who is both initiator and sustainer of this particular covenant, are situated within the broader framework of God's char-

14. Eichrodt, *Theology of the Old Testament,* I:37.

acter as one of hospitality and loving-kindness, as evidenced in liberating the people from Egypt. This refrain is picked up in Hosea 13: "Yet I have been the LORD your God ever since the land of Egypt; you know no God but me, and besides me there is no savior. It was I who fed you in the wilderness, in the land of drought" (vv. 4-5).

Nevertheless, the unfolding of this relationship creates a number of interpretive challenges related to making sense of the identity and character of the One who self-identifies with this name. Such is the case in the example of Abraham himself. Soon after the birth of Isaac, the reader of Genesis is confronted with one of the most difficult passages of Scripture, the *Akedah* ("binding") in Gen 22. As a test of Abraham (so the narrator shares), YHWH demands the physical sacrifice of Isaac by Abraham. Naturally, this scene raises a number of questions for the reader: Why would God do this? Is this command not contrary to the promises made to Abraham? And — readers now and in ages past would likely wonder most pressingly — is the request itself not blatantly, scandalously, and irremediably immoral?

Commentators have debated this incident from a variety of angles across the centuries. Yes, YHWH is the One who promised Isaac in the first place (so that without YHWH there would be no Isaac), and the narrator explicitly remarks at the beginning of Gen 22 that this event is a trial and form of testing. Furthermore, the angel of the LORD did prevent Abraham from completing the act, and Abraham hears the blessing upon his offspring once more and is lauded for his obedience. All of these details factor into the contemporary reading of the *Akedah,* yet interpreters often find it difficult to move beyond the particular moment in which YHWH commands Abraham to sacrifice Isaac. But does the focus on the command of YHWH, to the exclusion of the other narrative features of the story, result in a charitable reading? Obviously, the command itself is disturbing at one level; past and contemporary readers have recognized the strangeness and felt the visceral turmoil of this passage. From a strictly modern, Western perspective, this situation makes no sense, for child sacrifice is deemed by our own sensibilities as unquestionably deplorable.

Genesis 22 depicts a God who is in some sense beyond scrutiny and understanding. Yes, this One is good, trustworthy, merciful, and faithful, but those characterizations are not necessarily obvious to the covenant partner at a given moment or situation. Perhaps Abraham's understanding of YHWH is different after the binding, yet if so, it is an understanding that has been broken and reconstituted in a very specific way. The tendency for many is to isolate the existential conditions and moral intricacies of Gen 22 apart from a working sense of what preceded and followed this passage, particularly in terms of God's self-revealed character. The God who grants life can in turn demand it, and this

God may (in Abraham's case) or may not (in Jesus' case) let the trial of sacrifice and "godforsakeness" *(Gottverlassenheit)* pass.[15]

The pressing concern becomes the moral evaluation of YHWH when the moral frameworks that we the readers inhabit seem irreconcilable with what we see the agents of the biblical narrative — most importantly, YHWH — exhibiting and promoting.[16] Perhaps a tendency of ours would be to say that YHWH has the right to ask of Abraham a duty that "teleologically suspends the ethical" in a given situation, and because God is God and we are not, we should be perfectly fine with such an arrangement.[17] The posture piously and rightfully recognizes the gap that exists between these two specific covenant partners. At the same time, such a view might prematurely incite hermeneutical closures, sensibilities, and practices that would themselves be difficult to modify given the haste with which they are facilitated and adopted. Stemming from such closures, the outcome most difficult to reconcile would be the cultivation of blindness regarding the particularity of what constitutes "the ethical" in the first place. If God does ask Abraham to "teleologically suspend the ethical,"[18] and that is fine because God is God, then, among other things, whatever calls itself "the ethical" is not questioned and is destabilized as a result.[19]

15. The allusion here is to Gerhard von Rad's use of this term for the *Akedah;* see *Genesis* (rev. ed.; trans. John Marks; Philadelphia: Westminster, 1972), p. 244.

16. A work in which believers and nonbelievers alike explore these themes is Michael Bergmann, Michael J. Murray, and Michael C. Rea, eds., *Divine Evil?* (Oxford: Oxford University Press, 2011). For a helpful representation of the nonbeliever's perspective, see chapter 2, titled "The God of Abraham, Isaac, and Jacob," by Edwin Curley (pp. 58-78).

17. This view is associated with Søren Kierkegaard's *Fear and Trembling;* see "Problema I" in *Fear and Trembling/Repetition* (vol. 6 of *Kierkegaard's Writings;* ed. and trans. Howard V. Hong and Edna H. Hong; Princeton: Princeton University Press, 1983), pp. 54-67. Ethically, the approach is sometimes referred to as "divine command" theory.

18. And this admission is no small matter, for one should note Immanuel Kant's assessment of the *Akedah:* "But in some cases the human being can be sure that the voice he hears is *not* God's; for if the voice commands him to do something contrary to the moral law, then no matter how majestic the apparition may be, and no matter how it may seem to surpass the whole of nature, he must consider it an illusion" ("The Conflict of the Faculties," in *Religion and Rational Theology* [ed. and trans. Allen Wood and George Di Giovanni; Cambridge Edition of the Works of Immanuel Kant; Cambridge: Cambridge University Press, 1996], p. 283). Of course, testing has always been part of the Christian understanding of discernment, but then again the possibility of divine discourse has been present as well, at least within the biblical narrative; for a treatment of the latter theme in philosophical perspective, see Nicholas Wolterstorff, *Divine Discourse* (Cambridge: Cambridge University Press, 1995).

19. Notice that a "teleological suspension" is itself a certain kind of ethical framing; perhaps another way of getting at this matter would be to say that at play is an "eschatological suspension of the deontological." At any rate, the major point being pursued here is that what makes moral sense to contemporary readers may not have made moral sense to members of prior civilizations,

This outcome is very much a problematic one. The moral frameworks used to evaluate YHWH may in fact be suspended when pious readers simply do not know what to do with what *they see* in a given passage. By contrast, more brazen interpreters may not shy away from "calling it as they see it" in the text, and in their case what *they see* could be a god who is a vile sadist or powermonger.[20] In both cases, readers have different evaluations of the moral character of YHWH because of the particularity of their own embeddedness or situationality,[21] which in turn leads them to evaluate differently specific actions of YHWH and YHWH's character overall. Because of the multiplicity of interpretive outcomes from specific hermeneutical postures, the reading of the Bible and the significance of its happenings are deeply contested matters.

Obviously, moral evaluation of YHWH is not a "neutral" activity, but then again neither is the evaluation of the other covenant partner within the covenant bond, namely Israel. Upon leaving Egypt under the providential auspices of YHWH, Israel enters into an existential and practical situation of God-dependence, a development that in some sense would be ideal given God's steadfastness and mercy. They are led by a pillar of cloud by day and a pillar of fire by night, and when a besieging Egyptian army threatens to overtake them, the Israelites are assuringly told: "The LORD will fight for you, and you have only to keep still" (Exod 14:14). Once that ordeal passes and the demands of a people in the desert start to press in (as the case with drinking water shows), the people are given the following promise by YHWH: "'If you will listen carefully to the voice of the LORD your God, and do what is right in his sight, and give heed to his commandments and keep all his statutes, I will not bring upon you any of the diseases that I brought upon the Egyptians; for I am the LORD who heals you'" (Exod 15:26). Curiously, the people are told that the plight of the Egyptians is a possibility for them if they do not listen to and obey YHWH. The remark is not so much a threat (given the conclusion of the verse) as it is an admonition that God's people have to be about God's work in the world. This theme is picked up by the Twelve: "I sent among you a pestilence after the manner of Egypt" (Amos

---

and therefore the presumption of a universal and timeless value to contemporary morality simply because it is contemporary is deeply unsatisfactory and anachronistic *a priori*. These matters will be pressed further in the final theological chapter of this commentary.

20. Take Richard Dawkins's opinion: "The God of the Old Testament is arguably the most unpleasant character in all fiction . . . A petty, unjust, unforgiving control-freak; a vindictive, blood-thirsty ethnic cleanser; a misogynistic, homophobic, racist, infanticidal, genocidal, filicidal, pestilential, megalomaniacal, sadomasochistic, capriciously malevolent bully" (*The God Delusion* [Boston: Houghton Mifflin, 2006], p. 31).

21. I owe this term to James K. A. Smith; see *The Fall of Interpretation* (2d ed.; Grand Rapids: Baker Academic, 2012), pp. 30, 49.

4:10). Covenant dynamics suggest that Israel participates in an existential condition of God-dependence that will lead either to their healing (if they follow and obey God) or their destruction (if they deny and disobey the LORD).

But as all readers of the Bible know, Israel does not fulfill these covenant obligations; in fact, the vast amount of contention that arises within the covenant bond is due to Israel's rebellion and disobedience over generations.[22] More often than not, Israel fails in its role as a covenant partner. Why is this so? Interpreters have a number of possibilities at their disposal. Some of these point to a historical characterization and explanation (the people of Israel at that time and place happened to be obstinate), while others invite supersessionist and maybe even anti-Semitic sensibilities. Some readers may simply puzzle over Israel's behavior and ask, "Why don't they just get it?" But notice the irony in this last case: Readers may not understand YHWH's character, but then again, they may not understand Israel's either, despite the fact that the latter is thoroughly creaturely and typical of the human condition. In the first case, the agent is too strange and otherworldly, but in the other, the agent is too common and available since it relies on features of the human condition that are symptomatic not only of others but also of those who read and are claimed by these texts. Given the human constraints of being "in the middle" of these conditions, readers are simply further entwined in the complexity of morally situating Israel, human beings, and (by implication) themselves as contemporary readers.[23]

These challenges show that the task of morally evaluating the covenant partners in the YHWH-Israel bond is not a simple affair. Quite the contrary, this particular interpretive gesture (as with moral evaluation in general) is difficult to sustain in the contemporary milieu, since competing moral narratives create cultural cacophonies and only expose a culturally-fostered inability to evaluate and sustain serious moral inquiry. Morally evaluating this covenant partnership is thus fraught with challenges that reflect very much the formation and limitations of contemporary cultural and societal conditions. These remarks should serve a precautionary role as one interprets Hosea.

---

22. "But they [the tribe of Judah] have been led astray by the same lies after which their ancestors walked" (Amos 2:4); also note Mal 3:7: "Ever since the days of your ancestors you have turned aside from my statutes and have not kept them."

23. To harken back to the *Akedah,* one realizes how the evaluation of Abraham in this scene varies considerably by interpreters. In light of a sampling of the literature, R. W. L. Moberly remarks, "Does Gen 22 portray a model of true responsiveness to God, to be emulated by others, a source of strength and fortitude when life falls apart? Or does it portray a fundamentally mistaken view of God and an Abraham who is at best misguided and at worst ruthlessly self-seeking? The guides who would help the reader understand the text could hardly disagree more than they do here" ("Living Dangerously," in *ARS,* p. 187).

*4) This Name is to be worshiped, because the covenant extends for genera-
tions.* Despite repeated failures on the part of Israel, the Name of YHWH is to
be praised and proclaimed for generations, because the covenant continues to
be an ongoing reality due to YHWH's unwavering commitment to the promises
made to Israel. Because of God's character, goodness, and beneficent posture
towards YHWH's people, God's Name is to be revered, honored, sanctified, and
worshiped. One sees such themes at pivotal moments in the covenant relationship. For instance, when YHWH delivers the Israelites from the Egyptians at
the Red Sea, Moses and the people break into song: "The LORD is my strength
and my might, and he has become my salvation" (Exod 15:2); "The LORD is a
warrior; the LORD is his name" (Exod 15:3); "In your steadfast love you led the
people whom you redeemed; you guided them by your strength to your holy
abode" (Exod 15:13); and "You brought them in and planted them on the mountain of your own possession, the place, O LORD, that you made your abode,
the sanctuary, O LORD, that your hands have established. The LORD will reign
forever and ever" (Exod 15:17-18). The call to worship the Name of the living
God is something that Jews and Christians can agree is pivotal for those who
understand themselves as members of God's chosen people. Worship is not
simply a single act which people undertake on choice holy days; rather, it is an
existential, participatory, and active way of leading one's life. Worship involves
the cognitive register to be sure, but it also invites other registers as well, including (as the singing of the people in Exod 15 shows) affective ones.

Once one offers the possibility of a multitude of registers for doxological
existence, questions immediately present themselves, including the interaction
between the "mind" and the "heart." The relationship between intelligibility
and devotion in worship of God is a difficult one, because it does not admit of
easy "either-or" answers. Intelligibility has to be in some sense part of devotion
(we need to have some workable understanding of the One to whom we are
devoted), and increased intelligibility can lead to increased devotion in terms
of leading a people to richer and deeper dimensions of thought and life. At the
same time, intelligibility cannot function as a thoroughgoing and necessary
requirement for devotion if intelligibility is considered synonymous with com-
prehension or circumscription. The latter notions are often associated with the
reification of concepts, and such developments are one step removed from a
more generalized account of idolatry.

In his treatment of Hosea, Abraham Heschel cites this theme of God-
knowledge as especially pertinent for this prophetic book since he believes that
"Hosea's central complaint against the people is that they do not know God."[24]

---

24. *The Prophets* (2 vols.; New York: HarperCollins, 1962), 1:57.

Heschel goes on to emphasize the expression *daath elohim* as a running notion in Hosea, but this Jewish scholar emphasizes more pressingly the Hebrew notion of *yada* to make the point. As he elaborates: "In Hebrew *yada* means more than the possession of abstract concepts. . . . It involves both an intellectual and an emotional act. An analysis of the usage of the verb in biblical Hebrew leads to the conclusion that it often, though not always, denotes an act involving concern, inner engagement, dedication, or attachment to a person."[25] Heschel is raising the affective dimension as an oft-neglected but vital feature of God-knowledge within Hosea in particular, and the point is generalizable to the rest of the prophets and beyond. We suggest that this feature of creaturely existence is best fostered within covenant arrangements and through worship. We can only learn to know and feel properly when the true object of such activities is cognitively and experientially relatable and accessible. Only through an existential modality, a kind of being-in-the-world[26] that is doxologically framed and enacted, can the proper affective dispositions of a reading community be shaped and formed.

What would some of these proper affective dispositions be? Wonder and awe, for instance, have often been highlighted within Christian forms of spirituality and mysticism as ways of knowing that are more suitable for the cultivation of God-knowledge than explanation and logical deduction. The NT and Christian understandings of faith, particularly when taken as involving the notion of trust, yoked to the OT account of "the fear of the LORD,"[27] represent other such possibilities. Furthermore, with the *Akedah* in mind no less, Ellen Davis has made a case for depicting vulnerability "as the condition, the enabling condition, for covenant relationship with God."[28]

If awe, trust, vulnerability, and the like (i.e., affective dispositions) are considered more fundamental in terms of modes of knowing God than discursive reasoning and reflection (i.e., intellectual activities), then worship becomes an architectonic word for describing those processes, practices, and forms of life that can cultivate both the affective and intellective registers of human selves as they seek the particular kind of God-knowledge that God requires. Worship denotes a "master modality" that can encompass both liturgical and ordinary

25. *The Prophets*, 1:57.

26. I take this language from James K. A. Smith's appropriation of Heidegger; see for instance *Thinking in Tongues* (Grand Rapids: Eerdmans, 2010). Also note Hubert L. Dreyfus, *Being-in-the-World* (Cambridge: MIT Press, 1991). I have extended such logic in a particular way in *Revisioning Pentecostal Ethics — The Epicletic Community* (Cleveland: CPT Press, 2012).

27. Moberly draws a link between faith and fear in "Living Dangerously," p. 190. For an extensive account of the "fear of the LORD" as a guiding theological modality of knowing, see Daniel Castelo, "The Fear of the Lord as Theological Method," *JTI* 2 (2008): 147-60.

28. See "Vulnerability, the Condition of the Covenant" in *ARS*, p. 278.

time because it encompasses the sundry features of human life: our loves, our passions, our devotions, our self-understood purposes, and so on. The Name, then, is properly recalled, confessed, and proclaimed within worship, for it is this kind of rendering that God requires: "'Yet even now, says the LORD, return to me with all your heart, with fasting, with weeping, and with mourning; rend your hearts and not your clothing" (Joel 2:12-13).

This excursus into the logic of the covenant between YHWH and Israel is important for the study of Hosea because one sees this history already implied by the names used in the first verse of the book. The covenant relationship between these two partners is freighted with precedence, and attention to and remembrance of those features of the relationship are to be at the forefront of the minds of a community that reads this text. Such precedence is embedded within the text itself: "Yet I have been the LORD your God ever since the land of Egypt; you know no God but me, and besides me there is no savior" (Hos 13:4, with apparent allusion to Exod 20:2-3).

As in times past, YHWH once again speaks in this prophetic work. This text represents yet another episode in the covenant life of YHWH and Israel. And once again, Israel has fallen short of its covenant obligations. The pattern noted earlier that is guiding our subdivision of Hosea — the movements of rebellion, judgment, and possible hope — is not only indicative of the book but also representative of many of the dynamics of the covenant arrangement as it has played out in YHWH's responsiveness to Israel's disobedience. For instance, in a gesture contrary to God's noticing the people's hardships in Egypt (cf. Exod 2:25), YHWH remarks in terms of Hosea's second child: "Name her Lo-ruhamah, for I will no longer have pity on the house of Israel or forgive them" (Hos 1:6). Furthermore, in direct contrast to Exodus 6:7 ("'I will take you as my people, and I will be your God'"), YHWH stipulates with regard to Hosea's third child: "Name him Lo-ammi, for you are not my people and I am not your God" (Hos 1:9). Nevertheless, the restoration is on the horizon in Hos 2: "I will have pity on Lo-ruhamah, and I will say to Lo-ammi, 'You are my people'; and he shall say, 'You are my God'" (v. 23 [25]).

God is faithful to God's promises, and the covenant continues even to today, albeit in new and unexpected forms, as indicated in the prophecy of Jeremiah that a "new covenant" is on the horizon: Unlike the old covenant, the new covenant is depicted as being placed within the people and written in their hearts so that all will know YHWH (cf. Jer 31:31-34). Christians believe this covenant has been verbally sealed with the words of Jesus (Mark 14:24) and its logic extended in a variety of passages in the NT (including Rom 4 and Heb 8–10).[29] Simply put, covenant logic

---

29. The language of a "new" covenant, of course, creates the conditions for the possibility

still governs the relationship between YHWH and this One's followers and disciples; in typical Christian terms, a covenant framework still applies to the relationship between the Trinity and the church.

This last point raises the question of the Christian reader of Hosea and her relationship to the covenant arrangements between YHWH and Israel in their varying forms. The reading of this text is significantly inflected by whether the reader would identify herself existentially and practically as part of this "living process." Roughly put in the form of a question: Is the reader an "insider" or an "outsider" in relation to the covenant arrangements echoed at the very beginning of Hosea through the names of the covenant partners? If one self-identifies as an outsider, then little is at stake in the running narrative of the unfolding relationship between YHWH and Israel, of which Hosea is a constituent part. One cannot help but think that Christians have often taken this "outsider's" posture as they read OT texts, including Hosea. They may view these covenant dynamics as inherent to the relationship between YHWH and historical Israel, but then they often go on to affirm that these have been fulfilled, or maybe even superseded, by Jesus. After all, Christians today do not ritually perform circumcision, observe Passover, or celebrate the Sabbath on Friday evening/Saturday morning. In terms of Hosea, Christians also do not belong to a covenant nation with kings who in turn participate in political compromises and intrigue for which they are subsequently judged by YHWH. These differences are obviously readily available.

The matters involved here are significant, and a commentary of this kind cannot do them justice; however, we wish to contend that a reading strategy that assumes contemporary Christians to be strict outsiders to the covenant arrangements between YHWH and Israel as depicted throughout the Old Testament carries with it the potential for damaging, and maybe even irremediable, consequences. For instance, this *a priori* theological commitment would promote a "hermeneutic of rupture" rather than a "hermeneutic of continuity" in the assessment of the developments within the YHWH-Israel bond in terms of their ongoing relevance for communities of faith. With the privileging of rupture as a guiding hermeneu-

---

of supersessionistic thinking. What we would offer here is similar to what we would say regarding the unity of the OT and NT: Diversity among a number of covenants does not imply irreconcilable divisions. After all, the same God is making these covenants, and understandings and depictions learned in one covenant arrangement can be applicable in the other. The diverse covenants as well as biblical testaments point to one covenant-making God, YHWH. Robert Louis Wilken captures the idea fittingly in terms of the testaments: "Two histories converge in the biblical account, the history of Israel and the life of Christ, but because they are also the history of God's actions in and for the world, they are part of a larger narrative that begins at creation and ends in a vision of a new, more splendid city in which the 'Lord God will be their light'" (*The Spirit of Early Christian Thought* [New Haven: Yale University Press, 2003], p. 63).

tical orientation, readers would find those features of the covenant outlay that are strange, unpalatable, or offensive to be easily dismissed, so as to be conveniently brushed to the side as examples of those things that have been left behind by the new covenant initiated by Jesus. What this species of privileging underwrites is the further marginalization of the OT witness as an "irrelevant other" because its status has been deemed as nonviable through theological justification. This method could then result in a self-selective approach of looking to the text for only those things that can be fit into a regnant conviction set and its enabling plausibility structures. Under these conditions, the OT witness would not be "truly other" as a witness that can call into question or maybe even re-narrate or reconstitute the reader.

In contrast to these tendencies, we wish to emphasize a "hermeneutic of continuity." We have already made this stance clear by suggesting that YHWH is the Trinity and the Trinity is YHWH. Now before us is the challenge of relating Israel to the church. Do Christ followers stand in the covenant that YHWH made with Abraham, Isaac, and Jacob? If, according to Christian confession, Jesus is the Messiah, and the promises made to Abraham now extend to all peoples who have been "circumcised in the heart," then Christians have some theological warrants for claiming themselves as part of the ongoing story between YHWH and Israel, even with the twists and turns this story has taken (including the development of what can be termed a "new" covenant). If readers approach the book of Hosea in this way, then its prophetic oracles can be considered as Christian Scripture in that they speak of a historical and existential dynamic that is best expressed through a logic of covenant.[30]

If a "hermeneutic of continuity" is available, then the question of the reader's identity is pushed to the forefront once more.[31] Is the reader part of this covenant arrangement in the sense that the God speaking is the God of her own confession and piety? If the answer is positive, then a bevy of hermeneutical options and dynamics opens up for the reader, not as unavoidable necessities in the reading of the

---

30. This reading strategy is on display in Jesus' own allusion to Hosea 6:6 when he remarks, "Go and learn what this means, 'I desire mercy, not sacrifice'" (Matt 9:13). Here Jesus not only draws a connection between his words and the OT, but more importantly his allusion suggests that features of the OT covenant logic, ones that may be subsumed or overlooked by other subsequent pressures, continue to stand and be relevant for an emerging Christian context.

31. Following the work of Umberto Eco, Markus Bockmuehl has made the case that the NT envisages a certain kind of reader, one who 1) "has a personal stake in the truthful reference of what it asserts," 2) "has undergone a religious, moral, and intellectual *conversion* to the gospel of which the documents speak," 3) "takes a view of the New Testament as authoritative," 4) is "ecclesially situated," and 5) "is evidently assumed to be 'inspired,' in the sense of Spirit filled" (*Seeing the Word* [Studies in Theological Interpretation; Grand Rapids: Baker Academic, 2006], pp. 69-72). We think it appropriate (and explicitly warranted by Bockmuehl, given the next quote) to extend corollaries of these suggestions for Christian readers of Hosea.

text, but as potentialities that can be enacted and lived into when the reader assumes that "the meaning of the sacred text is understood not primarily by intellectual genius or once-and-for-all scientific dissection, but by the interplay of divine gift with human welcome and delight."[32] As Bockmuehl continues, "Both testaments of Scripture clearly presuppose such an interpreter. The implied interpreter of the Christian Scripture is a *disciple*," so that hermeneutics and performance are integrally tied.[33]

One such possibility stemming from a "hermeneutic of continuity" is the growing awareness and ensuing conviction that erupt when God's word can challenge a particular *Sitz im Leben*, including the reader's. An operational understanding of what is meaningful, true, good, beautiful, and lasting can be called into question and reconfigured when one comes to this text willing and ready to hear the word of the LORD. It is hard to imagine that a hermeneutic of rupture or a posture of suspicion can cultivate the sensibilities of receptivity, trust, and vulnerability that are needed for the worshipful apprehension of God's name and voice. A hermeneutic of continuity does not guarantee such an outcome, but it at least orients the reading community to recognize this possibility as worth seeking in a humble and reverent fashion. Given the contentious readings and reactions to Hosea over the centuries, one cannot help but recognize that a faithful reading of this text has to transcend in some sense the deleterious determinations of one's traditioned and formed self; such a reading is only viable through a deliberate and sustained appreciation for the Spirit's work of illuminating and clarifying the Word of God.[34]

Another possibility within the reading modality being proposed is that the role of a reading community qua community is indispensable. In communal terms, the reader is not just part of a covenant with relevance to the past, but one that very much has a bearing on one's own life here and now. And so the affective dispositions of awe, faith, trust, and vulnerability are not so much self-willed determinations of a single individual as much as they are communally-sustained sensibilities made available to those who worship and continually participate in the triune life of God. Within this communal way of reading, the story of Abraham and Isaac is not simply a logo-centric text read periodically according to the lectionary, but one that is enacted and glossed by a people's pilgrimage in the life of faith. Such communal dynamics can in turn provide imaginative channels and restraints[35] in the

32. Bockmuehl, *Seeing the Word*, p. 91.

33. *Seeing the Word*, p. 92.

34. A working account of this theme can be found in John Webster, *The Domain of the Word* (London: T & T Clark, 2012), chapter 3.

35. To take the *Akedah* once again, Moberly comments on the importance of communal memory and restraints: "For in the extensive history and use of Gen 22 up to modern times, there is *no* recorded example of Jews or Christians using the text to justify their own abuse or killing

interpretive process. All this is possible when the reader comes to the text with the firm belief, trust, and vulnerability that are assumed with a proclamation typical of such readers: "YHWH is my God, this story is my story, these people are my people, these failures are my failures, and this hope is my hope."[36]

Knowing and Speaking of YHWH within the Dynamic of the Covenant Bond

If the reader of Hosea makes the deliberative, orienting, hermeneutical moves outlined above, she participates within a modality of reading that constitutes and narrates 1) oneself, 2) everything else that is, and 3) the activities that help constitute the interrelationships between both. Such activities would include Christian metaphysics and Christian speech.

Metaphysics

We have already acknowledged that theological readings of Scripture have the goal of fostering God-knowledge. This kind of knowledge was distinguished from other forms of knowledge in that it was suggested that God-knowledge is transformational, participative, and reconstituting of the knowing subject, all for the fostering of a particular species of love of God and neighbor. Nevertheless, knowing in the West has often been governed by an intellective bent so that knowledge typically in this context has circulated around a person's mental and cognitive activities and capacities to the neglect of one's material and affective constitution. Another way of relating the concern is that knowledge has often focused on one's mind so that one's heart and body were overshadowed as a

---

of a child. This means that the metaphorical significance of the text was always (until recently) taken for granted, because it was read within a wider scriptural and communal context that provided guidelines and constraints for understanding and appropriating the story . . . in accordance with the story's intrinsic character. To take the story in isolation from the context that enabled its meaningful appropriation and then proclaim it a problem in terms of its apparent face value is to be confronted by a problem of one's own making; analysis of parts in separation from their contextual whole can sometimes enable understanding, but can also impede it" ("Living Dangerously," in *ARS*, p. 195).

36. This realization and identification in turn contribute to the understanding of the Bible as authoritative for a reader, thereby localizing her within the unfolding of the story. N. T. Wright's analogy of the unfinished Shakespearean play is apropos here; see *The New Testament and the People of God* (Minneapolis: Fortress, 1992), pp. 140-3.

result. This predilection led to the tendency to abstract and trade in terms of concepts, categories, and specific logics of coherence. From this general disposition, the field of metaphysics took its preeminence in the West until the modern onset of epistemological queries. These shifts in Western intellectual history have had their effect on Christian endeavoring as a result. One form of such endeavoring has been Christian metaphysics, which emerged as an attempt to formulate some working sense of God's being and attributes. This kind of work became a tradition all its own, and subsequent analysts have often employed a single category to speak of these developments in their early forms. The category is conveniently referred to as "classical theism."

Critics of "classical theism" often assume a non-problematized and non-nuanced uniformity for this term on their way to denouncing it. Essentially, "classical theism" is depicted as the god-construct of ancient Hellenistic thought that made its way through the centuries as a staple of Christian God-talk. This construct involved privileging the category of "being" so that the Christian God was assumed to be subsumable and understood through an ontological framework. In fact, many Christian apologists took their biblical cue from the etymological nature of the proper divine name: YHWH is a variant of the verb "to be" in Hebrew, so ontology/philosophy and the Bible/revelation were assumed by some as going hand in hand. In this regard, some early Christians, particularly in the apologetic era, followed the tendencies of Philo of Alexandria in believing that the God of the biblical materials and the "Divine Shaper" of Plato's *Timaeus* or the "Unmoved Mover" of Aristotle's *Metaphysics* were functionally the same entity.[37] With this conflation, patterns of speech and thought were employed by Christians as spoils from their Hellenistic culture, and in time, the practice of speaking of God as "immovable," "immutable," "impassible," "omnipotent," and the like became conventional. On account of this development, contemporary denouncers of "classical theism" have tended to follow Adolf von Harnack's thesis that Christian theology suffered a process of Hellenization in which metaphysical patterns of thought and speech overdetermined Christian intellectual culture for centuries. Within such a depiction, individuals such as Justin Martyr, the Cappadocians, Peter Lombard, and Thomas Aquinas are collectively said to be exemplars of this corruption; they exhibit in one shape or form the category of "classical theism."

In recent times, critics of "classical theism" have postulated what they call a "more biblical" way of thinking and talking about God. This group of alternatives is generally called "open" or "process" theism, and the regnant sensibility of these alternatives oftentimes follows from a desire to observe biblical patterns

---

37. Justin Martyr, *First Apology*, in ANF, 1:182.

of theological speech, especially those found in the Old Testament. One need only take an important example from Exodus: In Exodus 32, after the golden calf incident, YHWH's judgment is kindled to destructive proportions as God remarks to Moses: "'I have seen this people, how stiff-necked they are. Now let me alone, so that my wrath may burn hot against them and I may consume them; and of you I will make a great nation" (Exod 32:9-10). After all the experiences related to Moses' preparation and rise as a leader of the people, the back and forth exchanges between Pharaoh and Moses in light of the plagues, and the final liberation of the people at the Red Sea, YHWH desires at this moment in the covenant history to start all over again simply with Moses' posterity. Yet Moses implores YHWH to reconsider, making an appeal on several rhetorical grounds — God's power and might, the opinion of the Egyptians, God's promises to the patriarchs — and the result is an alteration of the divine disposition: "And the LORD changed his mind about the disaster that he planned to bring on his people" (Exod 32:14).

This example is not atypical of the biblical witness: Countless examples show a species of dynamism between God and God's people so that God's mind is changed, God's ire subsides, God's mercy prevails, and so on. Plenty of similar instances could be cited within the Book of the Twelve. One of the most famous of these is found in the book of Jonah: Here the prophet finally heeds his call and proclaims the judgment of God among the Ninevites, but when the people repented and "God saw what they did, how they turned from their evil ways, God changed his mind about the calamity that he had said he would bring upon them; and he did not do it" (Jonah 3:10). This example, and the varying pathos-laden passages within the Book of the Twelve, spur in the minds of some thinkers and believers the need for an alternative metaphysics to the regnant patterns available in Western theology. If one follows the plotline of Scripture, YHWH is not distant or disengaged but very much active, to such a degree that exchanges take place in which the covenant people sometimes even influence YHWH's decision-making. Rather than being the "Unmoved Mover" of Aristotle, this God appears to be an exceptional covenant partner; as a matter of contrast, one could call God the "Most Moved Mover."[38] Those who espouse such an alternative are adamant in reminding their hearers that God's mercy and grace are unfailing, God's judgment is ultimately restorative, and God is active, responsive, and conditioned by developments within the historical process.

What to make of this depiction of "classical theism" as something different from the biblical portrayal of the Trinity? On the surface, the simplicity

---

38. See Clark Pinnock, *Most Moved Mover* (Grand Rapids: Baker Academic, 2001).

of the narration invites a suspicion in terms of its operative assumptions. On the one hand, "classical theism" is not a unitary conceptual conglomerate that can adequately account for over fifteen hundred years of Christian God-talk. The span of epochs, figures, and theological emphases is simply too great to be summed up in a single descriptor. Within the variety that exists in this trajectory of figures, not only can words like "simplicity" or "impassibility" mean different things to different people, but the case could also be that these differences yield something distinctive on their own terms.[39] In other words, Christian appropriation of such terms does not necessarily mean their unqualified endorsement. The localization of such terms within a Christian ethos could in turn reconfigure their possibilities and connotative implications to such a degree that their espousers in the broader, non-Christian context might find them unrecognizable or unfitting in their Christian formulation. Because of the potential for such alterations and transfigurations, these purported "classical theists" often thought that their proposals were very much in the spirit of fundamental Christian convictions. One need only look at the example of a thinker often maligned in these discussions: Some would be surprised to recall that Pseudo-Dionysius — the great mystical theologian of the sixth century — at the beginning of his work on *The Divine Names,* locates his reflections within the boundaries set forth in Scripture. As he notes, "We must not then dare to speak, or indeed to form any conception, of the hidden super-essential Godhead, except those things that are revealed to us from the Holy Scriptures."[40] In short, scholars who render a counter-proposal to "classical theism," professing it as the truly "biblical" approach to God-talk, not only flatter themselves with the descriptor of being exclusively the "biblical" option, but also adopt a strategy that uncharitably constricts those whom they deem "classical theists."

How can one upset this rigidly dyadic presentation? In addition to the problematization of the term "classical theism," one can also delve into the challenge of what a "biblical metaphysics"[41] could look like and how it could be

39. I have argued repeatedly that each figure should be taken on his particular terms because grades of nuance and qualification exist from thinker to thinker; see "Toward Pentecostal Prolegomena II," *Journal of Pentecostal Theology* 21 (2012): 168-80.

40. *The Mystical Theology and The Divine Names* (trans. C. E. Rolt; Mineola: Dover, 2004), p. 51.

41. I render this phrase quite loosely as a tag for the activity of making sense of the biblical portrayals of God. As such, I do not intend to involve myself in the particular discussions related to the propriety and adequacy of metaphysics for theological endeavoring; on this point, see Kevin Hector, *Theology without Metaphysics* (Cambridge: Cambridge University Press, 2011). Having made that claim, I find Kevin Vanhoozer's theodramatic proposals agreeable to much of what I am proposing; see *Remythologizing Theology* (Cambridge: Cambridge University Press, 2010).

pursued. Naturally, a number of complexities exist for such a task, including the non-existence of a singular "biblical" alternative. The assumption that the Bible contains or suggests only one possible metaphysics is a reductive construal. Perhaps the quest for a singular biblical alternative betrays the fact that all readers bring to the table their own plausibility structures, methodological preferences, and metaphysical commitments, which in turn determine what they see in the text.[42] Therefore, from the very beginning, those seeking a "biblical portrayal of God" should recognize the tentative and provisional limits of such a task. We intend to heed our own advice by offering only one — but nevertheless crucial — component of what we believe should constitute such endeavoring.

Beginning with the primordial relationship between God and cosmos as one of Creator and creation, as set forth early on in Genesis and reiterated in other passages, a definitive pattern and condition are established. The relationship is one of creation's dynamic dependence and relative independence vis-à-vis its Creator. The Creator-creation link is one of dynamic dependence because creation both stems from, and is directed back to, the One named in the covenant. As the prophet Amos proclaims, "For lo, the one who forms the mountains, creates the wind, reveals his thoughts to mortals, makes the morning darkness, and treads on the heights of the earth — the LORD, the God of hosts, is his name!" (Amos 4:13). Without the goodwill and hospitality of the Creator, no creation would ever have come to be, nor would it have perdured for as long as it has; therefore, creation exhibits a form of contingency and dependency that is basic to its status as creaturely. This understanding is exceedingly difficult to sustain since many of our contemporary methodological and practical schemas do not assume the presence of a God who is involved in some active way. Obviously, knowing and speaking of God in the everyday is a tricky matter because such claims always rely on faith-conditioned sensibilities, but the demythologization of our lives means that God is often pushed to the periphery, to that space where our explanatory prowess inevitably falls short and we are pressed to admit (however reluctantly) our own ignorance.[43]

The relationship of Creator-creation can also be understood as one of relative independence, in that creation is something definitively distinct from

42. Abraham Heschel had this challenge in mind: "The principle to be kept in mind is to know what we see rather than to see what we know" (*The Prophets*, 1:ix).

43. What is being denounced here is in part a "functional deism," one in which God is not a clockmaker per se, as is usually assumed in deist portrayals, but is nevertheless cast at the periphery of life and action within the world. I explore this matter in *Confessing the Triune God* (Eugene: Cascade, forthcoming), chapter 7. For a helpful essay that illuminates this condition and offers ways forward, see Steven D. Boyer and Christopher A. Hall, *The Mystery of God* (Grand Rapids: Baker Academic, 2012).

the Creator. From a Christian understanding, the bond is one between two separately-identifiable entities. The Creator is not the creation, and the creation is not the Creator. In creating, God creates that which is not-God. In this sense, everything that happens in the theater of the world is not somehow caused by the Creator, for the way the creation is set up gives it a certain level of self-determination that is Creator-made and Creator-enabled, yet distinctly creation-enacted.[44] This understanding casts the creation as active and involved without it being threatening or competitive with the Creator. The creation can work alongside, obey, accept, and reject the Creator's promptings and beckonings without such gestures diminishing the divine glory.

How can this be? How is it that Creator and creation can work responsively and cooperatively without such dynamism involving the diminishment of the divine character? The Creator-creation dynamic entails that these entities interact with each other based on the infinite difference between the two. The matter is not simply that a vast expanse exists between YHWH and Israel or Trinity and church. The situation is also inaccurately framed in terms of a sole, fundamental dialectic.[45] The issues go deeper still because the agents in question *do not operate on the same ontological plane.* YHWH is not just a higher being when compared to creation or even "Being" itself. God is beyond any ontological formulation that we as creatures construct and devise for the sake of intelligibility and meaning-making. God is not even exclusively an "agent," because YHWH is more expansive than any such term can generate.

What is being proposed here is that the Creator-creation dynamic is of such unusual and incomprehensible proportions that an underlying sensibility of tentativeness and fragility surrounds all Christian metaphysical constructs.

---

44. What I am invoking here is the possibility of primary and secondary causality, a theme that has been repeatedly championed in the work of David Bentley Hart, usually under the heading of providence. An extended quote should elaborate this depiction of causality in terms of creation: "Providence works at the level of what Aquinas would call primary causality: that is, it is so transcendent of the operation of secondary causes . . . that it can at once create freedom and also assure that no consequence of the misuse of that freedom will prevent him from accomplishing the good he intends in all things. This is the same as saying that the transcendent act of creation, though it grants existence to creatures out of the plenitude of God's being, nonetheless brings forth beings that are genuinely other than God, without there being any 'conflict' between his infinite actuality and their contingent participation in it" (*The Doors of the Sea* [Grand Rapids: Eerdmans, 2005], pp. 83-84).

45. This danger is always lurking, even in this commentary. Maintaining this difference thoroughly has proven difficult for biblical interpreters and theologians in the past, partly because of the ease with which Christian reflection and speech involve YHWH as an active agent. This ease is a double-edged sword because, whereas some would say that this feature is distinctive of Christianity, it also invites with alarming ease the tendencies toward projection.

And yet because this expanse is both created and bridged by YHWH, conceptual formulation is possible and admissible given divine gratuity and hospitality. In this sense, patterns of theological reflection within Scripture ought to be employed and even relished by the faithful worshiping community, but these speech forms are contingent upon a deeper underlying claim, namely God's undetermined and so free self.

Speaking

Divine speech, both in terms of us speaking of God and God speaking to us, retains challenges similar to those registered above. In terms of humans speaking of God, Barth's famous remark about the admission of our inability and requirement to speak of God leading us to praise rings true:[46] In one sense, words cannot circumscribe or describe God in God's fullness, so that speaking of God is impossible on simply rational grounds. A divine entity, especially One who is said to be the beginning and end of all things, cannot be limited or controlled, which are features associated with the act of description. And yet within the covenant bond, God discloses Godself so as to be available to human speech. This availability makes an implicit and often explicit demand on those who "hear" and "see," one that presses them to testify to that which they have witnessed. Therefore, the dialectic of impossibility and obligation are at play in God-talk, and that admission, in Barth's estimation, drives the "theologian" to praise. But this call to praise is not just rendered because humans run up against the limits of their own capacities and capabilities in God-talk. More basically, the call to praise grows out of the singularity and uniqueness of this One. For this reason, despite all its difficulties, the Jewish practice of not pronouncing the divine name has a degree of theological merit. Our naming of God in no way means that we can grant for ourselves the profane impossibility of circumscribing or delimiting the presence and character of God.

Once this orienting hermeneutical horizon is admitted, the possibilities do run deep in terms of the way humans can speak of God. These possibilities vary, for they extend to material and immaterial objects, masculine and feminine roles, and various vocational depictions. What believers in turn can render to God runs the gamut of possibilities. Yes, many liturgical and doxological formulas are viable, but intimate and deeply emotive possibilities exist as well. The Song of Solomon often is cited as one such example, for it has occupied some of

46. See Karl Barth, *The Word of God and Theology* (trans. Amy Marga; London: T & T Clark, 2011), p. 177.

the ablest theological interpreters with its invitation to relate to God in the most intimate of ways. At another affective register, one is reminded of the "problematic" lament psalms, those that use strongly visceral and apparently accusatory language directed to God. Take for instance the latter part of Psalm 88 (vv. 13-18):

> But I, O LORD, cry out to you;
> In the morning my prayer comes before you.
> O LORD, why do you cast me off?
> Why do you hide your face from me?
> Wretched and close to death from my youth up,
> I suffer your terrors;
> I am desperate.
> Your wrath has swept over me;
> your dread assaults destroy me.
> They surround me like a flood all day long;
> from all sides they close in on me.
> You have caused friend and neighbor to shun me;
> my companions are in darkness.

One of the remarkable features of the ending of this psalm is that it does not conclude with the assurance and thanksgiving one tends to associate not only with the psalms, but with the life of piety in general. Strictly from the text itself, one cannot derive an account of hope, but rather a feeling of loss and despair. Now, as with the case of Hosea, so here: This part of Psalm 88 employs the Tetragrammaton, and in doing so, the history of God's covenant faithfulness is implied as a result. The Psalmist is here speaking of the same One who delivered the people of Israel and who is in an ongoing fashion the covenant-enabler and sustainer. Nevertheless, given the existential situation in which the Psalmist finds himself, the covenantal narrative runs counter to his experience and desperation. One could argue a number of claims against the Psalmist's sentiments: How can the Psalmist know if YHWH has actually cast him off? Has God really hidden God's face from him? Has the Trinity's wrath swept over him and God's dread destroyed him? Was God really the source of his friends shunning him? These queries can function as attempts to soften the visceral evocativeness at play in the words of this psalm. They certainly are typical reactions and feelings within the life of faith, but the fact that they are expressed in no less than Holy Scripture is a challenge to the reading community. Are these normative feelings within the YHWH-Israel covenant bond? Or was the Psalmist simply having an "off" day when he wrote Psalm 88? Should the form of this psalm's ending be taken seriously?

Another example of visceral language — and one that is especially pertinent to the themes at play in Hosea — is the poetry of John Donne. Donne was a Christian, and the language he often used in his poetry was of a species that some would find enriching, whereas others would see as blasphemous (and maybe even erotic or pornographic). Take his poem "Batter My Heart":

Batter my heart, three-personed God; for, you
As yet but knock, breathe, shine, and seek to mend;
That I may rise and stand, o'erthrow me and bend
Your force, to break, blow, burn and make me new.
I, like a usurped town to another due,
Labour to admit you, but oh, to no end.
Reason your viceroy in me, me should defend,
But is captived, and proves weak or untrue,
Yet dearly I love you, and would be loved fain,
But am betrothed unto your enemy,
Divorce me, untie, or break that knot again.
Take me to you, imprison me, for I
Except you enthrall me, never shall be free,
Nor ever chaste, except you ravish me.[47]

What Donne has ventured in this poem is to employ the themes of covenant faithfulness and sexual fidelity so as to push them to the limits of their sensible appropriation within the life of faith. The language is gripping, even scandalizing: "*batter* my heart," "*o'erthrow* me and *bend your force, to break, blow, burn*" me, "*divorce* me," "*imprison* me," "*enthrall* me," and "*ravish* me." These verbs are strongly suggestive, their range appallingly vast. How does Donne present himself here? Devoted? Conflicted? Does he demonstrate pathology? Is he asking for an abusive relationship?

The challenges associated with reading certain strands of the biblical witness and some exhibits of Christian literature are simply results of us speaking of God. As Augustine reminded us many centuries ago, language is largely a semiotic construct: an ordering of signs that represent and point to other things. Part of the difficulty with the hermeneutical process is that the *res* is not always clear, and the reader is herself complicated in the reading process by her own experiences. For instance, would a reading of Psalm 88 suggest something different to a survivor of genocide than to a citizen of a relatively

47. As found in *John Donne: The Complete English Poems* (edited by A. J. Smith; New York: Penguin, 1996), pp. 314-15.

peaceful nation? Would a victim of domestic violence read "Batter My Heart" differently from a person who has experienced relatively healthy relationships? Language, like metaphysical constructs, is a medium that breaks down under its own inadequacy, yet it retains some usefulness for purposes of communicability and formation. After all, language is one of the few resources humans have towards these ends.

The other side of divine speech, God speaking to us, is another linguistic consideration often quickly passed over by those who have grown accustomed to biblical patterns of speech. Inevitably involved in this gesture is the idea of condescension, a point picked up countless times in the past: Since God cannot be circumscribed by words, God's self-revelation through words is a form of accommodation or adjustment to our limits as humans. This admission, however, has some difficulties. First, this understanding has sometimes been used as a mechanism by which to "explain away" features of the text that were not readily available or relatable to a particular cultural and philosophical situation. One thinks for instance of Philo's remarks regarding Genesis 6 in his treatise on the immutability of God: According to Philo, the notions that God changed his mind and repented were strategies aimed at lesser minds who could not be reached or corrected otherwise.[48] Such a hermeneutical posture has the potential for making the text a "domesticated other," a testimony that cannot call attention to and reconfigure the plausibility and coherence mechanisms of the reader. Second, the strategy of accommodation for explaining the phenomenon of divine self-disclosure through speech depicts the act of God speaking as something artificial to the divine being.[49] This perspective has a way of diminishing the impact of the Johannine witness in which the One who was "in the beginning" is also the One who bore flesh and lived among us. Another way of expressing the concern would be: Is divine self-disclosure through the medium of language at its core some kind of artificial gesture on the part of God? Is not the link (or in written form, the dash) in the Creator-creation relationship one that is energized by this very God who communicates? Is it not the case that simply the act of creation demonstrates that this God is One who

---

48. *On the Unchangeableness of God*, XI; see *The Works of Philo* (trans. C. D. Yonge; Peabody: Hendrickson, 1993), pp. 162-63.

49. Obviously, accommodation is at work in some fashion with divine self-revelation, for issues of language, context, and the like are at play. But I wish to register a difference between what could be termed "soft" and "hard" forms of accommodation. "Soft" forms would involve the complexity associated with the phenomenon of mediation generally; "hard" forms, however, would be those cases in which apophatic possibilities are understood as off the table and one's own cultural predispositions are uncritically held and promulgated as the only viable plausibility structures. Philo would appear to be in the latter camp, given how he describes accommodation.

is *ekstatic,* moving out, spilling over, and superabundantly self-expressive, so that the word — written or oral — is not so much a sign of self-limitation but of freedom and abundance?

God's Manner of Speaking through Hosea to the Covenant People

In the oracles of Hosea, the principal speaker is YHWH, and so with this recognition come all of the preliminary considerations mentioned above: Such speech occurs within a history of divine self-communication that is enacted within a particular covenant relationship, one that has its very own dynamics, patterns, and assumptions. This One thus is self-communicating and is so quite naturally and appropriately. Hearers and readers of Hosea in turn are to engage this self-communication within a dynamic of dependence, trust, vulnerability, and worship.

Hosea tests its engagement by Christian readers, however, simply by virtue of being a very difficult text. Its difficulty is significantly related to the intensity, range, and rapid variance of affectivity displayed by none other than YHWH. This form of affectivity, what one could call *theopathy,* is often enough explicitly related: Hosea makes reference to God's indecisiveness (6:4; 11:8), anger (8:5; 13:11; 14:4 [14:5]), hatred (9:15), love (11:1; 14:4 [14:5]), compassion (11:8), and wrath (13:11). In this regard, Hosea is not unique compared to other voices in the Book of the Twelve. However, these particular examples from Hosea contribute to something greater than their collective sum, and that contribution is nothing short of a deeply complex, variable, and ranging gestalt of affective interiority on the part of YHWH.[50] In other words, explicitly or implicitly, YHWH's self-presentation in Hosea admits of an expansive affectivity, so much so that its reading teeters on the breakdown of theological language on one side and projectionist indulgence by the reader on the other.

What can the reading community do with the theopathic flair of Hosea? The guidelines established above can contribute to the shape of an approach to this matter. In terms of Christian metaphysics, examples like those present in Hosea may require a reconfiguration of what typically traffics as divine impas-

---

50. As Brueggemann notes, the "plenitude of images [in Hosea] is daring, offensive and evocative, for Hosea, in the depth of his passion and the richness of his imagination, was permitted to say the unsayable. What is unsayable and here said includes a) the conviction YHWH has a complex relation to the life of Israel that fits no ordinary formulation because b) YHWH has a complex, unsettled internal life. Hosea dares to take us inside that complex interior life of YHWH and thus to be exposed to a range of divine impulses not elsewhere available in Israel's ancient text" ("The Recovering God of Hosea," p. 6).

sibility. The notion of impassibility is a deeply contested one in the history of Christian dogmatics, and its reception in modernity has been marred by the overall approaches to "classical theism" alluded to above. In fact, some have gone on to say that divine impassibility is the most egregious exemplification of the errors attributable to the Hellenization of Christianity, since the affirmation that God is "not passionate" or is "apathetic" runs directly contrary to the claim that God is "steadfast love"[51] (the phrase of Exod 34:6-7 that serves as a refrain to the Book of the Twelve, as mentioned by Lim previously). Sundry Christian thinkers in the past, however, have maintained that impassibility is reconcilable with divine *caritas* and the range of theopathy one finds in biblical books like Hosea.[52] The source of rapprochement is precisely the covenant dynamics implied in the relationship between YHWH and Israel.

Within the covenant logic, YHWH is the ground and basis upon which all else depends. Hosea points to this feature of God-talk: "I will not execute my fierce anger; I will not again destroy Ephraim; for I am God and no mortal, the Holy One in your midst, and I will not come in wrath" (11:9). One must acknowledge the vast difference between covenant partners when one reads texts such as Hosea. In this way, an apophatic dimension of God-talk is sustained throughout interpretive endeavoring and not simply at the end once it is deemed that nothing else can be said. This beckoning of the apophatic is precisely the kind of work the espousal of divine impassibility has sometimes

51. Andrew M. Fairbairn remarked, "Theology has no falser idea than that of the impassibility of God" (*The Place of Christ in Modern Theology* [New York: Charles Scribner's Sons, 1899], p. 483), and Douglas White believed that "the doctrine of the impassibility of God, taken in its widest sense, is the greatest heresy that ever smirched Christianity" (*Forgiveness and Suffering* [Cambridge: Cambridge University Press, 1913], p. 84).

52. I take this approach in *The Apathetic God* (Milton Keynes: Paternoster, 2009); other works that rehabilitate divine impassibility along these lines include David B. Hart, "No Shadow of Turning: On Divine Impassibility," *Pro Ecclesia* 11 (2002): 184-206, and certain chapters in the collection *Divine Impassibility and the Mystery of Human Suffering*, edited by James F. Keating and Thomas Joseph White, OP (Grand Rapids: Eerdmans, 2009). Others, however, will disagree, as one can see in Roy Clements' sermon on Hosea 11 (see *Nothing Greater, Nothing Better* [ed. Kevin J. Vanhoozer; Grand Rapids: Eerdmans, 2001], pp. 203-15). The way Clements pictures the scenario, "We can certainly err like Erasmus by having thoughts of God that are too human, but we can err also by having thoughts of him that are not human enough" (p. 207). The difficulty with this approach is that the resolution is perceived to be one of striking a balance, one that teeters between divinity and humanity; however, sufficiency is an impossible goal given the very constitution of God-talk. Put bluntly, our words do not have the capacity to strike the balance that seems desirable in this case, for they are, on their own, deeply inadequate. Following the lead of Hart, I would argue that a reconstrual of divine impassibility offers theology precisely a way forward from the kind of binary thinking that keeps such matters as God's love within an entrenched stalemate not simply in terms of an "either/or" but also of a "both/and."

performed in Christian discourse. Stating from the beginning that God is impassible or apathetic is a way to register the claim that divine affectivity, as on display within the Scriptures, is of a different order than human affectivity, since God is not on the same ontological plane or spectrum as humans are.

Covenant constraints also suggest that the range of theopathy on display within Scripture is usually in reaction to, or on behalf of, the covenant people. Therefore, God's wrath or anger is usually incited *because of* Israel's obstinacy and rebellion. These are reactive, secondary affective responses fitting to the occasion of covenant infidelity on the part of the elect. Hosea has numerous instances of such examples. One is 9:15: "Every evil of theirs began at Gilgal; there I came to hate them. Because of the wickedness of their deeds I will drive them out of my house. I will love them no more; all their officials are rebels." Furthermore, YHWH's gracious disposition of mercy, love, and forgiveness is also directed to Israel as a way of restoring the relationship Israel has disrupted. Hosea has occasions of this tendency. Take the following as an example: "I will heal their disloyalty; I will love them freely, for my anger has turned from them. I will be like the dew to Israel; he shall blossom like the lily, he shall strike root like the forests of Lebanon" (14:4-5 [14:5-6]). All in all, the range of theopathy has to be situated within a covenant logic rather than simply taken in isolation, for it is within this context that one can make sense of such phenomena as God's judgment, anger, and wrath.

The vast difference at play between covenant partners, and the vicissitudes of the covenant history, create the conditions for a fascinating — and dare we say dangerous — dynamic. This dynamic occasions the possibility of thinking of God-talk generally, and the prophetic oracles particularly, through the mechanism of analogy. The value of analogy is that it pivots on both equivocity and univocity in the sense that two different entities are brought together in some kind of shared or proportional way.[53] YHWH is infinitely greater than Israel (equivocity), yet the shared link between the two is the covenant bond, which occasions communicability, shared expression, the exchange of names, and the like (univocity).[54] What this matrix occasions is a richness of language

53. As such, analogy is integral to the study of metaphysics, a point made by Gerald Phelan in accordance with Cajetan (see *Saint Thomas and Analogy* [Milwaukee: Marquette University Press, 1941], p. 1).

54. One should note that analogies come in different forms, and the theme is much more complex than what can be considered in the space of a footnote. For a helpful summary of some of the literature, see Alan Torrance, "Is Love the Essence of God?" in *Nothing Greater, Nothing Better*, pp. 114-37. Drawing from the work of Battista Mondin (*The Principle of Analogy in Protestant and Catholic Theology* [The Hague: Martinus Nijhoff, 1968]), Torrance concludes that, in the case of Aquinas's views on analogy in God-talk, two pertinent features apply in terms of the "analogy

and expression that on first blush is difficult to accommodate apart from the outright recognition of analogy, because the link and its possibility rest on this unimaginable discrepancy that can only be bridged from God's side.

As such, one finds within Hosea corollaries to the forms of expression outlined above from the human side of covenant. Similar to the way the Psalmist accuses God of casting him off, YHWH demonstrates through the prophet a range of expression that is astonishing, moving, and disturbing all at once. Putting to the side the marriage and sexual imagery (which will occupy a subsequent chapter), one finds in Hosea intense imagery and corresponding affective displays. Apart from the expression of judgment and ire, other "troublesome" passages exist: Take for instance the contention against the priesthood where the LORD threatens, "I will destroy your mother" and "Since you have forgotten the law of your God, I also will forget your children" (4:5-6). Chapter 5 has a series of startling images: the rise of the new moon devouring the people and their fields (5:7); the desolation of Ephraim so that YHWH's wrath is poured out like water and YHWH's presence functions like maggots to Ephraim (5:10, 12); and the depiction of YHWH as a lion who proclaims, "I myself will tear and go away; I will carry off, and no one shall rescue" (5:14). This imagery of YHWH as a lion reaches higher dramatic proportions in Hos 13: "So I will become like a lion to them, like a leopard I will lurk beside the way. I will fall upon them like a bear robbed of her cubs, and will tear open the covering of their heart; there I will devour them like a lion, as a wild animal would mangle them. I will destroy you, O Israel; who can help you?" (vv. 7-9). Repeated threats of infertility and barrenness are leveled throughout Hos 9 (vv. 11-14, 16, the latter being especially difficult: "Even though they give birth, I will kill the cherished offspring of their womb"). Mothers with their children being dashed to pieces (cf. 10:14) is an image picked up in 13:16: "Samaria shall bear her guilt, because she has rebelled against her God; they shall fall by the sword, their little ones shall be dashed in pieces, and their pregnant women ripped open." Obviously, these many instances create cognitive (and maybe even faith) dissonances for many readers. How is it that God could be good, loving, and holy when leveling such threats?

---

of intrinsic attribution" (in which a relationship of efficient causality exists): 1) The relationship must be "of one to another" *(unius ad alterum),* meaning that the relationship is between God and creatures and not subsumable to some quasi-Platonic category, and 2) it must be "according to priority and posteriority" *(per prius et posterius),* suggesting God is first and foremost in the relationship as Creator and that creation is essentially dependent and derivative as a result, making God a primary analogate and creation a secondary one (see pp. 120-21). Both claims fit well with what we have been trying to maintain about Christian God-talk as inherently requiring a creational and covenantal logic for its intelligibility.

At the same time, one finds startling expressions of YHWH's vulnerability and tenderness within the oracles of Hosea, moments that distinguish Hosea in a significant way. YHWH shows in Hos 7 a form of sadness for Israel's evil ways: "I would redeem them, but they speak lies against me. . . . It was I who trained and strengthened their arms, yet they plot evil against me" (vv. 13, 15). The most moving demonstration of YHWH's tenderness can be found in Hos 11. The sheer beauty of this passage is worth emphasizing. The chapter employs a parental and developmental model as a figuration of the covenant history: "When Israel was a child, I loved him, and out of Egypt I called my son" (v. 1). A wayward child, however, creates deep, inward pain for the parent who has the best of intentions for the child: "The more I called them, the more they went from me . . . Yet it was I who taught Ephraim to walk, I took them up in my arms; but they did not know that I healed them" (vv. 2-3). And with an expression that conjures a mother's nurturing care for her child, YHWH remarks: "I led them with cords of human kindness, with bands of love. I was to them like those who lift infants to their cheeks. I bent down to them and fed them" (v. 4).

Can the same entity be behind both forms of expression? Can one agent be both a roaring lion and a tender mother? Similar kinds of queries could be leveled at the examples lifted above: Could a faithful follower of the triune God register the sentiments found in Psalm 88 and in Donne's "Batter My Heart"? If one could answer in the affirmative from the human side of the covenant bond, then why could one not express a similar affirmation concerning the divine side of the covenant? Here is the value of analogical thinking: Once one continually affirms the vast difference between YHWH and Israel as covenant partners, that admission itself creates the possibility, in covenant history and speech, for a more radical and daring depiction of the interstices of covenant interaction. In other words, as the difference between covenant partners is registered primarily and thoroughly throughout covenant thinking, so the language marking their interrelationship can be stretched to scandalizing proportions, because the language itself is vigilantly recognized as provisional throughout; it relies on a history and relationship and not simply an isolated hermeneutical orientation or conceptual apparatus. By this measure, such dangers as projection and sentimentalism are at least recognized *as* dangers within a hermeneutical register, and in being so, they can be checked and resisted in what one goes on to say about the interrelationship between YHWH and Israel. All these concerns necessarily play a role in a churchly reading of Hosea, since this book will stretch a reading community's tolerance for scandalous God-talk and its implications for fitting God-knowledge.

7. Hosea 4:1–5:7

Bo H. Lim

Hosea 4:1-3 serves as an introduction to 4:1–5:7, 4:1–11:11, and even 4:1–14:9 [4:1–14:10]. Hosea 4:1–11:11 forms a distinct unit, opening with "Hear the word of the LORD" (4:1) and closing with the idiom "says the LORD" (11:11). Commentators have long observed that chapters 4–14 inherently possess a greater amount of unity than one finds between it and chapters 1–3. Clearly, chapters 4–14 differ from 1–3 in genre and tone; the former lack any prophetic sign-acts and any mention of the prophet Hosea or Gomer. For these reasons, scholars have often treated 4–14 in isolation from 1–3, and have focused on Hosea and Gomer's marriage to the neglect of these prophecies.[1] Whereas an earlier generation of commentators separated these units by assigning them different forms or sources, more recent scholars have argued that these two sections cannot be harmonized at a literary or ideological level.[2] Yet those who argue that the purported textual instability leads to interpretive chaos neglect the normative function of the prophetic book and the book's function within the Twelve and the canon. In the final form of the book, chapters 4–14 are prefaced by chapters 1–3 under the headings "The word of the LORD that came to Hosea son of Beeri" (1:1) and "The beginning of the word of the LORD to Hosea" (1:2). The mention of the "word of the LORD" (4:1) at the opening of this new section recalls 1:1 and 1:2 and signals to the reader that this section is a continuation of Hosea's prophecy.

As in 1:2, the prophetic word in 4:1 focuses on Israel's sin against the land. While these texts do not possess all the characteristics of a prophetic lawsuit, they confront Israel by exposing its moral failures and calling for the people to repent. The mention of an "indictment" (רִיב/*rîb*) in 4:1 recalls the repeated

---

1. See Brad E. Kelle, "Hosea 1–3 in Twentieth-Century Scholarship," *CurBR* 7 (2009): 180.
2. Sharon Moughtin-Mumby, *Sexual and Marital Metaphors in Hosea, Jeremiah, Isaiah and Ezekiel* (Oxford Theological Monographs; Oxford: Oxford University Press, 2008), pp. 77-79.

"pleading" (ריב/*rîb*) of 2:2 [2:4], and suggests that the disputation taken up against the woman of chapter 2 is continued against Israel in 4–11. Just as the disputation of 4:1 threatens to devastate the land in 4:3, so too, in the disputation of 2:2-3 [2:4-5], YHWH threatens to "make her like a wilderness, and turn her into a parched land, and kill her with thirst" (Hos 2:3 [2:5]). The indictment is directed at "those who dwell in the land" (4:1), that is, Israel.

Before any moral or ethical failure is identified, Israel's conduct is assessed according to the criteria of covenant faithfulness. The canonical prophetic books do not merely recount the words and deeds of radical individuals fighting against social inequity and political corruption; instead their ethical vision is thoroughly theological. "Faithfulness" (אמת/*'ĕmet*) and "loyalty/steadfast love" (חסד/*ḥesed*) in Hos 4:1 comprise a word pair that frequently describes the attributes of God. Both words appear in YHWH's self-description in Exod 34:6, "the LORD passed before him, and proclaimed, "The LORD, the LORD, a God merciful and gracious, slow to anger, and abounding in steadfast love (חסד/*ḥesed*) and faithfulness (אמת/*'ĕmet*)." Hosea 4:1 contains the only occurrence of "faithfulness" (אמת/ *'ĕmet*) in the book, and its derivative "faithfulness" (אמונה/*'ĕmûnāh*) also appears just once, in 2:20 [2:22]. Both passages include steadfast love in its immediate context (חסד/*ḥesed*, 2:19 [2:21]) and speak about the knowledge of YHWH/God (2:20 [2:22]; 4:1). In addition, Hos 6:6 also reiterates YHWH's desire for steadfast love and the knowledge of God. Repeatedly, the book of Hosea emphasizes that "knowing God" (i.e., covenant faithfulness) is as much a cultic as a non-cultic activity, and so moral lapses in one sphere of life inevitably corrupt all the others.

While knowing God is thoroughly theological, it is practiced in covenantal obedience to YHWH's revealed instruction. In 4:6, YHWH specifies that "My people are destroyed for lack of knowledge; because you have rejected knowledge." Hosea goes on define this absence of knowledge as "you have forgotten the law of your God." Many commentators have wondered if this reference to law and in particular the sins outlined in 4:2 are a direct reference to the Decalogue. While certainly definite correspondences exist between Hos 4:2 and Exod 20 and Deut 5, textual reliance is not conclusive. The sins of murder, theft, and adultery appear in Exod 20:13-15, Deut 5:17-19, and Jer 7:9 ("Will you steal, murder, commit adultery, swear falsely, make offerings to Baal, and go after other gods that you have not known"). In addition, Lev. 19:11 also prohibits lying and stealing. Dearman claims that the reference in Hos 3:1 ("though they turn to other gods") is dependent on the first commandment of the Decalogue ("You shall have no other gods before me" [Exod 20:3; Deut 5:7]) because of the repeated phrase "other gods."[3] Given that the correspondences between Hos 4:2

---

3. J. Andrew Dearman, *Book of Hosea* (NICOT; Grand Rapids: Eerdmans, 2010), p. 134.

and the Decalogue passages are loose and sparse, it is likely that Hosea "point[s] to a general understanding of these types of actions as paradigmatic of those that lead a society to destruction."[4] While the Decalogue in its final form may not have been available to Hosea, one need not conclude that "the prophets were far from originating a new conception of God, [for] they none the less were founders of what has been called 'ethical monotheism.'"[5] Law was assumed by the prophets, not invented. Hosea's ethical vision is not innovative, but rather traditional; he was "neither radical nor revolutionary but conservative, at every point calling Israel back to its foundations."[6] While the Decalogue may not have been completely codified in written form during Hosea's time, nonetheless Law as an ethical and theological category did exist and was understood covenantally. To violate Law was an abrogation of covenant (cf. Hos 8:1).

Once again, Hosea draws an inseparable connection between covenant and creation. As observed above, the ethical violations listed in v. 2 are not unique to Israel; they violate every community's code of conduct since they depart from God's design for creation. Covenant does not impinge upon creation but rather partners with it, as demonstrated in the Sabbath commands. Therefore Hosea's moral vision is not to be equated with natural theology, nor is it bound exclusively to Israel's law codes. Halton observes, "According to the diversity of the prophetic witness, God's law is found in many forms: Sinaitic revelation, Deuteronomistic reflections, prophetic oracles and visions, the natural world, and human moral consensus."[7]

The three categories of creatures listed in 4:3 match the three spheres of animal life described in Gen 1 (the land [1:24-25], the skies [1:20], and the seas [1:21]) as well as the pattern of human dominion over creation in Gen 1:28 ("Be fruitful and multiply, and fill the earth and subdue it; and have dominion over the fish of the sea and over the birds of the air and over every living thing that moves upon the earth"). This pattern is recalled in Ps 8:7-8 and in YHWH's declaration of judgment in Zeph 1:2-3 ("I will utterly sweep away everything from the face of the earth, says the LORD. I will sweep away humans and animals; I will sweep away the birds of the air and the fish of the sea. I will make the wicked stumble. I will cut off humanity from the face of the earth, says the

---

4. Ehud Ben Zvi, *Hosea* (FOTL 21A; Grand Rapids: Eerdmans, 2005), p. 109.

5. Julius Wellhausen, *Prolegomena to the History of Ancient Israel* (New York: Meridian Books, 1957), p. 474.

6. Gene M. Tucker, "The Law in the Eighth-Century Prophets," in *Canon, Theology, and Old Testament Interpretation: Essays in Honor of Brevard S. Childs* (ed. G. M. Tucker, D. L. Petersen, and R. R. Wilson; Philadelphia: Fortress, 1988), p. 214.

7. J. C. Halton, "Law," in *Dictionary of the Old Testament Prophets* (ed. M. J. Boda and J. G. McConville; Downers Grove: InterVarsity, 2012), p. 500.

Lord"). DeRoche observes that within the Prophets the verb "to sweep away" (אסף/*'āsap*) serves as an antonym for "to create" (ברא/*bārā'*); therefore, he interprets Zeph 1:2-3 as a warning about the reversal of creation.[8] This verb appears in Hos 4:3 to describe the fate of the fish, and the two verbs "to mourn" and "to languish" occur in lament and judgment oracles and elicit the dual association of physical and psychological diminishment.[9] As noted in the commentary to chapter 2, the announcement of a new covenant in 2:18 [2:20] is framed in similar terms ("with the wild animals, the birds of the air, and the creeping things of the ground"). Given the literary allusions to the primeval traditions, the mention of "bloodshed follows bloodshed" (4:2) recalls Abel's blood shed upon the ground (Gen 4:10), Cain's subsequent exile from the land (Gen 4:14), and the Noahic prohibition against shedding the blood of humanity in Gen 9. Numbers 35 extends the principle in Gen 9:6 ("whoever sheds the blood of a human, by a human shall that person's blood be shed") to the earth because of YHWH's presence among humans in the land. The law states, "You shall not pollute the land in which you live; for blood pollutes the land, and no expiation can be made for the land, for the blood that is shed in it, except by the blood of the one who shed it. You shall not defile the land in which you live, in which I also dwell; for I the Lord dwell among the Israelites" (Num 35:33-34). Similarly, Ezek 36:16-18 describes Israel defiling the land through their idolatry and bloodshed. While neither pollution nor defilement is explicitly mentioned in Hos 4:2, this concept appears later in the book. Hosea 9:3-4 describes Ephraim's defilement in exile due to eating the unclean foods of Assyria.

In Hosea, flood and exile are equated, and the collapse of the covenant signals an implosion of creation. Katherine Hayes sums up the relationship between creation and ethics in this passage:

> The phraseology of Hos 4:3 is reminiscent of the listing of living things to be destroyed by the flood, just as the concept of total devastation in this verse is reminiscent of that described in Gen 6–7. Further, the phrase "bloodshed strikes against bloodshed" in Hos 4:2 recalls traditions concerning the pollution caused by aberrant human behavior, especially bloodshed. Hosea 4:3 may suggest, then, that the corrupt state of the community of Israel is about to ensue in a massive ablution that entails unleashing the waters of primeval chaos on the earth.[10]

8. Michael DeRoche, "The Reversal of Creation in Hosea," *VT* 31 (1981): 405.

9. Katherine M. Hayes, *The Earth Mourns: Prophetic Metaphor and Oral Aesthetic* (Boston: Brill, 2002), pp. 42-43.

10. Hayes, *The Earth Mourns*, p. 57.

Thankfully, Hos 4:1-3 is not the last word on the future of Israel or the land. Hosea 1:10–2:1 and 3:5 have already signaled that a future return from exile will take place, and 2:14-23 [2:16-25] announces that there will be a renewed covenant with creation in the future. For the present, this passage warns that deceit, lust, and violence not only sever one's knowledge of God, but they threaten to dissolve God's obligation to care for creation in a providential way. This passage should cause alarm for all, particularly in our contemporary situation where social and economic disparities are increasing in epic proportions and at dizzying rates, and sexual immorality and violence have become integrated into the social fabric of whole societies. In this manner, Hosea affirms Martin Luther King Jr.'s famous words, "Injustice anywhere is a threat to justice everywhere. We are caught up in an inescapable network of mutuality, tied to a single garment of destiny. Whatever affects one directly affects all indirectly."[11]

A "spirit of whoredom" pervades over prophet, priest, king, and people in 4:1–5:7. These passages address a crisis of leadership in Israel that directly stems from the moral and spiritual corruption of the people. The most prominent class of leaders addressed in this section is the priesthood. They are the first to be mentioned in 4:4, and, of the five references to the priesthood in Hosea, four appear within 4:4–5:7 (4:4, 6, 9; 5:1). While Hosea directly faults Israel's leadership at times (5:1), the prophet also recognizes the symbiotic relationship between the people and priesthood (4:9). Israel is culpable even for the failures of its leadership, since 4:1–5:7 falls under the heading of "Hear the word of the LORD, O people of Israel; for the LORD has an indictment against the inhabitants of the land" (4:1).

Most commentators textually emend 4:4 to read, "Yet let no one contend, and let none accuse, for with you is my contention, O priest" (NRSV). This change is not due to the fact that the text is incoherent; rather, it reflects an attempt to harmonize the verse with its context. The MT reads, "But let no man bring a charge, let no man accuse another, for your people are like those who bring charges against a priest" (NIV).[12] This latter rendering seems at odds with the surrounding context, which is a disputation taken up against the priesthood and not against those who contend with the priests. As it stands, the text appears to be supportive of the priesthood rather than antagonistic

11. "Letter from Birmingham City Jail" in *A Testament of Hope: The Essential Writings of Martin Luther King, Jr.* (ed. James Melvin Washington; San Francisco: HarperCollins, 1986), p. 290.

12. The NJPS attempts a *via media* between the two translations, "'Let no man rebuke, let no man protest!' For this your people has a grievance against *you*, O priest!" This translation follows the suggestion by Anderson and Freedman that the initial phrase is the quoted words of the priest to Hosea in the same manner Amos cites his opponent, Amaziah, the priest at Bethel (7:10-13). The LXX largely follows the MT.

towards them. Jack Lundbom suggests that 4a concludes the previous section and that 4b ought to be translated not as "and your people are like those who contend with a priest," but rather "and your people are like the contentions of a priest."[13] This view finds support in the LXX ("that no one either go to law or accuse. But my people will be like a priest being contradicted" [4:4]), as well as the Babylonian Talmud ("your people are like quarrelsome priests" [Shab. 149b; Kid. 70b]). This rendering finds further support in v. 9, which again compares the people to priests: "And it shall be like people, like priest."

Regardless how one translates 4:4, 4:4-19 is clear that the priesthood, prophets, and people have each failed one another so that Israel has committed gross sins and will be destroyed because of them. In this chapter, references to God shift back and forth between the first and third person, and Israel (or populations within Israel) are referred to in the second and third person. Ben Zvi observes that while this inconsistency does not occur in oral communication, it is a literary pattern common to prophetic books, and therefore should be understood for its rhetorical effects upon the reader.[14] Readers are to perceive themselves as the "you" and identify with the people of Israel (4:1) and their various representatives in the drama of the prophetic book. The precise tragedy of Israel is that the boundaries between people and priesthood have been transgressed (4:9), so it is not crucial to identify the particular audience of each direct address in the text, or the social role of each character. While the priesthood is the primary target of Hosea's indictment, in 4:5 the prophet is also faulted. The role of the prophet in ancient Israel is not uniform, so the prophet mentioned in 4:6 ought not to be understood as a charismatic, marginalized opponent of the state cult as in other texts. In this case, the prophet appears to be collaborating with the priests and king.

Hosea 4:6 makes clear that the people's lack of knowledge (cf. 4:1) is directly tied to the corruption and incompetence of the priesthood. Repetition is utilized throughout 4:4-6 with the rhetorical purpose of communicating reciprocal justice to Israel or to one of its various representatives. Both Israel and its leaders are contentious; it is they who stumble, and they will be destroyed, rejected, and forgotten. Proper knowledge is gained through proper instruction, and 4:6 describes the priesthood's failure in neglecting God's Torah. The disregard of Torah is defined as both cultic and moral corruption. Hosea 4:7-8 describes a situation where the increase in prestige, power, and number of priests has only multiplied their sinful activity. Dearman believes that Hosea

13. Jack R. Lundbom, "Contentious Priests and Contentious People in Hosea 4:1-10," *VT* 36 (1986): 52-70.

14. Ben Zvi, *Hosea*, pp. 102-3.

makes a word play on חטא/*ḥāṭā'* which means "to sin" but also "to expiate sin," signifying that their attempts to expiate sin have only multiplied it.[15] This idea is repeated in 8:11 ("When Ephraim multiplied altars to expiate sin, they became to him altars for sinning"). The noun form חטאת/*ḥāṭṭa't* appears in 4:8, and there Hosea accuses the priesthood of exploiting sin offerings such that the more the people sin, the more the priesthood profits from their offerings. Hosea offers a sober warning — then and now — for the moral abuses incurred by clergy when religion becomes a commercial enterprise.

In addition to greed and religious exploitation, the priests engage in promiscuous sex, drunkenness, and idolatry. The word "to be promiscuous" (זנה/*zānāh*) is concentrated in this text, appearing nine times (4:10, 12, 13, 14 [2x], 15, 18 [2x]; 5:3), and the uncommon form "promiscuity" (זנונים/*zĕnûnîm*) occurs twice (4:12; 5:4). The word in either form occurs only once more in Hosea, in 9:1.[16] On four occasions (4:10, 18 [2x]; 5:3), the verb זנה/*zānāh* appears in the *hiphil* form, which suggests causation. While an object is not mentioned in these cases, the causative sense is implied; therefore, these passages suggest that the priests not only engaged in promiscuous activity themselves, but also encouraged the people to do so.

While זנה/*zānāh* functions primarily as a metaphor for the spiritual and political unfaithfulness of Israel and Samaria in chapters 1–3, in chapter 4 the word describes drunkenness, idolatry, and sexual promiscuity, and also serves as a metaphor for apostasy. The first use of this word occurs in the *hiphil* form in 4:10. It occurs in a parallel phrase with "they shall eat, but not be satisfied," and refers to the priesthood's unsuccessful attempts to encourage fertility. The next instance of the word in 4:11 occurs at the end of a phrase where "whoredom" is the object of the verb "to observe." The verb "to observe" (שמר/*šāmar*) typically takes "ways" or "commandments" as its object. Yet in an ironic twist, in 4:10-11 Hosea states that instead of obeying Torah, God's people "observe" (i.e., devote themselves to) promiscuity.[17]

The text does not precisely define the nature of the "spirit of promiscuity" in 4:12; but it does clearly describe its effects and origins. This "spirit" leads God's people into apostasy (4:12), prevents repentance (5:4), and nullifies any knowledge of God (5:4). The "spirit" runs counter to all the purposes of God in Hosea, and it resides *within* Israel rather than without. That is, the spirit of promiscuity is the spirit of Israel. Hosea 4:16 likens Israel to a heifer which, out of its own stubbornness, is unable to graze, and in 4:19, a wind — the same

15. Dearman, *Book of Hosea*, p. 159.
16. In addition, the noun form זנות/*zĕnût* occurs in 4:11 and 6:10.
17. Ben Zvi, *Hosea*, pp. 105-6.

word as "spirit" (רוח/*rûaḥ*) in 4:12 and 5:4 — wraps Israel up in her own wings or skirts. Hosea 5:4 locates "the spirit of whoredom within their inner parts" (בקרבם/*bĕqirbām*), and 5:5 describes Israel's own pride testifying against itself and Ephraim stumbling in its own sin. The feminine particle used in 4:18-19, and the image of Israel bearing foreign children in 5:7, correspond to the feminization of Israel in chapter 2 and contribute to the promiscuity motif.

If any external influence can be blamed for Israel's behavior, it is alcohol. Hosea 4:11 identifies wine and fresh wine as that which takes away understanding (or literally, "takes away the heart"). In 4:18 it is following the consumption of liquor that Israel's promiscuity is described in the most emphatic terms. Also, the verb זנה/*zānāh* appears in the infinitive absolute, with the only other occurrence in Hosea being 1:2. The double use of the verb "to love" (אהב/*'āhab*) appears to be an emphatic form of Northern Israelian Hebrew.[18]

Promiscuity is described as improper cultic activity in vv. 12-13 in sexually suggestive terms. The wood and rod in v. 12 refer to instruments of divination, yet also serve as phallic symbols. The use of the prepositions "from under/under" (מתחת/תחת/*mittaḥat/taḥat*) in 4:12-13, coupled with the numerous references to "on/upon" (על/*'al*) in 4:13, not only describe forbidden cultic practices but also carry innuendoes of sexual positions. While Hos 4:13 describes men engaging in illicit, yet unspecified, sacrificial worship, v. 13b and v. 14a go on to accuse the women of sexual impropriety. Although most modern translations of v. 14 mention a class of "temple prostitutes" (קדשות/*qĕdēšôt*), there is no evidence of "sacred prostitution." Hosea 4:14 equates cultic sacrifices facilitated by female temple functionaries (literally, "holy women") with the sexual promiscuity of prostitutes. The promiscuity here is metaphorical, and therefore functions rhetorically as a shocking indictment of the Israelite cult.[19]

Beginning in 4:17, the mention of Ephraim will occur frequently until the end of the book. Ephraim was the dominant tribe of the Northern Kingdom since its first king, Jeroboam I, son of Nebat, originated from it. Throughout Hosea, Ephraim will be synonymous with the Northern Kingdom, Israel, as demonstrated in the parallelism in 5:3: "I know Ephraim, and Israel is not hidden from me; for now, O Ephraim, you have played the whore; Israel is defiled." Hosea 4:15 cites cultic sites particular to the Northern Kingdom. Beth-aven ("House of Iniquity") is clearly a polemical reference to Bethel ("House of God"), and it and Gilgal served as the primary targets of Amos's criticism of the

18. A. A. Macintosh, *A Critical and Exegetical Commentary on Hosea* (ICC; Edinburgh: T & T Clark, 1997), p. 169.

19. Phyllis A. Bird, *Missing Persons and Mistaken Identities* (OBT; Minneapolis: Fortress, 1997), p. 234; Moughtin-Mumby, *Sexual and Marital Metaphors*, pp. 72-75.

Northern Kingdom (Amos 4:4; 5:5). The mention of Judah in Hos 4:15 demonstrates that the prophecy does not solely address an eighth-century Israelite context, but operates on multiple levels. This verse serves as a hermeneutical cue to the people of Judah that the contents of this whole book — and not merely the sections that mention Judah — apply to them as well. From the outset of the Twelve Prophets, Hosea signals to the readers the typology of Israel-Judah-the Nations that will serve as a hermeneutical guide for the LXX Twelve Prophets as a collection. Judah is mentioned again in 5:5, yet here Ephraim, Israel, and Judah are to be understood as separate entities. In this case, Ephraim refers to the city-state of Samaria and Israel to a different tribal union located possibly at Gilgal.[20] Originally, the author may have distinguished Ephraim from Israel, and certainly 5:9 identifies Ephraim as one among the tribes of Israel. Yet in 5:13-14, Ephraim functions as a synonym or metonymy for Israel in the same manner as in 5:3. The final form of the book does not specify the precise referent for the whoring woman and land of Hos 1–3. Instead, the prophecy implicates all of Israel with this metaphor, so sharp distinctions ought not to be made between Ephraim and Israel. In fact, 6:11b–7:1a views the people, Israel, Ephraim, and Samaria in a parallel relationship: "When I would restore the fortunes of my people, when I would heal Israel, the corruption of Ephraim is revealed, and the wicked deeds of Samaria."

If the word כנף/*kānāp* in 4:19 is translated as "skirts," it supports the image of sexual licentiousness in the passage. Yet if it is understood as "wings," the phrase indicates that Israel's sacrifices were unable to spare them from exile. The latter view, as understood by most commentators, depicts Israel caught up in forces beyond its control and supports an exilic interpretation of this passage. Hosea 5:7b indicates that the sacrifices associated with new moon festivals will not increase Israel's fertility but rather devour their portion. Amos provides a similar report of God's judgment during that period: "This is what the Lord GOD showed me: the Lord GOD was calling for a shower of fire, and it devoured the great deep and was eating up the land" (Amos 7:4). The "now" that prefaces Hos 5:7b situates the reader in exile, experiencing the consequences of the destruction of the land.

LeCureux classifies the use of "return" (שׁוב/*šûb*) in 5:4 under the semantic category of "repentance," and interprets the verb as the refusal to repent due to Israel's misdeeds.[21] Yet in this case "return" can also carry the sense of restoration from exile, as in 3:5. Hosea 5:6 describes Israel and Judah seeking

20. Dearman, *Book of Hosea*, p. 175.

21. Jason T. LeCureux, *The Thematic Unity of the Book of the Twelve* (HBM 41; Sheffield: Sheffield Phoenix Press, 2012), pp. 84-85.

YHWH but unable to find God because YHWH has withdrawn from them. In addition to the word "return," the verb "to seek" (בקשׁ/*bāqaš*) also occurs in 3:5, and describes the eschatological day when Israel seeks and returns to YHWH. In the meantime, YHWH will withdraw from Israel through the act of exile until Israel admits its guilt. This set of events is described in 5:15 ("I will return again to my place until they acknowledge their guilt and seek my face. In their distress they will beg my favor").

Hosea 5:1 indicts not the general populace but rather the royal house of the Northern Kingdom and the priesthood. The geographical references in 5:1-2 may have held particular meaning to an eighth-century audience, but that significance has been lost. Instead, these place names serve to evoke Israel's religious and literary traditions, similar to the way Jezreel functions in chapter 1. Mizpah is the site of the anointing of Israel's first king, which is portrayed as an act of disobedience to YHWH in 1 Sam 8–12. Tabor is the site where a number of tribes failed to unite as a common people in Judg 4–5, and Shittim is the location of Israel's worship of Baal-Peor in Num 25. Sweeney points out that "All of these sites were important to the formation of the Israelite nation, including its monarchy, its identity as a united people, and its priesthood."[22] Hosea's allusions to them suggest that the Northern Kingdom, particularly its ruling class, is thoroughly corrupt.

Sweeney observes that Hos 5:3-7 presupposes a situation of divorce in the manner addressed in Deut 24:1-4, a passage that prevents a man from remarrying a woman that he has previously divorced. The rationale behind this restriction is that the woman, now having married another man, is "defiled" (טמא/*ṭāmē'*) (Deut 24:4). Hosea 5:3 describes Ephraim/Israel in this manner because of its promiscuity. The language of "testifying against" (5:5) is legal terminology (e.g. Exod 20:16), and "withdrawing" (5:6) is used in Levirate marriage cases. "Dealing faithlessly" (בגד/*bāgad*, 5:7) is a general term for treachery in general, and in Jeremiah it is used to describe the adulterous actions of Israel and Judah. In fact, Jer 3:8 employs the legislation of Deut 24:1-4 to describe YHWH's actions toward the people, "She saw that for all the adulteries of that faithless one, Israel, I had sent her away with a decree of divorce; yet her false sister Judah did not fear, but she too went (בגד/*bāgad*) and played the whore." Reading 5:3-7 within the context of divorce proceedings reinforces the disputational character of 4:1–5:7. As indicated earlier, this pericope is characterized as an indictment against Israel and the land. Adultery is among the sins mentioned in 4:2, and it is to be noted that Deut 24:4 states that Israel's violations of marriage laws

---

22. Marvin A. Sweeney, *The Twelve Prophets* (2 vols.; Berit Olam; Collegeville: Liturgical Press, 2000), 1:55.

would "bring guilt on the land that the LORD your God is giving [them] as a possession." While Hos 4:1–5:7 does not demonstrate that Israel has violated particular legislation in a strict sense, the correspondences between this passage and Israel's legal codes demonstrate that Israel has disobeyed Torah, broken covenant, and committed adultery.

8. Hosea 5:8–7:2

Bo H. Lim

The interpretation of this section of Hosea has been dominated by an influential article written by Albrecht Alt in 1919.[1] Alt argued that Hos 5:8-6:6 is a series of five oracles spoken by the prophet Hosea in response to the struggle over the territory of Benjamin within the backdrop of the Syro-Ephraimite war in 733-32 BCE. According to 2 Kgs 16 and Isa 7, King Ahaz of Judah refused to join the anti-Assyrian coalition along with Ephraim and Syria, and instead sought the help of Assyria against his neighbors to the north. 1 Kings 15:16-22 depicts Benjamin as the site of tension and conflict between the Northern and Southern Kingdoms that would date back 150 years prior to Hosea. Alt interpreted 5:8 as an alarm sounded in Benjamin due to the invasion by hostile Judeans. He emends v. 11 to read, "Because he was determined to follow after his enemy," and interprets the passage as a criticism of Ephraim's alliance with Damascus. Verse 11 is one of several emendations Alt makes of the text, and in 5:13 he changes מלך ירב/*melek yārēb* ("a king who contends [*yārîb*]") to read מלכי רב/*malkî rāb* ("a great king"). Assuming that synonymous parallelism is operative in 5:13, he inserts "house of Judah" into this verse so that it reads, "then Ephraim went to Assyria, and the house of Judah sent to the great king." Alt believes 5:13 refers to Ahaz's submission to Tiglath-pileser III in 732 (cf. 2 Kgs 16:7-10) and interprets Hos 5:15–6:6 as a reaction to this political crisis.

While scholars have differed with Alt over his historical reconstruction and textual emendations, his view has continued to dominate the interpretation of the passage. For example, Macintosh rejects major portions of Alt's proposal,

---

1. Albrecht Alt, *Kleine Schriften zur Geschichte des Volkes Israel* (Munich: C. H. Beck, 1953), 2:163-87. Rashi also interpreted 5:13 as a reference to Ahaz's request for assistance from Tiglath-pileser III. See A. A. Macintosh, *A Critical and Exegetical Commentary on Hosea* (ICC; Edinburgh: T & T Clark, 1997), p. 209; Ehud Ben Zvi, *Hosea* (FOTL 21A; Grand Rapids: Eerdmans, 2005), p. 142.

yet he writes, "Thus, the section from vv. 8 to 14 constitutes in its present form (whatever the history of its composition) a reasoned, *impartial* and mature interpretation of the Syro-Ephraimite War and its consequences."[2] One wonders if the Syro-Ephraimite crisis ought to be determinative in properly interpreting Hos 5:8–7:2 if it requires numerous textual emendations in order to make the case. These readings presuppose that the biblical authors were precise in their correlation between text and event, and that modern scholars possess the means to reconstruct the historical background. Neither of these scenarios is the case. The book of Hosea conflates various locations, events, and traditions, so historical precision does not seem to be a concern for the author. Attempts to get "behind the text," based upon speculative historical or liturgical[3] settings, often compete with the theological message of the text, which does not find its basis in such reconstructions.

Theories abound as to the events surrounding a supposed invasion of Benjamin in 5:8, Judah's boundary violations in 5:10, and Ephraim's appeal to Assyria in 5:13, with no definitive solutions. Modern historians can only speculate as to the reasons for naming the various cities in 5:8, but with no persons identified, a definitive event cannot be ascertained. In fact, the geographical references in 5:8 may function rhetorically or literarily by recalling Israel's past traditions associated with those locales. If it is Ephraim who sends for Assyria in 5:13, then Judah's only correlation between this passage and the Syro-Ephraimite War is the supposed annexation of Benjamite territory in 5:10, an event that cannot be corroborated in any biblical or non-biblical sources. No king of Israel, king of Assyria, or princes of Judah are named in Hos 5:8–7:2, and Aram, who plays a key role in the Syro-Ephraimite War narrative, is never mentioned. Ben Zvi summarizes the political outlook of the book of Hosea:

> The book of Hosea as a whole (7:11; 9:3; 11:5, 11; 12:2) reflects (and construes) a general world of memory in which there were two main powers in the region: a northern power and a southern one, which in the pre-late monarchic period (see Hos 1:1; cf. Isa 1:1 and Mic 1:1) were Assyria and Egypt, respectively — Aram is not construed as playing the role of the main alternative power to Assyria in the books of Micah and Isaiah, nor in the book of Hosea.[4]

2. Macintosh, *Hosea*, p. 203, emphasis mine. It is surprising how Macintosh can be so confident in the ability to reconstruct the historical events surrounding the text when in the very next paragraph he acknowledges, "It is unfortunately impossible to give details of the annexation of Benjamite land by Judah since, other than this verse, there is no evidence for or about it" (p. 203).

3. See Edwin M. Good, "Hosea 5:8–6:6: An Alternative to Alt," *JBL* 85 (1966): 273-86.

4. Ben Zvi, *Hosea*, p. 142.

Clearly the events that serve as the backdrop to 5:8-15 are general and not precise. What can be garnered from the text is a situation in the late monarchical period that was characterized by internecine conflict between the Northern and Southern Kingdoms, Benjamin threatened by attack, and Ephraim's reliance upon Assyria.

The cities listed in 5:8 — Gibeah, Ramah, and Bethel (i.e., Beth-aven) — are all in the territory of Benjamin, and were of strategic importance because they fell along the road between Ephraim and Jerusalem. At the time of the division of the kingdoms, it is reported that Benjamin joined Judah to oppose Jeroboam I (1 Kgs 12:20-24), yet later Ramah was built by King Baasha of Israel for the expressed purpose of serving as an outpost to buffer Israel from an attack from Judah (1 Kgs 15:16-24).

Judah is given a favored status in 1:7, and in 4:15 and 5:5 it suffers due to the sin of Ephraim. With the exception of 11:12 [12:1],[5] from 5:10 to the end of the book Judah will be considered guilty of covenant disobedience in the same manner as Ephraim. Judah is typically named alongside Israel or Ephraim in YHWH's indictment of the people, which many scholars interpret as evidence of a Judean redaction. Hosea 5:10 is distinct because here Judah is singled out for specific sins committed against Ephraim. Judah's princes are accused of violating the boundaries of Ephraim by encroaching upon and annexing territory in Benjamin, which was a violation of Deuteronomistic law (Deut 19:14; 27:17) and the Wisdom instruction (Prov. 22:28; 23:10; Job 24:2). The effects of Judah's aggression upon Ephraim are that the Northern Kingdom is oppressed and "crushed in judgment" according to 5:11. While the term "oppressed" (עשק/ 'āšaq, 5:11) can speak of mistreatment in general, it often describes the victimization of the poor by the rich and powerful (Deut 24:14; Jer 7:6; Ezek 22:29; Amos 4:1; Zech 7:10; Prov. 14:31; 22:16; 28:3; Eccl 5:8). The phrase "crushed of justice" (רצוץ משפט/rĕṣûṣ mišpāṭ, 5:11) is an unusual word pair since typically the Bible speaks of justice being extended to the oppressed (cf. Isa 42:3, 4; 58:6); yet in this case the justice does the crushing. Rather than describe a historical event, perhaps this odd lexical combination serves to call attention to other texts. This vocabulary appears in Amos 4:1: "Hear this word, you cows of Bashan who are on Mount Samaria, who oppress (עשק/'āšaq) the poor, who crush (רצץ/rāṣaṣ) the needy, who say to their husbands, 'Bring something to drink!'" The issue of justice (משפט/mišpāṭ, 5:11), particularly on behalf of the poor and oppressed, features prominently in the book of Amos (5:7, 15, 24; 6:12). Given

---

5. Although the LXX of this verse associates Judah with both the sinfulness of Israel as well as a renewed relationship: "Ephraim has surrounded me with a lie, and the house of Israel and Ioudas with impiety; now God has come to know them, and the holy people shall be called God's."

Ephraim's prosperity, it is unlikely that 5:11 literally describes the social conditions of the Northern Kingdom during the time of Hosea. Rather, since Hosea
and Amos were to be read conjointly (see my introduction), it appears that Hos
5:11 serves as a theological response to Ephraim's oppression of the poor indicated in Amos 4:1, especially given the lexical and thematic correspondences
between the texts. Hosea indicates that YHWH's act of justice is to oppress and
crush Ephraim because of the fact that its inhabitants treated the vulnerable
among them in exactly the same manner. Judah's military aggression toward
Ephraim is viewed as an act of just retribution such that it can be labeled a "day
of chastisement" (5:9, NJPS).

In the immediate context, Ephraim's sin is its pursuit of "vanity" (צו/*ṣaw*,
5:11). This is a rare word in the Bible, only occurring elsewhere in Isa 28:10, 13,
and signifies the slurred speech of Judah's inebriated priests and prophets and
the unintelligible words of its foreign captors. Hosea 4–6 addresses corrupt
priests (4:6, 9; 5:1; 6:9) and prophets (4:5), and prophesies of Israel's captivity
to foreign powers (5:13-14). Hosea 5:13 speaks specifically of Ephraim going to
Assyria and sending for the great king. Most commentators consider the MT's
מלך ירב/*melek yārēb* "a king who contends" a misrendering of מלכי רב/*malkî
rāb* or מלך רב/*melek rab* "great king," the standard term of Assyrian kings found
in inscriptions and treaties. Since this term appears again in Hos 10:6, Ben
Zvi finds no reason to disregard the MT and translates the term "a king who
champions," "a protecting king," or "a patron king" (NJPS).[6]

Ephraim makes a serious political miscalculation and will soon discover
that, rather than bring healing, Assyria will destroy the nation. In 5:12-13 YHWH
is compared to invasive moths and rot, and Ephraim and Judah are depicted as
suffering slow deaths due to infected wounds. In 5:14 the attack upon Ephraim
and Judah is more vicious and their deaths more rapid. The simile of a lion in
its various stages of a hunt — capturing, killing, and dragging off its prey — is
employed to describe the actions of YHWH to both nations. The metaphor of
a lion here and throughout the book (11:10; 13:7) would not be lost on Hosea's
audience, since such language was often featured on Assyrian royal propaganda.
By use of this comparison, "Hosea insists that Ephraim and Judah have more to
fear in a theological and historical sense from YHWH. In Hosea's mind YHWH
is the real king and the only lion that Ephraim should fear."[7] Given that this
section resonates in several ways with Amos' prophecy, it is unsurprising that
YHWH is also depicted as a lion in Amos 3:4, 8, 12; 5:19. Judah is included in
Ephraim's judgment in Hos 5:12, 13, and 14, so it ought to be included among the

---

6. Ben Zvi, *Hosea*, p. 143.

7. J. Andrew Dearman, *Book of Hosea* (NICOT; Grand Rapids: Eerdmans, 2010), p. 187.

tribes of Israel in 5:9 who will face a day of chastisement. While Judah retains its distinct identity, the outlook of 5:8-15 is one in which both kingdoms have sinned and been punished by YHWH. Similar to the perspective of 1:10-11, Hos 5:15 indicates that the future hope for both kingdoms involves the acknowledgment of guilt, seeking the presence of YHWH, and calling upon God in distress.

While the term "place" (מקום/*māqôm*, 5:15) can serve as a technical term for the temple at Jerusalem (Deut 12:5, 14; 14:23, 25; 1 Kgs 8:29, 30; Isa 18:7), it seems unlikely that it would refer to Zion in this case, since God's departure to his "place" is to serve as an act of judgment against Judah. More likely, God's reference to "my place" is to the heavens above. Later within the Twelve Prophets, Micah describes YHWH going out from "his place" (מקום/*māqôm*, Mic 1:3) or "his holy temple" (Mic 1:2) to descend upon Samaria and Jerusalem and crush them in judgment for their sins (Mic 1:3-5). The prologue to Micah shares with Hosea the language of stripping Samaria (גלה/*gālāh*, 1:6; cf. Hos 2:10 [2:12]), promiscuity (זנה/*zānāh*, 1:7), and the imagery of incurable wounds (1:9; cf. Hos 5:13). Excluding a passing reference to Samaria in Obad 19, Micah will be the last book of the Twelve to address Samaria. The superscription to Micah shares three of the kings mentioned in Hos 1:1 and describes its prophecy as concerning Samaria and Jerusalem (Mic 1:1), much in the way Hosea indicts both Ephraim and Judah in 5:8-12:2. While the full implications of these literary connections cannot be explored here, these intertexts signify that, in its canonical context, particularly LXX Twelve Prophets where Hosea-Amos-Micah form the first three books, Micah is to be read as an extension of the prophecies of Hosea.

Hosea 6:1–7:2

The interpretation of this section centers on two issues: 1) how one understands the literary genre of 6:1-3 and its relationship to its wider context, and 2) how one understands the seeming reference to resurrection in 6:2 and the passage's parallels with Baalism. In regard to the first issue, the two prevailing views differ on to whom the speech is ascribed, and how it is to function. The traditional understanding of these verses has been to identify the speech as the words of either the people or the prophet, so that they function prescriptively as a model of penitence. The alternative view interprets 6:1-3 as the speech of the people or their leaders that is deemed unacceptable to YHWH and serves as an instance of inadequate repentance.[8]

---

8. Davies catalogues five different interpretations of this passage. See G. I. Davies, *Hosea* (NCBC; Grand Rapids: Eerdmans, 1992), pp. 150-51.

The numerous thematic and lexical links between Hos 6:1-3 and the preceding passage demonstrate that the author intended for the verses to be understood within the wider rhetorical context. The word "tear" (טרף/*ṭārap*) appears in Hosea only in 5:14 and 6:1, and "heal" (רפא/*rāpā'*) occurs in 5:13 and 6:1. When read in context, the phrase "Come let us return (שוב/*šûb*) to the LORD" (6:1) naturally serves as a response to YHWH's claim in 5:15, "I will return (שוב/ *šûb*) again to my place." The LXX even includes the word "saying" (λέγοντες/ *legontes*) at the end of 5:15 to introduce the words of 6:1-3. Viewed in this manner, 6:1-3 ought to be in quotations, as in most translations, to represent the speech of the people. This people consist of Ephraim and Judah who, because of their mistreatment of each other and disobedience to YHWH, find themselves sick and wounded and in need of a healer. Ephraim and Judah seek healing in Assyria only to be rebuffed by YHWH the lion, who wounds both peoples and withdraws from them until they acknowledge their own guilt and seek God's presence. Within its literary context, Hos 6:1-3 describes Ephraim and Judah's act of penitence and worship. They are currently in a state of distress and believe such actions will move YHWH to return to the people.

The passage contains the summons to worship, "Come let us return to the LORD" (6:1), which also appears in liturgical texts such Isa 2:3; Mic 4:2; and Ps 95:1. In addition, the text resembles calls to communal laments of repentance such as Lam 3:40 ("Let us test and examine our ways, and return to the LORD"), which addresses the aftermath of Jerusalem's destruction by the Babylonians. Given these formal similarities, some commentators have suggested that the saying originates from the priesthood and the cult in the same manner that Amos embeds the words of Amaziah within his prophecy in Amos 7:10-13.[9] Given the connection to the preceding passage in chapter 5, other scholars interpret 6:1-3 and the verses to follow in light of the Syro-Ephraimite crisis. Alt classifies these verses as a liturgy of political repentance for two wounded states,[10] and believes the passage reflects their rejection of Assyrian dependence and a turn toward YHWH. According to these interpretations, the priestly cult or eighth-century politics provide the context to understand this passage.

Hosea 6:2 continues to be an interpretive conundrum, particularly in regard to its seeming reference to resurrection and its similarity to non-Israelite religions. Many early fathers cited this verse as a prophecy of Christ's resurrection,[11] and the Targum viewed it as a reference to the eschatological resurrec-

9. For example, Hans Walter Wolff, *Hosea* (Hermeneia; Philadelphia: Fortress, 1974), pp. 116-17; Good, "Hosea 5:8–6:6," 280.

10. Good, "Hosea 5:8–6:6."

11. Wolff, *Hosea*, pp. 117-18; Alberto Ferreiro, ed., *The Twelve Prophets* (ACCS OT 14; Downers Grove: InterVarsity, 2003), pp. 27-28.

tion of Israel.[12] Modern scholars propose that the motif of a dying and rising God is borrowed from Canaanite religion. Wijngaards suggests that it is technical terminology to indicate the renewal of covenants,[13] while others conclude that the language does not refer to resurrection, nor should much significance be made of the third day.[14] A consensus seems to be emerging that the language describes the recovery of the sick in a relatively short period of time, and this view seems particularly convincing given the parallels between 2 Kgs 20 and Hos 6:2, "After two days he will revive (חיה/*ḥāyāh*) us; on the third day (ביום השלישי/*bayyôm haššlîšî*) he will raise (קום/*qûm*) us up, that we may live (חיה/*ḥāyāh*) before him." In 2 Kgs 20, Isaiah initially announces to Hezekiah, "you shall die; you shall not recover (חיה/*ḥāyāh*, v. 1)," but later communicates to him the words of YHWH, "I will heal you (רפא/*rāpā'*, cf. Hos 6:1); on the third day (ביום השלישי/*bayyôm haššlîšî*) you shall go up (קום/*qûm*) to the house of the LORD" (v. 5). The passage clearly speaks of the wounding and recovery of the people, not the God of Israel.

Regardless of the origins of Hos 6:1-3, it was incorporated into the prophecy of Hosea such that it represents the speech of Ephraim and Judah, who have been wounded by God as described in 5:13-15. YHWH withdraws from the people and vows to return to them only upon their acknowledgement of their guilt. Within the context of the book of Hosea, Hos 6:1-3 clearly represents the speech of the people, not the prophet. In the larger context of 5:1–7:2 or 4:1–7:2, the role of the prophet is not to reassure Israel that it will be healed and recover, but rather to bring an indictment (4:1) and message of judgment (5:1) against the people. Hosea 6:5 describes the preaching of Hosea and his contemporaries in the following manner: "Therefore I have hewn them by the prophets, I have killed them by the words of my mouth, and my judgment goes forth as the light." While certainly 1-2 Samuel describes a series of prosecutorial prophets preceding Hosea, Odell observes that the syntax of the verbs in Hos 6:5 ties the prophetic activity to contemporaneous events; he concludes, "Hos 6:5 comments on the manner in which YHWH has effected judgment through the prophets in the events described in the preceding verses."[15] At this point in the prophetic book, Hosea's words do not "revive" but rather "kill."

Certainly designating 6:4 as a new unit would avoid the challenge of harmonizing its contents with the preceding passage, but interpretive difficulties

---

12. Macintosh, *Hosea*, p. 222.

13. J. Wijngaards, "Death and Resurrection in Covenantal Context (Hos. 6:2)," *VT* 17 (1967): 226-39.

14. M. L. Barré, "New Light on the Interpretation of Hosea 6:2," *VT* 28 (1978): 129-41.

15. Margaret S. Odell, "Who Were the Prophets in Hosea?" *HBT* 18 (1996): 81.

alone should not justify exegetical decisions.[16] The reuse of the word "heal" in 7:1 (רפא/*rāpā'*, cf. 5:13; 6:1) and other common lexemes suggests that 5:8–7:2 should be read as a unity. Furthermore, the imagery of a morning cloud and early dew in 6:4 serves as a contrastive response to the declaration in 6:3 that YHWH's return is as assured as dawn, showers, and spring rain.

Interpreting 6:4-6 as YHWH's response to 6:1-3 raises a host of interpretive questions, particularly if one understands 6:4-6 as God's rejection of the people's confession. Interpreters have attempted to resolve this dilemma by positing that the speech contains Canaanite ideology and is subsequently rejected by God, but as we have noted, 6:2 does not describe the death and resurrection of YHWH. Others have posited that 6:4-6 serves as a rejection of the cult and priesthood represented in 6:1-3, but the prehistories of these texts and their social contexts cannot be verified. What is clear is that there is nothing in the confession itself that is so unorthodox as to warrant YHWH's response in Hos 6:4-6. One can then conclude that Hos 6:4-6 is not a per se rejection of the contents of the penitential speech in 6:1-3.[17] Hosea 6:4-6 demonstrates YHWH's displeasure with Israel, not on the basis of what is expressed by Israel in 6:1-3, but rather on what is lacking. This interpretation is suggested by the metaphor of mist and dew in 6:4 to describe Israel's loyalty (חסד/*ḥesed*). The problem is not that loyalty is absent; rather, it is evanescent. Israel does not lack in orthodoxy or sincerity, but rather in orthopraxy. Hosea 6:6 ought not be read as a wholesale rejection of the institution of the cult, but rather the recognition of its insufficiency. YHWH's displeasure with sacrifice and burnt offerings in 6:6 should not be limited merely to those two cultic activities, but also to the worship activities reflected in 6:1-3, given its liturgical elements. To learn what kind of loyalty and knowledge God expects requires reading beyond Hos 6:1-6.

As articulated in my introduction and illustrated throughout this commentary, Hosea functions as a prophetic book where individual pericopes are to be read dialogically, in light of the literary context of the whole book. In this case, the answer to why Israel's confession is rejected lies not in 6:1-3, but in the rest of the prophecy to follow. Although the people are called to "come" (6:1), "return" (6:1), and "know" (6:3), the passage gives no specific instruction as to what repentance entails, but instead describes the specific actions YHWH has done to the people. Within the internal logic of the book, Hos 14:1-5 [14:2-6] clearly serves as a response to 6:1-6 due to its numerous intertexual connections, and provides clear instruction on how to return to YHWH. The implications of

16. Davies, *Hosea* (1992), pp. 149-50.
17. Macintosh, *Hosea*, p. 229.

Bakhtin's insights, as they apply to Hos 6:1-6 and other difficult passages within the book, is the absolute necessity of reading such texts in conversation with other texts in the book. In the task of theological interpretation, hermeneutical patience is required, and there is no room for laziness since truth claims are always provisional. This same hermeneutical logic applies to those who assert that, because Hosea describes YHWH as sharing some similarities with foreign deities, YHWH is indistinguishable from them.[18]

The theological and pastoral implication of reading Hosea dialogically is that confessional orthodoxy and sincerity alone do not constitute knowledge of God. *Sola orthodoxa* or *sola veritas* will not do. Loyalty to YHWH requires a commitment to justice and righteousness for one's neighbors, as evidenced in 6:7–7:2. Prior to chapter 6, the word loyalty (חסד/*hesed*) appears two times. In Hos 2:19-20 [21-22] the word is collocated with the terms "righteousness," "justice," "compassion," "faithfulness" and "know[ing] YHWH." In Hos 4:1 it is combined with "faithfulness" and "knowledge of God," and the verses to follow describe how Israel lacks these qualities; because of this lack, social injustice is rampant in the land. True knowledge and loyalty involve a commitment to a politics of peace rather than one of violence and oppression. Although many Christians quote Hosea 6:6 as if the verse condemns cultic religion and extols inward piety, such is a misreading of this verse within both the context of Hosea and Jesus' citation of it in Matthew 9:13 and 12:7. In Matthew, as in Hosea, the knowledge of God and the morality God requires inevitably carries social and political implications.

The political aspect of the passage ought not to be tied to the events of the Syro-Ephraimite War since, as observed above, the text speaks more in historical generalities than in specifics. References to Ephraim and Judah are to serve as markers of their trans-temporal roles within the rhetorical logic of the book. While references to Adam (v. 7), Gilead (v. 8), and Shechem (v. 9) are specifically mentioned, not all their geographical locales are clear, nor is their significance directly related to eighth-century events. Hosea 6:7 indicates that Israel transgressed the covenant "like Adam" (כאדם/*kĕ'ādām*) or "like a person" (ὡς ἄνθρωπος/*hōs anthrōpos*, LXX). Read in this manner, the word "there" of 6:7 links Israel with Eden, Israel's abrogation of covenant with the disobedience

---

18. According to Jobling the text "ends up equating YHWH structurally with Baal. The text sets itself the (impossible) task of mediating between these incompatible options" ("A Deconstructive Reading of Hosea 1–3," in *Relating to the Text* [ed. Timothy J. Sandoval and Carleen Mandolfo; JSOTSup 384; London: T & T Clark, 2003], p. 214). See also Niels Peter Lemche, "The God of Hosea," in *Priests, Prophets and Scribes: Essays on the Formation and Heritage of Second Temple Judaism in Honour of Joseph Blenkinsopp* (ed. E. Ulrich, et al.; JSOTSup 149; Sheffield: JSOT Press, 1992), pp. 241-57.

of Adam, and exile with Adam's and Eve's expulsion from the garden.[19] Because of the mention of "there" in 6:7b, others have concluded that אדם/*ādām* cannot refer to a person. They emend the text to read "at Adam" (באדם/*bĕ'ādām*) and suggest that it refers to the city of Adam mentioned in Josh 3:16. Both readings communicate that Israel has been a covenant violator from the very beginning: either since the beginning of creation ("like Adam"), or since the beginning of Israel's entry into the promised land ("at Adam"). Gilead in v. 8 refers to the whole Trans-Jordanian region, which served as the location of intertribal conflict in Josh 22, and the base of operations of Jehu's bloody massacre of the Omrides, an event that led to Israel's alliance with Assyria.[20] The mention of Shechem in v. 9 recalls the rebellion of the northern tribes against the Davidic house and the division of the kingdom in 1 Kgs 12. Certainly events contemporary to Hosea are also signified by these names, particularly the revolt of Pekah mentioned in 2 Kgs 15:25, but they are to be understood within the backdrop of Israel's traditions. Sweeney observes that the term "evildoers" (פעלי און/*pōʿălê 'āwen*) in 6:8 recalls Hosea's mention of Beth-Aven, "house of evil" (בית און/*bêt 'āwen*, 4:15; 5:8; 10:5), which serves as a commentary on Beth-El, the ancient city of the Northern Kingdom associated with the patriarch Jacob.[21] In addition, the phrase in 6:8, "tracked with blood" (עקבה מדם/*'ăqubbāh middām*), contains the Hebrew root עקב/*'āqōb*, which serves as the basis for the name Jacob, a term that Hosea will feature prominently in chapter 12. The net effect of these references to Israel's past communicates to Hosea's readers that Israel's abrogation of its covenant relationship with YHWH reaches far back to the nation's beginnings.

The theme of restoration occurs again in 6:11, although the language is unclear. Most English versions translate the phrase שוב שבות/*šûb šĕbût* as "return the fortunes," yet it can also be understood as "return the captivity," since the word שבות/*šĕbût* may stem from the root שוב/*šûb* "to turn, return" or שבה/*šābāh* "to take captive." Of the 27 occurrences of this phrase in the OT, roughly a third are to be understood as "return the captivity," and this translation is

---

19. For the rabbis, Hos 6:7 served as the link between Gen 3:9, "But the LORD God called to the man, and said to him, 'Where are you (איכה/*'ayyekkâ*)?'" and Lam 1:1, "How (איכה/*'ēykâ*) lonely sits the city that once was full of people!" The Targum of Lamentations begins: "Jeremiah the Prophet and the High Priest told how it was decreed that Jerusalem and her people should be punished with banishment and that they should be mourned with *'eykah*. Just as when Adam and Eve were punished and expelled from the Garden of Eden and the Master of the Universe mourned them with *'eykah*." Christian M. M. Brady, *The Rabbinic Targum of Lamentations: Vindicating God* (Leiden: Brill, 2003), p. 18.

20. Marvin A. Sweeney, *The Twelve Prophets* (2 vols.; Berit Olam; Collegeville: Liturgical Press, 2000), 1:75.

21. Sweeney, *The Twelve Prophets*, 1:75.

reflected in the LXX ("when I return the captivity of my people"). Bracke revisits the various interpretations of this phrase and concludes that it is to be understood more broadly as a general reversal of God's judgment that takes the form of a tangible and concrete restoration; he concludes that its use in Hos 6:11 is ambiguous.[22] LeCureux observes that Hosea's use of this phrase is the only occurrence within the Twelve that does not clearly speak of an eschatological restoration (Joel 3:1; Amos 9:14; Zeph 2:7; 3:20). Grammatically, this phrase is set in parallel relationship to YHWH's action to heal Israel in 7:1.

The grammatical forms of the verbs "to restore" and "to heal" are not finite verbs and ought to be understood in a temporal manner:[23] "when I restored . . . when I healed." In addition, they carry the subjunctive mood: "When I would restore . . . when I would heal" (NRSV), and possibly even the optative: "When I wished to heal Israel."[24] The reason Israel's restoration and healing do not occur is clear: Ephraim is filled with wickedness, corruption, and violence (7:1-2), such that the people are so ill that they are beyond healing and restoration (cf. 5:13-14). The requirements for restoration and healing are stated in 7:2: Israel needs to make sincere confession of all its wickedness. The opening phrase in 7:2, "they do not consider," can literally be translated "they do not speak with their hearts" (בל-יאמרו ללבבם/*bal-yō'mĕrû lilbābām*). While 6:1-3 in itself is inconclusive, other texts, such as 8:2-3 ("Israel cries to me, 'My God, we — Israel — know you!' Israel has spurned the good; the enemy shall pursue him"), demonstrate that Israel's speech can be at great odds with its conduct, which suggests insincerity. Hosea 7:13 identifies Israel's speech as that which betrays them and causes them to forfeit redemption: "I would redeem them, but they speak lies against me." Although Israel may engage in fervent religious activity, YHWH recognizes that "They do not cry to me from the heart (לב/*lēb*)" (7:14). In further support of the necessity to read chapters 6 and 14 in a dialogical manner, chapter 14 demonstrates that genuine turning, both in human repentance and God's restoration, can occur when Israel confesses its wickedness:

> Take words with you and return to the LORD; say (אמר/*'āmar*) to him, "Take away all guilt; accept that which is good, and we will offer the fruit of our lips. Assyria shall not save us; we will not ride upon horses; we will say (אמר/*'āmar*) no more, 'Our God,' to the work of our hands. In you the orphan finds mercy" (Hos 14:2-3 [14:3-4]).

22. John M. Bracke, "šûb šebût: A Reappraisal," *ZAW* 97 (1985): 233-44.

23. Bruce K. Waltke and M. O'Connor, *An Introduction to Biblical Hebrew Syntax* (Winona Lake: Eisenbrauns, 1990), 36.2.2b.

24. Macintosh, *Hosea*, p. 248.

Throughout Hosea the people will make much confession to YHWH, but not all of it is from the heart. True knowledge of God requires genuine confession from the heart, and until the latter is displayed, Israel will not be restored or healed.

Many have rightly noted that Hos 6:4-6 functions as a theodicy to address the absence of YHWH (cf. Hos 5:15). While the people expect a relatively short period until restoration (cf. Hos 6:2), 6:4-6 provides an explanation for why Israel's recovery is delayed. Hosea 6:2 possesses similarities to Ezek 37, a passage that prophesies the resurrection of the nation of Israel in the midst of exile, and viewed in this manner, 6:2 may be understood as the description of restoration from exile. The wait of three days recalls the "many days" (3:3-4) YHWH withdraws from Israel, and the critique of the cult in 6:6 evokes the absence of the cult during the exile described in 3:4. While for an eighth-century audience שׁוּב שְׁבוּת/*šûb šĕbût* in 6:11 would be understood in the more general terms of "restore the fortunes," in the final form of the book, God's judgment takes the concrete form of exile (cf. 3:3-5), and thus the phrase should read, "restore from captivity." In the final form of the book, 5:8–7:2 serves as a theodicy, directed at an exilic audience, for why Israel has yet to return from captivity. For a postexilic people, it explains why so many of the prophecies of restoration remain unfulfilled.

9. Hosea 7:3–8:14

Bo H. Lim

Hosea 7:3-16

Whereas Hosea's contention with Israel and Judah in chapter 4 began with a focus on covenantal and creational violations, by chapter 7 the prophet's attention will increasingly shift towards Israel's political sins. While Hosea acknowledges the complicity of the princes (5:10; 7:5, 16; 9:15), judges (7:7; 13:10), kings (7:7), and priests (4:4, 6; 5:1), the blame for Israel and Judah's moral failures is repeatedly directed towards the people as a whole. Unlike 1-2 Kings, which targets the monarchies of both kingdoms for the breach of covenant, in Hosea the failure of Israel's leaders rests with the people themselves. The absence of royal leadership is perceived as an act of judgment and means of discipline for the people of Israel (Hos 3:4-5). While monarchical Israel was far from a modern democracy, the Scriptures nevertheless place the responsibility of leading the nation on the people (cf. 1 Sam 8; 1 Kgs 12).

Hosea 7:3-16 forms one unit, in which vv. 3-7 address corruption within Israel's domestic policies, and vv. 8-16 focus on Israel's disloyalty in foreign affairs. This section is replete with third masculine plural verb forms and pronouns. The repeated emphasis on "all of them" (7:4, 7) emphasizes Israel's corporate identity and the communal ramifications of sins committed by its individuals, particularly the leaders. These third masculine plural references signify Israel, Ephraim, and Samaria, which were mentioned in 7:1-2. Judah is mentioned in 6:11[1] and later in 8:14, so it seems the Northern Kingdom is primarily in view in this section. As mentioned previously, the progression within the Book of the Twelve from an initial focus on Israel to an emphasis on

---

1. Many commentators consider this reference to Judah a later gloss, and it is altogether missing in the LXX.

Judah signals for readers that the lessons originally intended for eighth-century Israel apply later to Judeans as well. While the historical setting is unspecified, because of the passage's references to Ephraim, Samaria, Assyria, and Egypt, the narrative backdrop for this prophecy appears to be late-eighth-century Israel.

Various proposals have been made for the historical setting of this section, but the texts remain unswervingly unspecific as to exact events. Deception, literally "lying" (7:2; cf. Hos 4:2); a "day of our king" (7:5), which may refer to a coronation event; the political threats of Egypt and Assyria; and regicide are all mentioned. Commentators variously associate this text with the regicide of Zechariah (746 BCE), Shallum (746 BCE), Pekahiah (737 BCE), and Pekah (732 BCE), narrated in 2 Kgs 15:8-30. Hosea earlier criticized the bloodshed incurred against the house of Omri by Jehu (1:4), so this text ought not to be understood to refer solely to the events of 747-732. Given the scarcity of evidence, it is difficult to determine the extent of Egypt's influence in Palestinian politics during this period. References to Egypt in the text may represent Israel's theological understanding of Egypt within its religious traditions rather than a historical entity. Clearly, Hosea's assessment of Israel's politics is thoroughly theological: Israel is to be loyal to YHWH alone, and unaligned with foreign powers. Pentiuc suggests that the reference to "their rulers" (שפטיהם/ *šōpṭêhem*) in 7:7 refers not to any contemporary rulers, but rather to the pre-monarchical leaders found in the book of Judges.[2] If viewed in this manner, Hosea reprimands Israel not only for its corruption and violence in the final years of the Northern Kingdom, but for a legacy of failed leadership that stems from the period of the Judges.

Whereas the sins of Judah were mentioned in the previous section (5:10, 13; 6:4, 11), the focus of chapter 7 and the texts to follow will consistently be on Samaria. For the final time in the book, Israel is deemed "adulterers" (מנאפים/ *mĕnā'ăpîm*, 7:4). This designation is applied to all the people of Israel, and functions as a metaphor for Israel's political treachery. Hosea 7:1 records the first reference to "Samaria" in the book, and from here to the end of the book, Hosea will consistently address the northern capital (7:1; 8:5, 6; 10:5, 7; 14:1). Both the prominence placed on this city in the latter half of the book and the metaphorical use of the term "adulterers" in 7:4 are consistent with the view, as argued in this commentary, that the promiscuous and adulterous woman in chapter 2 serves as a metaphor for Samaria, and the violence incurred upon her represents the destruction of Israel's capital at the hands of the Assyrians.

Hosea 7:4-7 employs the metaphor of a burning oven to illustrate the de-

---

2. Eugen J. Pentiuc, *Long-Suffering Love: A Commentary on Hosea with Patristic Annotations* (Brookline: Holy Cross Orthodox Press, 2002), p. 106.

ception and violence within the ranks of Israel's leadership. The oven described is likely a clay cylinder where the bottom would contain fire, and dough would be placed against its walls on top.[3] The image described in vv. 4-6 is that of a baker who does not need to stoke the fire because it smolders successfully on its own and creates such an intense heat that by morning it is ready for cooking and baking. One can liken it to cooking with charcoal. The simile suggests deceptive plots constantly smoldering within Israel until their heat engulfs all parties. Ben Zvi suggests that the word for "baker" (מאפה/*mēʼōpeh*, v. 4) forms a pun with "adulterers" (מנאפים/*mĕnāʼăpîm*, v. 4), and both words form a pun with "to be angry" (אנף/*ʼānap*), which is commonly associated with heat and fire.[4] The image of a burning oven occurs in vv. 4 and 6 and runs parallel to the descriptions of a plot to inebriate and murder the king, described in vv. 3 and 5. Admittedly, verse 5 is ambiguous and can also describe the king as the assailant.[5] Perhaps the text is intentionally unspecific in order to emphasize the larger point that there are no winners in partisan politics.[6] Conspiracy is self-destructive for Israel's rulers and results in the downfall of all Israel's kings.

Hosea 7:8 switches topics to international relations, yet continues to rely on the metaphor of baking from the previous verses. Now Ephraim is no longer compared to a smoldering oven, but is compared rather to the bread, and those consuming it are no longer Israelites but foreigners. In Hosea 7:8, Ephraim is compared to a dough that is mixed with the nations. The verb "to mix" (בלל/*bā-lal*) describes the process of combining flour and oil in order to make sacrificial cakes. It resembles the Akkadian word *balālu* used to describe kneading and the mixing of populations. Shalom Paul believes the author intends a double entendre of both the political and culinary use of the word in Hos 7:8, since both contexts fit the passage.[7] The end result of this mixing is a half-baked cake that is inedible. This metaphor suggests that foreign influence and reliance have corrupted Israel's national identity and vocation as a holy people. Later, Hos 8:7

---

3. A. A. Macintosh, *A Critical and Exegetical Commentary on Hosea* (ICC; Edinburgh: T & T Clark, 1997), p. 258.

4. Ehud Ben Zvi, *Hosea* (FOTL 21A; Grand Rapids: Eerdmans, 2005), p. 151.

5. The phrase "he stretched out his hand with the mockers" (NRSV) is ambiguous and can also be understood as "he deploys the conspirators with a signal" (Macintosh). The first interpretation describes the king and the officials as the victims of an unidentified attacker, while the latter view suggests that the king is the aggressor.

6. Freedman and Andersen suggest that the priesthood is responsible for the conspiracy, given Hosea's criticism earlier in the book. While certainly the priesthood is included in Hosea's repeated reference to "all of them" (7:4, 7), the emphasis is not on a single party within Israel. Hosea's criticisms of the priesthood are concentrated in chapters 4–6.

7. Shalom M. Paul, "The Image of the Oven and the Cake in Hosea 7:4-10," *VT* 18 (1968): 117-18.

and 8:8 appear to form a pun on "to mix" (בלל/*bālal*) when the prophet speaks of Israel being swallowed up (בלע/*bālaʿ*) by foreigners. To add to this image of consumption, in 7:7 all Israel "devours" (אכל/*ʾākal*) its rulers; the same word appears in 7:9 to describe the way "foreigners devour (אכל/*ʾākal*) his [Ephraim's] strength."

The phrase "Israel's pride testifies against him" in Hos 7:10 is an exact repetition from Hos 5:5, "Israel's pride testifies against him; Ephraim stumbles in his guilt; Judah also stumbles with them." Hosea 5:6 goes on to describe how, due to the people's failure, "they shall go to seek (בקש/*bāqaš*, cf. 7:10) the LORD, but they will not find him; he has withdrawn from them." In 7:10, Israel is blinded by its pride, and fails to learn from the discipline YHWH inflicts upon Israel in the form of domestic and international strife. Unlike 5:6, Israel in 7:10 does not even attempt to return to God or seek YHWH. Rather than assume a psychological rationale for the repeated phrase "Israel's pride testifies against him,"[8] the repetition is but another reminder of the necessity to read the prophecy in a dialogical manner.

Hosea 7:11 signals a shift in metaphors to avian imagery. Ephraim is compared to doves, which were well known for their naiveté. They were easily captured by trappers because, in their single-minded pursuit for food, they would be unaware of suspicious activity. Even though Israel is informed of "all this" (7:10) foreign treachery, they still refuse to return and seek God. Because they do not take seriously the spiritual and political consequences of foreign alliances, Hos 7:11 describes Ephraim as "silly and without sense." The word "silly" (פתה/*pātāh*) describes someone who is gullible and easily deceived, and occurs on one other occasion, in Hos 2:14 [16]. In that passage, YHWH "deceives" the promiscuous woman, and because she is pliable, God is able to redeem her. The phrase "without sense" is literally "without heart" (אין לב/*ʾên lēb*) and ought not to be understood as indicating a lack of emotion. Earlier, in 7:2, Hosea accused Israel that its speech is not from the heart; in 7:6 Israel's heart smolders in anger and plots treachery; and 7:14 will go on to claim the people do not cry out to God from their hearts. The absence of "heart" results, not in hate or apathy, but rather in foolishness and pride (7:10).

Continuing the avian imagery, v. 12 describes God trapping Ephraim like birds in a net, and v. 13 suggests that this is due to their propensity to stray from YHWH. The verb "to stray" (נדד/*nādad*, v. 13) can also describe the fluttering of wings (e.g. Isa 10:14). This seems to support the avian imagery used in 7:11-12, and 8:1 will later describe the diaspora existence of God's people (9:17) as a consequence of their disobedience.

---

8. Macintosh, *Hosea*, p. 273.

Hosea 7:12-16 describes how YHWH will discipline the people because they continue to rebel against their God. The word "to discipline" (יסר/*yāsar*) appears in 7:12 and 7:15, and possesses nurturing connotations such as "to teach, instruct, bring up," as well as the punitive associations of "to chastise, rebuke." Earlier, 5:1-2 contained the noun form "discipline" (מוסר/*mûsar*) as well as the word "net" (פרש/*pāraś*, cf. 7:12). The word יסר/*yāsar* and the concept of discipline are prevalent in the wisdom tradition to describe parental responsibility, and often occur in the covenantal discourse of Deuteronomy. These ideas are brought together in Deut 8:5, "Know then in your heart that as a parent disciplines (יסר/*yāsar*) a child so the LORD your God disciplines (יסר/*yāsar*) you." Hosea will similarly incorporate both definitions of the word, as well as their various contexts. YHWH's relationship to Israel is described in parental (cf. 11:1-7) as well as covenantal (6:7; 8:1) terms, and in chapter 7 יסר/*yāsar* communicates chastisement as well as nurture. The discipline spoken of in 7:12 becomes destruction in v. 13, yet in v. 15 the verb יסר/*yāsar* is set in a parallel relationship with "to strengthen arms" (חזק זרוע/*ḥāzaq zěrôʿa*), an idiom for encouragement and support. Both verbs describe the magnanimous actions of Job in Job 4:3, "See, you have instructed many; you have strengthened the weak hands (וידים רפות תחזק/*wěyādayîm rāpôt těḥazzēq*)". Later, in Hos 11:3, YHWH will describe the care extended to a young Israel: "It was I who taught Ephraim to walk, taking them by the arms (זרוע/*zěrôʿa*)" (NIV). While the language of discipline is not prevalent throughout the book of Hosea, its concept serves as one of the main themes of this prophecy. Although Israel will witness devastation, the message of Hosea is that God's actions toward the people are those of loving discipline.

When Hosea states in 8:1 that Israel has broken covenant, the evidence is abundant, since the people engage in political intrigue (7:12), lies (7:13), rebellion (7:14), and evil plots (7:15) against YHWH. The phrase "report to their assembly" in 7:12 is ambiguous. It has been understood as an assembly gathered to negotiate with international suitors,[9] translated as "report of their testimony" to describe terms of a treaty with Assyria or Egypt,[10] or emended to "report of their wickedness."[11] The desire for grain and wine in 7:14 recalls the grain and new wine given to Baal in 2:8 [10], and Israel's idolatrous and lecherous behavior as a result of wine in 4:11. Like these passages, Hos 7:14 similarly possesses both sexual and idolatrous connotations. While "wailing" (ילל/*yālal*) is most

9. J. Andrew Dearman, *The Book of Hosea* (NICOT; Grand Rapids: Eerdmans, 2010), p. 210.
10. Marvin A. Sweeney, *The Twelve Prophets* (2 vols.; Berit Olam; Collegeville: Liturgical Press, 2000), 1:81.
11. Hans Walter Wolff, *Hosea* (Hermeneia; Philadelphia: Fortress, 1974), pp. 107-8.

often associated with lamentation or mockery, the reference to "their beds" may suggest the imagery of sexual activity, given that 7:4 characterizes all their behavior as "adultery." The verb יתגוררו/*yitgôrārû* in 7:14 is difficult to translate and can mean either "to gash," "to gather," or "to fear." The first option is preferable, and suggests cultic activity in the manner of the priests of Baal in 1 Kgs 18:28. Regardless of the specifics, the conduct described in v. 14 is understood as rebellious activity.

The first line of Hosea 7:16 ישׁובו לא על/*yāšûbû lō' 'āl* is one of the most difficult phrases to translate, resulting in more than ten different suggestions.[12] Given the similarity in language and thought with 11:7 ("My people are bent on turning away from me. To the Most High they call, but he does not raise them up at all"), McComiskey seems correct in translating the phrase, "they do not return upward."[13] The consequences of Israel's lack of repentance are military impotency and defeat. The phrase "the rage of their tongue" likely refers to Israel's political negotiations with the Egyptians, alluded to earlier in 7:11. The last phrase of 7:16, "So much for their babbling in the land of Egypt," mocks the negotiations with the Egyptians, since they will result in Israel's subjection to the verbal abuse of their foreign conquerors (cf. commentary on 5:11; Isa 28:11). Ephraim's mixing with Egypt will eventuate in the reversal of the exodus, where the people of God return to Egypt (8:13; 9:3, 6; 11:5).

Hosea's political theology is absolutely clear: Allegiance to YHWH involves no negotiation with international powers. Yet such an international policy was utterly impractical given the constant threat of conquest by the Assyrian empire, for which the militaries of Israel and Judah were no match. Assyrian kings inherited the title "king of the four regions,"[14] and of Esarhaddon it was said, "Aššur has given him the whole world. From the place where the sun rises to where it sets there is no king to set beside him."[15] These oracles proclaimed Assyrian kings as rulers over the entire world, and it was assumed that they would invade and conquer foreign territories. The only recourses Israel and Judah had to survive were either to submit to Assyrian control, or to participate in alliances with regional powers and work collectively to repel Assyrian encroachment. Because the cooperation of all the Syro-Palestinian nations was vital in order to oppose Assyria, oftentimes several states would

12. For a list see Jason T. LeCureux, *The Thematic Unity of the Book of the Twelve* (HBM 41; Sheffield: Sheffield Phoenix Press, 2012), pp. 85-86.

13. Thomas Edward McComiskey, "Hosea," in *The Minor Prophets* (ed. T. E. McComiskey; Grand Rapids: Baker, 1992), 1:116.

14. Nin A line i 4 in Martti Nissinen, C. L. Seow, and Robert K. Ritner, *Prophets and Prophecy in the Ancient Near East* (Atlanta: Society of Biblical Literature, 2003), p. 137.

15. SAA 9 3.2 line ii 3-6 in Nissinen, *Prophets and Prophecy*, p. 119.

attack an unwilling king and force him to participate in the alliance.[16] In such an environment, neutrality was not an option for Israel; a rejection of Assyria meant that Israel was to ally itself with regional powers, or vice versa. In this regard Ben Zvi rightly points out, "The image of the past that is construed and communicated through this book is not historically accurate in contemporary terms but strongly shaped the 'memory' of later communities of Israel and as such created a past that carried a strong significance to them."[17] Hosea does not provide political strategies, but rather adopts a memory of Israel's past in order to communicate a theology of covenant faithfulness and loyalty. Israel's kings certainly made political concessions to foreign powers in order to survive politically, as demonstrated even in biblical narratives. Under the threat of empire, Hosea calls for a complete dependence on YHWH and a peaceable kingdom, a call that potentially threatens the political survival of the nation. On this point, McConville writes, "Whether the Old Testament emerges in dialogue with Assyria or another power, it is clear that Israel's Yahwism never takes the form of the domination of the weak by the strong. On the contrary, it is advocated in political weakness, and in the face of such power."[18]

Hosea 8:1-14

In chapter 8, Hosea returns to the central tenets of YHWH's indictment of Israel, namely that they have abrogated their covenant relationship with YHWH. Israel has failed to understand what it truly means to "know" God, and their idolatry and reliance upon foreign powers will result in destruction and deportation. Since Israel is repeatedly described as sick and rebellious, it appears that what may be perceived as redundant rhetoric on Hosea's part is necessary to address its deep-seated and pervasive corruption. In Israel's case, a few counseling sessions will not do; comprehensive therapy is needed (to anticipate Castelo's imagery later). With each new section of the book, previous themes are revisited, yet they are reframed so as to persuade the audience to come to terms with their illness; the past is more fully probed so as to address the core of Israel's destructive addictions. To read Hosea as a book takes the reader on an uncomfortable

16. Nadav Na'aman, "Forced Participation in Alliances in the Course of the Assyrian Campaigns to the West," in *Ah, Assyria: Studies in Assyrian History and Ancient Near Eastern Historiography Presented to Hayim Tadmor* (ed. M. Cogan and I. Eph'al; Jerusalem: Magnes Press, 1991), pp. 80-98.

17. Ben Zvi, *Hosea*, p. 159.

18. J. G. McConville, *God and Earthly Power: An Old Testament Political Theology: Genesis-Kings* (London: T & T Clark, 2006), p. 29.

journey into places of Israel's past that its people would rather forget. But if healing is the goal, Israel must acknowledge the root causes of its illness. In this regard, the book of Hosea offers its readers a model for the long road of restoration and reconciliation when dysfunction has been the norm for generations.

The opening command to signal a trumpet call in 8:1 is reminiscent of the warning in 5:8 ("Blow the horn in Gibeah, the trumpet in Ramah. Sound the alarm at Beth-aven; look behind you, Benjamin!"). The שׁפר/šôpār, or animal horn, was used in Israel as a signal in religious ceremonies, military battles, and to announce a theophany of YHWH or the Day of YHWH. These three associations with the animal horn occur in the Twelve Prophets (Hos 5:8; 8:1; Joel 2:1, 15; Amos 2:2; 3:6; Zeph 1:16; Zech 9:14). Here in 8:1 it announces both impending military conflict and also the judgment of YHWH, a phenomenon associated with the Day of the LORD. The avian imagery is continued from chapter 7, and the bird mentioned in 8:1 may refer to either a vulture or eagle, but more likely the latter for two reasons. First, the eagle was commonly used as a symbol of Assyrian kings or the god Asshur; second, this image is used in the context of covenant making and Torah giving in Exod 19:4. Hosea 8:1 explicitly mentions covenant and Torah, and the Assyrian threat is prevalent throughout chapters 7–8 (7:11; 8:9). Dearman identifies a "saving eagle" tradition found in Deuteronomy, where Yahweh is depicted as the hovering eagle who protects Israel through the wilderness (Deut 32:10-12). In contrast, in the "predatory eagle" tradition, a foreign nation swoops upon Israel and carries them off into exile as part of a covenant curse (Deut 28:49). The opening announcement, "Set the trumpet to your lips! One like a vulture is over the house of the LORD" (Hos 8:1), is itself ambiguous as to which tradition of the two it represents. The surrounding context reveals that Hosea is proclaiming the "predatory eagle" concept, since the latter half of the verse describes Israel's abrogation of covenant and Torah. In addition, the previous verse's description of "babbling in the land of Egypt" (7:16) is consistent with the curse of Deut 28:49 ("The LORD will bring a nation from far away, from the end of the earth, to swoop down on you like an eagle, a nation whose language you do not understand"). Deuteronomy 28:51 ("[A fierce nation] shall consume the fruit of your livestock and the fruit of your ground until you are destroyed, leaving you neither grain, wine, and oil") also resonates with the judgment described in Hos 8:7-8.

Several commentators consider the reference to covenant and Torah in the latter half of 8:1 a postexilic addition, in accordance with an evolutionary concept of Israelite religion. In this view, covenant and Law emerged in the postexilic period, in contrast to their placement within the narrative of the Scriptures and their placement within the canon. Yet for Hosea, the concepts of covenant and Torah are so embedded and pervasive throughout the book that they cannot be merely a redactional addition. Wellhausen himself acknowledged that the marriage metaphor "certainly presents us as clearly as possible with the thing [covenant]."[19] As discussed previously, the words "covenant" and "Torah" found in Hosea ought not to be equated with their Pentateuchal forms, but they need not be completely disassociated from them either given Hosea's role within the canon. Hosea assumes a long-standing tradition of covenant and instruction so that he could legitimately indict his audience for these violations. John Day observes parallels between Hos 8 and Ps 78 — a psalm dated prior to 722 since it lacks any knowledge of an Assyrian diaspora — and concludes that the concept of covenant was pre-deuteronomistic. Like Hos 8, in Ps 78 it is the people of Ephraim (78:9) who "did not keep God's covenant, but refused to walk according to his law" (Ps 78:10), and whose "heart was not steadfast toward him; they were not true to his covenant" (78:37).

The word "instruction" (תורה/*tôrāh*) occurs once more in 8:12, and there it is understood as something documented and substantive: "I wrote for them the many things of my law" (NIV).[20] Hosea 8:12 can also be translated, "Though I write for him the principal requirements of my law."[21] In this case, "תורה/*tôrāh* refers to a divine torah/instruction that is written, read, and interpreted (by the authorities of the period), and complemented with less weightier [sic] matters that are not written in the text, and which one would assume remain in the hands of the accepted authorities of the period."[22] Viewed in this manner, Hosea faults Israel for violating the most important aspects of YHWH's instruction, and any supposed citations of תורה/*tôrāh* by Hosea are never direct quotes from a law code, but rather Hosea's own interpretation of the central tenets of God's instruction. Such a reading would be consonant with the prioritization of loyalty and knowledge of God over cultic activity, expressed earlier in 6:6. In addition, the scarce references to Mosaic legislation in Hosea ought not to be understood as the absence of Pentateuchal law in Hosea's day, but rather as the prophet's free interpretation of its most important teachings.

In Hos 8:2-3, Hosea once more addresses the dissonance between Israel's speech and deeds. The outcry in v. 2, "My God, we — Israel — know you!"[23]

---

19. Ernest W. Nicholson, *God and His People: Covenant and Theology in the Old Testament* (Oxford: Clarendon Press, 1986), p. 188.

20. The *Qere* appears to be a form of the word רב/*rab* "great, many"; and the *Kethib* רבוא/*rîbbô'* "ten thousand, multitude." The *Qere* is to be preferred since it better parallels the previous verse, where רב/*rab* speaks of the multiplication of sacrifices.

21. Macintosh, *Hosea*, p. 325.

22. Ben Zvi, *Hosea*, p. 178.

23. Since the LXX and the Peshitta lack the word "Israel" (e.g., LXX: "O God, we know you") and its absence makes the phrase more grammatically sound, it is possible that "Israel" is a gloss.

appears to be an expression of trust in response to a liturgical exhortation in the manner of Ps 46:10 [11] ("Be still, and know that I am God!") or Ps 100:3 ("Know that the LORD is God" [cf. Pss 9:10 [11]; 36:10]). Throughout Hosea, Israel's eschatological goal is that it "knows YHWH" (2:20 [22]) and confesses, "You are my God" (2:23 [25]). The only other instance of the word "cry" (זעק/*zāʿaq*) occurs in 7:14, where Hosea acknowledges that Israel does not cry to YHWH from the heart. Israel's rejection of "the good" in 8:3 is demonstrated in the previous chapter's description of their wickedness (רעה/*rāʿāh*, 7:1, 2, 3) and their plotting of evil (רע/*raʿ*, 7:15).

In Hosea, Israel is self-deluded into thinking they know God even while they have rejected YHWH and nullified the covenant. As a result, YHWH is no longer Israel's covenant partner. Exodus 34:7 describes YHWH as "keeping steadfast love for the thousandth generation, forgiving iniquity (עון/*ʿāwôn*) and transgression and sin (חטאה/*ḥaṭṭâ*)," but in Hos 8:13 a change occurs, and "now he will remember their iniquity (עון/*ʿāwôn*), and punish their sins (חטאה/*ḥaṭṭâ*) and return Israel to Egypt." The reference to "the good" (טוב/*ṭôb*) in Hos 8:3 may also allude to YHWH's description of this same covenantal presence of God described in Exod 33:19: "I will make all my goodness (טובי/*ṭûbî*) pass before you, and will proclaim before you the name, 'The LORD'; and I will be gracious to whom I will be gracious, and will show mercy on whom I will show mercy." Most versions end Hos 8:4 with the phrase, "With their silver and gold they made idols for their own destruction," and leave untranslated the verb "he/it is cut off" (יכרת/*yikkārēt*). The verb commonly describes the making — literally the "cutting" — of covenants between YHWH and Israel (Gen 15:18; Exod 24:8; Hos 2:18 [2:20]) and treaty ratification with foreign powers (Deut 7:2; Hos 10:4; 12:1 [12:2]). Both senses of the word occur in 8:4, such that Israel's cutting or proliferation of treaties with the nations results in the "cutting off" of covenant with YHWH. In a variety of ways, Hosea communicates in this chapter that the covenant between Israel and YHWH is no more.

Hosea 8:4 summarizes Israel's two primary covenant violations, idolatry and treaties with foreign nations, and vv. 5-11 elaborate on these sins and the judgment to follow. Because of the confluence between religious, military, and national identity and authority in the ANE, it is unsurprising that these two issues are raised. Prophets and priests worked in conjunction with kings for political and religious leadership, so certainly they are among the "they" in v. 4 who are held responsible for royal and cultic failures.

Scholars have posited several historical scenarios regarding Israel's dealings with Assyria that may lie behind the text of vv. 8-9, from as early as pre-743-739, to 738, 735-732, or 725-722/20.[24] Whatever scenario this text addresses,

24. See Ben Zvi, *Hosea*, pp. 176-77.

Hosea is not interested in merely critiquing recent political moves, but rather providing a theological assessment of Israel's foundational narratives by overturning its national myths. Hosea's critique in 8:4-11 bears much resemblance to prophetic polemics against the idolatry of foreign nations (cf. Isa 44:6-20; 45:20-21). By offering a revisionist history of popular views, he directs a similar verbal attack against the most foundational and cherished beliefs of his own people. Prophetic ministry involves much more than behavior modification on a personal or social level; it entails challenging mythologies in their various forms and persuading one's own community to be willing to read their own story afresh. Prophetic ministry is to persuade people to forsake their previous identities and embrace a new understanding of themselves.

Rather than merely critique the regicide in the latter years of the Northern Kingdom, Hosea's assessment that "They made kings, but not through me; they set up princes, but without my knowledge" (Hos 8:4) delegitimizes every king of the Northern Kingdom beginning with Jeroboam I. The statement also criticizes treaties made with foreign empires, where a foreign suzerain reigned over Israel.[25] The reference to the calf at Samaria has puzzled commentators, since 1 Kgs 12:26-33 places the calves at Dan and Bethel, a point confirmed later in Hosea 10:5. Whether a calf or calves existed at the site of Samaria is of little consequence since Samaria takes the role of unfaithful lover within the rhetorical argument of Hosea. Hosea's point is that Samaria is guilty of idolatry in the manner of Jeroboam I, as well as Aaron in Exod 32. Clearly, 1 Kgs 12:26-33 is to be associated with golden calf narratives in Exod 32 (cf. 1 Kgs 12:28), as well as Hos 8:5. The phrase "anger burns" (אף חרה/ḥārāh 'ap) in Hos 8:5 occurs four times in the Sinai narrative (Exod 32:10, 11, 19, 22), and the destruction or removal of the calf in Hos 8:6[26] is reminiscent of the fate of the golden calf at Sinai (Exod 32:19-20). With the reference to unauthorized rulers in 8:4, Hos 8:4-6 associates the entire history of the Northern Kingdom with the idolatrous creation of the golden calf at Sinai.

Hosea 8:7 introduces a new metaphor, that of sowing, to describe both Israel's idolatry, which was mentioned in the previous verses, as well as its re-

---

25. Sweeney, *The Twelve Prophets*, 1:87. Sweeney also observes that 8:4 resembles Israel's words to Samuel in 1 Sam 8:5, "Appoint for us, then, a king to govern us, like other nations," which may suggest that Hosea views the monarchical institution as a departure from YHWH's plans for Israel. Such need not be the case, since elsewhere Hosea views the absence of a king as a form of discipline and the return of the Davidic monarch as an eschatological blessing (3:4-5).

26. The verb "broken to pieces" (שבבים/šĕbābîm) is a *hapax*, so one can only speculate as to its meaning. Macintosh finds the common understandings of the word — as referring to "splintering" or "burning" — unconvincing and opts for translating it as "removal" (Macintosh, *Hosea*, pp. 308-10).

liance on foreign powers, described in the verses to follow. The particle "for" occurs twice in v. 6, and thereafter introduces the thought of vv. 7, 9, 10, and 11. It functions to distinguish the unit of vv. 7-10, but also ties this section into the preceding and following passages. The word "to sow" (זרע/*zāra'*) in 8:7 recalls the theme of Jezreel in chapters 1–2. This word, coupled with the references to grain in 8:7 and the mention of lovers in 8:9, recalls the text and imagery of chapters 1–3. Hosea draws attention to the futility of idolatry and foreign treaties by comparing such activity to sowing the wind. Idolatry is futile because the idol is not divine (8:6), and foreign alliances similarly lack substance according to the metaphor of empty grain in 8:7. The imagery of a destructive storm developing from what initially began as a breeze illustrates the calamitous effects of these misplaced investments. Similarly, Hos 8:7c–10 describes Israel's huge miscalculation in appealing to foreign nations for assistance, particularly Assyria. The two occurrences of the verb "to swallow" (בלע/*bāla'*) in Hos 8:7-8 allude back to 7:9 ("Foreigners devour his strength"), and point forward to the eating and devouring in 8:13-14. The word "to swallow" בלע/*bāla'* is a pun on the verb "to mix" (בלל/*bālal*) in 7:8, as well as the name of the Phoenician deity Baal (בעל/*ba'al*) that is associated with Ephraim's past (11:2; 13:1).

Verse 9 employs another pun by comparing Ephraim (אפרים/*'eprayîm*) to a wild ass (פרא/*pere'*). Like an ass, which is typically a gregarious animal, Israel is now abandoned and powerless.[27] The mention of "lovers" (אהבים/*ăhābîm*) in 8:9 recalls Hos 2–3, in which the word occurs nine times (2:5 [7], 7 [9], 10 [12], 12 [14], 13 [15]; 3:1 [4x]), yet the metaphor in chapter 8 differs from 2-3. Samaria was depicted as a promiscuous woman and adulterous wife in chapters 1–3, yet in Hos 8:9 Ephraim is now a man soliciting sex from paramours. The verb "to bargain" or "spend" (תנה/*tānāh*) occurs again in 8:10, yet now nations are set in a parallel relationship with lovers in the previous line, implying that Ephraim's lovers are foreign nations. Israel's payment of tribute only backfires, so that they are oppressed by the Assyrian "king of princes."[28] Ephraim the wild ass now becomes a domesticated beast of burden. The verb "writhe" in 8:10 may not stem from the root חיל/*hāyal*, but rather be the *hiphil* form of חלל/*hālal*, "to begin," or "pollute or profane." In the latter sense, the Israelites will not only be victimized by Assyria by possibly being forced into labor, but they will also be defiled through, among other things, exposure to unclean food

---

27. Göran Eidevall, *Grapes in the Desert: Metaphors, Models, and Themes in Hosea 4–14* (ConBOT 43; Stockholm: Almqvist & Wiksell International, 1996), p. 134.

28. Most translations understand מלך שרים/*melek śārîm* as "king *and* princes," yet given Hosea's other references to the Assyrian king in construct form (מלך ירב/*melek yārēb*, 5:13; 10:6), the phrase is likely a reference to the Assyrian king. See also Ezek 26:7 where Nebuchadnezzar, the king of Babylon, is given the title "king of kings."

(cf. 9:3). The word "gather" (קבץ/*qābaṣ*) in Hosea and other parts of the Bible typically describes deliverance *from* exile (1:11 [2:2]); Isa 11:12; Jer 29:14), yet in 8:10 it refers to a gathering *for* exile. Essentially, Hosea reinterprets the national myth of Israel. Whereas previously Israel's story involved a deliverance from the nations and a conquest of them in the promised land, now it will include a defeat and dispersion among the nations.

Thankfully, Hosea makes clear Israel's story does not conclude with exile, but rather with restoration (1:10-11 [2:1-2]; 3:4-5; 11:10-11). Similarly, the Twelve Prophets conclude not with a gathering *to* the nations but rather an ingathering *from* the nations and a return to the land. The last mention of the word (קבץ/*qābaṣ*; εἰσδέξομαι/*eisdexomai*) within both the Hebrew and Greek versions of the Twelve Prophets occurs in Zech 10:10. In this case, it reverses the "gathering to Assyria," "gathering to Egypt," (Hos 9:6), and the "returning (שוב/*šûb*) to Egypt" (Hos 8:13; 9:3) motif that so marks the first book of the Twelve Prophets:

> Though I scattered them among the nations, yet in far countries they shall remember me, and they shall rear their children and return (שוב/*šûb*). I will bring them home from the land of Egypt, and gather (קבץ/*qābaṣ*; εἰσδέξομαι/*eisdexomai*) them from Assyria (Zech 10:9-10a).

With the announcement of a great eschatological ingathering, the canonical Scriptures ingrain into Israel's consciousness that they are survivors. As a people, they may face defeat, but they will never be utterly destroyed.

Pisano has demonstrated that LXX Hosea differs significantly from the MT regarding the significance of Egypt.[29] In MT Hosea, Egypt plays an important role in Israel's past, present, and future, whereas in LXX Hosea, Egypt is consistently only an actor in Israel's past. In MT Hos 8:13, the judgment of a future deportation to Egypt is threatened ("they shall return to Egypt" [המה מצרים ישובו/*hēmmāh miṣrayim yāšûbû*]). A similar threat is repeated in 9:3, yet here Assyria and Egypt are collocated together as future sites of exile ("but Ephraim shall return to Egypt [ושב אפרים מצרים/*wĕšāb 'eprayim miṣrayim*] and in Assyria they shall eat unclean food"). In 8:13 the Greek text reads, "they have returned to Egypt (αὐτοὶ εἰς Αἴγυπτον ἀπέστρεψαν/*autoi eis Aigypton apestrepsan*) and will eat unclean things among the Assyrians." It appears the Greek translator borrowed the note concerning unclean food in Assyria from 9:3. LXX Hosea 9:3 reads, "Ephraim settled in Egypt (κατῴκησεν Εφραιμ εἰς

---

29. Stephen Pisano, "'Egypt' in the Septuagint Text of Hosea," in *Tradition of the Text: Studies Offered to Dominique Barthélemy in Celebration of His 70th Birthday* (ed. G. J. Norton and S. Pisano; OBO 109; Freiburg: Universitätsverlag Freiburg Schweiz, 1991), pp. 301-8.

Αἴγυπτον/*katōkēsen Ephraim eis Aigupton*), and among the Assyrians they shall eat unclean things." According to Pisano, the Greek text appears to have "undergone an almost systematic alteration in order to place this return to Egypt in the past. In this way, the statement that Ephraim has gone back to Egypt . . . [is] a symbolic statement concerning Ephraim's current situation at the time of Hosea's writing: by its infidelity Ephraim, and Israel, has in effect placed itself in a relationship to the Lord which was similar to its sojourn in Egypt."[30] According to LXX Hosea, Egypt is either an event in Israel's historical past, or it represents the current state of affairs where Israel finds itself in a state of bondage and exile.

Hosea 8:11-14 describes how Israel and Judah have forgotten their maker even though both kingdoms bustle with activity. Ephraim's multiplication of sacrifices, intended to atone for sin, backfires and only increases the nation's guilt. Hosea condemns Israel for idolatry in 8:4-6 and has already criticized the people for forsaking loyalty in favor of cultic practice in 6:6, so vv. 12-13 may or may not describe the proliferation of idolatrous acts. Regardless of the specific nature of their sin, Israel's folly leads to increased blindness to YHWH's instruction (v. 12) and exile to a foreign land (v. 13). Judah multiplies fortified cities and strongholds (v. 14; cf. 5:10), yet receives a judgment similar to Ephraim so that they too stand guilty. Israel tries to compensate for its covenantal disobedience through increased cultic activity and Judah attempts to do so through militarism, yet both actions result in conquest by foreign powers. Ben Zvi observes that the masculine and feminine pronouns in the judgment formula, "I will send a fire upon *his* cities, and it shall devour *her* strongholds" in 8:14 refer to Israel and Judah, respectively, emphasizing Israel's core identity as a united kingdom.[31] This formulaic speech occurs again in Amos 1:4, 7, 10, 12; 2:2, 5 to describe God's judgment against the nations and Judah, and it emphasizes YHWH's concern for justice among the nations within the Twelve Prophets. Election and covenant do not exempt Israel from discipline; rather, they provide a different rationale for its employment. Not only is Israel to exercise justice and righteousness within their nation and to treat others humanely, as emphasized by Amos, but Israel is also to demonstrate loyalty to YHWH alone and reject any other god or king, as emphasized by Hosea. Conservatives tend to focus on the religious message of Hosea and liberals gravitate to the social concerns of Amos, yet when one reads the Twelve Prophets canonically, the question is not whether God cares about idolatry *or* injustice; rather, both are an affront to the holy one of Israel.

30. Pisano, "'Egypt' in the Septuagint Text of Hosea," p. 306.
31. Ben Zvi, *Hosea*, p. 173.

10. Hosea 9:1–10:15

Bo H. Lim

Throughout this commentary, the primary literary unit has been the prophetic book of Hosea, and proposed structures within it have been viewed largely as heuristic devices. While establishing the boundaries of texts may be a priority for modern scholars, particularly those in the form-critical school, ancient scribes and readers did not draw sharp distinctions between literary units. Even so, consideration of structure is helpful in understanding the rhetorical argument of the prophetic book. Different proposals regarding the book's structure prioritize different features of the text, so examining them closely aids readers in appreciating the various textures of this multilayered book.

Scholars have observed a strong affinity between Hos 9:10-17 and 10:1-15, primarily because of shared agricultural metaphors. But these texts do not share the same level of congruence with the previous pericope, Hos 9:1-9. Otto Eissfeldt proposed that Hosea 4–14 ought to be divided into two sections, 4:1–9:9 and 9:10–14:9. Scholars have since treated 9:10–10:15 as a subunit, such that Eidevall writes, "It is uncontroversial to regard 9:10 as the beginning of a new discourse unit."[1] Certainly Hos 9:1-9 demonstrates literary links to chapter 8. The phrase in 8:13, "Now he will remember their iniquity, and punish their sins," is repeated in 9:9. The announcements of Ephraim's return to Egypt in 9:3 and Egypt's gathering of Israel in 9:6 recall the mention of Israel's return to Egypt in 8:13. In Hosea, new tropes are introduced to unify previously-covered texts with subsequent sections of the book.

Yet other scholars do not read 9:1-9 as a conclusion of the discourse in chapter 8, but rather as an introduction to the argument of 9:1–10:15 (and possibly further into the book). Links can also be drawn between 9:1-9 and

---

1. Göran Eidevall, *Grapes in the Desert: Metaphors, Models, and Themes in Hosea 4–14* (ConBOT 43; Stockholm: Almqvist & Wiksell International, 1996), p. 145.

9:10–10:15, as demonstrated in the reference to Gibeah in both sections (9:9; 10:9). Sweeney has proposed that 9:1–13:16 functions as the prophet's condemnation of Israel in the form of a historical overview of Israel's repeated rejection of YHWH.[2] Several commentators have proposed the festival of Sukkoth as the backdrop for 9:1-9, yet Sweeney goes further and argues that it serves as the context for 9:1–10:15,[3] since fertility is a major concern throughout these chapters. Proposals such as Sweeney's support reading 9:1–10:15 as a cohesive unit, especially given that the agricultural motif (which is one of the suggested reasons for separating out 9:1-9) applies to this text as well. The natural progression — from the references to wine and threshing floor in 9:1-2, 4 to the metaphors of grapes in the wilderness (9:10) and to a luxuriant vine (10:1) — serves to unify 9:10–10:15.

Hosea 9:1-17

Prophetic imperatives begin a new section at Hos 9:1, in the same way that previous units of the book (4:1; 5:8) have been introduced. The commands in 9:1, "do not rejoice" and "do not exult," presume an occasion for celebration. Scholars have suggested that Hosea spoke these words on the occasion of a religious festival, since 9:5 mentions a day of an appointed festival and a day of feasting. Sukkoth, also known as the Feast of Booths, is likely the context, since Deut 16:13 associates threshing (cf. Hos 9:1, 2) and wine presses (Hos 9:1) with this festival. This feast commemorated God's provision for Israel during its wandering in the wilderness and entry into the promised land. During this time, grapes and olives were gathered, and grain was planted for the spring harvests. Given these aspects of the celebration, Hosea's instructions in 9:1-3 reverse every expectation for this feast. Deuteronomy characterizes Sukkoth as a time of rejoicing (Deut 16:14, 15), yet Hosea commands Israel not to do so in 9:1. Sukkoth is a time of harvest and feasting, yet in 9:2 Hosea indicates that both threshing floor (where grain is processed) and wine press (where wine is produced) will fail them. On a religious level, Sukkoth celebrates Israel's settlement in the land of promise, yet in 9:3 Hosea informs them that they will return to Egypt and Assyria.

Consistently, this commentary has argued that hypothetical life settings for individual pericopes ought to be eschewed because of their speculative na-

---

2. Marvin A. Sweeney, *The Twelve Prophets* (2 vols.; Berit Olam; Collegeville: Liturgical Press, 2000), 1:93.

3. Sweeney, *The Twelve Prophets*, 1:93-112.

ture. In addition, I have argued that, in the process of grafting texts into prophetic books, literary and theological interests were prioritized to the extent
that historical markers are no longer reliable. So in the case of Hos 9, rather
than attempting to identify a precise date and location for Sukkoth, readers
ought to read the prophetic word against a generalized narrative background
of celebratory festivals involving harvest, wine, and sex. Sukkoth functions as
a literary motif of wealth, abundance, and pleasure, anchored in Israel's exodus
and wilderness traditions. Hosea utilizes this narrative backdrop to communicate his message of covenant reversal. So while the festival may have functioned
initially as the social context for the prophecy in 9:1-6 or 9:1-9, the prophet
thereafter adopts the related *literary* motif of gardening for the remainder of
chapters 9 and 10.

Admittedly, the two references to "day of" in v. 5 and the two references to
"days of" in v. 7 do not fit the criteria of the "Day of the LORD" references within
the Twelve Prophets. Yet we have already seen the close parallels between this
chapter and Amos 7, and the close tie between Hosea and Amos has been noted
in my introduction. So when readers reread the Twelve Prophets, a connection
can be made between the reference to the "Day of the LORD" in Amos 5:18-20
and the day/s references in Hos 9. Both Hos 9 and Amos 5 assume a context of
religious festivals; instruct Israel to lament rather than rejoice; communicate
YHWH's rejection of Israel's cultic activities; and reveal that rather than a day
of salvation, a day of judgment is imminent. In addition, Amos 7:17 ("Therefore
thus says the LORD: 'Your wife shall become a prostitute [זנה/*zānāh*] in the city,
and your sons and your daughters shall fall by the sword, and your land shall be
parceled out by line; you yourself shall die in an unclean [טמא/*ṭāmē'*] land, and
Israel shall surely go into exile away from its land'") appears to be a summation
of Hos 9. Both texts mention promiscuity (זנה/*zānāh*, Hos 9:1), the execution
of children (Hos 9:16), defilement among the nations (טמא/*ṭāmē'*, Hos 9:3, 4),
and exile among the nations as an act of punishment. Given such an unpopular
message, it is not surprising that, in both Amos 7 (vv. 10-16) and Hos 9 (vv. 7-8),
the legitimacy of the prophet's ministry is challenged.

Hosea 9:7-9 is considered the most difficult speech to decipher in the
entire book, so any interpretation ought to be accepted with a degree of tentativeness.[4] Each option requires varying degrees of emendation, atypical punc-
tuation, or the addition of clarifying speech, because the text as it stands is
incomprehensible. In terms of its message, the key point of difference lies in
the identification of the prophet in vv. 7-8. Some view v. 7 as a quotation of

---

4. See J. Andrew Dearman, *The Book of Hosea* (NICOT; Grand Rapids: Eerdmans, 2010),
pp. 242-48 for a survey of the various options.

Hosea's opponents describing the prophet, and interpret v. 8 as the prophet's response to their criticism. For example, Seow suggests that v. 7 reflects the sentiments of Hosea's opponents who, influenced by a sapiential tradition that prized temperance and marital fidelity, were critical of his quarrelsomeness and association with a promiscuous woman and therefore called him a fool.[5] Another view understands vv. 7-8 in its entirety as a condemnation of the false prophets in Ephraim, which were mentioned earlier in Hos 4:5 and 6:5. A third option depicts v. 7 as Hosea's condemnation of the false prophets, and v. 8 as Hosea's contrastive definition of a true prophet. While it is unclear and less important exactly to whom v. 7 refers, it is vital that v. 8 be identified with the true prophet Hosea. The first person pronominal suffix in v. 8, on "my God," identifies Hosea with the prophet and is vital to the message of this passage. In addition, Jeremiah 6:17 and Ezekiel 3:17; 33:2-7 will also describe the role of the prophet as watchman or sentinel. Hosea teaches that the way of wisdom (cf. 14:9) and prophetic ministry is foolishness to the world, a lesson that will later be reiterated by the apostle Paul (cf. 1 Cor 1–4).

Hosea clarifies to the people that obedience is not merely the observance of cultic practices or priestly instruction, but that covenant faithfulness requires obedience to *prophetic* word. The rejection of God's prophet and his message is a rejection of the very person of God. Israel's "great hostility" (רבה משטמה/ *rabāh maśṭēmāh*) mentioned in v. 7 is further defined as a "hostility" (משטמה/ *maśṭēmāh*) directed against the prophet of God in v. 8. The days of punishment and recompense described in v. 7 — that is, Israel's imminent threat of foreign conquest and deportation — are predicated upon the people's reception or rejection of the prophet's message. The viability of the covenant rests not only upon the Law but also upon the *Prophets*. This link between the voice of the prophet and Israel's covenant relationship is vital to subsequent generations receiving the prophetic word. And, given Hosea's position as introducing the Twelve Prophets, it authorizes the rest of the collection of the Twelve as covenant prophets.

The references to "my God" in 9:8 and 9:17 function on a rhetorical level to set apart those loyal to the prophet, in distinction to the majority of Ephraimites who are identified by the references to "his God" in v. 8 and "they" in v. 17. While distinct from the "I" speech of God in vv. 10-15, the first-person speech of the prophet in vv. 8 and 17 functions to align the prophet with the will of YHWH. God does not treat Israel as a monolithic entity, but distinguishes those who heed the voice of God's prophet from those who reject the prophet's message. Verse 17 makes this clear: "Because they have not listened

---

5. C. L. Seow, "Hosea 14:10 and the Foolish People Motif," *CBQ* 44 (1982): 221.

to him, my God will reject them; they shall become wanderers among the nations." The people's reception or rejection of the prophetic word becomes the decisive measure by which God's people will be judged. When readers of the Twelve reach the third vision of Amos and read of how God will no longer show compassion because of Israel's rejection of Amos, they are reminded of Hosea's instructions concerning the treatment of prophets in Hos 9. Schart observes, "God's patience comes to an end because Israel had driven out from Bethel the very same prophet, who had in the two previous visions prevented God's punishment through intercession. *God's patience ends when Israel expels God's prophet.*"[6] Ben Zvi describes the ongoing rhetorical effect of this discourse: "The text not only reinforces the sinful construction of past Israel, but also allows the readers who are also Israel to identify with YHWH and separate themselves from the sinful manifestation of trans-temporal Israel that is portrayed in the book, and which is part of their social memory and story about themselves."[7] Hosea's message instructs every generation that they cannot ignore the written prophetic word and the prophets in their midst if they wish to continue as the people of God.

The repetition of the phrase in Hos 9:9 ("he will remember their iniquity, he will punish their sins") from 8:13 signifies to the reader that 9:1-9 is a continuation of the previous chapter. In addition, the phrase "They have deeply corrupted themselves" (העמיקו־שחתו/*he'mîqû-šiḥētû,* Hos 9:9) recalls the phrase in 5:2, "In their wicked condition, they have sunk deep into corruption" (CEB, ושחטה שטים העמיקו/*wĕšaḥăṭâ śēṭîm he'mîqû*). The return to Egypt serves as a recurring threat of judgment (7:16; 8:13; 9:3), and in 9:6 Egypt signifies a "vast burial place, a land of no return."[8] The combination of the words "nettles" and "thorns" in 9:6 appears only one other place in the OT, in Isa 34:13, a passage that describes eschatological judgment against Edom. If the terms function in the same manner in this passage, then the announcement of the "day of the festival of the LORD" in Hos 9:5-6 mirrors the description of the inescapable judgment of the Day of the LORD in Amos. In both cases, the people assume the day to be one of celebration, only to discover that, in the words of Amos, it will be a day of darkness and not light (Amos 5:18, 20), and in Hosea, it will be a day of punishment and recompense (Hos 9:7).

Eidevall has proposed the following structure to 9:10-17, situating the prayer for barrenness at the center of the unit:

6. Aaron Schart, "The First Section of the Book of the Twelve Prophets: Hosea-Joel-Amos," *Int* 61 (2007): 146, emphasis mine.

7. Ehud Ben Zvi, *Hosea* (FOTL 21A; Grand Rapids: Eerdmans, 2005), p. 191.

8. Eidevall, *Grapes in the Desert,* p. 145.

> 10a Election (past)
>> 10b Apostasy
>> 11-13 Childlessness
>>> 14 Imprecation
>> 15 Apostasy
>> 16 Childlessness
> 17 Rejection (future)[9]

This structure is not symmetrical, but its topics, focus, and thematic progression reflect key features of the text. Even though Israel is God's elect people, Hosea will pray an imprecation upon them because of their apostasy, signifying God's rejection of them. Eidevall observes that the references to grapes and figs in 9:10 likely serve as metaphors for righteous persons. Given the fact that grapes do not appear in the desert, YHWH's discovery of Israel under such circumstances indicates that the election of Israel is viewed as a miracle. He writes, "In a 'wilderness of paganism,' YHWH discovered a people meant to be faithful."[10] In this instance the wilderness is chosen as the origins of Israel (cf. Jer 2:2), demonstrating that the prophet possessed multiple narratives for Israel's beginnings and drew upon those traditions that would best serve his rhetorical and theological aims.

The characterization of Israel here is one of apostasy. Hosea 9:10 recalls the incident at Baal-peor referred to in Num 25, where the men of Israel profaned themselves by engaging in promiscuous sex (זנה/*zānāh*, Num 25:1) with Moabite women, worshipping foreign deities, and devoting themselves to Baal of Peor. According to Hos 9:10, this episode cannot be overlooked as a minor or uncharacteristic incident; instead, Israel's actions are portrayed as an act of "consecration" (נזר/*nāzar*) — the word used to describe Nazarite vows — as well as "love" (אהב/*'āhab*). The reasons for choosing this episode are obvious given the references to promiscuity, idolatry, and Baal in Hosea. Hosea describes this episode in Israel's past as a liturgical act in order to highlight the dangers of desires that are shaped by false worship. James Smith offers the reminder, "We are, ultimately, liturgical animals because we are fundamentally desiring creatures. We are what we love, and our love is shaped, primed, and aimed by liturgical practices that take hold of our gut and aim our heart to certain ends."[11] Worship and devotion always result in imitation; therefore, the end result of Israel's misguided devotion is shame and abhorrence.

---

9. Eidevall, *Grapes in the Desert*, pp. 148-49.

10. Eidevall, *Grapes in the Desert*, p. 151.

11. James K. A. Smith, *Desiring the Kingdom: Worship, Worldview, and Cultural Formation* (Grand Rapids: Baker Academic, 2009), p. 40.

In Hos 9:10, the grape simile recalls the lack of grapes in the wilderness in contrast to Canaan (Num 13:17-20; 20:5); the use of "consecrate" (נזר/*nāzar*) recalls the Nazarite instructions in Num 6:1-21; and the reference to Baal-peor suggests that Israel is deserving of the same fate as those who died at the hands of Phineas because of their involvement in idolatry and sexual immorality (Num 25:1-18). While the word "jealousy" (קנא/*qānā'*) does not appear in Hosea, the Numbers narrative justifies God's anger and violence with this word (Num 25:11, 13), and it characterizes YHWH's covenantal relationship with Israel (cf. Exod 20:5; 34:12; Deut 4:24; 5:9; 6:15). Righteous jealousy is consistent with the covenantal character and commitments of Israel's God.

What is shocking is the punishment that will be inflicted upon Israel for its sins. Because of Ephraim's refusal to acknowledge its source of fertility, Hos 9:14 appropriates and then reverses Israel's tradition of YHWH's sovereign care of the breast and womb.[12] The threefold repetition of the word "give" (נתן/*nātan*) in 9:14 subverts Israel's expectations, since the word is oftentimes used in requests for the well-being of God's people. The word occurs four times in Hos 2 (vv. 5 [7], 8 [10], 12 [14], 15 [17]) as a key term to describe the woman's ascription of her provisions to other lovers and YHWH's commitment to lavishly provide for her. In 9:14, the opening exhortation "give" suggests that a blessing will follow, yet instead the prophet subverts expectations by invoking a curse. The word "giving," then, acknowledges YHWH as the giver of all good things, even as Ephraim receives judgment. Within the book of Hosea, God's ultimate "gift" is not barrenness, and the final reaction of God is not one of jealousy or anger. The only other multiple occurrence of the word "give" is in 11:8, where God admits that God cannot give Ephraim over to destruction in the manner of Sodom and Gomorrah because God's compassion overrules judgment.

The combined reference to "wombs" and "breasts" in 9:14 recalls the blessing of Jacob upon Joseph, the father of Ephraim, in Gen 49:25 ("By the God of your father, who will help you, by the Almighty who will bless you with blessings of heaven above, blessings of the deep that lies beneath, blessings of the breasts and of the womb"). Earlier, in Gen 49:22, Joseph is characterized as "a fruitful vine, a fruitful vine near a spring, whose branches climb over a wall," imagery also found in Hos 9:10-15. The promise of miscarrying wombs and dry breasts nullifies the patriarchal promises of fertility and becoming a great nation made to Abraham, Isaac, Jacob, and Ephraim (cf. Gen 48:1-20). In 9:16, the use of "fruit" (פרי/*pěrî*) functions as a pun of "Ephraim" (אפרים/

---

12. Deborah Krause, "A Blessing Cursed: The Prophet's Prayer for Barren Womb and Dry Breasts in Hosea 9," in *Reading Between Texts: Intertextuality and the Hebrew Bible* (ed. D. N. Fewell; Louisville: Westminster John Knox, 1992), pp. 191-202.

'eprayîm), but also serves as a metaphor for children and cherished offspring. The curse of 9:10-17 is a comprehensive annihilation of all living children and any hope of conceiving any new children. Hosea 9:11 denies the possibility of conception; Israel's days are numbered since it lacks the capacity to reproduce. Verse 12 indicates that YHWH will abandon the children currently within God's household, and v. 16 goes further by describing the slaughter of Israel's children. Since the creation of Israel was a miracle from the start, God's retraction of the Abrahamic promise suggests that the very continued existence of Israel as a people is a demonstration of the grace of God.

Yet like the double reversal of "giving," so too Hosea reverses the imprecation of barrenness. Krause observes that 14:8 [9] reasserts YHWH as the true source of Israel's fertility and upholds YHWH as the provider of Israel's fruitfulness through the declaration, "your fruitfulness (פרי/*pĕrî*) comes from me" (NIV).[13] In addition, when situated within the larger book, Hosea 9:10-17 does not provide the final word on the future of Israel's progeny. Not only do the concluding words of the book (Hos 14:4-8 [14:5-9]) indicate a hopeful future for Israel, but the book's opening chapter ends with an eschatological prophecy of the fulfillment of the Abrahamic promises of great progeny (1:10 [2:1]). One should not read 9:11-16 as a literal description of infanticide, but rather as the prophet's rhetorical challenge to Israel's understanding of its identity as the people of God. Israel is not entitled to election but rather is gifted with it. The concrete result of these judgment speeches is exile, as indicated in v. 17. Verse 17 ought not to be read as a judgment condemning Jews to a perpetual diaspora existence, in the manner of the "eternal Jew" interpretations.[14] Rather the word "wandering" (נדד/*nādad*) is better translated "flight," and is often used in conjunction with avian imagery. In the context of Hosea, this word ought to be understood as synonymous with "exile" (גלה/*gālāh*, cf. 10:5), and is likely employed because of the use of avian metaphor in 9:11.

The contrastive language of "hate" and "love" in 9:15 is not unusual in prophetic rhetoric (Isa 61:8; Ezek 16:37; Amos 5:15; Mic 3:2; Zech 8:17; Mal 1:2-3). Moran argues that the "love language" of Hosea is based upon the covenantal discourse of Deuteronomy, where love serves as a political term to signify fear, reverence, loyalty, service, obedience to law, and devotion from vassals to suzerains.[15]

---

13. Krause, "A Blessing Cursed," pp. 191-202.

14. See Hans Walter Wolff, *Hosea* (Hermeneia; Philadelphia: Fortress, 1974), p. 168; David Allan Hubbard, *Hosea: An Introduction & Commentary* (TOTC 22a; Downers Grove: InterVarsity, 1989), p. 169. See also the discussion in A. A. Macintosh, *A Critical and Exegetical Commentary on Hosea* (ICC; Edinburgh: T & T Clark, 1997), pp. 381-82.

15. William L. Moran, "The Ancient Near Eastern Background of the Love of God in Deuteronomy," *CBQ* 25 (1963): 77-87.

Lohfink, building upon Moran's thesis, argues that the language of hate in 9:15 condemns Ephraim for covenant disloyalty to YHWH as king.[16] He believes that the word "house" in 9:15 is a royal designation, and the reference to Gilgal alludes to the anointing of Saul as king at God's disapproval, and Saul's subsequent rejection as ruler. According to Lohfink, the language of hatred in 9:15 signals YHWH's rejection of Israel as God's covenant nation on account of their leaders seeking alliances with foreign powers. Ackerman adds that the term for "love" (אהב/*'āhab*) can be used interchangeably to describe personal and political relationships, because both assume hierarchical relationships where one party is superior to the other, whether he be a king, husband, or parent.[17] Sweeney observes that the words "to hate" (שׂנא/*śānāʾ*) and "drive out" (גרשׁ/*gāraš*) employed in 9:15 are technical terms to describe divorce. In the legislation regulating divorce in Deut 24:1-4, verse 3 states, "and the latter man hates (שׂנא/*śānāʾ*) her and writes her a certificate of divorce" (ESV). The root גרשׁ/*gāraš* is used to describe a divorced woman in Lev. 21:7, 14; 22:13; Num 30:9 [10]; and Ezek 44:22. In Ezek 23:29, Assyrian conquest is characterized by hatred and sexual humiliation in terminology similar to that of Hosea: "And they shall deal with you in hatred (שׂנא/*śānāʾ*), and take away all the fruit of your labor, and leave you naked and bare, and the nakedness (ערוה/*'erwâ*, cf. Hos 2:9 [11]) of your whorings (זנונים/*zěnûnîm*, cf. Hos 1:2 [2x]; 2:2 [2:4]; 2:4 [2:6]; 4:12; 5:4) shall be exposed (גלה/*gālāh*, cf. Hos 2:10[12])." In sum, God's hatred of Israel involves the dissolution of the covenant with Israel, with the possibility of Israel experiencing a violent conquest by foreigners, coupled with the implications of a divorce.

The language of love and hate signifies covenant election and rejection. As indicated in my introduction, the themes of marriage and divorce unify the Twelve Prophets and feature prominently within its bookends, Hosea and Malachi. In fact, the last book of the Twelve begins with the language of love and hate: "I have loved you, says the LORD. But you say, 'How have you loved us?' Is not Esau Jacob's brother? says the LORD. Yet I have loved (אהב/*'āhab*) Jacob but I have hated (שׂנא/*śānāʾ*) Esau; I have made his hill country a desolation and his heritage a desert for jackals" (Mal 1:2-3). Hill observes that the phrase "yet I have loved Jacob" in 1:2 implies an ongoing emotional response, and finds its closest parallel in the first book of the Twelve Prophets, in Hos 11:1, "When Israel was a child, I loved him."[18] Malachi, writing in the postexilic period, reminds Israel that God's love has not wavered, even as the people experienced

16. Norbert Lohfink, "Hate and Love in Osee 9:15," *CBQ* 25 (1963): 417.

17. Susan Ackerman, "The Personal Is Political: Covenantal and Affectionate Love ('ĀHÊB, 'AHĂBÂ) in the Hebrew Bible," *VT* 52 (2002): 437-58.

18. Andrew E. Hill, *Malachi: A New Translation with Introduction and Commentary* (AB 25C; New York: Doubleday, 1998), p. 150.

the collapse of the monarchy and the exile. Even though the language of hate in Hos 9:15 suggests that God divorces Israel and will inflict violence upon the nation, Malachi reverses such a notion when God declares, "For I hate (שׂנא/ *śānaʾ*) divorce, says the LORD, the God of Israel, and covering one's garment with violence (חמס/*ḥāmās*), says the LORD of hosts" (Mal 2:16). The final word of the Twelve Prophets is not one of hatred but rather of love, and likewise the final chapter of Hosea ends with YHWH's promise, "I will love them freely, for my anger has turned from them" (Hos 14:4 [14:5]). From the first book of the Twelve Prophets to its last, the prophets declare that God is love.

Hosea 10:1-15

The next unit opens with an image of Israel that appears to be in stark contrast to the barren and childless Israel of the previous chapter. The prophet employs the metaphor of a vine, which, because of its ability to produce wine, evokes notions of national prominence and prosperity. The agricultural motifs of grapes in a wilderness (9:10) and a young palm tree (9:13) are recalled by this reference. Eidevall suggests that the vine's vigorous growth and productivity "almost sounds like a piece of chauvinistic panegyric,"[19] given the author's propensity to privilege maleness. Even so, the prophet subverts the notion of virile masculinity, since the word used to describe the vine as "luxuriant" (בקק/ *bāqaq*) in 10:1 can also be translated "damaged" or "ravaged" (NJPS). Israel possesses damaged goods; the only fruit it can produce are altars and pillars that increase its guilt (10:1-2). Earlier, in 8:11, Hosea sarcastically associated the multiplication of altars with the proliferation of sin. In Hos 10:1 he revisits this theme, and in 10:2 he announces the destruction of these altars and pillars. The destruction of "pillars" (מצבות/*maṣṣēbôt*) recalls the disciplinary action of 3:4, in which Israel will remain without king, prince, sacrifice, pillar, ephod, or teraphim for many days.

The people are faulted in 10:2 for possessing hearts that are false. The phrase literally means, "their heart is smooth, slippery." The verb חלק/*ḥālaq* suggests dishonesty and divided allegiance, and it is oftentimes used to describe flattering and manipulative speech. Sweeney observes that Gen 27:11 describes Israel's eponymous ancestor Jacob as a "smooth man" (איש חלק/*ʾîš ḥālāq*), and the phrase also describes the character of this duplicitous patriarch in the Genesis narratives.[20] The name "Jacob" first appears in Hosea in 10:11, and it will

19. Eidevall, *Grapes in the Desert*, p. 156.
20. Sweeney, *The Twelve Prophets*, 1:103.

feature prominently in 12:2, 12 [3, 13]. Sweeney suggests that the verb שׁוה/*šāwâ*, from the phrase "yields its fruit" in 10:1, may possess a double entendre due to its similarity to שׁוא/*šāw'*, which expresses "emptiness" and "vanity," as in Exod 20:7: "You shall not take the name of the LORD your God in vain" (ESV).[21] If Sweeney is correct, Hosea 10:4 elaborates on the false heart of Israel when it characterizes Israel's speech as mere words and its oaths as empty or vain (שׁ וא/*šāw'*). The lesson Israel needs to learn is that words are never merely words. Oaths are either true or false, and whereas an honest oath demonstrates a promise, a dishonest oath is a form of self-imprecation.[22]

Given that Israel is deemed untrustworthy in 10:2 and 10:4, it is difficult to decipher Israel's comments concerning the monarchy in 10:3. Unsurprisingly, numerous attempts have been made to identify a historical referent to the dual mention of kings. The admission, "We have no king," if true, could describe the turbulent period between 749 and 732, which was marked by the assassinations of Zechariah, Shallum, Pekahiah, and Pekah. Or, if "a king — what can he do for us" refers to the impotence of an Israelite monarch because of his submission as a vassal to Assyria, then scholars locate this text within the reigns of Jehu, Menahem, or Hoshea. Given the mention of the "great king" in 10:6, Hos 10:3c may also criticize covenants made with, or tribute paid to, the Assyrian king. Based upon the generic character of the writings, Freedman and Andersen suggest that the reference is to the divine king, and the subsequent admission "we do not fear the LORD" is a parallel statement.[23] Given the lack of historic specificity and the typological and transhistorical character of the prophecy, Ben Zvi correctly argues that "the lack of a king cannot refer only to Hoshea's capture and the downfall of the northern kingdom, but also to their own situation, to their being without a king, and implicitly to the downfall of the last Judahite monarch."[24] Earlier, in 3:4, Hosea announced that Israel would remain many days without a Davidic king. Read within the immediate context of chapter 10, v. 3 reflects the despair the people of Israel experienced due to foreign domination and corrupt politicians. Israel's powerlessness to Assyrian kings is an act of judgment and discipline stemming from Israel's failure to fear the LORD. Yet when read within the context of the whole book, 10:3 resonates with an exilic or postexilic audience who have lost hope in the restoration of the Davidic monarchy.

21. Sweeney, *The Twelve Prophets*, 1:103.

22. Dearman, *Book of Hosea*, p. 263.

23. Francis I. Andersen and David Noel Freedman, *Hosea* (AB 24; New York: Doubleday, 1980), p. 553.

24. Ben Zvi, *Hosea*, p. 215. I would not attribute the text to the literati of Yehud in the same manner as Ben Zvi; otherwise his point is well taken.

Hosea 10:5-8 focuses on the idolatrous practices of the Samaritans at Bethel. Once again (cf. 4:15; 5:8), the prophet sarcastically refers to Bethel, the "House of God," as Beth-Aven, the "House of Iniquity," or in the vernacular, "Sin City." The Samaritans are condemned for the reverence and devotion shown to the calves at Bethel (10:5) as well as the idolatry practiced at the high places in the same location (10:8). Chung argues that Jeroboam's use of the calves in 1 Kgs 12 was not idolatrous in nature. He believes they initially served as the footstool upon which YHWH stood, and in this manner functioned much like the cherubs on the ark. Chung suggests that, during the 8th century, syncretism between the worship of YHWH and Baal increased, resulting in the Israelites beginning to identify the calf with Baal.[25] For the readership of the book, the earlier reference to the calf in 8:6 evokes the sin of Sinai as well as Jeroboam, and in 10:5, the mention of "the glory that has departed from it" recalls the loss of the ark to the Philistines in 1 Sam 4:22 ("She said, 'The glory has departed from Israel, for the ark of God has been captured'"). Ben Zvi interprets the feminine form of "heifer" (עגלה/*'eglāh*) in 10:5 as an intentional feminization of the male deity in an attempt to polemicize and deride Baal worship. The reference to a calf at Samaria in 8:6 is unusual, yet if the mention of the king of Samaria in 10:7 refers not to a monarch but rather to the calf itself, then both texts suggest the demise of calf worship. Although the specific king is not mentioned, 10:6 indicates that the Assyrian "king who contends" (מלך ירב/*melek yārēb*), previously mentioned in 5:13, will seize the calf as tribute and transport it to Assyria. In this event, Samaria's "glory" departs (10:5; cf. 9:11) and it exchanges its glory for shame (10:6; cf. 4:7).

The reference to the "days of Gibeah" in 10:9 is difficult to identify precisely. Some have suggested that it, along with the mention of Gilgal in 9:15, is to be associated with the establishment of the monarchy under Saul. Gibeah is Saul's hometown (1 Sam 10:26; 15:34), and features prominently in the narratives that describe Saul's rise to power, as well as God's rejection of his anointing in 1 Sam 10–15. Gilgal is known as the locale where Saul failed in obedience and Samuel pronounced God's rejection of his kingship in 1 Sam 13–15. The failure of Israel's kings, and the people's complicity in their downfall, are prominent themes throughout chapters 7–10. If 10:3 is interpreted as Israel's rejection of YHWH as king and 10:15 represents God's desire to rid Israel of its human monarchs, then 10:9 may identify Israel's sin with the establishment of the monarchy.

25. Youn Ho Chung, *The Sin of the Calf: The Rise of the Bible's Negative Attitude Toward the Golden Calf* (LHBOTS 523; New York: T & T Clark International, 2010). Chung observes a clear progression in Canaanite glyptic art from a young bull ridden by a storm god, to a bull carrying only lightning bolts, to a bull with nothing on its back. Chung believes a similar development took place with regard to YHWH, Baal, and the calf.

The other suggestion is to associate the "days of Gibeah" with the violence perpetrated by the inhabitants of Gibeah against the Levite's concubine, and the ensuing war against Benjamin that nearly extinguished the tribe, as told in Judg 19–21. Although the terms are not exactly the same, in both instances war is waged against the "sons of anarchy" (בני עלוה/*běnê ʿalwāh,* Hos 10:9; cf. בני־בליעל/*běnê běliyyaʿal* in Judg 19:22; 20:13). The text of 10:9 is difficult to translate. Interpreting 10:9c as an interrogative, "Shall not war overtake them in Gibeah?" (NRSV), carries no grammatical basis, so it is better to read the phrase as a simple statement, "the war against the sons of iniquity did not overtake them in Gibeah."[26] The mention of war in 10:9 and the "the nations gathering against them" conjures up the memories of all Israel assembling together to fight against Benjamin in Judg 20:1-2. Just as the story in Judges takes place in the backdrop of the absence of kingship (Judg 19:1; 21:25), so too does Hosea address a situation involving the failure of the monarchy (Hos 10:3). Hosea identifies Israel with the scoundrels of Gibeah, the rebellious tribe of Benjamin, and possibly the failed reign of Saul. Because of Israel's double iniquity (10:10), Ephraim will be chastised through war, yet in this case the foreign nations will be the instrument of God. But just as Benjamin was punished but not extinguished in the Judges narrative, Israel need not ultimately despair at the words of the prophet. Hosea will go on to describe the components of true repentance in the following verses. Hosea 10:9-10 instructs that genuine repentance involves claiming one's sinful ancestry rather than distancing oneself from it. Whitewashing the past atrocities of individuals, communities, and nations only forestalls the process of restoration.

In Hosea 10:11-13a, the prophet employs agricultural metaphors to exhort the people to repent. Whereas Hosea earlier compared Israel to a stubborn heifer (4:16), the prophet now recalls a nostalgic past when Ephraim was a trained heifer. The metaphor of Israel as a cow further disrupts any sacred associations with the calves at Bethel mentioned in 10:5-6. Rather than translate עברתי על/*ʿābartî ʿal* in 10:11 as "pass over" or "spare" (NRSV), Hos 10:11b reads "I passed by her good neck." The phrase recalls 9:10a, which describes how YHWH discovered something valuable in Israel in its early days.[27] In 9:10, 10:11, and later in 11:1, the prophet recalls how promising Israel was at its initial election, which is a far cry from the present reality. Commentators have puzzled over the collocation of Ephraim, Judah, and Jacob in 10:11, and have proposed various historical and editorial explanations for this seemingly anachronistic

---

26. Sweeney, *The Twelve Prophets,* 1:109. Cf. Macintosh, *Hosea,* pp. 411-12.

27. Eidevall, *Grapes in the Desert,* p. 160. He translates the phrase, "I passed by the beauty of her neck."

combination. Certainly, editorial activity may have been involved, but the text underscores the transhistorical and typological nature of the prophecy.

Whereas God is depicted as a farmer and Israel as a beast of burden in 8:10, in 10:11c-13b the metaphor switches so that now Israel takes on the role of farmer. In 10:12 Israel is called to sow righteousness (צדקה/ṣĕdāqāh) and reap steadfast love (חסד/ḥesed), and in return, God will rain righteousness back to them. Both terms are listed among the characteristics of YHWH's renewed marriage with the woman in 2:19 [21]. In 4:1 the prophet remarks that faithfulness, steadfast love (חסד/ḥesed), and the knowledge of God are completely absent from the land. In 6:4 Israel's חסד/ḥesed is deemed ephemeral, and in 6:6 YHWH makes clear that God desires steadfast love and the knowledge of God rather than cultic sacrifices. The call for Israel in 10:12 to seek steadfast love and righteousness evokes the earlier passages (in 4:1; 6:4, 6) that describe the absence of these qualities in Israel. In order to experience the eschatological promises of 2:19 [21], Israel is called upon to pursue steadfast love and righteousness in the present. Whereas earlier in 6:3 Israel presumed YHWH would come (בוא/bô') like the spring rains, in 10:12 the prophet calls upon Israel to seek the LORD so "that he may come (בוא/bô') and rain righteousness upon you." Hosea repeatedly describes the covenant relationship as a reciprocal one. Rather than sow steadfast love and righteousness, Hos 10:13 indicates that Israel has ploughed wickedness and reaped injustice instead. The remainder of chapter 10 goes on to describe how Israel reaps what it sows. Yet when read within the context of the book, Hosea presents a radical message of grace, since in 2:19-21 [2:21-23] YHWH promises to wed Israel and the land in righteousness, justice, steadfast love, mercy, and faithfulness, and instill the knowledge of the LORD. Although Ephraim is called upon to sow in 10:12, ultimately it is YHWH who will sow Israel for God's own sake (זרע/zāraʿ, 10:12; cf. 2:23 [25]).

As noted in my introduction, God sowing is not only a major theme in the book of Hosea but also in the Twelve Prophets. In Hos 10 this motif has less to do with the land and agriculture and instead functions as a metaphor for ethical instruction. In this regard, Hos 10 bears great affinity with the prophecy of Amos. Both prophets utilize agricultural and fertility metaphors, make sarcastic references to Bethel, mention Sodom and Gomorrah/Admah and Zeboiim, and threaten exile. Dearman observes that the terms "justice" (משפט/mišpāt) and "poisonous weeds" (ראש/rō'š) in 10:4 — "And justice degenerates into poison weeds" (NJPS) — also occur in Amos 6:12: "But you have turned justice (משפט/mišpāt) into poison (ראש/rō'š) and the fruit (פרי/pĕrî) of righteousness (צדקה/ṣĕdāqāh) into wormwood."[28] In addition, the term "fruit" (פרי/pĕrî) appears

28. Dearman, *Book of Hosea*, pp. 264-65.

in Hos 9:16; 10:1 (2x), 13; 14:9, and "righteousness" (צדקה/*ṣĕdāqāh*) occurs in 10:12. Of the seven occurrences of the verb "to seek" (דרש/*dāraš*) in the Twelve Prophets, four of them occur in Amos 5 (vv. 4, 5, 6, 14) and one in Hos 10:12. For the reader of the Twelve Prophets, Hosea's call to "seek the LORD" through just living (Hos 10:12) is not merely a suggestion for Israel, but carries the urgency and force of Amos' threefold cry, "Seek good and not evil, that you may live" (Amos 5:14; cf. 5:4).

This section ends in Hos 10:13c-15 with a critique of militarism and a prophecy of impending, devastating conquest. Hosea 10:13 criticizes Israel for trusting in its own "way" (דרך/*derek*, NJPS), a reference likely to Israel's political strategies. Israel's "way" is to seek solutions through the proliferation of warriors and fortresses; yet as already indicated in 8:14, YHWH considers militarization a rejection of God's care for the people. In 10:14, Hosea recalls Israel's utter inability to withstand Assyrian power at Beth-arbel's defeat, when they had to witness the murder of mothers and children. The historical referent for v. 14 cannot be determined since the location of Beth-arbel cannot be verified. It may be associated with Shalmanesser V, who is mentioned in 2 Kgs 17:3 and 18:9, or it may be a nonspecific memory of war in general. While certainly the death of mothers and children would horrify any people, such a prophecy also threatened the very heart of God's covenant promises to Abraham.

In the face of constant threat by the Assyrians and subsequent empires, Hosea's call for Israel to relinquish its diplomatic and militaristic efforts in order to secure national security must have been received with utter incredulity. In this regard, ancient Israel is no different than countries today, where altar and fortress, religion and militarism, and worship and war are two sides of the same coin, working in tandem to advance national interests. Hosea provides a critique of civil religion, particularly when military power is used to maintain it. The North American church continues to face the challenge of American ideologies, such as exceptionalism, messianism,[29] and zealous nationalism,[30] which run counter to the scriptural narratives of the kingdom of God. Rather than expose and subvert these myths, oftentimes the church propagates civil religion motivated out of its own political and economic interests. The stakes are much higher for the church in countries like the U.S. where the military threat is not from without but rather within.

---

29. See Michael J. Gorman, *Reading Revelation Responsibly: Uncivil Worship and Witness* (Eugene: Cascade Books, 2011), pp. 44-56.

30. See Robert Jewett and John Shelton Lawrence, *Captain America and the Crusade against Evil: The Dilemma of Zealous Nationalism* (Grand Rapids: Eerdmans, 2003). In this book, Jewett and Lawrence provide a reading of Hosea's critique of the mystique of violence (see pp. 261-69).

11. Hosea 11:1-11

Bo H. Lim

As indicated in our introduction, Hos 11:1-11 concludes the second major unit of the book, Hos 4:1–11:11, with a message of hope. The previous section of this unit, Hos 10:1-15, concludes with the pronouncement of impending warfare for Ephraim, and its devastating effects upon Israel's cities, people, and king. While Hos 11:1-11 lacks salvation pronouncements, its hopeful message lies in the fact that YHWH renounces his decision to destroy the people. While Hosea is known for its difficult Hebrew, chapter 11 is particularly notorious for its fragmentation of speech, unintelligible phrases, and confounding metaphors. Many have surmised that this "artful incoherence"[1] results from its emotionally-charged contents, and possibly the unstable disposition of the prophet. Despite the difficult language, the main thrust of the message remains clear.

As in 9:10, 13; 10:1, 11, Hos 11:1-2 recalls the hope associated with the initial election of Israel, which later resulted in great disappointment. In 11:1 Israel is called a "child" or "youth" (נער/*na'ar*), which places God in the role of parent and describes Israel's deep dependence upon YHWH from the outset. Hosea 11:1 makes clear that the relationship is characterized by love (אהב/*'āhab*), a term that describes hierarchical relationships and is associated with Israel's unmerited election (cf. Deut 4:37; 7:7-8).[2] Since love functions as a dominant theme within the chapter (cf. 11:4), particularly with God's declaration of his compassion in 11:8, God's love ought to be understood as laden with pathos. The word נער can also describe a servant under the authority of a master and, given the mention of Egypt in v. 1, it also suggests Israel's pitiable state prior to its redemption through the exodus.

The phrase "I called my son" (קראתי לבני/*qārā'tî libnî*) conveys God's act

1. J. L. McKenzie, "Divine Passion in Osee," *CBQ* 17 (1955): 287-89.
2. See commentary on 9:15.

168

of summoning Israel from Egypt. In this regard, Hos 11:1 resembles Exod 4:22 — "Thus says the LORD: Israel is my firstborn son" — since both texts associate the nation's sonship with the exodus event. In addition, the language "call my son" may signify the appointment of a royal figure, as commonly understood in the ANE. In the OT, God claims to be a father to David (2 Sam 7:14), and to the Messianic ruler YHWH announces, "You are my son, today I have begotten you" (Ps 2:7). Commentators have suggested that the extension of the sonship language to the nation in Hos 11:1 democratizes royal identity.[3] Such a view is unlikely, given that God's punishment to Israel is to remove its king (10:15) and its national hopes are for the reestablishment of the Davidic monarchy (3:5). It is more likely that this passage recalls a period prior to the establishment of the monarchy where Israel as a nation was granted royal status, and this role would later be centralized in the Davidic king. In the LXX, Hos 11:1 reads, "Out of Egypt I have called *his children* (τὰ τέκνα αὐτοῦ/*ta tekna autou*)" rather than "my son." The Greek text lacks any Messianic connotations, so it is no wonder that the author of Matthew follows the Hebrew in his quotation of Hos 11:1 in Matt 2:15, "Out of Egypt I have called my son (τὸν υἱόν μου/*ton huion mou*)."

The majority of translations, including the NRSV, emend the first verb of 11:2, "they called" (קראו/*qār'û*), to "I called," particularly since the verb appears at the end of v. 1. Yet this change is unnecessary since "they called" makes for an intelligible reading. "They called" and "they went" function as a word pair, and since Egypt is named in v. 1, the phrase may serve as a modified repetition of 7:11, "they call upon Egypt, they go to Assyria." In addition, the "they" within the larger context of the book of Hosea could be understood as the prophets sent by God to both deliver and judge the people. Later, in 12:10 [12:11], Hosea announces, "I spoke to the prophets; it was I who multiplied visions, and through the prophets I will bring destruction," and in 12:13 [12:14], he says, "By a prophet the LORD brought Israel up from Egypt, and by a prophet he was guarded." Both Israel's calling into sonship and the Davidic monarch's anointing as king were mediated through God's prophets, Moses and Samuel, respectively. The connection is clear: God's calling comes in the form of the prophets' calling. Unfortunately for Israel, though the prophets called the people, the people departed from YHWH. While Hosea will speak of Israel literally going/walking to Egypt or Assyria in 11:5, v. 2 defines their "going" into idolatry and sacrifices made to Baals.

Nissinen observes similar structure, themes, and vocabulary between the opening words of the Decalogue and Hos 11:1-2:[4]

---

3. E.g., Ehud Ben Zvi, *Hosea* (FOTL 21A; Grand Rapids: Eerdmans, 2005), pp. 233-34.
4. Martti Nissinen, *Prophetie, Redaktion und Fortschreibung im Hoseabuch: Studien zum*

Exodus 20:2-5	Hosea 11:1-2
I am the LORD your God, **who brought you**	When Israel was a child, **I loved him**
out of the land of Egypt, out of the house of slavery	and **out of Egypt** I called my son
you shall have no other gods before me	The more [they] called them, **the more they went from me**
You shall not make for yourself **an idol**	they kept sacrificing to **the Baals**
You shall not **bow down to them or worship them**	and **offering incense** to idols

Since the words are not reproduced verbatim, Nissinen does not argue for direct literary dependence, but he does believe a prior version of the Decalogue may have influenced the author of Hosea. If Nissinen is correct, then Hos 11 is but one more example[5] that the Law and Prophets ought to be read conjointly. When read in light of the canon, the covenant violations of Israel described in Hosea are also those revealed in Mosaic Torah.

The language and metaphors in Hos 11:3-4 are difficult to decipher. Eidevall denies the presence of a parental motif in these verses, instead arguing that a shepherd metaphor unifies these texts. He finds that the translation of the *hapax* תרגלתי/*tirgalti* as "I taught to walk" lacks merit, and instead suggests that the verb describes guiding activity. He emends the reference "his arms," to "my arms," and translates v. 3 as "But I, I led the way for Ephraim, I carried them on my arms." According to this reading, rather than a fatherhood metaphor, Hos 11:3 employs a shepherd metaphor in the manner of Isa 40:11 ("He will feed his flock like a shepherd; he will gather the lambs in his arms, and carry them in his bosom, and gently lead the mother sheep"). Eidevall believes that readings suggesting that God takes the role of father, with Israel as prodigal son, find "more textual support in Luke 15 than in Hosea 11."[6]

Yet considerable evidence exists to argue that the metaphor of God as mother and father appears in Hos 11. Recent versions such as the NRSV and

---

Werdegang eines Prophetenbuches im Lichte von Hos 4 und 11 (AOAT 231; Neukirchen-Vluyn: Neukirchener Verlagsgesellschaft, 1991), pp. 321-22.

5. See the commentary on 4:1-2.

6. Göran Eidevall, *Grapes in the Desert: Metaphors, Models, and Themes in Hosea 4-14* (ConBOT 43; Stockholm: Almqvist & Wiksell International, 1996), p. 179, n. 82.

the CEB follow the suggestion to emend עֹל/ʿōl "yoke" to עוּל/עֹל/ʿul / ʿûl "infant, suckling," and translate 11:4, "I was to them like those who lift infants to their cheeks. I bent down to them and fed them" (NRSV). Nissinen observes that Neo-Assyrian oracles and ANE iconography commonly portrayed goddesses as mothers or wet-nurses to the king, who was depicted as a child or even a suckling. He observes the following common motifs between Neo-Assyrian prophecy and Hos 11:1-4: 1) the divine love for a child; 2) the child's designation as son of God; 3) the nursing of the child; 4) the rearing of the child; 5) the carrying of the child upon the arms.[7] Melnyk examines ANE adoption formulas and concludes that Hosea possesses the same declarative statements regarding adoption, as well as similar stipulations for raising a child, providing an inheritance, and punishing a rebellious child.[8] The expression "human cords" (בחבלי אדם/běḥablê ʾādām) in v. 4 can be understood as "bonds of friendship"[9] and signify parental guidance. The word חבל/ḥēbel appears on only one other occasion in Hosea, in 13:13, and there it refers to labor pains. For this reason, Sweeney translates 11:4, "with human labor pains, I drew them out."[10] The parental metaphor finds further support if YHWH's conflicted emotions, which are expressed in 11:8-9, arise out of an inability to punish Israel in the manner instructed by Deut 21:18-21. This passage prescribes the stoning to death of a son who repeatedly rebels against his father and mother. If this legislation serves as the subtext for Hos 11:8-9, then the metaphor of an anguished parent over a disobedient child applies to this text.

From ancient times to modern, Matt 2:15 has been cited as an occasion where purportedly "Matthew Twists the Scriptures."[11] Jerome claims that Julian the Apostate (4th c.) commented concerning Matt 2:15, "What is written of Israel, the Evangelist Matthew has transferred to Christ, in order that he might make a laughing stock of the ignorance of those who from among the Gentiles had believed."[12] In addition to the Messianic features of Hosea 11 mentioned above, the passage bears similarities to other ANE royal prophecies. Parpola

---

7. Nissinen, *Prophetie, Redaktion und Fortschreibung im Hoseabuch*, p. 290.

8. Janet L. R. Melnyk, "When Israel Was a Child: Ancient Near Eastern Adoption Formulas and the Relationship between God and Israel," in *History and Interpretation: Essays in Honour of John H. Hayes* (ed. M. P. Graham, W. P. Brown, and J. K. Kuan; JSOTSup 173; Sheffield: JSOT Press, 1993), pp. 245-59.

9. A. A. Macintosh, *A Critical and Exegetical Commentary on Hosea* (ICC; Edinburgh: T & T Clark, 1997), p. 446.

10. Marvin A. Sweeney, *The Twelve Prophets* (2 vols.; Berit Olam; Collegeville: Liturgical Press, 2000), 1:114.

11. S. Vernon McCasland, "Matthew Twists the Scriptures," *JBL* 80 (1961): 143-48.

12. Jerome, *In Osee* III.xi.1-2; CCSL 76: 121-22. I wish to thank my colleague Steve Perisho for his assistance in identifying and translating these Latin sources.

observes the similarities between Hos 11 and Neo-Assyrian prophecies regarding Esarhaddon's unprecedented triumphant rise to power against all odds. He describes Esarhaddon as a savior king, refers to him as "messianic," and draws a comparison between the prophecies concerning both Esarhaddon and Jesus.[13] While readers such as McCasland may be scandalized by Matthew applying to Jesus a prophecy concerning Israel, they fail to realize that Hos 11 possesses numerous Messianic features. It seems Matthew never twisted the Scriptures after all. Jerome observes that the prophecy is typologically fulfilled in Christ in the following manner, " 'Israel was a child, and I loved him, and out of Egypt I have called my son' is assuredly said of the people of Israel, which in that time, after the error of idolatry, is summoned somewhat like an infant or a child; yet it perfectly refers to Christ."[14]

While one can read a metaphor of a toddler and suckling child in vv. 3-4 because of the ambiguous Hebrew, one can also observe an animal husbandry metaphor in these verses. The verb תרגלתי/*tirgaltî* "taught to walk" (NRSV) in v. 3 is the only occurrence of the *Tiphel* form of רגל/*rāgal,* which in noun form means "foot." Andersen and Freedman interpret the verb as leading or guiding along a way.[15] If one does not emend עֹל/*ōl* "yoke" in v. 4, then both verses depict YHWH as one who harnesses Israel (in this case a heifer rather than child) and leads it to fodder. While the designations of "cords" with "human kindness" and "bands" with "love" in 11:4 appear nonsensical, if understood as descriptions of a relationship between human and beast, they communicate the magnanimous attitude of a farmer gently training his livestock. Given the reference to Ephraim as a trained heifer in 10:11, this imagery would make sense to the reader.

The difficult Hebrew continues in Hos 11:5-7. Commentators have been puzzled by the particle "not" (לֹא/*lō'*) that opens v. 5, since 8:13 and 9:3 explicitly state that Ephraim will return to Egypt. Scholars have been quick to emend the text, as in the case of the LXX's "Ephraim settled in Egypt," or posit a historical scenario such as 2 Kgs 17:4, when Hoshea sought help from the king of Egypt only to be disciplined by the king of Assyria for his treachery. It does appear that v. 5a ought to be understood in a contrastive manner to 5b, so the negative particle "not" ought to be maintained. Since 10:15 announced that the king of Israel would be cut off, 11:5 appears to function as a follow-up, announcing that Assyria's king would rule in his place. Whereas Hosea earlier threatened a return to Egypt and suggested little differentiation between the two foreign

13. Simo Parpola, *Assyrian Prophecies* (State Archives of Assyria 9; Helsinki: Helsinki University Press, 1997), pp. 42-44.

14. Jerome, *In Osee* III.xi.1-2; CCSL 76: 121-22.

15. Francis I. Andersen and David Noel Freedman, *Hosea* (AB 24; New York: Doubleday, 1980), p. 579.

threats in 9:3, he now definitively identifies Israel's oppressor as Assyria, which will be corroborated by history. In contrast to the nurturing care of YHWH (cf. 11:3-4), 11:6 indicates that the rule of the king of Assyria will be characterized by violence and domination. The language of devouring (אכל/*'ākal*) in 11:6 first appears in Hosea with reference to the woman's horticultural greenery in 2:12 [14], and later describes how Israel and Judah's cities would be devoured (8:14). In Hosea and the rest of the Twelve, this language of devouring frequently describes Israel's mistreatment of others and the consequent judgment to fall on the people and the land.

Hosea 11:11 has puzzled interpreters because it names both Egypt and Assyria as the starting point for Israel's migration back to the land. Perhaps the best solution to this discrepancy is simply for readers to admit that the text is ambiguous. Hoffman wonders how Hosea arrived at the notion that a return to Egypt would serve as a national punishment when the Bible lacks any tradition that viewed slavery as a punishment for Israel. He observes that Hosea lacks historical specificity and concludes, "His [Hosea's] belief that the exodus had been a typological event stimulated the idea that the renewal of the broken covenant would be impossible unles [sic] a new exodus occurred, and since a new slavery in Egypt was a necessary logical precondition to a new exodus, he reached then the inevitable conclusion that the people's punishment should be to return to Egypt."[16] Hoffman describes typological interpretation as thoroughly theological, since a return to Egypt lacks any correspondence to the political situation of Hosea's day. Exile in Egypt instead corresponds to Israel's national myth and reflects Hosea's theological outlook on the future of God's people. In this regard, typology "demands generalization rather than specification which blurs the unique historical details in order to make the core of the tradition more flexible and adaptable to changing historical situations."[17] Since the prophecy in Hos 11:10-11 is eschatological, it is all the more likely to function in a typological manner and need not possess a historical referent. Hosea's announcement of an eschatological ingathering of the people from among the nations, in particular from Egypt and Assyria, is corroborated by the prophecies of Isaiah (cf. 11:11, 16; 19:23-25). In Hosea's case, as well as in Isaiah, these prophecies lack historical precedence, but that need not require emending the text in an attempt to harmonize it with Israel's other narratives. Macintosh observes that ibn Ezra also understands the reference to Egypt as a prelude to a return to the land; he therefore reads the prophecy "they should not return to

---

16. Yair Hoffman, "A North Israelite Typological Myth and a Judean Historical Tradition: The Exodus in Hosea and Amos," *VT* 39 (1989): 175.

17. Hoffman, "A North Israelite Typological Myth," p. 176.

the land of Egypt" in Hos 11:5 as a form of judgment that prevents Israel from initiating a process that would eventuate in a New Exodus.[18]

When interpreting Hos 11:8-9, one ought to pay attention not merely to its contents but also to its rhetorical form. The fascinating and puzzling aspect of this passage is that God speaks in the interrogative. The particle "how" (איך/*'êk*) occurs twice in 11:8 but is implied in the first four phrases: "How can I give you up, Ephraim? How can I hand you over, O Israel? How can I make you like Admah? How can I treat you like Zeboiim?" The word "how" is an expression of bewilderment and grief,[19] and it occurs rather infrequently among the Prophets, with the exception of Jeremiah, in which it occurs 17 times. In Jer 9:7 it appears in a manner similar to that of Hos 11:8: "Therefore thus says the LORD of hosts: I will now refine and test them, for what else [איך/*'êk*] can I do with my sinful people?" Interpretations that assume that this question is existential as opposed to rhetorical, and conclude that a transformation *in* God occurs in these verses, collapse the categorical differences between creator and creation.[20] Hosea 11:9 is emphatic in maintaining ontological distinctions between God and humanity: "for I am God and no mortal, the Holy One in your midst." As Castelo observes, only when these differences are honored can meaningful dialogue and authentic relationship occur between these parties.

Hosea 11:8 is written in poetic form, where Ephraim is set in parallel relationship with Admah, and Israel with Zeboiim. In Genesis, Admah and Zeboiim are located in the same region as Sodom and Gomorrah and associated in the same sinful activities (10:19; 14:2, 8). The author of Deut 29:23 [22] groups these cities together when he recalls "the destruction of Sodom and Gomorrah, Admah and Zeboiim, which the LORD destroyed in his fierce anger." Sodom and Gomorrah function as archetypes for a wicked society throughout the Old Testament, and therefore the mention of Admah and Zeboiim in Hos 11:8 both condemns Israel and also justifies God's decision to destroy Ephraim.

Hosea 11:8 describes God as having a "change of heart," or, interpreted literally, "my heart is overturned upon me" (נהפך עלי לבי/*nehpak 'ālay libbî*). Semantics and structure are closely linked, and since this phrase is set in a parallel relationship with the clause "all my compassion is aroused," these phrases ought to be understood as mutually glossing. Viewed in this manner, the language does not provide a precise description of the internal mind of God; rather it

18. Macintosh, *Hosea*, p. 451.

19. Macintosh, *Hosea*, p. 459.

20. J. Gerald Janzen, "Metaphor and Reality in Hosea 11," *Semeia* 24 (1982): 7-44. See the response by James L. Mays, "Response to Janzen: 'Metaphor and Reality in Hosea 11,'" *Semeia* 24 (1982): 45-51.

highlights the intense emotions involved in YHWH's decision to withdraw judgment from Ephraim. Several translations insert the word "again" in 11:9 so that it reads, "I will not *again* destroy Ephraim" (e.g., NRSV, ESV), even though the Hebrew contains no such adverb. Such emendations are likely based upon a desire to harmonize the passage with Assyria's conquest of Samaria in 722. Others date the text earlier and suggest that Ephraim was granted amnesty for the time being by the announcement of 11:8-9. They go on to propose that this decision was later reversed when Ephraim once again fell into sin, and Hos 13:7-8 was spoken to overturn YHWH's prior commitment, not to destroy Israel. Historical markers are absent in Hos 11, and the text is full of historical typologies with an eschatological outlook in mind, so it is most likely that the text is to be read in a trans-temporal manner.[21] Hosea 11 recalls the larger story of Israel, from its beginnings out of Egypt (vv. 1-4) to God's unfailing commitment to its preservation (8-9) and future restoration (10-11). Rather than introduce chapters 12–13, Hos 11:1-11 concludes the section chapters 4–11; therefore, Hos 13:7-8 ought not to be understood as a reversal of 11:8-9. Instead, Hos 4–11 demonstrates a movement away from Israel's present apostasy toward a renewed relationship with God in the future.

McKenzie observes that the description of God's holiness in 11:9 does not correspond to that of Num 23:19 and 1 Sam 15:29, both of which define holiness as God's unchanging nature. In Hosea God possesses conflicted emotions, and the prophet does not consider such activity a violation of the holiness of God. In this case, God's holiness does not mean that YHWH is not impassioned; rather it means that God is "set apart" from humans such that God is never overcome by rage. McKenzie writes that Hosea "has described a conflict of passions in YHWH, a conflict in which love moderates anger, as it does in man; but because YHWH is God and not man, His anger will never become a blind rage, His love will never curdle to hatred and the impulse to destroy."[22] The God of Israel is not unemotional, but unlike humans, God is never overcome by emotion, particularly anger, such that the Holy One will act irrationally or unjustly.

Ultimately, texts that speak of the im/passibility of God in the Old Testament highlight the dual features of covenant and election in Israel's dynamic relationship with God, as Castelo has discussed earlier. Moberly describes the tensions that the Scriptures maintain with regard to this relationship:

21. Ben Zvi, *Hosea*, p. 238.

22. McKenzie, "Divine Passion in Osee," p. 291. Yet McKenzie will go on to argue that Hos 11:8-9 represents God's penultimate response. According to him, the rest of Hosea's prophecy demonstrates that God's final choice is not of love, but of anger. For McKenzie, Hos 11:8-9 represents a moment of divine weakness, and God's sense of justice and integrity finally prevails.

On the one hand, God acts on God's own initiative, calling people with a call that is irrevocable precisely because it depends on God and not on the one called. On the other hand, the relationship thus initiated is a real one in which there is everything to be gained or lost according to how human beings live within that relationship with God. It depends on God, and it depends on human response. This is the dynamic tension at the heart of Israel's Scripture. It is a tension never to be "resolved," for it is definitional of what human life is and entails: a construal of humanity in relation to God that enlarges the scope and challenge and richness of what it means to be human.[23]

Rather than resist the dialectical nature of this relationship so as to demand a choice between God's love or justice, God's people are to embrace, live into, and even celebrate this dynamic tension. This view of God ought not to be designated the "God of the Old Testament," as if the "God of the New Testament" differs in some marked fashion. In Romans 9–11 the apostle Paul affirms Israel's irrevocable gift of election while defending God's justice in cutting off Israel because of its unbelief. Paul's response to Israel's story is to warn Gentile Christians to remain steadfast in faith lest they too are cut off. He concludes his discourse with a doxology: "O the depth of the riches and wisdom and knowledge of God! How unsearchable are his judgments and how inscrutable his ways!" (Rom 11:33). Similarly, the proper response to Hos 11 is obedience and worship rather than speculative and abstract theology.

23. R. W. L. Moberly, "'God Is Not a Human That He Should Repent' (Numbers 23:19 and 1 Samuel 15:29)," in *God in the Fray: A Tribute to Walter Brueggemann* (ed. T. Linafelt and T. K. Beal; Minneapolis: Fortress, 1998), p. 121.

12. Marriage, Sexuality, and Covenant Faithfulness

Daniel Castelo

If a person knows anything at all about Hosea, usually it has to do with his marriage and the underlying themes of steadfast love and faithfulness, themes that typically are associated with chapters 1–3, but which occur in other parts of Hosea as well. So far, through his elaboration of Hos 4:1–11:11, Lim has shown that there is more to Hosea than this imagery, and yet the marriage motif typically overwhelms the reception of Hosea. For this reason, we will revisit this theme here, because many contemporary readers — rightfully or wrongfully — have viewed much of the rest of the work as fitting within the marriage motif in one way or another.

For those readers who are inclined toward a "hermeneutic of trust," the strategy usually has been to show how Hosea's love and devotion to Gomer, despite the latter's infidelity, is a testament to the love God has for us despite our sin. Such an approach is on display in the 2012 film "Amazing Love: The Story of Hosea." The movie employs the story of Hosea to demonstrate God's "amazing love" for us despite our wayward ways and brokenness. The "us" here in the movie includes unfaithful Gomer, rebellious Israel, and a teen who is excessively arrogant and indifferent to a youth group camping adventure. The film self-admittedly embellishes the story[1] so as to illustrate how Hosea must have

---

1. In this light, the movie is self-critical in a way that other works are not. Take for instance, Richard L. Strauss's book *Living in Love* (Wheaton: Tyndale, 1978). In the chapter devoted to the marriage of Hosea and Gomer, he adds liberally to the account by saying that "the early days of their marriage were beautiful as their love began to blossom," as well as giving this running series of embellishments: "It was after the birth of Jezreel that Hosea seems to have noticed a change in Gomer. She became restless and unhappy, like a bird trapped in a cage" (p. 87); furthermore, with time, "Gomer seemed less and less interested in [Hosea's] ministry. In fact, she may have grown to resent it. She probably even accused Hosea of thinking more about his preaching than he did of her" (p. 87). Strauss adds that Hosea was convinced that the second child was not his (p. 88),

felt God's pain, yet loved Gomer unconditionally to the point of redeeming her for fifteen shekels of silver. Likewise, the movie suggests that Jesus demonstrates such love for us on the cross, for he pays the price for our redemption. In applying this story to our lives, we may not feel that we could love Gomer the way Hosea did, but, the movie goes on to say, through Jesus' help we could. Plenty of other popular examples show similar characteristics: Hosea 1 and 3 are often interweaved (contrary to Lim's reading) so as to express the unfaltering and devoted love of Hosea in making Gomer a respectable woman and beloved wife despite her repeated infidelities. In light of Hosea's prophetic sign-acts, we are to stand in awe of God's forgiveness and love for us and try to do so for others, even those who hurt us deeply, the way that Gomer must have pained Hosea.

Those who advocate a "hermeneutic of suspicion" also find this marriage worthy of attention, but in their case, the marriage is deplorable in that the text's imagery and themes suggest spousal abuse and violence against women. For instance, as Lim has already noted, Setel believes that there is congruence between the imagery of Hosea and pornography, since both 1) offer depictions and objectifications of women in ways that suggest their public degradation, 2) depict women's sexuality as negative, compared to a positive or neutral male account, and 3) describe women's ongoing submission to male power and domination.[2]

Hosean marriage imagery, therefore, splits opinion and excites interest, commentary, and questioning. As Joseph Blenkinsopp has remarked, "The marriage of Hosea has given rise to more questions and hypotheses than any other passage in [the] Latter Prophets."[3] The imagery sometimes overshadows everything else that is in Hosea, for it has been hailed by some as the key that unlocks everything else in the book.[4] The present climate has only exacerbated the interest and proliferation of scholarly and popular treatments of the subject.[5]

---

and that Hosea is a perfect example of the command in Scripture that husbands are to love their wives as Christ loved the church (pp. 88-90). These gestures, particularly as they are implicitly communicated to be part of the original account, are deeply misleading and disfiguring of the content of this prophetic book. Glen H. Von Wald's *Hosea and Gomer: A Love Story* (Baltimore: PublishAmerica, 2012) is a similar case.

2. See T. Drorah Setel, "Prophets and Pornography: Female Sexual Imagery in Hosea," in *Feminist Interpretation of the Bible* (ed. Letty M. Russell; Philadelphia: Westminster, 1985), pp. 86-95. Also note Athalya Brenner and Fokkelien Van Dijk-Hemmes, *On Gendering Texts* (Leiden: Brill, 1996).

3. *A History of Prophecy in Israel* (Philadelphia: Westminster, 1983), p. 102. Lim uses the more recent and updated version of this work, but interestingly, this quotation is missing from that edition.

4. Usually, this gesture is undertaken by those who subdivide Hosea into two sections, chapters 1–3 and chapters 4–14.

5. Popularly, the redemption of a prostitute because of love is a plot that writers of fiction

How can one make headway into this morass of investment and curiosity on the theme? Part of the strategy, of course, should involve looking to the text itself, which Lim has helped us to do. Despite its elaborate and flowery treatments by some interested readers, the marriage receives very little exclusive attention within the text of Hosea. Gomer is only mentioned in 1:3. She is never given a voice of her own, and her status and identity are deeply contested, in large part because of the scant evidence available from the book itself. Many questions remain unanswerable: Was she a prostitute when Hosea first met her? Was she wayward only after the marriage? What is her relationship, if any, with the woman depicted in chapter 3? And so on. As for Hosea, the reader is not privy to facts about much of his life and mindset as he enters into these arrangements. He is commanded by YHWH in 1:2, so he obeys the command, as evidenced in 1:3. As Lim has accurately observed, the rest of the first chapter focuses on the children and their names, not on Hosea and Gomer. In 3:1-3, Hosea discloses another detail about his life. This disclosure is the most elaborate interpersonal communication one finds between Hosea and the unnamed woman (who may or may not have been Gomer): "And I said to her, 'You must remain as mine for many days; you shall not play the whore, you shall not have intercourse with a man, nor I with you.'" The romanticization of this text in popular Christian culture is simply uncharitable, inaccurate, and misrepresentative; these readings tend to *eisegesis* more than *exegesis*, and as such, they lean toward projectionist distortion.

With so little textual evidence available, readers who focus inordinately on Hosean marriage imagery tend not to limit themselves to chapters 1 and 3; on the contrary, they derive much of their impetus from chapter 2 particularly, but also from chapter 4 and a variety of allusions and speech patterns in the rest of Hosea's oracles. These passages relate to YHWH's speech through the prophet Hosea, and as such, they are properly situated within the covenant logic developed in the previous theological chapter of this volume. Much of the work of contextualizing covenant arrangements therein was developed with one eye to this imagery since so much has been made of it in the history of Hosea's reception.[6] But when looked at exegetically, the text of chapters 2, 4 and the

---

have readily employed. Take for instance, Dorothy Clark, *Hosea's Bride* (New York: Steeple Hill, 2004), a work of Christian fiction in which a preacher by the name of Hosea "saves" Gelina/Angela from a life of prostitution and ends up marrying her because of his devotion and pursuit. A similar case is Francine Rivers's *Redeeming Love* (Chicago: Alabaster, 1997).

6. Lim has done an effective job of expanding the number of interpretive options available for readers of these early chapters of Hosea. For instance, the similarities between Hosea 2 and Assyrian warfare language are important to note. For my purposes in the following, I will consider Hosea 1–3 as setting up a nexus of concerns such as gender, sexuality, and marriage that endures across the book. In this sense, Lim's purposes are similar to mine, but we are working at different

rest of Hosea consist of YHWH's address to Israel, which is prefaced by Hosea's prophetic sign-acts. As a result, the rhetorical expressions, the figures of speech, the hyperbolic and reactionary cries — these can all be related back to the YHWH-Israel covenant bond.[7] Because of the embeddedness of such speech, a number of constraints, parameters, and possibilities are available only to those who make the hermeneutical choice to locate these oracles (and themselves) within that theological and existential context that is the covenant way of life.

If these demarcations hold, then why has the book of Hosea been plagued with such wide-ranging readings? One obvious culprit is simply the complexity of achieving a workable understanding of the relationship between YHWH's speech and the prophet's actions. When YHWH commands a prophet to perform prophetic signs and to speak to the people in light of those signs, it is unclear to the contemporary reader what exactly the link between sign and oracle is. This difficulty is further compounded by the sheer "strangeness" of prophetic texts. As Lim has pointed out, some of the speech patterns one finds in the opening chapters of Hosea are common among ancient Near Eastern cultures; these are often simply unrecognized by the contemporary reader of Hosea. Because of this, certain passages are simply read at face value, with contemporary sensibilities dictating what counts as the "obvious" meaning. Therefore, the way popular literature highlights Hosea's marriage to Gomer represents the strained attempt to "make a connection" with this book that appears so strange to the contemporary reader. Of course, in this effort to make the text relevant to present sensibilities, commentators show more of themselves than they would often care to admit. The projectionist distortion that particularly bedevils Hosean reception is often unbridled, romanticized sentimentality, the species of which is running amok in Christian circles within certain parts of the West.

This theological chapter explores the marriage imagery associated with Hosea — which we take as illustrative of the YHWH-Israel covenant bond — with the aim of probing this imagery in ways that push against its sentimentalization. Such efforts will take the form, in part, of showing how this imagery

---

registers: Lim proceeds to problematize dominant readings by looking at the micro-level and reading exegetically, whereas I have gone on to problematize the dominant reading theologically at a macro-level. Put another way, Lim has expanded the interpretive options, and I have gone on to pick up the most popular stream in order to discredit it.

7. I admit that I am taking a fairly broad stance on this point. As Nelly Stienstra remarks, "It is a matter of debate among exegetes at which point Hosea is describing his own marital situation, and at which point he is voicing YHWH's grievances against His people, speaking as if it is YHWH who speaks" (*YHWH Is the Husband of His People* [Kampen: Kok Pharos, 1993], p. 98). Nevertheless, given the liberties some take in highlighting the interplay, I find it prudent to emphasize what seem to be the aims of this motif's role within Hosea and the prophetic literature overall.

cannot work; that is, how its employment eventually breaks down under its own pressure. This strategy is suitable for all metaphors in Christian God-talk, but it is especially appropriate in this case.

Contemporary Difficulties with Marriage Imagery

Western culture often assumes a monolithic idea of marriage: People fall in love, and as a sign of their commitment to one another, they often get married. This commitment is often thought to involve the sharing of responsibilities, perhaps the upbringing of a family, as well as the kind of devotion that people often believe is unrivaled in its bliss, beauty, and humanizing potential. From these assumptions, modern Western society (as we the authors have experienced it) has had to deal with a number of challenges. For instance: Do same-sex couples fulfill the criteria outlined above? And if so, then shouldn't their partnerships be recognized as marriage-worthy? If not, on what specific grounds are we to deny them marriage? What about people who are single? If marriage is a humanizing arrangement, are single people "less developed" socially and relationally than their married counterparts? Both of these challenges also relate to the broader concern of sexuality. What is the relationship between marriage and sexuality, and is sexuality something best expressed through marriage arrangements, or are other possibilities available, and maybe even more advisable? These questions put pressure on our society's understanding of marriage. Sometimes people become exasperated in these discussions because of the strains and wounds that can erupt from the contentiousness associated with such matters. Perhaps it is of little consolation to those who feel these pressures, but such contention surrounding the institution of marriage in the West is nothing new; changes to the ways we understand marriage have been taking place for centuries in the West. And if this kind of flux contributes to the ways contemporary people evaluate and perpetuate marriage (or not), then it is questionable to what degree the marriage metaphor can illuminate certain features of the YHWH-Israel covenant relationship for us today.

What Does "Marriage" Mean?

I wish to argue that Western society has precious few resources for making sense of marriage — in terms of its rationale, purposes, appeal, and suitability — because of the drastic changes that have taken place around this issue. Given the way that marriage has been and continues to be defined and redefined, it is not altogether clear if contemporary readers can live into and appropriate the metaphor of a YHWH-Israel "marriage" without being significantly impeded by their own understandings and confusions.

Take for instance the American scene: In this context, marriage has become a political issue in ways that it has not in other Western countries. Much of this fervor surrounds two unique characteristics of marriage in the United States: Americans often see marriage as "an important status symbol . . . a marker of a first-class personal life," while at the same time they maintain a sacrosanct view of an individual's right for self-fulfillment so that "your partnership must provide you with the opportunity to develop your sense of who you are and to express that sense through your relations with your partner."[8] These two valuations create a condition of serious tension and heightened expectation, for these represent two different and competing cultural estimations:

> When [Americans] think about the way marriage should be, they tend to say that it should be for life. But when people think about individual satisfaction, they tend to give others wide latitude to leave unhappy living arrangements. Cue them in one direction, and you get one picture; cue them in another, and you get a different picture. Both pictures, contradictory as they may be, are part of the way that Americans live their family lives.[9]

Within this mix of competing valuations, Americans marry, divorce, and remarry at a higher rate and at a faster pace than any other Western nation. Andrew Cherlin remarks:

> Together these factors create a great turbulence in American family life, a family flux, a coming and going of partners on a scale seen nowhere else. There are more partners in the personal lives of Americans than in the lives of people of any other Western country. The most distinctive characteristic of American family life, then, the trait that most clearly differentiates it from family life in other Western countries, is sheer movement: frequent transitions, shorter relationships.[10]

These rapid and constant transitions have deleterious effects on all involved, including (perhaps most especially) children. This unstable situation reflects the incoherence and conflict-laden nature of American estimations of marriage.

8. Andrew J. Cherlin, *The Marriage-Go-Round* (New York: Vintage, 2009), pp. 121 and 130.
9. Cherlin, *The Marriage-Go-Round*, p. 32.
10. *The Marriage-Go-Round*, p. 5.

But how did Americans get to this point? How is it that Americans came to harbor such conflicting understandings of marriage in general? These questions require a broader and more complex investigation into marriage as an institution within Western civilization. For many Americans, the golden era of marriage and family life is believed to be the 1950s, when popular culture reflected a marriage model typified in television series such as *Ozzie and Harriet* and *Leave It to Beaver*. But experts actually view that era as an aberration within a trend of wider, sweeping changes that have been taking place for centuries.

Throughout the history of Western civilization, marriage was viewed as a social institution that brought with it social responsibilities and economic gains. Questions related to inheritance rights and the establishment of legitimacy lines, as well as matters tied to economic survival, labor distribution, and the formation of cooperative relationships for political and financial ends, were all tied to the institution of marriage. In fact, the financial aspect of marriage has probably been the single most important function of marriage throughout history.[11] As a result of these factors, a strategic and survivalist tenor has surrounded the institution of marriage for much of Western history.

Over two centuries ago, expectations surrounding marriage changed — for people in North America and Western Europe in particular — because marriage ceased to have the kind of social significance it once did. With time, married couples were assumed to start their own individual families, polygamy was outlawed, privacy of the nuclear family was increased, adultery was de-idealized, domestic violence was less tolerated, and sentimentality crept in as a fitting disposition toward the marriage bond. The rising prominence of the individual during the Enlightenment (and its implications for human rights and dignity, wage earnings, gender relationships, organizational structuring, and so on) meant that marriage became less of a socially-necessary institution and more of a humanizing partnership, one entered for the fulfillment of relational and intimacy-related needs. What once was deemed a precarious and unreliable reason to marry became the norm in the West: People began to marry largely for love, personal fulfillment, and happiness.

Interestingly, these Enlightenment ideals were curbed and transfigured when they pressed toward their natural consequences. For instance, after the revolutions in America and France, legislators and public purveyors of social norms pulled back from some of the radical calls made during the latter part of the eighteenth century. As Stephanie Coontz notes, "As the nineteenth

---

11. Stephanie Coontz, *Marriage, a History* (New York: Penguin Books, 2005), p. 31. Financial concerns played a very important role in ancient Near Eastern marriages as well; see David Instone-Brewer, *Divorce and Remarriage in the Bible* (Grand Rapids: Eerdmans, 2002), pp. 3-8.

century dawned, the control of husbands over their wives was reaffirmed, although it was now usually described as protection. Women as a gender were excluded from the new rights that were being extended to men."[12] With this control emerged the nineteenth-century phenomenon of the women's purity cult: Women were deemed "sexual innocents whose purity should inspire all decent men to control their own sexual impulses," a move that helped establish "separate spheres for the sexes," which collectively proved to be a power arrangement that could function as a "temporary reconciliation between the egalitarian aspirations raised by the Enlightenment and the fears that equality would overrun the social order."[13] Therefore, the feminist demands of the 1790s were curbed significantly in the early to mid-1800s. In terms of marriage, increased equality between the sexes and the subsequent imposition of the women's purity construct led to a cult of domesticity that made the nuclear family even more central to one's life than in previous eras, and it highlighted gender differences under the guise of men protecting — rather than dominating — women.[14] These proponents of the cult of domesticity were the Victorians, who "were the first people in history to try to make marriage the pivotal experience in people's lives and married love the principal focus of their emotions, obligations, and satisfactions."[15]

In Coontz's estimation, this heightening of the experience of love and marriage meant that "women . . . found in falling in love the kind of self-fulfillment that the previous generation had sought in religious revivals."[16] This was true for men to the same degree that it was true for women. Unsurprisingly, then, with this heightening of sentimentality came the increased sexualization of marriage. For instance, the "Roaring Twenties" created further expectations about love and marriage: Good sex, it was argued by experts of the day, "was the glue needed to hold marriages together," especially as patriarchy waned.[17] Sex appeal, rather than submission, was valued of wives. These views shifted, however, with the impact of the Great Depression and the two World Wars. After this deeply tumultuous period, the *Ozzie and Harriet* model of the 1950s was claimed by American society as a kind of return to Victorian principles. The rise of contraception and the sexual revolution of the 1960s quickly followed this "golden age," and these currents furthermore heightened the sexualization of intimate relationships that had begun prior to the Great Depression.

12. *Marriage, a History,* p. 153.
13. Coontz, *Marriage, a History,* pp. 159-60.
14. Coontz, *Marriage, a History,* p. 176.
15. Coontz, *Marriage, a History,* p. 177.
16. Coontz, *Marriage, a History,* p. 179.
17. Coontz, *Marriage, a History,* p. 204.

Marriage in the West, then, has endured an exceedingly variable and tumultuous history. In several phases of the story, what seemed viable in one generation was deemed impossible for the next. "For centuries, marriage did much of the work that markets and governments do today," and within such configurations were a number of practices and assumptions we would now deem horrifying, including a husband's right to beat his wife: For thousands of years, law systems "upheld the authority of husbands to punish their wives physically and to exercise forcibly their 'marital right' to sex."[18] With the increased privatization, sentimentalization, and sexualization of marriage, new sets of expectations and understandings were forged in the West from roughly the eighteenth century to the present day. So it is no wonder why, according to Cherlin, the American landscape in particular is riddled with perplexing and oftentimes contradictory assumptions and valuations of marriage. Depending on the particular subculture and features of history that determine a person's identity, the "optimal" marriage could take on any number of configurations.

What Does Hosea's Marriage Mean?

These outlined features of marriage's history as an institution in Western civilization make the use of marriage imagery for the covenant bond between YHWH and Israel difficult to employ, since we as contemporary readers are ourselves so conflicted about this particular social custom. Obviously, we cannot escape our embeddedness, even if we were to grant that ancient Near Eastern marriages — and their internal workings and dynamics — were different from ours, and that an ancient reader would most likely hear and react differently to the imagery of, say, Hosea 2 than we would. That kind of hermeneutical charity may help make such instances a bit more palatable historically, but the pressing question concerning contemporary relevance would still stand. In other words, if we grant that marriages were different back then, what do we do with this imagery now?

Rather than pursuing a historical treatment of marriages in the ancient Near East so as to situate the language of Hosea, this section will press the dissonance between contemporary approaches to marriage and features of the YHWH-Israel covenant bond in order to pave a way forward from the extremes of sentimentalized projection and outright rejection that readings of Hosea often yield. This strategy is thus theological in that it aims to particularize contemporary sensibilities in light of the narrative shape of the covenant arrange-

18. Coontz, *Marriage, a History*, p. 9.

ment, and to enumerate its possible implications for the Christian reading of Hosea today.

The associations, expectations, and practices of marriage referenced in the above section run up against YHWH-covenant logic in a number of ways. First, the way people — particularly Americans — enter and exit marriages so quickly is in direct contradistinction to the way YHWH interacts with Israel. Most obviously, the promises YHWH made with the patriarchs are everlasting. Admittedly, strife occurs, threats of covenant dissolution are made, and both judgment and exile are real (and enacted) possibilities, but God's commitment to God's people is unflappable. The crises that erupt within this covenant are from Israel's side, not God's. God's faithfulness to God's honor and God's promises is in direct contrast to the way people oftentimes negotiate marriage fidelity today. As a case in point, the vows made at wedding ceremonies often entail the phrase "till death do us part," but in light of the way half of marriages end up in divorce, such vow-making could be symptomatic of the confused and idealized notions of marriage our society maintains. The promissory dimensions of marriage, as we experience them, run counter to the way YHWH goes about making and sustaining promises to the covenant people.

Second, people often enter marriage on the basis of benefits that they believe can accrue in such relationships; these can include companionship, sexual intimacy and exclusivity, and various kinds of support. In other words, humans usually enter marriages in order to address particular needs they have. From the perspective of God-talk, the category of necessity has always proven difficult to negotiate. On the one hand, if one were to say that God needed creation, this affirmation would open the door to suggest that God is deficient and dependent in some way. Nevertheless, God created that which is not-God and delighted in it. In this sense, God is self-sufficient, but not self-enclosed or self-absorbed. Applied to biblical history, YHWH did not enter the covenant bond seeking to gain something from Israel, for Israel had nothing to give that would make God a more fully-realized deity. And yet God freely, willfully, and happily entered into a covenant arrangement with Israel and has been faithful to it ever since.[19]

If these and other qualifications are necessary for the employment of marriage imagery to describe the covenant bond between YHWH-Israel, then

19. Perhaps here is where the kinship covenant understanding can help correct the excesses of the marriage metaphor. God adopting or taking up Israel as a kind of progeny is perhaps a more compelling image than marriage for sustaining the point that God enters covenant arrangements so as to give of Godself, rather than to benefit from God's covenant partner. Naturally, the kinship covenant perspective would beg another extensive foray, this one into the reasons why people have children today.

what can marital language mean? After all, Hosea is not the only prophet to use such imagery,[20] and the language is not idiosyncratic to the prophetic witness of Scripture.[21] Its presence and prevalence within Scripture suggest that it can play a role in illuminating God's disposition to God's people, so what does such imagery mean, particularly as it is employed in Hosea?

We wish to suggest that the employment of marriage imagery within Hosea functions as a conduit for exploring depth dimensions of relationality that could not otherwise be demonstrable. In this sense, Hosea's marriage is a prophetic sign-act that points to a very elusive *res,* namely God's disposition and affect in light of Israel's rebellion, disobedience, and rejection. Such a *res* pivots on the Creator-creation distinction, but it does so in a tragic way. If God created creation so as to delight in it, to enjoy it, to love it, and so on, what is the corollary when creation exercises its agency and wills to reject its very source and end? The opposite of God's love has typically been thought to be God's wrath or anger, and many instances of God's anger are on display within Hosea and the Book of the Twelve broadly. But as those in the therapeutic professions will recognize, within the human domain, wrath or anger is a secondary, reactive sentiment. Anger is not a primary affect, as it is something derivative of other primary feelings such as pain and loneliness.[22] If this is the case with humans, and if one ventures to suggest a category of divine affectivity or emotions (what I have called "theopathy" for short[23]), then can the same logic apply to the way the worshiping faithful speak of God?

Let us be mindful of what we just averred. According to the logic previously considered, we stressed the vast difference between Creator and creation

---

20. One thinks of various passages in Jeremiah (e.g., 11:15; 31), Ezekiel (16; 23), and Deutero-Isaiah (e.g., 54:5-8). Because of chronological considerations, a reliance upon Hosea by these prophets could have been in effect (Gordon P. Hugenberger, *Marriage as a Covenant* [VTSup 52; Leiden: Brill, 1994], p. 295).

21. See for instance Ephesians 5 and Revelation 19.

22. I am working from the account of affectivity present in Leslie S. Greenberg and Susan M. Johnson, *Emotionally Focused Therapy for Couples* (New York: Guilford Press, 1988), pp. 4-9. Primary emotions are to some degree biologically determined, and are often shrouded by the reactionary secondary emotions that "often take the form of defensive coping strategies and [that] are counterproductive in creating change" (p. 6).

23. I have used the category of theopathy earlier, but let me stress the analogous nature of such language here: Silvan Tomkins (in *Affect Imagery Consciousness,* Volume 1: *The Positive Affects* [New York: Springer, 1962], chapter 10) delineates eight categories of (human) emotions: interest/excitement, enjoyment/joy, surprise/startle, distress/anguish, fear/terror, shame/humiliation, contempt/disgust, and anger/rage. I cannot possibly pursue in this chapter all the biblical interstices between human and divine affectivity on these eight emotions, but certainly some of these are very difficult to apply to YHWH even within the range of affectivity attributed to God in the Bible.

(and by implication, between YHWH and Israel), but in doing so, we have gone on to stress deep resonances of continuity through the category of affectivity. This is as it should be. God and humans are not on the same ontological plane, and yet because God has revealed Godself through language and particular forms of imagery within language, possibilities of convergence do take place in Scripture and can be sustained by believers. Therefore we are willing to go quite far in such convergences (following the prompts of Scripture), given the care that we have taken to secure the tentativeness and precariousness of such language itself. Equivocity is the ground for tentative univocity in God-talk. Once that point is affirmed, univocity can reach levels of depth and richness while having on its horizon the conditional restraints necessary to check natural human projections. Put another way, once the language is affirmed as analogous, the imagery can hold greater interpretive weight while staying true to its core identity as simply, and nothing more than, figures of speech.

The importance of this move is that it creates the conditions for extending the metaphor as far as it can go. Only now can the reading community affirm something like the following: "All right, let's say that the covenant is like a marriage and that the covenant partners can be talked about as if they were spouses: What can we gain from this thought-exercise that would not be available otherwise, and how far can it be taken?" And, at least at this stage, we are willing to grant that this imagery helps its readers see the complexity and polyvalence of a provisionally-constructed account of theopathy, a richness that goes beyond the love/anger dyad so prominent in popular construals of divine affectivity. God's love may be an orienting disposition of the divine life that helps solidify God's *ek-static* character of reaching out and extending Godself in a non-self-referential way, and God's wrath or anger may be the reaction often displayed in the Bible as proper to a rebellious people, but what Hosea pictures through the marriage imagery is a *spectrum* of divine affectivity, an "in-between" expanse between holy love and holy wrath. The prophetic sign-act of Hosea helps the believing faithful to imagine that there is more to God's affective life than love and anger. And such a conception is both alluring and shocking.

Covenant Faithfulness and Infidelity

Divine affectivity within Hosea revolves around the notions of fidelity and its opposite, infidelity, and these are themselves challenging notions. Evidently in Hosea's time, as in ours, marital in/fidelity was largely negotiated in terms of sexuality. In other words, marital fidelity has often been considered as synonymous with sexual exclusivity and infidelity with sexual promiscuity or adultery.

If in/fidelity is a metaphorical linchpin between the YHWH-Israel bond and human marriages, then the table is set for thinking of covenant faithfulness along the lines of sexual fidelity. The appeal of such language relates to its emotional depth, for a marriage ravaged by infidelity is deeply painful for those who have experienced it. The violation of trust, the sense of rejection, and a host of other features contribute to its significance. While the use of such imagery for the YHWH-Israel bond makes sense at some levels, it is also problematic at others, particularly when one has to take into account the vast differences in sexual mores across civilizations.

Lim previously highlighted the importance and extensiveness of the term "whoredom." As he suggested, the word implies fornication, or the act of having sexual relations outside of/apart from marriage. This term and its cognates are more general than the notion of adultery, which at the time of Hosea is a term that pivots on the sexual obligations of a woman to her husband. Obviously, both terms relate to sexuality and have different ranges of application. Both notions are applied to Israel's wayward behavior (not just religiously but politically, economically, and in other dimensions as well), so both are intended to carry negative connotations. Of the two ideas, one might think that "adultery" is perhaps more accessible than "fornication" for us today,[24] but contextual evidence from the ancient Near East shows that even our modern notions of adultery are inadequate for grasping adultery's full meaning in an ancient setting. In the Bible itself, adultery is banned in the Decalogue (Exod 20:14; Deut 5:18), but is not explained until Deuteronomy 22:22, where it is considered a capital offense.[25] Cyril Rodd comments on this last passage in the following way:

> Adultery is committed when a man has sexual intercourse with a married woman. No more and no less, although a woman who is betrothed counts as married (Deut 22:24). There is no hint that the man has committed a wrong against his own wife, were he married. The offence is entirely against the woman's husband,[26] and even if the man was not married he is still re-

24. Contemporary readers should eschew simplistic construals of ancient sexual customs and mores. David H. Jensen's reflection on the New Testament word *porneia* makes the point clearly: "The term, in short, has come to mean whatever each generation assumes it means, whatever departs from the supposedly self-evident mores of each era. Today's fornication, in short, often becomes tomorrow's sexual norm" (*God, Desire, and a Theology of Human Sexuality* [Louisville: Westminster John Knox, 2013], p. 3).

25. This is in keeping with ancient Near Eastern contexts; see Instone-Brewer, *Divorce and Remarriage in the Bible*, p. 9.

26. This feature suggests the deep connections between marriage and property rights in patriarchal societies such as ancient Israel.

garded as an adulterer. Nothing is said about having sexual intercourse with a woman who is not married. Laws regarding the seducing of unmarried women who are not betrothed are quite different. In that case the man has to pay the *mōhar* ("bride-price"), whether he is willing to marry the woman or not, since her value to her father is less because she is no longer a virgin.[27]

No written record exists that shows whether adultery was actually upheld as a capital offense within Israelite religion, and scholars have speculated about this topic on a number of points, but it is clear that the above stipulations make adultery a different kind of act from today's understandings and expectations. Consideration of the Holiness Codes of Leviticus (particularly Lev. 18) further expands our understanding of ancient attitudes, in that it declares that adultery and other sexual indecencies cause defilement and impurity among both people and land; because of these acts, the Holiness Code warns, the land will "vomit out" its inhabitants until those who are guilty are cut off from the people.[28] Adultery in this context, then, is not simply an interpersonal matter, but a cultural and religious infraction that involves a host of im/purity considerations that are simply foreign to the modern-day Western reader.

In spite of these very important considerations, what "work" can infidelity imagery accomplish for us today? As noted above, I believe that such imagery and language can introduce a fuller spectrum within theopathy, thereby helping to situate both God and human beings within covenant arrangements. As to the first covenant partner, this language helps render a God-visual in which YHWH is significantly affected by the disobedience of God's people. One need only recall the most prominent features of divine affectivity on display among the Twelve, but especially those registered in Hosea: If YHWH's primary disposition is love, and yet wrath (a secondary, reactive emotion) is occasioned by Israel's disobedience (these being running and prominent features of theopathy among the prophets), then something has happened within God's affective life for the transition from one to the other to take place. Possibilities that biblical scholars and theologians have registered to fill this in-between, affective "something" include pain, suffering, vulnerability, and others.[29] The image of

---

27. Cyril S. Rodd, *Glimpses of a Strange Land* (Edinburgh: T & T Clark, 2001), p. 28.

28. Rodd, *Glimpses of a Strange Land*, p. 30.

29. Jürgen Moltmann is often associated with this line of thinking in theology, particularly his claims regarding a crucified or suffering God (*The Crucified God* [trans. R. A. Wilson and John Bowden; Minneapolis: Fortress, 1993); on the side of Old Testament studies, see Terence E. Fretheim, *The Suffering of God* (OBT; Philadelphia: Fortress, 1984). An early work in this area is Kazoh Kitamori, *Theology of the Pain of God* (Richmond: John Knox, 1958). Rather than "suffering," I find the language of vulnerability more helpful for the reasons outlined in William C. Placher,

a wounded and betrayed lover and husband, an image that is lurking behind the most problematic features of theopathic speech in Hosea, captures that "something" in a powerful way.

Some observers of my work may be puzzled by these affirmations since I have repeatedly offered support for the notion of divine impassibility. What I am venturing here is not a complete turnaround of my earlier claims, but rather an exemplification of how I think those claims can make sense alongside the explicit speech patterns of Scripture. If language of and for God is at its core analogous, and if covenant arrangements and modalities are assumed of and fostered by readers of such texts as Hosea, then the language of sexual infidelity (and all that it may suggest) can exemplify a species of theological imagery by which a community can — in an ongoing, provisional, and revisable fashion — speak, reflect, and worship the triune God.[30] In other words, to say "God is like a wounded lover when God's people disobey God" is not an ontological claim, but rather a metaphorical construct registered in Scripture alongside many others (including the images found within Hosea of YHWH as a teacher, judge, farmer, and military leader). The point of these images is to illustrate holy mysteries inherent to the Creator-creation and YHWH-Israel bonds, but these images have to change repeatedly, be extended until they unravel, and be regulated over time by theological speakers so that no single one predominates, becomes staid, is reified, or possibly even abused or employed to justify abuse. The potential for this kind of nimble shuffling of metaphors exists within Hosea itself: In addition to its early marital metaphors (Hosea 1–3), one finds strong and extensive usage of both parental and juridical forms of speech throughout much of the latter parts of the book (Hosea 4–14).

Another way sexual infidelity language performs "work" for readers of Hosea is by reframing theological epistemology. Fascinating about this book is that its denunciation of "whoredom" and "adultery" is counterpointed to the call for "knowledge of God." Put differently, the opposite of the promiscuity

---

Narratives of a Vulnerable God (Louisville: Westminster John Knox, 1994). The language of "vulnerability" itself, however, has the potential, like "suffering," to be used to describe God ontically rather than to elaborate a certain feature of God-talk present within certain strands of the biblical witness.

30. I hope I make it as clear as possible: In my mind, the situation cannot boil down to one being "for" or "against" divine pathos; rather, the crux of the matter rests on how such pathos (given its inclusion in biblical forms of speaking and reflection) can be understood, elaborated, and marked as both similar to, and different from, human pathos. My repeated concern is that scholars, pastors, and readers often fail to mark the analogous nature of this language and instead leave it unqualified. Such lack of nuancing often leads to univocal assumptions regarding such speech, a move that is simply one step removed from projection, as is often the case with Christian readers of Hosea.

being denounced in Hosea is a certain kind of fidelity captured by a species of God-knowledge. Now, as Lim and others are inclined to point out, the Hebrew term for knowledge, *yada'*, does have sexual connotations of its own. So at the level of sexual imagery, knowledge fits well as a contrast to whoredom and adultery. At the same time, the word helps cast covenantal participation in a certain way: Rather than being devoted and faithful to idols, YHWH wishes for the covenant people to be faithful to Godself so as to know God intimately, vulnerably, and brokenly.

And this point is where sexual imagery somehow reconfigures us as disciples of the one, true, holy God. One way that this language alters our horizons of interpretation is the way worship and desire interplay. Knowing the things of God is not reductively intellective; rather, it is participatory and so self-involving. This view casts worship as not simply cognitive or involving verbal assent, but also requiring embodiment and affective devotion. As to the former, the practices of executing justice, vow-keeping, and obedience are very much part and parcel of the way God is known when the connotations of *yada'* are in the mix. This theme is one of the most prominent in the Book of the Twelve broadly and Hosea specifically. When cast this way, God-knowledge is inextricably tied to what we typically refer to today as social concern and advocacy.[31] As for affectivity, Israel's wayward ways are suggestive of corrupt and distorted desire. Of course, sexuality and desire go hand in hand for us as humans, and YHWH's employment of sexual imagery for the covenant bond heightens the link between covenant fidelity and desire for YHWH. The desire to know God is a topic of considerable debate within theological circles, but this much is plain in the text of Hosea: Israel was led astray not by conceptual, historical, or factual ignorance, but by unruly, disordered, and so perverted desire. The Baals were not superior to YHWH, yet the Israelites desired, delighted, and gave themselves voluntarily to them. Israel *wanted, yearned for, lusted after* other gods and powers. This perverted desire manifested itself in other ways as well, including political intrigue, injustice, and the entire lot of complaints and grievances YHWH levels at Israel in Hosea. As such, lust and idolatry are the perversions of love and worship. Sexual imagery thus heightens the emotional stakes for negotiating the constellation of worship, desire, knowledge, and religious devotion.

This point has implications that are bound to be especially controversial in Western culture (and particularly American society), for these contexts are

---

31. Such characterization works well with what Jesus commands and expects of his followers, thereby making the God-knowledge typified in Hosea concordant with the life of a Christ-follower.

shockingly and crudely hyper-sexualized, but the employment of sexual imagery for the covenant bond between YHWH and Israel can either exemplify projectionist ideas from a dominant culture, or it can call them into question so as to narrate rival accounts of the way sexuality is understood and practiced by disciples of Jesus. We simply see no other way around the matter. How can sexual imagery be productively employed theologically in the way Hosea uses it — including use of such terms as "whoredom," "fornication," and "adultery" — when sex is often viewed in our environs as recreational fun, a biological function typified strictly by the act of orgasm, a random activity undertaken for the release of stress and the satisfaction of hormonal urges, and so on? Ideas such as "hooking up" simply disfigure rather than illuminate what is at stake in Hosea's employment of such imagery.

Again, normative consideration of the matter is contentious because of competing discourses and accounts of human sexuality that run rampant both in the public square and in the church, but we wish to examine the way sex has been at once demythologized and glamourized in our society to the point that it has become increasingly commodified, instrumentalized, and materialized. As a case in point, it is a challenge for people in the West to do something as basic as develop a definition of sex.[32] When people do, it sometimes runs parallel to the notion of orgasm, but the equivocation between sex and orgasm does not help us to appreciate what is taking place in Hosea. The emphasis in Hosea is on relational breach, betrayal, dignity, fidelity, and pain. So much of what Hosea wishes to accomplish through sexual imagery is obstructed to those of us who live in oversexed societies. Hosea's sexual imagery beckons readers to become re-enchanted with sexuality as something holy, interpersonal, and mysterious, but this process cannot take place simply by reading Hosea; rather, it requires intentional reconfigurations of attitudes, dispositions, perceptions, and valuations. Outside of such a process, many of those who approach Hosea with a hermeneutic of trust will continue to think of it as "the greatest love-story ever told."

Marital Diagnostics Suggested by Hosea's Oracles and Sign-Act

Let us conclude this chapter with a final thought experiment. If, as Hosea invites us, we as the worshipful and reading community cast the YHWH-Israel bond not only in terms of a marriage, but a dysfunctional one at that, what kind of

---

32. See the introductory reflections by Jenell Williams Paris in *The End of Sexual Identity* (Downers Grove: InterVarsity, 2011).

pathologies exist in this relationship as evidenced by Hosea's rhetoric?[33] The exploration of such possibilities should render an account that is both suggestive and in need of supplementation, thereby showing the generative and degenerative potential such language has for describing the covenant bond.

Within the specific covenant arrangements depicted in Hosea's oracles, YHWH has been affected in some fashion so that God's love morphs into God's wrath. But in all of this, YHWH does not extensively claim the affective "middle" register, one of pain and brokenness.[34] On the contrary, the reader sees a number of other rhetorical devices. These include the following verses with their possible categorizations:

1) *Hyperbole/Exaggeration*
   "I will put an end to the kingdom of the house of Israel" (1:4)
   "I will no longer have pity on the house of Israel or forgive them" (1:6)
   "I will not save them" (1:7)
   "You are not my people and I am not your God" (1:9)
2) *Threat/Act of Divorce*
   "She is not my wife, and I am not her husband" (2:2)[35]

33. In what follows, I am going to extend the use of Emotionally Focused Couple Therapy (or EFT) to the marriage bond as depicted in Hosea. I have chosen this theory of Susan Johnson as opposed to others within the experiential camp (Carl Whitaker, Virginia Satir, John Gottman, and so on), as well as to other schools of thought in the field of marriage therapy (narrative, solution-focused, cognitive-behavioral, and so on), because I think it the most appealing model given the difficulties inherent in applying any form of couple therapy to Hosea's narrative of the marriage between YHWH and Israel. Essentially, I am trying to honor the rhetorical forms of Hosea's oracles in a way that does not fall victim to projectionist sentimentalization. Simply, if this relationship can be cast as a marriage, then it needs to be treated with the seriousness such a situation demands, for I believe that affairs within marriage bonds ought to be considered in terms of interpersonal trauma.

34. Although Brueggemann focuses on transitions (or, as he styles them, "turns") from wrath to redemption in Hosea 2:13-14, the same point holds as in my focus on the prior affective development of moving from love to wrath: "It is remarkable that Hosea, while taking us boldly into YHWH's internal life of turmoil, will not go so far as to open up the process between these verses. That process remains hidden, a hiddenness that invites us to interpret" ("The Recovering God of Hosea," *HBT* 30 [2008]: 15).

35. As Lim has already considered, the language of Hosea 2:2 is a formula for ancient Near Eastern divorces. Instone-Brewer wishes to make the case that a divorce actually did happen between YHWH and Israel, both because of this language and because of the use of the term "hate" in Hosea 9:15 (*Divorce and Remarriage in the Bible*, pp. 37-38). Further support can be found in Jeremiah 3:8, with the language of the certificate of divorce for Israel. However, in the case of Hosea, the matter is not clear (see Wang-Huei Liang, "Is She Not My Wife, and Am I Not Her Husband?" *HBT* 31 [2009]: 1-11). The theological difficulty with this reading is that it is not entirely clear what a divorce would entail at the theological register. Instone-Brewer's claim that

3) *Extreme and Quick Transitions in Affective Dispositions*
   Immediately following the hyperbole of 1:1-9, one sees the following:
   "Yet the number of the people of Israel shall be like the sand of the sea"
   (1:10)
   "Children of the living God" (1:10)
   "Great shall be the day of Jezreel" (1:11)
4) *Other Kinds of Threats*
   "That she put away her whoring from her face, and her adultery from
   between her breasts, or I will strip her naked and expose her as in
   the day she was born, and make her like a wilderness, and turn her
   into a parched land, and kill her with thirst" (2:3)
   "Upon her children also I will have no pity, because they are children of
   whoredom" (2:4)
   "Therefore I will hedge up her way with thorns; and I will build a wall
   against her, so that she cannot find her paths" (2:6)
   "Therefore I will take back my grain in its time, and my wine in its sea-
   son" (2:9)
5) *Assertions of Power*
   "Now I will uncover her shame" (2:10)
   "I will put an end to all her mirth" (2:11)
   "I will lay waste her vines" (2:12)
   "I will make them a forest" (2:12)
   "I will punish her for the festival days of the Baals" (2:13)

What to make of these rhetorical forms? Given the marriage metaphor, it is necessary to conduct what marital therapists term a "couples assessment." One strategy would be to obtain a communication sample in which the couple would be "instructed to find a topic that arouses emotions of moderate intensity, and then attempt to solve the problem on their own for 10 minutes."[36] Obviously, such a device is impossible to obtain in the case of the YHWH-Israel bond as depicted in Hosea, but, in the existing rhetoric of Hosea 1–2, the communication patterns are intense. From the oracular materials, one could say that this marriage has an overfunctioning-underfunctioning dynamic, in which one partner dominates communication and exerts more energy than the other. Now in terms of faith, believers will typically say that YHWH is in the right and has

---

it would be better to say that YHWH "suffered" a divorce, given Israel's infidelities, alleviates the ambiguous tension to some degree but not entirely.

36. Lee Williams, Todd M. Edwards, et al., *Essential Assessment Skills for Couple and Family Therapists* (New York: Guilford Press, 2011), p. 186.

supreme prerogative in this case, but Israel (similarly to Gomer) never speaks back within this specific dynamic. One does hear from Israel on occasion, but within the pages of Hosea, the people do not claim responsibility for their infidelity. Therefore, communication between YHWH and Israel has broken down severely, with the aggrieved party dominating communication, over-exerting, and overcompensating, whereas the offending party claims no responsibility for the breach in the relationship.

A second possibility for couples assessment would be the formulation of a relationship history. This exercise would include writing up the most significant moments, developments, and features of the relationship. Such an assessment tool would require extensive time and the sifting of massive amounts of data. In this commentary, a relationship history of sorts has been compiled on two levels. The first was the elaboration of the covenant history, beginning with Moses and the people throughout the exodus episode, and culminating at Sinai, which some might say is where YHWH and Israel were "married."[37] The other would be the dynamic on display in many of the prophets, one that we have used to subdivide Hosea: 1) Israel's rebellion, 2) YHWH's judgment, and 3) YHWH's extension of hope for healing the breach in the relationship. In both schematizations, Israel displays extensive and visible dysfunction across generations. This dysfunction is a systemic, repeated expression of an underlying pathology, one that requires assessment at the "individual" level; in other words, a personal, individual history is needed to uncover why such aberrant behavior repeatedly exists. Obviously, in the case of Israel, one is speaking of multiple generations and individuals; nevertheless, unhealthy patterns continue to present themselves, and developments from the past continue to haunt succeeding generations. This is especially apparent in the rise of the Israelite monarchy, with the many patterns and consequences erupting from this development, including political subterfuge and intrigue, the division between the Northern and Southern Kingdoms, etc.

How to account for the extremes of communication in YHWH's speech practices as depicted in Hosea, and what to make of the findings from the paltry little that can be derived from a hypothetical marriage assessment? One way to meaningfully cast YHWH's speech patterns in a contemporary idiom is with the category of "flooding." The term "flooding" denotes a case in which a partner is triggered by conflict in the relationship to such a degree that he or she is moved to extremes in speech or action. Such extremes can be said to be the case within the YHWH-Israel bond because of the perpetual (as opposed

---

37. There is midrashic precedent for this connection; see Instone-Brewer, *Divorce and Remarriage in the Bible*, p. 35.

to resolvable) problem of Israel's infidelity.[38] With flooding, a partner simply reaches the breaking point; a spouse is so desperate and frustrated at the state of the marriage that threats, put-downs, and other rhetorical forms are possible. The quoted passages above, therefore, can be understood in terms of YHWH being "flooded" by Israel's ongoing, unabated, and extensive infidelity.

The difficulty with this interpretation is that, if one assesses YHWH as having experienced "flooding" because of Israel's pathological disposition to be adulterous, one may find the possibility of reconciliation to be implausible. After all, those of us who are married have most likely participated in heated arguments in which we say things we later regret. Ultimately, we love our partners, but when we experience pain, hurt, or offense because of something they did (or something we thought they did), we sometimes end up overreacting and speaking "in the heat of the moment." According to EFT, a way forward in such a situation is to move behind the reactive emotions and rhetorical mechanisms so as to touch the pain that led to the reaction in the first place. Williams, Edwards, and their colleagues emphasize the need for such depth: "Can both partners accurately label or articulate their feelings? How does each partner handle the expression of emotions? Can they identify and express the softer or more vulnerable emotions like hurt and fear? Or, is anger the emotion that is primarily expressed?"[39] As noted above, this acknowledgment never occurs in Hosea. As for the penultimate question, if one takes Hosea 1–3 as a whole, YHWH's answer has to be negative. And in terms of the last question, for YHWH the answer is largely affirmative: Particularly in chapter 2, God is extremely reactive and angry in light of Israel's persistent infidelity. Little in terms of softness and care is available in light of the sheer rancor God expresses in these first chapters since — to use the language of Emotionally Focused Couple Therapy once again — an insecure attachment bond has been created between YHWH and Israel because of the latter's persistent infidelity. Pressing the analogy further, YHWH has experienced a certain kind of trauma — partly evidenced by the rhetorical forms of flooding — such that the rhetoric that follows is an attempt on God's part to regain some kind of control and order within the relationship.[40]

---

38. I learned the language of flooding from John Gottman, *The Marriage Clinic* (New York: Norton, 1999); another resource for this topic is Paul Ekman, "Expression and the Nature of Emotion," in *Approaches to Emotion* (ed. Klaus R. Scherer and Paul Ekman; Hillsdale: Lawrence Erlbaum, 1984).

39. *Essential Assessment Skills*, p. 194.

40. I am aware of how far I am pushing this analogy, but let me continue as a way of making sense of the rhetoric of Hosean marriage imagery: For EFT, "When attachment security is threatened, human beings respond in predictable sequences. Typically, anger is the first response. This

As noted above, Israel does not respond in Hosea apart from the first verses of chapter 6, which again do not treat seriously of the marital infidelity. According to Williams, Edwards, et al., the case of marital infidelity requires that the offending party take a number of concrete actions. An apology would be the very first step. Without this first move, it is doubtful that the relationship can be mended. Other responses include the acceptance of responsibility, acknowledgment of how the other person was hurt, atonement (activities demonstrating the desire to change), the accounting of why the affair happened, and the accumulation of trust.[41] Israel takes none of these actions in Hosea.

Therefore, the Hosean marriage metaphor, when pressed clinically, suggests that one partner (YHWH) is overfunctioning, overcompensating, and silent regarding the softer feelings that lie immediately behind the reactive ones of wrath and anger. Silence also marks Israel's response to the couple's dynamic (thereby demonstrating a thorough breakdown in communication), since Israel does not acknowledge fault for its infidelity and does not take the necessary steps toward reconciliation.

What these conclusions yield is a working sense of the real limits of the marital metaphor for readers of Hosea. This delimitation partly stems from the unavailability of a working sense of the extensive communication patterns between YHWH and Israel, and without this, the speech that is so troublesome to readers in Hosea cannot be adequately situated within a broader context of marital conflict-resolution. Because of this limit, the language stands as a perpetual puzzle or offense to readers, one that occasions speculation, distrust, and dismissal of Hosea as Holy Scripture. In other words, the limits of the marriage

---

anger is a protest against the loss of contact with the attachment figure. If such protest does not evoke responsiveness, it can become tinged with despair and coercion, and evolve into a chronic strategy to obtain and maintain the attachment figure's attention. The next step in separation distress is clinging and seeking, which then gives way to depression and despair. Finally, if all else fails, the relationship is grieved and detachment ensues. Separation from attachment figures can be conceptualized as a traumatic stressor that primes automatic fight, flight, and freeze responses. Aggressive responses in relationships have been linked to attachment panic, in which partners regulate their insecurity by becoming controlling and abusive to their partner" (Susan M. Johnson, "Emotionally Focused Couple Therapy," in *Clinical Handbook of Couple Therapy* [ed. Alan S. Gurman; 4th ed.; New York: Guilford Press, 2008], pp. 113-14). Obviously, I wish to preserve the divine character and the differences implied by a divine-human "marriage," but if this metaphor of marriage is to do real work for reading and understanding Hosea, then I believe its clinical consideration can help situate some of the most troubling parts of Hosea in a redemptive way, given that those parts are ones that some readers see as having the potential to reinforce patterns of domestic violence (see Julia O'Brien, *Challenging Prophetic Metaphor* [Louisville: Westminster John Knox, 2008], pp. 33-34).

41. *Essential Assessment Skills*, p. 219.

metaphor for the YHWH-Israel covenant directly contribute to Hosea's ongoing misreading and rejection by contemporary readers.

At the same time, and in light of these particular shortcomings, the Hosean marriage metaphor can serve as a specific kind of invitation for later covenant members, that is, subsequent "children of the living God" (Hos 1:10), in that one can take the silence of Israel in the oracles as an invitation to the worshiping community to "fill in the blanks," so to speak. This makes possible the community's own reconciliation with YHWH as people of the new covenant, a reconciliation foreshadowed in Hosea 2:18 and given fuller consideration in Jeremiah 31. From this perspective, the Hosean oracles can be the beginning, rather than a comprehensively-displayed process, of a reading community's reconciliation with YHWH. Of course, this kind of reading requires some kind of resonance between the faults committed by Israel and those committed by a contemporary reading community; in other words, the latter has to situate their collective life in these destructive patterns so that they can in turn seek a renewed alliance and attachment bond with YHWH. If Hosea is read this way, and the bond between God and people is pursued in this manner, a break in cyclical marital dysfunction can take place. For whereas the Israel in the text does not apologize, accept responsibility, acknowledge the pain caused to YHWH, make atonement (in the way that the authors cited above suggest), account for their infidelity, and build trust, nothing stands in the way of current covenant partners from doing so, particularly this side of the work of Christ and the empowering presence of the Holy Spirit. Put another way, the problematic passages of Hosean marriage imagery can serve as a prelude to both a prayer of confession and an act of reconciliation between the Trinity and the church, so that YHWH claims YHWH's people, and they claim YHWH as their God (Hos 2:23). Of course, dangers exist in the worshiping community's engagement of Hosea in this way (and some of these will be accounted for in the final theological chapter of this commentary), but the promise and potential for such churchly readings and outcomes do exist, thereby making the difficult and unsettling moments of Hosean discourse potential preludes to softening encounters that can occur when we as the worshiping community are vulnerable and transparent before a God who is pained by our unfaithfulness and contrary ways.

13. Hosea 11:12–13:16 [12:1–14:1]

Bo H. Lim

Hosea 11:12–12:14 [12:1-15]

In some regards, the last unit of the book, Hos 11:12–14:9, recapitulates chapters 1–3 and chapters 4–11:11, possessing the same thematic movement of judgment to restoration. Chapters 1–3 begin with an accusation against the land and a disputation (ריב/*rîb*, 2:2 [2:4]) against the woman/mother, and 4–11:11 similarly opens with an indictment (ריב/*rîb*, 4:1) against Israel. Hosea 12:2 [12:3] also begins with YHWH's indictment (ריב/*rîb*) of his people, suggesting that chapters 12–14 form a cohesive unit in the same manner as the previous two sections of the book. Literary recapitulation need not be equated with semantic repetition such that chapters 12–14 merely rehearse the teachings in the previous sections. The prophet's message is intensified in regard to both judgment and salvation so that this section, particularly chapter 14, functions as a climax to the book. The three units of Hosea — chapters 1–3; 4:1–11:11; and 11:12–14:9 [10] — ought to be read as complementary, with each section glossing the other while maintaining its distinct contribution to the message of the book. Viewed in this manner, the book is not to be read linearly, nor are these sections to be organized chronologically. While individual sections of the book may have been written against a particular historical backdrop, their function within the prophetic book follows the book's literary and theological logic. Scholars are certainly free to investigate the redactional history of the text, but they do not need to do so in order to understand the message of the book.

The references to Judah in the opening verses of this final section are difficult to decipher. In 12:2 [3], the prophet singles out Judah in his indictment without any corresponding mention of Israel or Ephraim, as typically found in Hosea. In addition, in 11:12 [12:1], Judah is spoken of in positive terms ("but Judah still walks with God, and is faithful to the Holy One"), which is in contrast to Israel and Ephraim, who are described as utterly deceitful. Given Hosea's consistent criticism of Judah throughout chapters 4–11 (5:5, 10, 12, 13, 14; 6:4; 8:14; 10:11), scholars have questioned whether 11:12 [12:1], with its positive view of Judah, is authentic to Hosea. The NIV casts the verse as a negative reference to Judah ("And Judah is unruly against God, even against the faithful Holy One"), which is similar to how Macintosh translates it ("[and Judah] still he seeks to gain the mastery with God, and with the Most Holy remains immovable").[1] The verb רד/*rād* appears to be a derivative of רוד/*rûd*, "to wander, roam," rather than רדה/*rādah*, "to rule," and the verb נאמן/*ne'ĕmān* modifies Judah rather than "holy one(s)"; therefore, the pro-Judean reading ought to be maintained: "Ephraim surrounds Me with deceit, The House of Israel with guile. But Judah stands firm with God and is faithful to the Holy One" (NJPS). The reference to Judah in 12:2 [3] may have replaced an earlier reference to Ephraim/Israel/Jacob, as scholars have suggested. Nevertheless, the "update" reflects the canonical form that was received as authoritative tradition and therefore cannot be dismissed. Rather than seek an original form, readers are to appreciate the varied assessments of Judah's character. The book of Hosea depicts Judah as the faithful kingdom in contrast to Israel, who has already gone astray (4:15). On other occasions, Judah is indicted for its own particular violations of God's will (5:10; 8:14). Most often, Judah is castigated alongside Ephraim, with little differentiation made between the two nations (5:5, 12, 13, 14; 6:4; 10:11), or both are named as recipients of God's eschatological blessings (1:11 [2:2]; 6:11). On two occasions, Judah is given a favored status in contrast to Ephraim (1:7; 11:12 [12:1]). Hosea subsumes all the national myths of Ephraim under Judah, including those regarding Israel's patriarch, Jacob, that would be deemed less savory. Judah may have possessed a favored status with God in Israel's history, but those days will come to an end. Whether Judah likes it or not, they will be the inheritors of Ephraim's tradition, both its promises and its failures.

Deceit (כחש/*kaḥaš*, 11:12 [12:1]) and deeds (מעלל/*ma'ălāl*, 12:2 [12:3]) appear to be two strong emphases of Hos 11:12–12:14 [12:1-15], and this thematic focus indicates that the unit serves as a response to chapters 4–11, where both lexemes and corresponding themes feature prominently. A summation of Israel's failures recounts its repeated lies and misdeeds. Prior to 11:12 [12:1], the word "lies" occurs four times in Hosea (4:2; 7:3; 9:2; 10:13) — solely within chapters 4–11 — and appears second on Hosea's list of sins in 4:2. "Deeds" also occurs four times in Hosea prior to 12:2 [3], and also solely within chapters 4–11 (4:9; 5:4; 7:2; 9:15). In 5:4, the word "their deeds" (מעלליהם/*ma'alĕlêhem*) is set in a

---

1. A. A. Macintosh, *A Critical and Exegetical Commentary on Hosea* (ICC; Edinburgh: T & T Clark, 1997), p. 473.

parallel relationship with the "spirit of whoredom," and this verse indicates that it is because of these factors that Israel does not know or return to God. In 7:2, "their deeds" are equated with "their wickedness" (רעתם/*rāʿātām*), and the prophet makes clear that God continues to remember their sinful actions. The word "surround" (סבב/*sābab*) occurs twice in Hosea: in 7:2 to describe how Israel surrounds itself and God's presence with evil deeds, and in 11:12 [12:1] when Ephraim surrounds God with lies. In 9:15 it is on account of "the wickedness of their deeds" that God withdraws love, banishes Israel to exile, and comes to even "hate" the people. The phrase "will punish Jacob according to his ways, and repay him according to his deeds" (12:2 [12:3]) serves as an *inclusio* for Hos 4:1–11:12 [4:1–12:1], since a similar form appears in 4:9 ("I will punish them for their ways, and repay them for their deeds"). In addition, the phrase functions as a bridging device to recapitulate the message of chapters 4–11 in 12–14.

Readers of Hosea may ask why a third cycle of prophecies appears in chapters 12–14, one that revisits many themes previously covered in 4–11. Admittedly, some of the text is redundant. Perhaps the repetition is due to the persistence of evil in Israel, Ephraim's very own stubbornness, and their unwillingness to respond to prophetic instruction. Israel will spout many words, some of them recorded by the prophet (cf. 6:1-3; 12:8 [9]), but none of them reflect authentic repentance. When the prophet makes clear that righteous action is the prerequisite to true repentance, words devolve into excuses and even lies (cf. 11:12 [12:1]). Perhaps the extended discourse of Hosea may provide a lesson to the church to practice not mere confession, but rather genuine penitence that is demonstrated in "faithful love and justice" (12:6 [12:7], CEB). Particularly for ecclesial traditions that emphasize momentary acts of conversion, Hosea demonstrates that the road to reconciliation and rehabilitation is more often a journey with fits and starts rather than an instantaneous achievement. Macintosh even employs the language of "penance" — a concept Protestants tend to be averse to — to describe the means by which Israel is reconciled to God in chapter 12.[2] Repentance is an activity that demands God's initiative as well as human response. Because people are so often unresponsive or under-responsive, the process to restoration may be lengthy and involved.

In Hos 12:3-14 [12:4-15], the prophet turns to the story of the patriarch Jacob, whose deception and subsequent contrition provide yet another window into the soul of God's people. While the Scriptures often call for a repentance wherein the crooked is made straight, the Jacob narrative demonstrates that the road of reconciliation often zigs and zags, involving unexpected encounters and discoveries that cannot be anticipated at the outset. Such unpredictability is to

2. Macintosh, *Hosea*, p. 509.

be expected when humans seek to be reconciled with a holy and loving God. Transformations in the hidden souls of persons, as well as of whole societies, will be exposed to the light of God's holy love.

In many regards, Hos 12:3-14 [12:4-15] is organized around the topic of identity, both the identity of God's people as well as the identity of the God of Israel. Names are the focus of this section, particularly "Jacob," "Israel," "YHWH," "Bethel," "Ephraim," and "Canaan." In the Scriptures, names not only identify individuals or peoples, but they also describe their character and often determine their destiny. The prophet will revisit the ancient narratives regarding the origins of these names, and through a reinterpretation of the tradition for his current audience, he reveals their true significance. This study will not explore the question of literary dependence and priority between Hosea and Genesis, for which definite answers are lacking. The focus of this commentary at this juncture will be on Hosea's interpretation of the Jacob tradition regardless of his sources.

The Hebrew of Hos 12:4 [12:5] has been notoriously difficult to interpret because of its ambiguous syntax and unspecified pronouns. While all the options cannot be covered here, the following interpretations approximate the various proposals:[3]

1. Jacob strove against God, a messenger, and Jacob prevailed. The messenger wept and sought the favor of Jacob. At Bethel the messenger found Jacob, and there God spoke with us.

2. Jacob strove against God, a messenger, and Jacob prevailed. Jacob wept and sought the favor of Esau. At Bethel the messenger found Jacob, and there God spoke with us.

3. God, the messenger, strove and prevailed. Jacob cried and wept and implored the favor of the messenger. At Bethel Jacob found the messenger and there the messenger spoke with us.

4. But Israel, the messenger, prevailed. Jacob cried and wept and implored the favor of the messenger. At Bethel Jacob found the messenger and there the messenger spoke with us.

What complicates matters is that the Jacob tradition is ambiguous in its moral assessment of the patriarch. While Jacob can be viewed as a trickster, a more

---

3. The variations are legion, so the suggestions above are but a composite of several proposals. In addition to the disputed syntax and the pronoun assignments, the differences lie in whether וישר אל/*wāyyāśar ʾel* "and God strove" in 12:4 [12:5] ought to be emended to וישראל/*wĕyiśrāʾēl* "and Israel." See J. Andrew Dearman, *The Book of Hosea* (NICOT; Grand Rapids: Eerdmans, 2010), pp. 305-6 for a list of options. This reading also assumes that וַיָּשַׂר/*wāyyāśar* ("he ruled," שׂרר/*śārar*) ought to be read as וַיִּשַׂר/*wayyiśar* ("he strove," שׂרה/*śārāh*).

sympathetic interpretation would view him as a resourceful and cunning hero. The Genesis narratives make no criticism of Jacob and instead blame Esau for despising his birthright. By divine election the elder is to serve the younger, yet throughout the story Jacob prospers because of his wily actions and overcomes his opponents. According to the first proposal mentioned above, Jacob does not face defeat at Jabbok, but rather triumphs over the messenger, who then submits to him. The mention of Jacob fleeing to Aram to serve for a wife in 12:12 [12:13] is not viewed as a humiliation of the patriarch, but rather the occasion for the outpouring of God's favor, much like the parallel experience of Israel in Egypt in v. 13 [14]. Ackroyd believes that Hosea retells the Jacob narratives within the P material in Genesis virtually without embellishment for the purpose of rebuking his audience, prompting them to emulate their patriarch rather than dissociate from him. He writes, "Contrasted with the indications of divine willingness to bless and protect, exemplified in Israel's ancestor, is the marked unfaithfulness of the present community. The recall of the past points to the responsibility of the present."[4] Given this commentary's focus on reading the canonical text, in which Law and Prophets function as a hermeneutical dialogic, one need not read Genesis over and against Hosea or vice versa. The largely positive portrayal of Jacob in Genesis can be appreciated for its unique contribution, and not be taken as opposed to Hosea's criticism of the patriarch.

While the following interpretation may be a minority view, most likely 12:4 [5] describes the defeat of Jacob at the Jabbok. Even if Israel's patriarch managed to triumph over the messenger of God (view 2), the passage goes on to describe how he wept when he was reunited with Esau. Clearly the verb "to supplant" (עקב/'āqab, v. 3 [4]) is a pun off the name Jacob (יעקב/ya'ǎqōb, v. 2 [3]). If v. 3 [4] is to be read in the context of v. 2 [3], then the assessment of the Jacob tradition is clearly negative, since v. 2 [3] makes clear that Jacob will be punished for his ways and deeds. The verb עקב/'āqab can also be translated "to deceive" (cf. Gen 27:36), an accusation leveled against Ephraim in 11:12–12:1 [12:1-2]. Just as Jacob is deemed "deceitful" (מרמה/mirmâ) in Gen 27:35, the same word describes the house of Israel in Hos 11:12 [12:1] and Canaan in 12:7 [12:8].

The word "manhood" (און/'ôn) in v. 3 [4] can refer to strength or virility (Gen 49:3; Deut 21:17), but in v. 8 [9] it clearly indicates wealth. In Hos 12, Jacob is described as possessing both strength and riches, a theme consistent with the Jacob narratives in Genesis. Yet like the profit gained from Laban's flock, Ephraim's wealth is acquired through deceptive and oppressive means and is therefore illegitimate (cf. 12:7-8 [12:8-9]). The Rabbinic commentator

4. Peter R. Ackroyd, "Hosea and Jacob," *VT* 13 (1963): 259.

Qyl argues that v. 8 [9] is a parody of Jacob's protest of innocence before Laban in Gen 31.[5] Rather than translate כנען/*kĕna'an* as "trader" in v. 7 [8], the proper name "Canaan" ought to be maintained (cf. LXX), signifying that not only has the conduct of Ephraim and Canaan become indistinguishable, but their identities have become blurred as well. In v. 6 [7], YHWH urges that love, justice, and trust might be found in Ephraim. While Ephraim claims that it is free from sin and iniquity (עון/*'awôn*) in v. 8 [9], v. 11 [12] makes clear that iniquity (אָוֶן/*'āwen*) is found in Gilead. Hosea has already referred to "Beth-el" ("house of God") as "Beth-aven" ("house of iniquity," 4:15; 5:8; 10:5); therefore, its mention in 12:4 [5] as the site of Jacob's communion with God serves as a rebuke for Israel at that time.

Hosea 12:4 [5] ("He strove with the angel and prevailed" [וישר אל־מלאך וַיֻּכָל/*wayyāśar el-mal'āk wayyûkāl*]) bears close resemblance to Gen 32:28 [29] ("for you have striven with God and with humans, and have prevailed" [כי־שרית עם־אלהים ועם־אנשים ותוכל/*kî-śārîtâ 'im-ĕlōhîm wĕ'im-'ĕnāšîm wattûkāl*]). Genesis describes Jacob's opponent at Jabbok as a person (איש/*'îš*, Gen 32:24 [25]) and makes no mention of a messenger (מלאך/*mal'āk*), as in Hos 12:4 [12:5]. In addition, the Hosea account differs by reversing the order of the wrestling match and the encounter with God at Bethel. In Genesis, weeping occurs not at the Jabbok, but only afterwards in Jacob and Esau's tearful reunion (Gen 33:4).

While virtually all translations emend עִמָּנוּ/*'immānû* in 12:4 [5] to read "with him," such a change is not necessary. The language "with us" demonstrates that Israel's traditions function as revelatory word to every generation, and that Israel is prefigured in its narratives of the past. Fishbane finds that the net effect of this typological reading of the Jacob story reveals the core identity of transtemporal Israel. He writes:

> It would appear that for the prophet, in so far as the individual Jacob-Israel is the ancestor of Israel, his behavior has to some degree *determined* the behavior of his descendants. Indeed, because of the eponymous link between the person Israel and the nation, the parallelism drawn between the actions is not mere rhetorical trope, but drives deep into the very 'nature' of Israel. The nation is not just 'like' its ancestor, says Hosea, but *is* its ancestor in fact — in name and in deed. Thus, in this instance, aggadic typology discloses the inner nature of Israel, its rebellious core *ab origine*.[6]

5. Macintosh, *Hosea*, p. 498.
6. Michael Fishbane, *Biblical Interpretation in Ancient Israel* (Oxford: Clarendon, 1985), p. 378, emphasis his.

Hosea 12:8 [12:9] demonstrates that Israel continues in self-delusion, and in order for genuine reconciliation to take place, God's people need to come to grips with not only *what they do* but with *who they are*. Whether Israel and Judah like it or not, they continue to be Jacob, in terms of both strength and deception. While not all people possess the status of election unique to Israel, ancestry inevitably shapes individuals and communities. Cultural heritage alone does not dictate the present and future, yet its formative influence cannot be ignored if genuine transformation and reconciliation are to take place. History-telling is an act of identity formation for individuals as well as communities. The prophetic task is one of a historian: to call forth those aspects of the past that have been hidden from view yet continue to shape the present from unseen places. Since Israel serves as a type for the church, Hos 12 reveals to every community of faith that, like Israel, they possess at their core a heritage of great strength as well as rebellion. Rather than distance itself from past atrocities, the church is called to claim them as its own. For example, in regard to racism Bantum reminds us, "To imagine a life in Christ we must begin to reimagine the shape of our unfaithfulness, our complicity in the economy of race, in order to faithfully imagine what it might mean to participate in the renunciation of the old life marked by the tragedy and violence of race."[7] The exploration of Israel's national identity provides a resource by which the church can address its own myths and lies.

This prophecy aligns with Calvin's maxim, "true and sound wisdom, consists of two parts: the knowledge of God and of ourselves,"[8] because chapter 12 addresses not only the identity of the people, but also the identity of God. The prophet's vision is not only anthropological but also theological. Genuine repentance requires the reexamination of one's understanding of self as well as the character of God. Hosea 12:5 [6] places great emphasis on names and identifies the God whom Jacob wrestled at Bethel as YHWH, the God of hosts. As mentioned previously, names function as a unifying motif in this chapter, and the person most clearly identified is none other than YHWH. The word for "name" in 12:5 [12:6] is the word "memorial" (זכר/*zēker*). The first occurrence of this word in the book occurs in 2:17 [19] in the context of a discussion regarding the naming of God. Hosea 2:16-17 [2:18-19] reads, "On that day, says the LORD, you will call me, 'My husband,' and no longer will you call me, 'My Baal.' For I will remove the names of the Baals from her mouth, and they shall be

---

7. Brian Bantum, *Redeeming Mulatto: A Theology of Race and Christian Hybridity* (Waco: Baylor University Press, 2010), p. 16.

8. John Calvin, *Institutes of the Christian Religion* (ed. John T. McNeill; 2 vols; Philadelphia: Westminster, 1960), 1:35.

mentioned by name (זכר/*zēker*) no more." The reuse of this term in 12:5 [12:6], and the subsequent exhortation for repentance in v. 6 [7], reminds Israel that in order for Israel to "remember" or "name" YHWH, they must first "forget the names" of the Baals (cf. 11:2; 13:1). When read in conjunction with chapter 2, Hos 12 reminds God's people that the name of Israel's "husband" (איש/*'îš*, 2:16 [18]) is none other than YHWH.

Dearman observes that 12:5 [12:6] ("The LORD the God of hosts, the LORD is his name!") is a formulaic expression that is also found in Amos 4:13 and 9:5-6. In addition, it recalls Exod 3:15, "God also said to Moses, 'Thus you shall say to the Israelites, "the LORD, the God of your ancestors, the God of Abraham, the God of Isaac, and the God of Jacob, has sent me to you: This is my name forever, and this my title (זכר/*zēker*) for all generations."'" Earlier in 1:9, Hosea indicated that the name YHWH was to be obliterated from Israel's vocabulary, signifying the termination of the covenant. Furthermore, the divine name was mediated through the prophetic ministry of Moses, so the loss of this name also involved the termination of prophetic mediation. Yet Hos 12:5 [6] reminds Israel that it can call upon the name of YHWH, who is identified twice as "your God" in 12:6 [7]. The only other occasion where "love" (חסד/*ḥesed*) and "justice" (משפט/*mišpāṭ*) are collocated together in Hosea is 2:19 [21], where they describe the renewed covenant relationship between YHWH and Israel. The emphasis in 12:6 [7] is placed upon the people's obedience, signalled by the three imperatives, "return," "hold fast," and "wait," as well as the opening emphatic phrase, "But as for you." Yet this obedience is not generated solely from human effort, but rather through the grace of God. The ב/*b* preposition before "your God" (באלהיך/*bē'lōhêkā*) suggests instrumentality, so that the verse ought to be translated, "For your part you shall return *through the help of* your God."[9] Such reciprocity reflects the dynamic relationship between God and the people throughout the book.

Once again, in 12:9 [12:10], God is identified, this time according to the covenant formula "I am the LORD your God."[10] While the Hebrew text states, "I the LORD have been your God ever since the land of Egypt" (NJPS), the Greek text reads, "But I the Lord, your God, brought you up from the land of Egypt." With the addition of the phrase "brought you up" (ἀνήγαγόν σε/*anēgagon se*), the Septuagint makes a more explicit identification of YHWH as redeemer. In 12:10 [11], YHWH is identified as a God whose message is mediated through

---

9. Macintosh, *Hosea*, p. 491, emphasis mine. This view originates from the medieval commentators Rashi, ibn Ezra, and Kimchi. Macintosh also suggests that, given the context, the verb "to return" alludes to God's promise to Jacob, "I will bring you back to this land" (Gen 28:15).

10. Regarding covenant formulae, see comments on 1:9.

prophets. Since Hos 12 extensively reflects upon Israel's past, the prophets mentioned in v. 10 [11] ought not to be identified with Hosea's contemporaries,[11] but rather with all covenant prophets beginning with Moses. Although Moses is not explicitly named, in v. 13 [14] he is clearly identified as the prophet who delivered and guarded Israel as they departed Egypt. As a covenant mediator, Moses in this case is not identified as a lawgiver, but rather as a prophet, the very role of Hosea. Earlier, Hosea described his instruction as communicated through written text (cf. 8:12), and it is likely that Hosea's audience received the message of past prophecy according to the same medium. Whether or not 12:10 [12:11] initially referred to prophetic speech, readers of the book of Hosea would understand this verse to grant the authority of Moses to the writings of Hosea.

Hosea 12:10 [11] catalogues the varieties of prophetic speech: "... When I spoke to the prophets; For I granted many visions, and spoke parables (דמה/*dāmāh*) through the prophets" (NJPS). The NRSV understands דמה/*dāmāh* in the same manner as its use earlier in the book (4:5, 6; 10:7, 15), and translates the last phrase as, "and through the prophets I will bring destruction." But the alternative use of the word, "to liken," better fits the context of 12:10 [12:11]. Macintosh writes concerning this word, "From the fundamental notion of comparison, then, there is to be detected here the sense of thought consisting of appropriate analogy and reasoning, devised for the purpose of instruction in regard to truth and morality."[12] Prophets teach in parables that require faithful interpretation. The prophetic word comes in the form of comparisons, analogies, parables, and typologies, and therefore a discerning mind is a prerequisite for understanding prophetic speech. Christian discipleship involves cultivating the skills, knowledge, and virtues necessary to draw the proper connections between God's word and one's world.[13]

The mention of Gilead (גלעד/*gil'ād*, Gen 31:21, 23, 25, 47, 48) and stone heaps (גל/*gal*, Gen 31:46, 48, 51, 52) in Hos 12:11 [12:12] recalls the covenant made between Jacob and Laban. In this story, Jacob pleads innocence to the accusations of Laban in language similar to 12:8 [9] (cf. Gen 31:36). Nevertheless, the patriarch continues to deceive and steal from his uncle, albeit unwittingly, owing to the schemes of Rachel. Adjacent to the stone heap in the Genesis narratives is a pillar (מצבה/*maṣṣēbâ*, Gen 31:45, 51, 52), and in Gen 28 and 35,

11. Contra Margaret S. Odell, "Who Were the Prophets in Hosea?" *HBT* 18 (1996): 78-95.

12. Macintosh, *Hosea*, p. 502.

13. Briggs argues, "All this is to say that almost any significant discussion of biblical texts has a *self-involving* dimension: the interpreter must interact with the subject matter of the text in ways that in turn shape or at least respond to the character of the interpreter" (Richard S. Briggs, *The Virtuous Reader: Old Testament Narrative and Interpretive Virtue* [Studies in Theological Interpretation; Grand Rapids: Baker Academic, 2010], p. 40, emphasis his).

these pillars function as a witness to God's presence with Jacob. The mention of altars (מזבח/*mizbēaḥ*) in 12:11 [12:12] also recalls the altar Jacob erected at Bethel to commemorate God's favor upon him in allowing him to be reconciled with Esau (Gen 33:20; 35:1, 3, 7). Within the book of Hosea, pillars and altars are collocated together (cf. Hos 10:1, 2) such that mention of stone heap, pillar, or altar is suggestive of the others and of the Jacob narratives. Hosea 12:12-13 [12:13-14] is linked by the repetition of the verb "to guard" (שמר/*šāmar*), which results in the conflation of Jacob's servitude to Laban with Israel's bondage in Egypt. Given Hosea's previous statements equating the destruction of pillars with the removal of the king (3:4; 10:2), Hosea draws the typological connection between Jacob's experience of chastisement followed by homecoming with the disciplinary events of the exile and the promise of restoration.

By the repetition of the verb "to guard" (שמר/*šāmar*) in Hos 12:12-13 [12:13-14], an analogous relationship is drawn between Jacob guarding sheep in order to wed Rachel, and YHWH guarding Israel on the journey out of Egypt. Macintosh believes Israel is to understand its upcoming exile living in tents again (cf. 12:9 [12:10]) as a "penance," analogous to Jacob's flight from the land of promise (12:12 [12:13]), as well as Israel's bondage in Egypt (12:13 [12:14]). Yee describes this event as Israel's "dark night of the soul," an experience of divine absence that leads to spiritual transformation through one's struggle with God.[14] Just as Jacob wrestled with a man during the night, so too will Israel experience the darkness and hardship of exile. Yet "guarding" also signifies the hope of redemption. Macintosh writes, "Hosea seems to suggest that YHWH's providential care of the nation ('Israel') through a prophet is of a sort with Jacob's ('Israel's') devotion to a woman for whom he toiled in order to win her as his wife."[15] God's people are to remember that, although they may be Jacob, a deceiver, their God is YHWH, the liberator of the Exodus. Hosea combines both traditions to capture Israel's penchant for sin and consequent discipline, but also YHWH's propensity to redeem out of longsuffering love. When caught in sin — particularly of the likes of sexual misconduct which results in catastrophic familial, vocational, social, and spiritual loss — Hosea teaches that God both disciplines as well as redeems. The path towards restoration and reconciliation involves embracing both from the hand of God.

Although the Jacob tradition highlights the weaknesses in Israel's character, it also provides hope for a positive outcome, should God's people choose to repent. The call to return to God, to hold fast to loyalty and justice, and to wait

---

14. Gale A. Yee, "The Book of Hosea: Introduction, Commentary, and Reflections," in *The New Interpreter's Bible* (ed. L. E. Keck; 12 vols.; Nashville: Abingdon, 1996), 7:287.

15. Macintosh, *Hosea*, p. 511.

for God in Hos 12:6 [12:7] assumes the possibility for a hopeful future. The Jacob tradition also includes how Israel's patriarch remained loyal and loving to Rachel. The narratives recall how he served 14 years for her hand in marriage, and upon her death placed her sons, Joseph and Benjamin, in positions of prominence over the sons of Leah. Also, Jacob eventually returns to the promised land at the end of the story. Sweeney writes, "It is Jacob's fidelity to Rachel and his return to Israel that prompts Hosea's use of the image to call for Israel's fidelity and return to YHWH. In the prophet's view, if Jacob could change, so can northern Israel."[16] Jacob remains a symbol of both judgment and salvation. The beauty of the biblical narratives is the manner in which they repeatedly demonstrate how God can redeem deeply-flawed persons and use them as a means of blessing others.

Hosea 13:1-16 [13:1–14:1]

Hosea 13:1-16 [13:1–14:1] appears to be a clear unit, with the references to Samaria's and Ephraim's guilt — "but he [Ephraim] was exalted in Israel; but he incurred guilt through Baal and died" (13:1), and "Samaria shall bear her guilt, because she has rebelled against her God" (Hos 13:16 [14:1]) — serving as an *inclusio*. If any section of Hosea requires the reader to consider the wider context of the book, it is chapter 13. As will be demonstrated below, on several occasions chapter 13 alludes to previous texts and in doing so brings the judgment speech of Hosea to a climax.

Hosea functions as a prophetic dialogue that requires its readers and audience to participate in its drama as it unfolds. Therefore, interpretations based primarily upon historical grounds misread the intention of the text, since they fail to account for the text's primary point of reference: its literary context. Isolated readings of texts often ascribe an absolute status to them, when instead they were intended to carry provisional truths. Readers of chapter 13 are required to know chapters 1–12, continue reading until the end of the prophecy, and only then draw conclusions regarding its message.

Israel's Sin

Various proposals have been suggested as to the precise historical referent of "through Baal" in 13:1, but it is to be understood in a generic sense. Chapters 11,

---

16. Marvin A. Sweeney, *The Twelve Prophets* (2 vols.; Berit Olam; Collegeville: Liturgical Press, 2000), 1:120.

12, and now 13 (vv. 4-6) explicitly mention Egypt and the exodus, so undoubtedly this tradition serves as the narrative backdrop of Hosea's message. The word "cast image" (מסכה/*massēkâ*) recalls the molten calf at Sinai (Exod 32:4, 8; Deut 9:12, 16; Ps 106:19), and the mention of calves at the end of v. 2 also suggests the Horeb episode. The calf episode in turn invokes the sin of the Omride dynasty because of Jeroboam's repetition of the announcement, "Here are your gods, O Israel, who brought you up out of the land of Egypt" (1 Kgs 12:28; cf. Exod 32:8). While 13:2 indicates that Israel "keep[s] on sinning," the inception of this rebellion reaches back to the beginning of the Northern Kingdom, but also to the constitution of Israel at Sinai.

In addition to the intertextual links with the Sinai narratives, chapter 13 contains numerous allusions to other texts in Hosea, particularly chapter 8. The mention of idols (עצב/*'āṣāb*) in 13:2 recalls the earlier condemnations of idolatry in 4:17 and 8:4. Hosea 2:8 [10] describes how the woman used the very silver given to her by YHWH on behalf of Baal, and 8:4 indicates that Ephraim's idols were made of silver (כסף/*kesep*, cf. Hos 13:2). The phrase "work of artisans" (מעשה חרשים/*ma'ăśēh ḥārāšîm*) in 13:2 alludes to the description of the calf in 8:6, "an artisan made it" (חרש עשהו/*ḥārāš 'āśāhû*). Hosea mentions calves (עגל/*'ēgel*) only in 8:5, 6 and 13:2, and each text considers them an abomination. The word "to know" (ידע/*yāda'*) is a key term connecting 13:4b-5: "you know no God but me, and besides me there is no savior. It was I who knew you in the wilderness" (RSV). This word also carries a crucial role in Hos 8:2, "Israel cries to me, 'My God, we — Israel — know you!'" as well as 8:4, "They made kings, but not through me; they set up princes, but without my knowledge."

The need for a monarch or royal court is put into question in 13:10-11, and this theme also appears in 8:4, "They made kings, but not through me; they set up princes, but without my knowledge." Hosea 13:2 states that Israel "keep[s] on sinning (חטא/*ḥāṭā'*)," and earlier, 8:11 spoke about the proliferation of altars because of Israel's continued sinfulness. The net effect of these intertextual links between chapters 8 and 13 is to suggest that they ought to be read in tandem. Chapter 8 identifies Israel's primary sins as idolatry and alliances with foreign nations; therefore, when 13:1 speaks of Israel incurring guilt through Baal, this expression describes a broader category of covenant violations than Baal worship.

Not only does chapter 13 allude to chapter 8, but Israel's comparison to "the morning mist or like the dew that goes away" in 13:3 is almost a direct quotation of 6:4, "like a morning cloud, like the dew that goes away early." In 6:3 the people indicate with their lips that they seek to know YHWH, and in 6:4 God considers their loyalty (חסד/*ḥesed*) to be fleeting. Hosea 6:6 makes clear that their evanescence is equated with a lack of loyalty (חסד/*ḥesed*) and knowledge. Later, Hos 10:12 equates loyalty (חסד/*ḥesed*) with righteousness, and in 12:6 it is synonymous with justice. While chapter 13 lacks the language of loyalty, it returns full circle back to the dilemma raised in chapter 6, with its focus on knowing God; apparently no spiritual progress has been made by the people. According to 13:4-5, at one point Israel did demonstrate loyalty by knowing no other God and savior but YHWH, and God in turn knew Israel in the wilderness (cf. Hos 2:14 [16]; 9:10; 13:5). Hosea 13:4 repeats the identification of God stated previously in 12:9 [10], "Yet I have been the LORD your God ever since the land of Egypt," and in doing so creates overlapping memories of the past. The same God who is remembered as redeeming Israel from Egypt in chapter 12 is the one who judges Ephraim in chapter 13 for its apostasy. Earlier, Israel's heart was found to be insincere (7:14) and deceptive (10:2). According to 13:6, it is also proud and forgetful, and for this reason, God will tear it out (13:8).

The precise meaning of how Ephraim's iniquity is bound up and kept in store in 13:12 is not absolutely certain, but its significance is clear enough. Some believe the language of "bound up" (צרר/*ṣārar*) suggests a sealed written record of Israel's sinfulness (cf. Isa 8:16),[17] while others find that this language is suggestive of labor pains (cf. Jer 48:41; 49:22),[18] because this motif continues on in v. 13. Regardless of its precise meaning, Ben Zvi is correct to emphasize, "Whereas Israel may be evanescent (see v. 3), its sin . . . is portrayed as well established, well kept, and permanent."[19]

Israel's Death

The exact nature of Ephraim's death is not specified in 13:1, but the remainder of the chapter indicates that it refers to the devastation of the Northern Kingdom. In a surprising move, in 13:7-9 God recalls the covenant name and likens himself to the destructive power of wild animals devouring their prey. Sweeney suggests that the opening phrase of 13:7, "So I am" (ואהי/*wā'ĕhî*), is a variation of the covenant name "I am" (אהיה/*'ehyeh*), which appears earlier in Hos 1:9, "I am not your God."[20] Up to this point in the book, the only other first person common singular form of this verb is found in 11:4, "I am (ואהיה/*wā'ehyeh*) as one who lifts a yoke onto their jaws" (translation mine), which may also represent God's

---

17. Cf. Macintosh, *Hosea*, p. 542.
18. Dearman, *The Book of Hosea*, p. 326.
19. Ehud Ben Zvi, *Hosea* (FOTL 21A; Grand Rapids: Eerdmans, 2005), p. 273.
20. Sweeney, *The Twelve Prophets*, 1:132-33.

covenant name. This name, associated foremost with loyalty, compassion, and the forgiveness of iniquity,[21] is now to be identified as the destroyer of Israel.

Whereas God is portrayed in 13:5-6 as the shepherd who nourishes and protects Israel (cf. 12:13 [12:14]), in vv. 7-8 YHWH morphs into the role of predatory beast and turns against the flock under his care. The comparison of God to lion, leopard, and bear in 13:7-8 recalls God's warning earlier in 2:12 [14], "I will make them a forest, and the wild animals shall devour them," particularly since the word pair "wild animals" (חית השדה/*ḥayyat haśśādeh*) is repeated in 13:8. The pairing of lion and bear in comparison to God occurs in Lam 3:10, and the three-fold comparison of a lion and two other beasts appears in Amos 5:19 and Jer 5:6. God as lion is the dominant image in this passage since it is the first and last beast mentioned, and unlike the other two beasts, it occurs elsewhere in Hosea (cf. 5:14; 11:10).[22] As in 5:14, in 13:7-8 the lion image is suggestive of Assyria, since the verb describing the leopard's actions, "lurk" (אשור/*'āšûr*), is most certainly a pun on the name Assyria (אשור/*'aššûr*). While the precise syntax of v. 9 is difficult to determine, the meaning appears to be clear: Israel's helper is now its destroyer, with the haunting reminder that this change is on account of YHWH.[23]

The final section of chapter 13, vv. 13-16 [13:13–14:1], speaks of Israel's future with regard to the womb and the tomb. The first half of v. 13 is clear: "The pangs of childbirth come for him, but he is an unwise son." The second half can either be understood as a reference to a breech position ("for at the proper time he does not present himself at the mouth of the womb" [NRSV]), or to the ability to survive labor ("For this is no time to survive at the birthstool of babes" [NJPS]). In either case the image is clear: The child, and possibly the mother as well, will die in labor due to the foolishness of the child. While certainly it is unusual to assign blame to an unborn child, Hosea has already done so in the case of Jacob in 12:3 [4]. The reference to sonship recalls chapter eleven's description of Israel as the rebellious son, as well as chapter twelve's reflections on Jacob, the patriarchal supplanter and deceiver. The moral failure of the child is its lack of wisdom, an accusation leveled throughout the book by its emphasis on a true knowledge of God. In addition, the book ends with a sapiential exhortation in 14:9 [10] that further reinforces the need for wisdom. Sweeney suggests that Hosea employed this imagery because of the widespread phenomenon of stillborn deaths in the ANE and as a polemic against Baal wor-

21. See commentary on 1:9.

22. See comments on 5:14.

23. It seems best to understand שחתך/*šīḥetkā* as a noun, "your destruction," so that 13:9 reads, "Your destruction, Israel, is on account of me, your helper."

ship, since Baal supposedly possessed the power to grant fertility and children.[24] Hosea 13:13 places the blame for Ephraim's infant mortality and maternal death upon the shoulders of the people themselves; the people's own foolishness has led to its death.

The Hebrew of Hos 13:14 is difficult to translate, so there are varying possibilities regarding its meaning.[25] Scholars differ over whether an interrogative particle is implied in the first bicolon, given that the next two clauses begin with the particle "where?" (אהי/*'ĕhî*). Thus the first two phrases can be understood as a pair of rhetorical questions ("Shall I ransom them from the power of Sheol? Shall I redeem them from Death?" [NRSV, CEB, ESV]), or as declarative statements ("I will ransom them from the power of the grave; I will redeem them from death" [NIV, NJPS, LXX]). The declarative statement that concludes the verse, "Compassion is hidden from my eyes," serves as a response to the preceding interrogatives, and it appears likely that the first two clauses ought to be understood as rhetorical questions as well. In other words, Hos 13:14 raises the question, Will God rescue Israel from its impending death and destruction? The answer seems to be no.

For the Christian interpreter, the question is raised, How is such a reading to be reconciled with other passages in Hosea, as well as Paul's reading of the verse in 1 Cor 15:55? The only other occurrence of the word "compassion" (נחם/*niham*) in Hosea appears in 11:8, though it is a variation on the Hebrew root: "How can I give you up, Ephraim? How can I hand you over, O Israel? How can I make you like Admah? How can I treat you like Zeboiim? My heart recoils within me; my compassion (נחומם/*niḥūmîm*) grows warm and tender." In both passages, YHWH asks rhetorical questions regarding whether to bring destruction upon Israel, and in the case of 11:8 the answer is clear: God will not execute judgment. The next verse provides declarative statements indicating Ephraim will be spared because of the holy character of God. While some argue that 13:14 functions as a counterpoint to or reversal of 11:8-9, such a reading need not be the case. As argued in our introductory chapters, the book of Hosea possesses a threefold structure, where chapters 1–3, 4:1–11:11, and 11:12–14:9 each possess a movement from judgment to salvation. On the basis of form, chapter 13 ought not to be compared to chapter 11, a passage of salvation, but rather to the preceding chapters on judgment within Hos 4–10.[26]

---

24. Sweeney, *The Twelve Prophets,* 1:133.

25. Ben Zvi lists nine different readings for the verse. Ben Zvi, *Hosea,* pp. 274-75.

26. In addition, "compassion" (נחם/*niham*) may function as a synonym for death and Sheol. In Ezek 31, the prophet speaks of death, Sheol, the pit, and the underworld interchangeably; v. 16 announces, "I made the nations quake at the sound of its fall, when I cast it down to Sheol with those who go down to the Pit; and all the trees of Eden, the choice and best of Lebanon,

While most scholars admit that Hos 13:14 is not a promise of deliverance, oftentimes they decontextualize it from the book of Hosea in order to support Paul's use of the text in 1 Cor 15:55, "Where, O death, is your victory? Where, O death, is your sting?" In Hosea the passage declares the certainty of death, whereas in 1 Cor 15:55 it celebrates the victory over death. These scholars justify Paul's reading on the basis of features external to the text: Christ's resurrection is appealed to as the hermeneutical warrant to reverse the text's original intent. Ciampa and Rosner explain, "An eschatological hermeneutic is employed in the use of Hos. 13:14. Paul turns a text about judgment into one declaring salvation, for we are not under the law, and the resurrection of Christ signals the beginning of the new age of redemption."[27] In addition, Isa 25:8a ("he [YHWH] will swallow up death forever") appears to have influenced Paul's reading of Hos 13:14.

While chapter 13 provides no indication that v. 14 would be understood as a taunt over death, such a reading is possible with the inclusion of chapter 14. When Hos 14 is read as a postlude to Hos 13, the reader is made keenly aware that Israel will be redeemed from death and Sheol. Whereas in Hos 13:14 YHWH declares that "compassion is hidden from my eyes," God makes clear in 14:4 [5], "my anger has turned from them." Chapter 14 may provide the warrant to reread 13:14a as a declaration ("I will ransom them from the power of the grave; I will redeem them from death") and 13:14b as a taunt ("O Death, where are your plagues? O Sheol, where is your destruction?"). While the mechanism for this transformation from judgment to salvation is unidentified within the book of Hosea, mystery alone ought not to discredit the possibility for resurrection.

If chapter 13 concluded Hosea, the book would end with the same themes and tone as it began. Hosea begins with the condemnation and rejection of a woman and her children (1:2, 9), and ends with a prophecy of infanticide and the violent murder of pregnant women (13:16 [14:1]). While the language ought not to be understood as mere metaphor, the threefold combination of death by sword, infants dashed, and violence against women (cf. 2 Kgs 8:12; Isa 13:15-16) appears to be a convention signifying utter humiliation and defeat and the termination of a covenant.[28] Not only does 13:16 [14:1] bring to a climax this

---

all that were well watered, were consoled in the world below." Given that Sheol and death are also topics in Hos 13:14, the passage may function in a similar fashion to Ezek 31. If so, YHWH's announcement that "compassion is hidden from my eyes" may indicate that God will not bring about death and Sheol.

27. Roy E. Ciampa and Brian S. Rosner, "1 Corinthians," in *Commentary on the New Testament Use of the Old Testament* (ed. G. K. Beale and D. A. Carson; Grand Rapids: Baker Academic, 2007), p. 748.

28. See comments on Hos 2.

motif appearing elsewhere in Hosea (9:11-16; 10:14), but it also provides a concrete expression of the metaphor of a breech or stillborn child in 13:13. All three sections of Hosea (chapters 1–3; 4–11:11; 11:12–14) contain salvation oracles that reverse this judgment and announce a hopeful future for children (1:10; 11:1, 4, 10; 14:3 [14:4]). In addition, the feminine reference in 13:16 [14:1] ("Samaria shall bear her guilt, because she has rebelled against her God") recalls the devastating judgment on the woman of chapter 2. While God's audience takes the form of a feminine figure repeatedly throughout chapters 1–3, 13:16 [14:1] is the only occurrence where Ephraim or Samaria is explicitly referred to in feminine terms within chapters 4–13. The reference to Samaria as female in 13:16 [14:1] supports the view taken in this commentary that the woman of chapter 2 ought to be understood primarily as Samaria.

While 13:7-9 and 13:15-16 [13:15–14:1] describe the ferocity of Assyrian conquest, they do not necessarily suggest a finality of judgment. Jeremiah 50 transfers the judgments that befall Israel in Hosea over to Assyria and Babylon; it also promises the restoration of those things lost in the course of foreign conquest. Jeremiah 50:17-20 shares motifs and concerns with Hos 13, including the metaphors of sheep and lions, the acknowledgement of the sin and iniquity of both kingdoms, the promise of a restoration to northern territories, and the satiation of hunger:

> Israel is a hunted sheep driven away by lions. First the king of Assyria devoured it, and now at the end King Nebuchadrezzar of Babylon has gnawed its bones. Therefore, thus says the LORD of hosts, the God of Israel: I am going to punish the king of Babylon and his land, as I punished the king of Assyria. I will restore Israel to its pasture, and it shall feed on Carmel and in Bashan, and on the hills of Ephraim and in Gilead its hunger shall be satisfied. In those days and at that time, says the LORD, the iniquity of Israel shall be sought, and there shall be none; and the sins of Judah, and none shall be found; for I will pardon the remnant that I have spared.

When read within the context of the larger prophetic collection, the final verdict of Hos 13 is not that Israel and Judah will be completely destroyed, but rather that God's judgment will fall on Assyria and Babylon. Israel in turn will be completely forgiven and returned to its homeland with all its needs restored.

14. Hosea 14:1-9 [14:2-10]

Bo H. Lim

Hosea 14 reverses the expectations of Hos 13 in dramatic fashion; therefore, its message is bound up with the preceding text. Chapters 13 and 14 function as a diptych, where each "panel" of text glosses the other and meaning is found in the interaction between the messages. When read together, Hosea 13–14 announces the death and resurrection of Israel. Yet chapter 13 provides no indication that a message of hope will follow; instead, it depicts the devastation of Israel in a manner that implies finality. So even though these texts function as a diptych, they are not required to function in this manner. Chapter 13 can function independently of chapter 14 as a legitimate conclusion to the book of Hosea, so the very inclusion of an additional chapter that provides a different ending to the book is a surprise. Therefore, Israel's resurrection and restoration ought not to be understood as a given or as inevitable, but rather as a dramatic and unexpected act of YHWH's grace.

Chapter 14 is focused on repentance, yet it is also an eschatological passage. In this case repentance is not viewed as a precursor to the last days, but rather as a characteristic of the eschaton. Viewed in this manner, repentance is both a means and an end; it is not to be viewed as an act of humiliation and judgment, but rather as the mechanism to receive eschatological blessing. Hosea 1–3 also possesses an eschatological orientation, yet these texts speak little of Israel's role in ushering in future blessing; there it is the prerogative of God to redeem Israel and creation. Chapter 14 focuses on the human response to God's invitation, and demonstrates that salvation involves a willing acceptance of divine forgiveness and renewal. Earlier in the book the prophet spoke of the necessity for discipline and the "penance" of exile. Viewed from the perspective of the end of the book, any judgment brought upon the house of Israel and Judah is restorative justice. Genuine repentance ought not to be viewed as punitive, since the call to repentance is motivated out of love. The prophet has not led his audience on a thirteen-chapter literary journey of penitence only to end in judgment. Turning to YHWH, renouncing sinful ways, and receiving the love and forgiveness of God are the gift and the goal of repentance. The pilgrimage of penitence, then, ought to be viewed not as a precursor to condemnation, but rather as a gateway to salvation.

That the main theme of chapter 14 is repentance is demonstrated by the fact that its opening word, "turn/return" (שׁוּב/*šûb*), occurs four times in this chapter (1 [2], 2 [3], 4 [5], 7 [8]). It has been argued in my introduction that this motif runs throughout the book, and a case can be made that it is the central theme of the book, since it ends on this note. Since Hosea also serves as the first book of the Twelve Prophets, the emphasis on "turn/return" in its conclusion may signal the importance of this theme for the rest of the Twelve. Regarding its conclusion, Schart observes, "The reader is not provided with information concerning how Israel responded. As a result, Hosea remains open-ended, and readers await further treatment of this topic. And indeed, they will not be disappointed: the topic of return will become a major thematic thread as the Book of the Twelve progresses."[1] Sure enough, the language of Hos 14:1-3 [2-4] occurs in the very next book of the Twelve, in Joel 2:12-14. In Joel, the word "turn/return" (שׁוּב/*šûb*) appears three times (2:12, 13, 14), and 2:13 quotes Exod 34:6-7, a passage that deeply influenced the author of Hosea. Amos picks up this theme in 4:6-11, and emphatically states that Israel failed to repent by repeating five times the phrase "yet you did not return (שׁוּב/*šûb*) to me, says the LORD" (4:6, 8, 9, 10, 11). Certainly the Assyrian and Babylonian conquests confirm Amos' words, yet Hosea's prophecy that Israel would return (שׁוּב/*šûb*, 3:5) in the future finds confirmation in the postexilic prophets. Zechariah indicates that the people heard the former prophet's words, "Return (שׁוּב/*šûb*) from your evil ways and from your evil deeds" (1:4), and that "they repented (שׁוּב/*šûb*) and said, 'The LORD of hosts has dealt with us according to our ways and deeds, just as he planned to do'" (1:6). Hosea's call to return is announced by Zechariah, "Thus says the LORD of hosts: Return to me, says the LORD of hosts, and I will return to you, says the LORD of hosts" (1:3). The last prophet of the Twelve will reiterate this plea for repentance, "Return to me, and I will return to you, says the LORD of hosts" (Mal 3:7). Even after God's people returned to the land from Babylonian exile, the prophets continued to call God's people to return. This demonstrates the ongoing struggle for Israel to remain faithful to YHWH despite its political circumstances, and indicates

---

1. Aaron Schart, "The First Section of the Book of the Twelve Prophets," *Int* 61 (2007): 141. For a full treatment of this theme within the Twelve see Jason T. LeCureux, *The Thematic Unity of the Book of the Twelve* (HBM 41; Sheffield: Sheffield Phoenix Press, 2012).

that the eschatological promises of Hosea and the Twelve have not yet been completely fulfilled.

Many have observed that chapter 14 resembles liturgical penitential prayers similar to Pss 51, 85, and 126. While this passage is to be understood primarily with regard to its role in the prophetic book of Hosea, its liturgical elements — both in form and in content — are not without significance. While Hosea has been critical of the cult, it is striking that the prophet utilizes cultic practices and imagery in his attempts to call the people to repentance. Perhaps the prophet does so because he understands that humans are liturgical beings, and that the solution to false worship is never to abolish worship altogether, but always to reform it. James Smith observes that liturgies "shape and constitute our identities by forming our most fundamental desires and our most basic attunement to the world. In short, liturgies make us certain kinds of people, and what defines us is what we *love*."[2] Because humans are inherently worshipping creatures, Hosea communicates in liturgical forms. Repentance requires the transformation of the totality of one's being, so Hosea appropriately addresses Israel in liturgical forms in order to reform the heart and not just the mind.

The recognition in 14:1 [14:2] that Israel has stumbled (כשׁל/*kāšal*, cf. 4:5; 5:5) in its iniquity suggests that some form of judgment has already occurred. Even though Israelites were not to appear before YHWH empty-handed (cf. Exod 23:15; 34:20), the prophet calls on Israel to "take words" rather than sacrifices in the act of returning in v. 2 [3]. The words Israel offers to God come in the form of a litany that includes the request that God 1) forgive all guilt, 2) take that which is good, and 3) receive the bulls of their lips (i.e., the bulls they have promised). Many translations follow the LXX and emend שׁפתינו פרים/*pārîm šĕpātênû* to read "fruit of our lips." Yet in this case, it seems "bulls" ought to be maintained since bulls and calves feature so prominently in the book of Hosea (8:5, 6; 13:2). Instead of the offering of bulls or kissing calves with their lips (cf. 13:2), Israel is to use its lips to offer contrite confession unto God. Once again, true repentance and the true knowledge of God cannot be confined to cultic observance. In this case, Hosea uses liturgical language to describe non-cultic practices in order to redefine what truly constitutes true worship.

In pluralistic environments in which there are competing claims for loyalty, genuine believers are often required to make both affirmations and denials. In this manner, Hos 14:3 [4] contains three negative statements: 1) Assyria shall not save us; 2) we will not ride upon horses; 3) we will say no more, "Our God," to the work of our hands. It also contains one positive affirmation, "in you the

2. James K. A. Smith, *Desiring the Kingdom* (Grand Rapids: Baker Academic, 2009), p. 25, emphasis his.

orphan finds mercy." In the commentary on chapter 13, several intertextual links were observed between chapters 13 and 8. Beginning in 14:3 [14:4], chapter 14 makes several allusions to chapter 8 as well. Hosea 8:9 describes how "they have gone up to Assyria," yet in 14:3 [4] Israel confesses, "Assyria shall not save us." Hosea 8:6 describes how an artisan made an idol in Israel, yet in 14:3 [4] Israel denounces those idols that are "the work of our hands." Hosea 8:5 is the first mention in the book where YHWH admits, "My anger burns against them," and in 14:4 [5] God reverses course, stating, "for my anger has turned from them." Hosea 8:4 describes Ephraim making "idols for their own destruction," and in 14:8 [9] YHWH once and for all denounces idolatry, saying, "O Ephraim, what have I to do with idols?" Two lines of literary development, either from chapter 8 to chapter 13, or from chapter 8 to chapter 14, result in two endings to the book of Hosea. These conclusions represent two different moral choices for the reader of the book: either the devastating judgment of chapter 13 or the divine healing and love of chapter 14. The key to avoiding destruction and to unlocking a future filled with forgiveness, abundance, love, and security is repentance.

While caring for the orphan was a common expectation of ANE kings, here in Hos 14:3 [4] this commitment bears even greater significance. Within the near context of chapters 11-13, Israel has been portrayed as a child who has been rejected due to his unfaithfulness (11:1-2) and foolishness (13:13). As noted in the comments to chapter 13, it is children in particular who bear the harsh consequences of the judgment to befall Israel (cf. 13:16). Lastly, the mention of "mercy" (רחם/*rāḥam*) in 14:3 [4] recalls the name "No Mercy" (לא רחמה/*lō' ruḥāmāh*) that was bestowed upon Hosea's child in 1:6. Hosea's affirmation that the orphan can now find mercy in YHWH signifies a reversal of God's previous claim, "I will no longer have pity (רחם/*rāḥam*) on the house of Israel or forgive them" (Hos 1:6). Just as Lo-Ruhamah served as a concrete sign of the abrogation of covenant relationship, God's care for the orphan represents the renewal of the covenant. Repeatedly, Hosea has given witness to the importance of children as a sign of God's favor and the covenant relationship. If such is the case, the people of God should consider the degree to which children are valued and integrated into communities of faith.

Reflecting the liturgical character of the passage, God's response to the people carries cultic associations. In 14:4 [5] the word "freely" (נדבה/*nĕdābāh*) almost always refers to "freewill offerings" in the OT. Freewill offerings were spontaneous acts above and beyond the necessary sacrifices in Israel's cult, and were given as an expression of love and thanks to YHWH. Once again, God uses a cultic term to describe a non-cultic act, and in this case, it is love. Unsurprisingly, liturgy is the mode of communication since it is the most effective pedagogy to train the heart. While the people offer sacrifices and burnt offerings but lack loyalty and the knowledge of God (cf. 6:6), God responds with "freewill" love.

The language of healing in 14:4 [5] (רפא/*rāpā'*, cf. 6:1; 7:1) and dew in 14:5 [6] (טל/*ṭal*, cf. 6:4) recalls the discourse in Hos 6:1–7:2. Earlier it was argued that the oracles of Hosea ought to be read dialogically, and that Hos 14:1-5 [14:2-6] serves as a conclusion to the provisional claims of Hos 6:1–7:2. In Hos 6:1, Ephraim presumes that YHWH would heal the injured nation, yet 7:1 indicates that such would not be the case because of Israel's continued wickedness and corruption. Whereas Hos 6:1–7:2 is inconclusive about whether Israel will be healed, Hos 14:4 [5] makes a definitive announcement that Israel can expect healing in its future. A discrepancy exists between the diagnoses of Israel's illness and the prescribed treatments. Whereas Israel seeks healing from foreign oppression and dominance (cf. 5:13–6:1), God focuses instead on the disease within Ephraim itself. One reason why the healing has been delayed, and the discourses of repentance in Hosea extended, is because of Israel's refusal to acknowledge that its illness is self-induced. Hosea 14:4 [5] identifies the problem as "disloyalty" (משובה/*mĕšûbāh*), derived from the word "return, turn" (שוב/*šûb*), a term that features so prominently in Hosea and the Twelve. This word appears earlier, in 11:7, and besides one other occurrence, the only other book it appears in is Jeremiah (2:19; 3:6, 8, 11, 12, 22; 5:6; 8:5; 14:7). This word appears in the context of Jeremiah's speech regarding whoredom and adultery, and like Hos 14:4 [5], Jer 3:22 offers the promise, "Return, O faithless children, I will heal your faithlessness (משובה/*mĕšûbāh*)."

Previously, dew has been a negative metaphor in the book, signifying the capriciousness of Ephraim and Judah. In 6:3-4 Israel, as evanescent dew, is set in contrast to God, who is like the substantive downpour of rains. Hosea 13:2-4 compares Ephraim's loyalty to dew that quickly evaporates, in contrast to YHWH, who has remained Israel's God and savior since the exodus. In Hos 14:5 [6], the dew metaphor is redeemed, and here it describes YHWH as an agent of life and nourishment. By taking an image used previously to define Israel and now applying it to God, the prophecy shifts the gaze of the reader from the attributes of the people to the character of God. Rather than Israel corrupting God through its faithless character, the prophecy repeatedly indicates that the attributes of God will be transferred over to the people (cf. 2:19-20 [2:21-22]). Because Israel is the child of YHWH, it was created to reflect the image of its father; therefore, its true identity rests only in God. The opening verb of 14:5 [14:6], "I will be" (אהיה/*'ehyeh*), in its first person common singular form, occurs only one other time in the book: when YHWH declares that God would no longer be "I am" to Israel in Hos 1:9. Its use in Hos 14:5 [14:6] indicates that God remains "I am" to Israel, and this name carries the reciprocal name "My people" (cf. 2:1 [2:3]) for Israel according to the covenant formula, "I will be God for you; you shall be a people for me."[3] In addition, it is noteworthy that the blessing of dew (טל/*ṭal*, 6:4; 13:3; 14:5 [14:6]), fat or oil (שמן/*šemen*, 2:5 [2:7]; 12:1 [12:2]), grain (דגן/*dāgān*, 2:8 [2:10], 9 [11], 22 [24]; 7:14; 9:1; 14:7 [14:8]), and wine (תירוש/*tîrôš*, 2:8 [2:10], 9 [11], 22 [24]; 4:11; 7:14; 9:2) that occurs so frequently in Hosea is featured in Isaac's blessing of Jacob in Gen 27:28 — "May God give you of the dew (טל/*ṭal*) of heaven, and of the fatness (שמן/*šemen*) of the earth, and plenty of grain (דגן/*dāgān*) and wine (תירוש/*tîrôš*)" — and stripped from Esau in Gen 27:37. It is no wonder that the Jacob traditions feature prominently in Hos 12. The mention of these particular blessings in Hos 14 signifies the fulfillment of God's promise to the patriarchs.

Excluding for the moment 14:9 [14:10], the book ends with the reiteration of Ephraim's identity in 14:8 [14:9]. The wordplay is not only suggestive of how Ephraim (אפרים/*'eprayim*) might once again be "fruitful" (פרי/*pĕrî*), it is also a clarification of the identity of God's people. This penultimate conclusion is unsurprising given the repeated emphasis on names signifying identity throughout the book of Hosea (e.g., Jezreel, [Lo-] Ammi, [Lo-] Ruhamah, Jacob). The prophet wants the audience to be absolutely clear from what — or rather from whom — they are named and defined as persons. The idols are to be rejected because they threaten to corrupt Israel's understanding of itself.

Since the wisdom saying at the conclusion of the book asks readers to process the contents of the prophecy with discernment, Hos 14:9 [14:10] in many ways functions as a hermeneutical introduction to the book. The fact that it appears at the end of the book supports the notion that this prophecy was to be read and reread. The book was designed so that readers might draw connections in the book, both backwards and forwards, and we have followed this reading strategy in this commentary. The ending to Hosea serves as a beginning; it calls for the reader to return to the beginning of the prophecy, as well as read further into the Twelve Prophets. The fact that an additional superscription besides Hos 1:1 was added to the text indicates that the prophecy was to be read from multiple perspectives. Hosea 14:9 [14:10] explicitly instructs the reader to read the prophecy from a perspective other than that of the historical prophet.

Since Hosea ends without a resolution to the question of whether Israel turns to YHWH or not, the book of Joel serves as a continuation of the prophecy. In a continuation of themes, language, and common intertexts from Hosea, Joel 2:12-14 continues to call for Israel to repent:

> Yet even now, says the LORD, return (שוב/*šûb*) to me with all your heart (לבב/*lēbāb*), with fasting, with weeping, and with mourning; rend your

---

3. See commentary on 1:9.

hearts (לבב/*lēbāb*) and not your clothing. Return (שוב/*šûb*) to the LORD, your God, for he is gracious and merciful, slow to anger, and abounding in steadfast love, and relents (נחם/*niham*) from punishing. Who knows whether he will not turn (שוב/*šûb*) and relent (נחם/*niham*), and leave a blessing behind him, a grain offering and a drink offering for the LORD, your God?

The language of turning and returning is clearly reminiscent of the double call for repentance in Hos 14:1-2 [14:2-3] that concludes the prophecy. The double mention of the "heart" recalls Hosea's description of Israel's insincere and deceiving heart in Hos 7:14 and 10:2. Joel quotes the self-description of the covenant God in Exod 34:6-7, a passage that features prominently within the prophecy of Hosea. Whereas Hos 13:14 declared that God would not relent or show compassion (נחם/*niham*), Joel 2:13 acknowledges that YHWH relents from punishing, and 2:14 recognizes this as a genuine possibility. The fact that Hosea's prophecy continues into Joel and the rest of the Twelve demonstrates that it is not bound to a particular historical moment. When read within its canonical context, Hosea's prophecy urges every community to receive it as a contemporary message.

As many have observed, Hos 14:9 [14:10] resembles the wisdom writings of Ps 107:43 ("Let those who are wise give heed to these things, and consider the steadfast love of the LORD"). Psalm 107:43 serves as the last verse of the opening chapter to book five of the Psalter; in a somewhat similar fashion, Hos 14:9 [14:10] serves as the last verse of the opening book of the Twelve. As noted in my introduction, Hos 14:9 [14:10] follows a pattern of adding a sapiential redaction to books in the OT canon so that wisdom functions as a hermeneutical lens to read the Torah and the Prophets. In addition, since wisdom features prominently in the Writings and Poetic books, Hos 14:9 [10] also links the Prophets with this last canonical collection. Petersen observes:

> Just as Mal. 3:22-24 [4:4-6] establishes connections with the torah and the former prophets, Hos. 14:10 [9] provides a linkage with the third section of the canon. The two epilogues work together to relate the book of the XII to the other sections of the canon. One may argue that these two epilogues act as a canonical envelope, which encloses the minor prophets. They not only mark off but also integrate the minor prophets with the rest of the canon.[4]

4. David L. Petersen, *Zechariah 9–14 and Malachi: A Commentary* (OTL; Louisville: Westminster John Knox, 1995), p. 233.

Like Hosea 14:9 [14:10], the book of Malachi ends with an emphasis on the importance of wisdom to discern between the righteous and the wicked: "Then once more you shall see the difference between the righteous and the wicked, between one who serves God and one who does not serve him" (Mal 3:18). The wisdom that is called for in Hos 14:9 [14:10] and Mal 3:18 is not of the speculative sort, but is rather wisdom concerned with ethics and piety. Perhaps Hosea concludes with a call for what Briggs identifies as interpretive wisdom, wisdom that "discerns the difference between questions that lead us forward (toward life, away from death) and questions that amount to the anxiety or futility of shouldering impossible interpretive burdens."[5] Rather than burden readers with interpretative conundrums, the message of Hosea ought to burden its hearers with the need to turn/return to God.

5. Richard S. Briggs, *The Virtuous Reader: Old Testament Narrative and Interpretive Virtue* (Studies in Theological Interpretation; Grand Rapids: Baker Academic, 2010), p. 99.

15. Readers of Terror: Brief Reflections on a Wise Reading of Hosea

Daniel Castelo

The last theological chapter ended with the claim that Hosean marriage imagery could be used among the worshiping faithful, but only with great care. The warning serves not to prohibit the church from employing Hosea as Sacred Scripture, but to alert readers that certain themes and passages of the Bible require directed and meticulous attention because they have the potential to strike a chord with our present situation in deeply stirring, obfuscating, and maybe even painful ways. Naturally, the Bible should always be approached with great care because of its role among God's people, which is its employment by the triune God to nourish, sustain, chastise, and transform them. But at the same time, Scripture is textual and thus requires interpretation, and because of this, wayward approaches to Holy Writ are always possible, approaches that complicate and even impede its God-given role in the formation of the faithful. That is why risk always exists just under the surface when people explicitly claim that their aim is to find the "biblical view" for any number of topics. In such cases, Scripture all too easily serves to legitimize, spiritually and theologically, a predetermined agenda.

We mentioned in the first chapter that theological interpretation is a kind of "interested reading" of the Bible and that, after the critical turn in hermeneutics, such self-understood forms of interpretation were justified. Nevertheless, the main challenge before the reading faithful is the identification of the interests involved whenever the Bible is read. Is the interest of reading Scripture the promotion of the knowledge and love of God? This is a salutary goal, one that has grounded our own work in this commentary. But other interests are possible, and these can be sinister, not only because of their detrimental effects, but also because of their obscurity. As noted above, some readers of the Bible are simply looking for ways to support what they already want to say. This process could take place purposefully or unintentionally by the readers involved.

Others, again possibly consciously or unconsciously, may employ the Bible so as to reinforce, directly or indirectly, forms of restrictive hegemony and systemic injustice that mark a given context's *Zeitgeist*. Could it be that multiple interests are involved in a given instantiation of Scripture's reading, and that some of these are less obvious and faithful than others? And if so, how would these be identified, disciplined, and corrected?

One way to address these questions would be to attend to how the church uses the Bible, but such a strategy is fraught with complications. For instance, to what degree is the reading of Scripture "communal" in its execution and forms? Take the local church context. When a preacher elaborates a biblical passage in the form of a sermon, the medium itself is not conversational but instructional and hortatory. Devotional reading of the Bible is often individualistic and privatized. Small group Bible study represents one potential venue for the identification of readerly interests, but these often gravitate to other goals, including application. Often, the Bible is mined and cast so as to be relevant to its Christian readers, and of course, one does need to see how Scripture could function within one's life. But relevance can be framed in any number of ways. The tension comes to the fore when one contrasts the alternatives: Does application coincide easily with confession and repentance? Is transformation understood as a "relevant" outcome from the reading of Holy Writ?

These difficulties point to the challenge of rendering an account of the church's communal reading practices. More often than not in the ecclesial contexts we know, the Bible is read by individuals, for individuals. Little in terms of communal deliberation, questioning, and critique can be found in the church's reading practices. Because of this, the identification, weighing, and discrimination of readerly interests rarely take place in a corporate and public way within churches. These tasks, we believe, are crucial and take priority over seeking relevance and rendering application, since the latter assume working accounts of a text's meaning. In other words, before seeking to apply a biblical text, should we not sit and dwell on what a text can mean?[1]

This absence of mechanisms by which to identify and purify readerly interests has at least two associated concerns for the theological interpretation of Scripture. First, apart from a communal identity and location, the fostering of the knowledge and love of God is significantly impaired. We realize that, in our individualistic contexts, such a claim appears nonsensical and perhaps

---

1. This line of inquiry goes back to our hermeneutical commitment that the meaning of texts is underdetermined. What we worry about with those who seek quickly to apply the biblical text is the assumption that one meaning for the text exists (usually an author-driven account), which in turn needs to be mined, universalized, and then applied. A text's meaning, we would contend, is much more dynamic and fluid.

offensive. But the depths and riches of the Christian life have never been promoted in terms of individualistic dynamics. Christian discipleship from its very beginnings has been cast in collective terms. Growth in the Christian life is properly and fittingly a communal phenomenon. Furthermore, the summation of the law is loving both God and neighbor, and often it is *through* our neighbor that God works and is made known. In terms of the praxis of the Christian life, one could argue that one cannot know and love God apart from knowing and loving one's neighbor. Therefore, if one reads the Bible to seek the face of God, one must be rooted in the company of those who are striving after that same goal and who reflect that same face.

Second, even if Christians lack a communal sense of their identity as readers of the Sacred Word, they are nevertheless bombarded as Christians with a multiplicity of interpretations of it. "Christian" as an identity construct is largely constituted by arrangements and configurations of biblical texts and their interpretations. A basic reason for this state is the way the Bible (especially for Protestants) is valued as central to Christian identity. Often one can find claims to the effect that the theological task rests directly upon the exegetical. Therefore, as Christians come and go in their faith peregrinations, listening to songs, seeing videos, hearing speakers, and reading books that are all embedded within the Christian ethos, they will inevitably be shaped and influenced by varying — and often competing — interpretations of the Bible. With so many options available, the question of identifying and evaluating the interests of readers becomes all the more necessary.

Given the absence of a diagnostic process for evaluating competing interpretations of biblical texts within many Christian fellowships, which readings ultimately prevail? Which ones stick, are picked up, and exert long-term influence? Usually, interpretations become normative when their source and logic fit and correspond to other determinations and evaluations. Take again the context of the local church: If my pastor, whom I already respect, elaborates a passage a certain way, I am predisposed to grant that reading some legitimacy. Furthermore, that reading's appeal is reinforced for me if it makes sense to my way of thinking and can be accommodated within my concerns, values, and desires. Notice how self-enclosed this hermeneutical process sounds: Readers see in the text what they are already disposed to see. They identify and cast the text in ways that fit their own structures of intelligibility and meaning.[2]

The challenge of Hosea is that many of its features do not fit very easily alongside contemporary sensibilities and thought forms, and apart from

---

2. This insight, as with so many in this chapter, is compellingly expressed by Hans-Georg Gadamer in *Truth and Method* (2d and rev. ed.; London: Continuum, 2004).

communally-deliberative practices of interpretation, the tendency by Christian readers is to pick up those readings that are most easily accommodated to their wider intuitions of what God and God's purposes must be like. We suspect this tendency is at play in those who are disposed to see in Hosea "the greatest love story ever told." A "hermeneutic of trust" may be proper in the sense of recognizing Scripture as a means of grace employed by the triune God for the formation of a godly people, but trustworthiness could also be misdirected so as to invite Scripture's domestication.

Those who are disposed to see the deleterious effects of hermeneutical enclosures are often roused to point them out through gestures of scholarly advocacy. Usually, their voices are inflected and grounded in specific experiences and circumstances. The suspicion they harbor often rests on precedent. Their readings and concerns are usually not on behalf of the spacious, removed, and privileged contexts of academia's ivory towers, but rather driven by the nitty-gritty situations of real life.[3] The promotion of these perspectives simply adds richer, otherwise inaccessible dimensions to the reading of texts; these mixtures allow the task of reading the Bible to be disrupted in meaningful ways. After all, "the greatest love story ever told" approach to Hosea often carries with it any number of assumptions related to gender roles, domestic violence and abuse, sexual intimacy, and forms of relating that are *only* identified as such once a variety of readers are allowed at the table of scriptural deliberation and conversation. Take again a feature of Hosea: As mentioned earlier, Gomer has no voice in the book of Hosea and, for the most part, neither does Israel within Hosea's oracles. Those who have been silent or silenced in their own experience of intimacy and marriage are more inclined to see this feature of the book, and the insight itself is an important and relevant dimension to its reading in the church today. These readers might fittingly ask: How can a love story be "great" when one partner never speaks?

The force of these concerns points to the following: Parts of Hosea may be considered "texts of terror" in some sense (to use the language of Phyllis

3. If one simply takes time to account for the statistics, they are overwhelming: According to one study, slightly more than a quarter (25.5%) of American women are "violently victimized at some time during their lives," with such victimization including "physical assaults, attempted and completed sexual assaults, and stalking" (see the "Introduction" to Claire M. Renzetti and Raquel Kennedy Bergen, eds., *Violence against Women* [Boulder: Rowman and Littlefield, 2005], p. 1). The issues reach into the church as well, for a survey of United Methodist women in the early 1980s demonstrated that "one in every twenty-seven . . . had been raped, one in every thirteen had been physically abused by her husband, [and] one in every four had been verbally or emotionally abused" (see Susan Brooks Thistlewaite, "Every Two Minutes: Battered Women and Feminist Interpretation," in *Feminist Interpretation of the Bible* [ed. Letty M. Russell; Philadelphia: Westminster, 1985], p. 96).

Trible[4]), but we tend to believe that the real culprits of Hosea's misappropriation are its readers and employers. We believe that "readers of terror" are much more sinister and dangerous than whatever one finds problematic within Hosea itself. That is not to say that motifs, images, and features of Hosea' oracles are not without their difficulty. Quite the contrary, we tend to think that Hosea's role within the canon of sacred writings is to shock and unsettle its readers. But we wish to focus the responsibility of Hosea's damaging reception upon those who read and utilize the book. A theological reading of Hosea lends itself to the promotion of the diagnostic and reparative work needed for a community's faithful reception of the Bible.

In what follows, we will address a common and perennial concern raised by Hosea's readers; it is a running question that theological interpreters of Hosea have to address at some point or another. We will conclude by offering some practical considerations for how to read Hosea in a responsible, fitting, and wise way. We hope to show that Hosea does indeed have a role to play in the church today *only if* the church is willing to prepare and regulate itself adequately to receive it.

Is Hosea Misogynistic?

One of the persistent concerns about Hosea relates to the question of whether it is essentially misogynistic, i.e., if it perpetuates a message that is inherently and ultimately hateful toward women. The question is deeply complex: For some people, it is unquestionably a ludicrous query because the Bible is Holy Scripture; God's Word simply could not promote something so blatantly sinful as hatred toward women because of what the Bible is. In this case, a "hermeneutic of trust" may be overriding some legitimate concerns raised by those who operate out of a "hermeneutic of suspicion," since the latter are aware of the countless examples in which people have read in God's Word things that are generally deemed contrary to an overall sense of God's purposes. At the same time, others would wish to press the rhetorical forms present in Hosea's oracles to significant and maybe even deleterious degrees. Rather than giving a "pass" to the Bible because it is Holy Writ, these readers would wish to sit in the tension of its strangeness and potential offensiveness with a sensibility of not "explaining away" what they believe is "obviously there" in the text.[5] With this

---

4. *Texts of Terror* (OBT; Philadelphia: Fortress, 1984).

5. If the reader will indulge me with an autobiographical note, this point hit home for me when I was a junior in high school attending a summer theology camp at a major university. At

approach, a "hermeneutic of suspicion" could ignore or unhelpfully destabilize the authority of the Bible for readers with such concerns. Both camps essentially show how, at a fundamental level — in the "background," so to speak — certain assumptions about meaning and legitimacy are operative and determinative of all that follows in one's hermeneutical orientation and execution.

At the beginning of her monograph on the sexual and marital metaphors in the prophetic literature, Sharon Moughtin-Mumby labels (however inadequately) the camps alluded to above as the "traditionalist" and "feminist" approaches, and makes a legitimate point about metaphors generally. One cannot help but agree with her view that variances between these two camps are due largely to "differing understandings of metaphor shifting beneath the surface of the debate."[6] The "traditionalists" are inclined to emphasize the way metaphors operate out of a principle of equivocity, so that these images can be translated or substituted by a more direct and available set of referents. Such gestures are generally seen as unproblematic so that — to take the present case — Hosea's sexual imagery would be a metaphor for the more relevant and applicable circumstances related to Israel's unjust political alliances with foreign powers, its faulty worship of YHWH, and so on. Given that the end or point of the metaphor is taken to be the highlighting of the scandalous nature of such alliances and practices, the sexual imagery in Hosea can be seen as functioning strictly to illustrate those points. Whatever problematic features subsequently arise related to a specific metaphor can be deemed incidental or misdirected in relation to the more relevant concerns for which the metaphor exists in the first place.

To continue with Moughtin-Mumby's categories, the "feminist" camp, on the other hand, believes metaphors function in more complex ways than the traditionalists suggest. These readers would resist the assumed ease with which metaphors could be put to the side, since "connotations surrounding any metaphorical word are intrinsic to its meaning."[7] As Moughtin-Mumby continues, "Indeed, metaphor, as a cognitive device, is often believed to *create*

---

one point, one of the event's leaders guided some of us through the pericope of Jesus and the Canaanite woman (Matt 15:22-28). The focus of the session was largely directed to Jesus' use of the metaphor of not throwing food to dogs, and of course, gender implications (among others) follow from it. To open discussion, the leader began, "Now, Jesus called this woman a 'bitch.' What do we do with that?" Right away, I was confronted with the way people "see" texts differently. For a helpful discussion of this hermeneutical point of various acts of "seeing," see Merold Westphal, *Whose Community? Which Interpretation?* (Grand Rapids: Baker Academic, 2009), chapter 1.

6. Sharon Moughtin-Mumby, *Sexual and Marital Metaphors in Hosea, Jeremiah, Isaiah, and Ezekiel* (Oxford Theological Monographs; Oxford: Oxford University Press, 2008), p. 3.

7. Moughtin-Mumby, *Sexual and Marital Metaphors*, p. 4.

meaning, having the ability to introduce new perspectives and outlooks."[8] These readers believe that metaphors are not so easily abandoned once their function is "realized"; quite the contrary, their usage has the potential to introduce or reinforce associations or stereotypes that are held, consciously or unconsciously, by those encountering texts with rich and complex imagery. As such, metaphors depicting women as inferior, their sexuality as deviant, and their very bodies as meriting physical constraint and force all work to create interconnected webs of signification in which women are anything but positively portrayed. When one adds patriarchal arrangements to the mix — not simply those of the text's orig-inating circumstances, but also those related to the contexts in which biblical texts are received — one can easily see how Hosea could aggravate or worsen the struggle for women's full equality, dignity, and respect.

It is worth noting several aspects of Moughtin-Mumby's mapping of the prophetic literature's varied reception in terms of the sexual and marital met-aphors as they are found in books like Hosea. We tend to agree at some level with Moughtin-Mumby: Operative in this differentiation of camps is not so much the particular question of the specific metaphors used, but varied ap-proaches to metaphor in general. This hermeneutical concern may go unno-ticed among interpreters until something controversial, such as a metaphor's relationship to violence against women, is brought to the fore; at those times, one's approach to metaphor becomes all-important simply because the stakes are so high. Nevertheless, one must examine the way approaches to metaphors are inculcated, sustained, and used, so that reactions to Hosea can be situated within a broader framework of meaning-generation. The consequences of this step should not be downplayed, for one's approach to metaphor will inevitably determine in a significant way what one "sees" in and outside the text. To take the two camps outlined above: The "traditionalists" may be so taken by their approach to metaphor that they fail to see how the language and imagery of Hosea can have deleterious consequences on readers. In such cases, agreement with a theory of metaphor trumps the legitimacy of a person's lived experience. On the other side, "feminists" may be so fixated on the potential abuse and pain that such imagery can inspire among readers that their general outlook toward such texts is irremediably tinged and affected as a result. For some of these readers, texts like Hosea can never be read for salutary ends, so they are best avoided because of their potential effects. Obviously, these conclusions are exceedingly disparate. They show in microcosmic form the wide array of outcomes possible from varying hermeneutical vantage points.

These concerns, and the decisions made in light of them, determine sig-

---

8. *Sexual and Marital Metaphors*, p. 4.

nificantly how one approaches a question such as the one that titles this sub-section. To ask "Is Hosea Misogynistic?" involves the prior consideration of whether a text and its metaphors can be said to be ontically constituted (the "is" of the question) by an ideology, perspective, and disposition such as misogyny. Another way of asking the question would be, "Can misogyny be a property of a text, and if so, is this the case with Hosea?" A commentary such as this one cannot entertain the complexity of such matters, much less offer an insight or treatment that will win the day among the majority of readers and interested parties. The pertinent concerns are simply too contested to be otherwise.

For us, both as authors of this commentary and Christian readers of Holy Scripture, we tend to side with those scholars who would say that texts are nei-ther ontically constituted ideologically nor that ideologies can be considered as properties of texts.[9] We derive this conclusion from the form of textuality itself: Texts, in being texts, have to be interpreted. Texts cannot be accessed apart from interpretation, given their nature as texts. And if one considers the receptive and effective histories of various passages of the Bible, sundry cases show that single texts can be interpreted as suggesting multiple (and sometimes even contradictory) ideological concerns across time.[10] Both in their composition and reception, texts can reflect the ideological tendencies of individuals, but texts and language generally are significantly underdetermined when isolated from the contexts that engage, foster, and perpetuate them.[11] Texts do not have ideologies, nor are they ideological. *But people have ideologies, and they can be ideological.*

In this sense, Hosea cannot be misogynistic; it can reflect misogynistic authors and trigger misogynistic tendencies in given readers, but such admis-sions are altogether different from making an ontological claim about a text itself. If these commitments are granted, then Hosea need not be marginalized by Christian readers, nor considered as antithetical to the Christian gospel, on the basis that it is misogynistic. We believe Hosea can be read profitably for the life of faith. Nevertheless — and the following is granted with utmost seri-ousness — the admission of a text's non-ideological essentiality does not mean that it is strictly a neutral phenomenon. As a "distinct other," a text does have qualities that pertain to itself. Certain words are used, others not; some images

9. We follow the lead here of Stephen Fowl; see his early article, "Texts Don't Have Ideol-ogies," *BibInt* 3 (1995): 1-34, and his subsequent work in *Engaging Scripture* (Malden: Blackwell, 1998), pp. 63-75.

10. See Fowl, *Engaging Scripture*, p. 65.

11. I make this point simply out of the sensibility of how most of our language "works" given the heavy influence of hermeneutical background concerns that drive a text's assumed meaning. See John R. Searle, *The Construction of Social Reality* (New York: Free Press, 1995), chapter 6.

are employed, others not at all. As we have noted of Hosea, some personages in the narrative speak, others do not. In fact, Hosea is blatantly one-sided in the use of sexual and marital metaphors, since women are exclusively depicted as the offending sex. Whatever one wishes to make of the nature of metaphor, we believe this judgment is available to an attentive reader. As Carol Dempsey remarks, "The text [of Hosea] gives a preference for and an affirmation of the male gender while offering a negative image of the female gender. The one who is faithful is male; the one who is unfaithful is female. . . . The text's metaphorical language communicates an image that could legitimate and support misogyny, both ancient and modern."[12] Were men and husbands depicted with some degree of regularity as offending parties in such imagery and women more positively portrayed, the gender-charged difficulties would be minimized for readers encountering Hosea today. However, no significant respite on the gender front presents itself along these lines, so one is faced with a reduction of operative motifs. In Hosea, womanhood is continually depicted as the image of choice for infidelity, impurity, and sexual lasciviousness; manhood simply is not. Despite our commitments to the nature of texts, we refuse to ignore that Hosea retains a distinctive shape by what it includes and avoids; therefore, we agree that reading this text as Holy Scripture is challenging, and we sympathize with how this collection of oracles could trigger or shape its readers in difficult and unhealthy ways.[13]

Interpretation as a Communal Activity

The camps as formulated by Moughtin-Mumby are problematic not only in that such framing posits the situation as an "either-or" contrast (that is, a person can hold only one or the other view), but also in the way that no guiding framework is provided for the way these approaches are to be embodied communally. Simply, these categories can be said to represent "positions," a term which itself could be taken as ideological in nature. As "positions," these views are highly abstracted and separated from contexts of performance, which is a problem since these contexts would in turn nuance and shape the way these "positions" are taken up and enacted. Without communal forms of reading, one wonders:

12. *The Prophets* (Minneapolis: Fortress, 2000), p. 154. We take Dempsey's claim of an image's potential legitimation and support of misogyny to rest on readerly interests and deployments.

13. For these reasons we join with Julia O'Brien's qualification of Fowl, that when a text's originating circumstances share ideological forms with those of a certain set of readers, ideological proclivities can be reinforced as a result; see *Challenging Prophetic Metaphor* (Louisville: Westminster John Knox Press, 2008), pp. xviii-xix.

Can readers be held accountable? And if so, by whom, and on what grounds? The issue for us is not Hosea per se, but how Hosea is read. To address these concerns, we wish to lift up the community known as the one, holy, catholic, and apostolic church.

We mention the church for several reasons. We remarked earlier that the Bible is properly the "church's book." The Bible is Sacred Scripture for this broad communion that includes many individual collectives. And it is only within communal forms of existence that guiding frameworks can be available for a fitting and appropriate reading. Communal forms of life set up ways of embodying and practicing a discipline — such as the reading of particular texts — so as to demonstrate tangibly and experientially what maturity and excellence look like in such activities. Only within a community can a person be held accountable, corrected pastorally, and urged to grow in accordance with known and admired precedents and models. For these and many more reasons, the church plays a vital role in the task of scriptural interpretation.

Some may find these claims inconsonant with approaches that emphasize the authority of Scripture. Particularly, Protestants may quibble with this estimation of the church's role as sounding too Roman Catholic, particularly in light of the Protestant inclination to affirm the sufficiency of Scripture. We cannot answer this charge adequately here. We would simply say in light of these concerns that we view biblical interpretation as a collective enterprise, since individual selves are constituted and shaped by their embeddedness and situationality within broader forms of life. When one considers the endeavors of translation, copying, transmission, canonization, preaching, teaching, and commentary, biblical interpretation is not a solitary affair. Others are always involved in this process, so the more pertinent questions would be the identity of those "others" and how they exert their influence.

Despite raising the importance of the church, we have also lamented that, within particular churches (as we have experienced them), the Bible typically is not so much deliberated as it is elaborated, not dwelt upon but hurriedly applied. Rarely do Christians gather around a table and "chew on" Scripture. For many, Scripture is not a conversation-starter but an answer-key. And if this is the case, then Hosea will continually suffer in its reception as Holy Word, for its challenge is such that only collectively can sense be made of how the Trinity can use this collection of oracles for teaching, reproof, correction, and training in righteousness (cf. 2 Tim 3:16). Through this line of reasoning, we are not suggesting a capitulation to groupthink or institutionalized mechanisms; rather, we are simply attempting to render the complexity involved in any account of theological reading. Reading Scripture is more an art than a science (as those terms function in English), involving an apprenticeship more so than a week-long seminar, a mentor-friend more than a guru.[14] Time, patience, trial-and-error: These and many other qualities and practices, so often contrary to our daily routines and habits, are required for faithful readings of Hosea. The transition from "readers of terror" to "readers of charity and grace" is characterized by nothing short of a conversion, a kind of renewal and transformation enacted by the Spirit in the midst of Christ's body. The criterion of excellence pertinent to this activity is the wisdom of Christ.

Wisdom has lately gained some prominence as a theological topic; however, as a form of practical reasoning, it is notoriously difficult to define. In fact, by its very nature it is best shown rather than explained. The cross-norming of the conceptual and the practical is of utmost importance with a topic like wisdom, and a commentary can only do so much to promote it. Because of this, we will pursue the following definitions of wisdom with the understanding that we are not doing justice to the notion itself, since no commentary on its own can do so. Wisdom can be cast as the integration of "knowledge, understanding, critical questioning and good judgment with a view to the flourishing of human life and the whole of creation," with "theological wisdom" attempting "all that before God, alert to God, and in line with the purposes of God."[15] From these working proposals, we would like to stress at least two features tied to the theological reading of Hosea, ones that bear directly upon the concerns raised by the camps outlined above.

1) The Need for a Community of Wise Practitioners of Theological Interpretation

If theological reading is more an art than a science, then one has to learn to read Scripture theologically in the context of wise readers. This model of theological interpretation would show "knowledge, understanding, critical questioning, and good judgment," but the point we would stress here is that they would demonstrate all of these *in the midst of challenging circumstances.* In other words, what makes readers wise is not simply their skill and ability as these have been honed through academic study. As important as this kind of

14. Ellen Charry makes the case for a particular kind of pedagogy in conversation with past Christian thinkers: "The church is responsible for providing mentors and guides for less experienced Christians. . . . Indeed, the church should take a pedagogical lesson from God, who, as Augustine pointed out, first had to assure us of how much he loves us before we could allow him to teach us" (*By the Renewing of Your Minds* [Oxford: Oxford University Press, 1997], p. 243).

15. David F. Ford and Graham Stanton, "Introduction," in Ford and Stanton, eds., *Reading Texts, Seeking Wisdom* (Grand Rapids: Eerdmans, 2003), pp. 2-3.

preparation is, it is no substitute for the actual practice of reading texts in the context of challenging circumstances, in which being faithful to God can come at great cost and require both risk and courage.[16]

We stress the location and circumstances of theological readings because these factors rarely are taken with appropriate seriousness in talk of biblical hermeneutics. Often, Scripture is read theologically in the context of a classroom or a church, but such readings are characterized by "conditions of distance." The latter phrase is employed to suggest that the Bible is approached at arm's length, with cool objectivity and a "healthy" sense of detachment. This is a mode of reading that stems from a particular mindset, one that demonstrates Eurocentric qualities. We have noted that the critical turn in hermeneutics has helped curb these tendencies, but the worry of "bias" continues to be a strong one in the culture at large; thus, a text's reading is often still governed by the kind of neutrality that is fostered in other forms of intellectual and scientific inquiry.

What we are proposing is a form of reading in which all participants bring to the table of deliberative scriptural interpretation their experiences, hardships, and joys as vital features of the hermeneutical process. In this sense, wise readers of Scripture need not be simply those who went to seminary or received formal training, though of course such people are welcomed to the table. But others should be welcomed as well. Readers must be united in this single task by both the commitment to Scripture as Holy Word, and the desire to see how it intersects with the variety of situations and circumstances in which we find ourselves. Readers must become a group of disciples, attuned to God's presence and to the work of healing and repair. The goal here is not to apply Scripture in some instrumentalized and accommodating way; rather, the aim is to see, patiently and imaginatively, how Scripture and lived life can inflect and condition one another within the practice of Christian discipleship. Wise readers of Scripture will not simply give up on a text because it appears on first blush to be irredeemable, but will go on to construe, prayerfully and meditatively, the intersections between the biblical story and their story, uncovering not simply a hermeneutical outlook, but a beautiful (and so desirable and imitable) life and ethos as a result.[17] For such an outcome to be available, all kinds of people

16. This point simply affirms the claim made by Stephen E. Fowl and L. Gregory Jones early on in their generative work: "The vocation of Christians is to *embody* Scripture in the various contexts in which they find themselves" (*Reading in Communion* [Eugene: Wipf and Stock, 1998], p. 1, emphasis theirs).

17. These proposals go along with A. K. M. Adam's account of biblical theology as a signifying practice; see "Poaching on Zion," in A. K. M. Adam, et al., *Reading Scripture with the Church* (Grand Rapids: Baker Academic, 2006), pp. 17-34.

from a variety of contexts and experiences should openly, critically, and constructively engage the text under the rubric of this common goal of discipleship.

Ultimately, the difficulty we find with Moughtin-Mumby's claim — that the differences in camps rest on varying approaches to metaphor — is that the observation operates out of the bifurcation between theory and praxis. What readers of Scripture require is not so much agreement on the ways metaphors work, but to belong to communities of rich experience and diversity that in turn read Scripture theologically with the entirety of their experiences and concerns available so that they have bearings on the hermeneutical task. In this way, theological readings are not simply evaluated on the basis of definitional predeterminations or standards, but also on communal forms of life that themselves show the range of possibilities and limits in the reading of challenging texts.

Naturally, different communities will come to different conclusions, but herein lies the challenge of the intentionality surrounding theological interpretation. If one is a part of a homogenous community in terms of gender, race, and class, then obviously the practice of theological interpretation within this context will take shape in a particular way. But if the Bible is "the word of God for the people of God," then obviously God's people are quite diverse along these and other strata. If one is seeking a wise reading of Scripture, then one must attend to this multiplicity within reading communities. Wise practitioners of theological interpretation do not all look and talk the same, nor do they come to the same conclusions regarding a text's meaning or applicability, but they do have the singular aim of seeking God's face at the intersection of the scriptural world and their worlds.[18] Reading Scripture with varied others, hearing their stories, and witnessing their reading practices at work are activities that contribute directly not only to a text's meaning, but also to the formation of communities of wise readers.

Simply put, the faithful reading of Hosea cannot take place among communities marked by a single gender, class, race, or context. The kingdom of God is simply too vast for one particular community to assume that their radical contingency need not influence their reading practices. The practical outcomes are simply too vast across the range of Christian embodiment for such an assumption to remain unchallenged. For instance, a group of men will read Hosea differently from a group of women. A Western community will engage Hosea differently from one in the global South. A context of privilege or of a ruling majority will read Hosea differently from a marginalized community. And a

---

18. Fowl's point of single-minded focus (drawing from Luke 11:34-35) is helpful here, since such a perspective keeps the activity theological while allowing for a multiplicity of readings; see *Engaging Scripture,* chapter 3.

group of recovering abusers will sound out different themes from those who have been abused and traumatized. This is not to say that reading is hopelessly relativistic; after all, these diverse people would be unified by reading the same text.[19] And the goal of reading Hosea is not so much a "right" reading as it is a "faithful" one, with such faithfulness being directed first to God and then to the lived experiences of those among us. Only within such conditions can interpretive self-regulation and accountability be fostered. With varied others at the table, Hosea cannot so easily be employed to promote or sustain misogynistic mindsets and agendas. Given the trust built by being at the same table with the same aim, readers can confront other readers pastorally but decisively when the biblical text is coopted for hurtful purposes.

2) A Humble Community Guided by the Aim of Worship

The kingdom of God is constituted by all kinds of broken people, all of them moving toward God on the basis of past promises and hopeful evidences of realized change. Christians read, come to love, and live by Scripture because they gradually see it as an instrument of God's Spirit to aid them in their healing. For these reasons, rather than securing Scripture's authority simply through a definitional account of inspiration, Christians would do well to think about and read Scripture by attending to its role and work in the life of the church. As such, Scripture can be deemed inspired *because* the Spirit uses it in a myriad of ways, "so that everyone who belongs to God may be proficient, equipped for every good work."[20]

Being "proficient" and "equipped" theological readers means attending to the aim of theological interpretation when reading Hosea, and as we have mentioned several times now, Christians read Hosea in order to encounter the Trinity, to seek and see God's face. However, Christians throughout history have found it difficult to find God's face in the Old Testament, particularly at those moments when the words and actions attributed to YHWH appear at odds with their understanding of Jesus' message and their own contextual sensibilities. Recently, a plethora of books have been written to address this challenge, in part because of the larger cultural pressures that question the viability of religion generally. Because of the wide range of relevant issues and concerns associated with these matters, easy answers are not satisfactory or helpful for the life of

---

19. Westphal is helpful in dispelling the anxiety of relativism within scriptural interpretation in *Whose Community? Which Interpretation?*

20. This issue has repeatedly been sounded in the oeuvre of our colleague Robert Wall.

faith in the long run, and such a prospect at times appears overwhelming as a result.

If we couple the aim of seeing God's face with the theme from the OT that anyone who would see God's face would inevitably die (cf. Exodus 33:20), we are faced with the realization that theological interpretation is an activity that will inevitably be provisional and revisable. A certain form of humility should mark theological interpretation, in part simply because of its lofty aims. The species of humility in question here, however, is not simply one marked by the limits of broken human beings (as important as those factors are), but also by the splendor of the Trinity. God's glory invites us to maintain an ongoing and adaptable disposition, one that is disposed to alter metaphors, ways of speaking, and forms of address when referencing the triune God of Christian confession. A single image or theme is simply inadequate to account for God's beauty and complexity in the life of the worshiping faithful. Both the brokenness of readers and the splendor of the Trinity suggest the need for a robust account of hermeneutical humility. We wish to stress two features of such an account.

First, humility before God and others entails avoiding metaphorical fixation of any kind. In a reluctant sense, we focused one theological chapter of this commentary on the marriage imagery of Hosea, knowing full well that this approach could be taken as feeding into the tendencies by interpreters of Hosea to make chapters 1–3 the key to interpreting the rest of the book. However, we saw no other way of addressing the current state of Hosea's reception than to direct our attention to its most dominant form. Nevertheless, we have striven to emphasize that there is more to Hosea than simply the marriage imagery, and we believe that when communities of faith engage and utilize Hosea in their worship, this variety of imagery should come through in one way or another. Through such a strategy, the richness of Hosean imagery can prevail. We believe this point is important to maintain, for a wise, self-regulating community of interpreters may find it necessary to resist the natural privileging of one metaphor or image in God-talk over others. The marriage imagery is not the only metaphor available in Hosea to illustrate the covenant bond between Trinity and church, nor is it always the most fitting given both the dynamics of Hosea itself and the range of experiences represented within a particular community. Depriviliging metaphors is not necessarily an act of hermeneutical fancy; quite the contrary, it can be a gesture of communally embodied charity.

A second feature of humility that ought to mark a community of wise readers of Scripture is the ability to risk being both deliberative and compassionate in its reading practices. Both deliberation and compassion are expressions of humility, because these activities require a way of tending to one another in which a hierarchical conception of power is questioned. Under this rubric, diverse opinions matter, and individual selves are recognized for the God-given dignity they retain, regardless of circumstances and estimations.

On the one hand, a fellowship can and should be marked by a healthy ethos of debate and reflection. As noted above, Scripture's complexity and richness cannot be subsumed under any one single gaze or approach, but require deliberation and conversation of varying kinds. This point is tied to the remarks about the provisionality of faithful reading made above; as Fowl and Jones have opined, "No particular community of believers can be sure of what a faithful interpretation of Scripture will entail in any specific situation until it actually engages in the hard process of conversation, argument, discussion, prayer, and practice."[21] Naturally, part of the difficulty in this process is maintaining a sense of unity and common purpose, despite the varied reading strategies and conclusions that may ensue within a community. But in no way should this sense of commonality be sustained in such a way that other readers are dismissed outright as a result. Common purpose and hegemony are two very different things.

A wise community of interpreters should also aspire to be compassionate. If wisdom is marked by the search for human flourishing, then wise Christian readers of Scripture will seek healing for themselves and others through their reading practices. These practices could take any number of forms, but the aim here is that the word of God actually be *for* the people of God in ways that aid them in their pilgrimage toward blessedness. This process does not mean simply affirming or dismissing all that people are or have experienced. Again, we as Christians are all broken in varying degrees and ways, and we operate out of the assumption that we are continually "on the mend." But the aim here is for a community to be attentive to who they are and where they are located on this journey to see God with the hope that, in the company of God and one another, they can mature and grow to be more whole and to experience increasingly YHWH's shalom.

In our calls for wisdom, humility, deliberation, and compassion, we do not mean to be overly romantic regarding the lived experience of Christian community. We the authors have been part of communities of faith whose characters were marked by significant pain and brokenness, to such a degree that we wondered about the power of the gospel to confront the powers of decay, evil, and brokenness. But we do wish to highlight that reading a book like Hosea as Holy Scripture is a radical moral challenge demanding serious communal commitment. Reading Hosea can quickly serve as a measure of how much trust, hospitality, and mercy exist within a particular fellowship. We believe all Christian fellowships should be challenged in these ways since

---

21. *Reading in Communion*, p. 20.

such is the path of sanctification and wisdom. But such a process is anything but easy; for this, we are communally reliant on the Holy Spirit to help us strive after that understanding and form of life which we may sense at times as beyond our reach, and which is yet a promise of the gospel. We choose to be realistic but also hopeful since our hope is in the Trinity.

We have found it fitting to conclude this theological commentary just as Hosea ends. Our source and end is God, and our lives (including our interpretive practices) can take any number of helpful and difficult forms. To continue with Lim's final remarks, may YHWH help us, through the means of grace that is Hosea, to re/turn to YHWH.

I am like an evergreen cypress; your faithfulness comes from me. Those who are wise understand these things; those who are discerning know them. For the ways of the LORD are right, and the upright walk in them, but transgressors stumble in them.

Bibliography

Abraham, William J., Jason E. Vickers, and Natalie B. Van Kirk, eds. *Canonical Theism: A Proposal for Theology and the Church*. Grand Rapids: Eerdmans, 2008.

Ackerman, Susan. "The Personal Is Political: Covenantal and Affectionate Love ('ĀHĒB, 'AHĂBÂ) in the Hebrew Bible." *Vetus Testamentum* 52 (2002): 437-58.

Ackroyd, Peter R. "Hosea and Jacob." *Vetus Testamentum* 13 (1963): 245-59.

Adam, A. K. M., Stephen E. Fowl, Kevin J. Vanhoozer, and Francis Watson. *Reading Scripture with the Church: Toward a Hermeneutic for Theological Interpretation*. Grand Rapids: Baker Academic, 2006.

Adam, Margaret A. B. "The Perfect Hope: More Than We Can Ask or Imagine." PhD diss., Duke University, 2011.

Alt, Albrecht. *Kleine Schriften zur Geschichte des Volkes Israel*. 2 vols. Munich: C. H. Beck, 1953.

Andersen, Francis I., and David Noel Freedman. *Hosea: A New Translation with Introduction and Commentary*. Anchor Bible 24. New York: Doubleday, 1980.

Augustine. *On Christian Teaching*. Translated by R. P. H. Green. New York: Oxford, 1999.

Bantum, Brian. *Redeeming Mulatto: A Theology of Race and Christian Hybridity*. Waco: Baylor University Press, 2010.

Barré, M. L. "New Light on the Interpretation of Hosea 6:2." *Vetus Testamentum* 28 (1978): 129-41.

Barth, Karl. *Church Dogmatics, I/1*. Translated by G. W. Bromiley. Edinburgh: T & T Clark, 1975.

———. *The Word of God and Theology*. Translated by Amy Marga. London: T & T Clark, 2011.

Barton, John. *The Nature of Biblical Criticism*. Louisville: Westminster John Knox, 2007.

Bauckham, Richard. *Jesus and the God of Israel: God Crucified and Other Studies on the New Testament's Christology of Divine Identity*. Grand Rapids: Eerdmans, 2008.

Baumann, Gerlinde. *Love and Violence: Marriage as Metaphor for the Relationship between YHWH and Israel in the Prophetic Books*. Translated by L. M. Maloney. Collegeville: Liturgical Press, 2003.

Beale, G. K., and D. A. Carson, eds. *Commentary on the New Testament Use of the Old Testament*. Grand Rapids: Baker Academic, 2007.

Bell, Daniel M., Jr. *Economy of Desire: Christianity and Capitalism in a Postmodern World.* Grand Rapids: Baker Academic, 2012.

Bellah, Robert N., Richard Madsen, William M. Sullivan, Ann Swidler, and Steven M. Tipton. *Habits of the Heart: Individualism and Commitment in American Life.* Berkeley: University of California Press, 1996.

Ben Zvi, Ehud. *Hosea.* Forms of Old Testament Literature 21A. Grand Rapids: Eerdmans, 2005.

———. *Micah.* Forms of Old Testament Literature 21B. Grand Rapids: Eerdmans, 2000.

Bergman, Michael, Michael J. Murray, and Michael C. Rea, eds. *Divine Evil? The Moral Character of the God of Abraham.* Oxford: Oxford University Press, 2011.

Bird, Phyllis A. *Missing Persons and Mistaken Identities: Women and Gender in Ancient Israel.* Overtures to Biblical Theology. Minneapolis: Fortress, 1997.

Blenkinsopp, Joseph. *A History of Prophecy in Israel: From the Settlement in the Land to the Hellenistic Period.* Philadelphia: Westminster, 1983.

———. *A History of Prophecy in Israel.* Rev. and enl. ed. Louisville: Westminster John Knox, 1996.

———. *Isaiah 1–39: A New Translation with Introduction and Commentary.* Anchor Bible 19. New York: Doubleday, 2000.

Bockmuehl, Markus. *Seeing the Word: Refocusing New Testament Study.* Studies in Theological Interpretation. Grand Rapids: Baker Academic, 2006.

Boda, Mark J., and J. G. McConville, eds. *Dictionary of the Old Testament Prophets.* Downers Grove: InterVarsity, 2012.

Bosman, J. P. "The Paradoxical Presence of Exodus 34:6-7 in the Book of the Twelve." *Scriptura* 87 (2004): 233-43.

Boyer, Steven D., and Christopher A. Hall. *The Mystery of God: Theology for Knowing the Unknowable.* Grand Rapids: Baker Academic, 2012.

Bracke, John M. "šûb šebût: A Reappraisal." *Zeitschrift für die alttestamentliche Wissenschaft* 97 (1985): 233-44.

Brady, Christian M. M. *The Rabbinic Targum of Lamentations: Vindicating God.* Leiden: Brill, 2003.

Brenner, Athalya, ed. *A Feminist Companion to the Latter Prophets.* The Feminist Companion to the Bible 8. Sheffield: Sheffield Academic Press, 1995.

Brenner, Athalya, and Fokkelien Van Dijk-Hemmes. *On Gendering Texts: Female and Male Voices in the Hebrew Bible.* Biblical Interpretation. Leiden: Brill, 1996.

Briggs, Richard S. *The Virtuous Reader: Old Testament Narrative and Interpretive Virtue.* Studies in Theological Interpretation. Grand Rapids: Baker Academic, 2010.

Brueggemann, Walter. "The Recovering God of Hosea." *Horizons in Biblical Theology* 30 (2008): 5-20.

Calvin, John. *Institutes of the Christian Religion.* Edited by John T. McNeill. 2 vols. Philadelphia: Westminster, 1960.

Campbell, Ken M., ed. *Marriage and Family in the Biblical World.* Downers Grove: InterVarsity, 2003.

Castelo, Daniel. *The Apathetic God: Exploring the Contemporary Relevance of Divine Impassibility.* Milton Keynes: Paternoster, 2009.

———. *Confessing the Triune God.* Eugene: Cascade, forthcoming.

————. "The Fear of the Lord as Theological Method." *Journal of Theological Interpretation* 2 (2008): 147-60.

————. *Revisioning Pentecostal Ethics — The Epicletic Community.* Cleveland: CPT Press, 2012.

————. "Toward Pentecostal Prolegomena II." *Journal of Pentecostal Theology* 21 (2012): 168-80.

Cathcart, Kevin J., and Robert P. Gordon. *The Targum of the Minor Prophets.* The Aramaic Bible 14. Wilmington: Michael Glazier, 1989.

Chapman, Cynthia R. *The Gendered Language of Warfare in the Israelite-Assyrian Encounter.* Harvard Semitic Monographs 62. Winona Lake: Eisenbrauns, 2004.

Chapman, Stephen B. *The Law and the Prophets.* Forschungen zum Alten Testament 27. Tübingen: Mohr Siebeck, 2000.

Charry, Ellen. *By the Renewing of Your Minds.* Oxford: Oxford University Press, 1997.

Cherlin, Andrew J. *The Marriage-Go-Round: The State of Marriage and the Family in America Today.* New York: Vintage, 2009.

Childs, Brevard S. *The Book of Exodus: A Critical, Theological Commentary.* Old Testament Library. Philadelphia: Westminster, 1974.

————. "Retrospective Reading of the Old Testament Prophets." *Zeitschrift für die alttestamentliche Wissenschaft* 108 (1996): 362-77.

Chung, Youn Ho. *The Sin of the Calf: The Rise of the Bible's Negative Attitude Toward the Golden Calf.* Library of Hebrew Bible/Old Testament Studies 523. New York: T & T Clark International, 2010.

Clark, Dorothy. *Hosea's Bride.* New York: Steeple Hill, 2004.

Clements, Ronald E. *Old Testament Prophecy: From Oracles to Canon.* Louisville: Westminster John Knox, 1996.

Coats, George W., and Burke O. Long, eds. *Canon and Authority: Essays in Old Testament Religion and Theology.* Philadelphia: Fortress, 1977.

Cogan, M., and I. Eph'al, eds. *Ah, Assyria: Studies in Assyrian History and Ancient Near Eastern Historiography Presented to Hayim Tadmor.* Jerusalem: Magnes Press, 1991.

Coontz, Stephanie. *Marriage, a History: How Love Conquered Marriage.* New York: Penguin Books, 2005.

Davies, Graham I. *Hosea.* New Century Bible Commentary. Grand Rapids: Eerdmans, 1992.

————. *Hosea.* Old Testament Guides. Sheffield: JSOT Press, 1993.

Davies, Philip R., ed. *First Person: Essays in Biblical Autobiography.* Biblical Seminar 81. London: Sheffield Academic Press, 2002.

Davis, Ellen F. *Scripture, Culture, and Agriculture: An Agrarian Reading of the Bible.* New York: Cambridge University Press, 2009.

Davis, Ellen F., and Richard B. Hays, eds. *The Art of Reading Scripture.* Grand Rapids: Eerdmans, 2003.

Dawkins, Richard. *The God Delusion.* Boston: Houghton Mifflin, 2006.

Dearman, J. Andrew. *The Book of Hosea.* New International Commentary of the Old Testament. Grand Rapids: Eerdmans, 2010.

————. "YHWH's House: Gender Roles and Metaphors for Israel in Hosea." *Journal of Northwest Semitic Languages* 25 (1999): 97-108.

Dempsey, Carol J. *The Prophets: A Liberation-Critical Reading.* Minneapolis: Fortress, 2000.

Deroche, Michael. "The Reversal of Creation in Hosea." *Vetus Testamentum* 31 (1981): 400-409.

Donne, John. *John Donne: The Complete English Poems*. Edited by A. J. Smith. New York: Penguin, 1996.

Dreyfus, Hubert L. *Being-in-the-World*. Cambridge: MIT Press, 1991.

Eichrodt, Walther. *Theology of the Old Testament*. Translated by J. A. Baker. Vol. 1. Philadelphia: Westminster, 1961.

Eidevall, Göran. *Grapes in the Desert: Metaphors, Models, and Themes in Hosea 4–14*. Coniectanea Biblica: Old Testament Series 43. Stockholm: Almqvist & Wiksell International, 1996.

Emerson, C., ed. *The Dialogic Imagination: Four Essays; Problems of Dostoevsky's Poetics*. Minneapolis: University of Minnesota Press, 1984.

Emerson, Michael O., and Christian Smith. *Divided by Race: Evangelical Religion and the Problem of Race in America*. Oxford: Oxford University Press, 2000.

Emmerson, Grace I. *Hosea: An Israelite Prophet in Judean Perspective*. Journal for the Study of the Old Testament: Supplement Series 28. Sheffield: JSOT Press, 1984.

Ewald, Heinrich. *Commentary on the Prophets of the Old Testament*. Translated by J. F. Smith. Vol. 1. London: Williams and Norgate, 1875.

Fairbairn, Andrew M. *The Place of Christ in Modern Theology*. New York: Charles Scribner's Sons, 1899.

Ferreiro, Alberto, ed. *The Twelve Prophets*. Ancient Christian Commentary on Scripture, Old Testament 14. Downers Grove: InterVarsity, 2003.

Fewell, Danna Nolan, ed. *Reading Between Texts: Intertextuality and the Hebrew Bible*. Louisville: Westminster John Knox, 1992.

Fish, Stanley. *Is There a Text in This Class? The Authority of Interpretive Communities*. Cambridge: Harvard University Press, 1982.

Fishbane, Michael. *Biblical Interpretation in Ancient Israel*. Oxford: Clarendon, 1985.

Ford, David F., and Graham Stanton, eds. *Reading Texts, Seeking Wisdom*. Grand Rapids: Eerdmans, 2003.

Fowl, Stephen E. *Engaging Scripture: A Model for Theological Interpretation*. Malden: Blackwell, 1998.

————. "Texts Don't Have Ideologies." *Biblical Interpretation* 3 (1995): 1-34.

————, ed. *The Theological Interpretation of Scripture: Classic and Contemporary Readings*. Oxford: Blackwell, 1997.

————. *Theological Interpretation of Scripture*. Eugene: Cascade, 2009.

Fowl, Stephen E., and L. Gregory Jones. *Reading in Communion: Scripture and Ethics in Christian Life*. Eugene: Wipf and Stock, 1998.

Freedman, David Noel, ed. *Anchor Bible Dictionary*. 6 vols. New York: Doubleday, 1992.

Fretheim, Terence E. *The Suffering of God: An Old Testament Perspective*. Overtures to Biblical Theology. Philadelphia: Fortress, 1984.

Gadamer, Hans-Georg. *Truth and Method*. 2d and rev. ed. London: Continuum, 2004.

Gentry, Peter J., and Stephen J. Wellum. *Kingdom through Covenant: A Biblical-Theological Understanding of the Covenants*. Wheaton: Crossway, 2012.

Glenny, W. Edward. *Hosea: A Commentary Based on Hosea in Codex Vaticanus*. Leiden: Brill, 2013.

Good, Edwin M. "Hosea 5:8–6:6: An Alternative to Alt." *Journal of Biblical Literature* 85 (1966): 273-86.

Gorman, Michael J. *Elements of Biblical Exegesis: A Basic Guide for Students and Ministers.* Rev. and exp. ed. Peabody: Hendrickson, 2009.

―――. *Reading Revelation Responsibly: Uncivil Worship and Witness.* Eugene: Cascade, 2011.

Gottman, John. *The Marriage Clinic: A Scientifically Based Marital Therapy.* New York: Norton, 1999.

Graham, M. Patrick, William P. Brown, and J. K. Kuan, eds. *History and Interpretation: Essays in Honour of John H. Hayes.* Journal for the Study of the Old Testament: Supplement Series 173. Sheffield: JSOT Press, 1993.

Green, Joel B. *Practicing Theological Interpretation: Engaging Biblical Texts for Faith and Formation.* Grand Rapids: Baker Academic, 2011.

―――. "The (Re)Turn to Theology." *Journal of Theological Interpretation* 1 (2007): 1-3.

Green, Joel B., and Max Turner, eds. *Between Two Horizons: Spanning New Testament Studies and Systematic Theology.* Grand Rapids: Eerdmans, 2000.

Greenberg, Leslie S., and Susan M. Johnson. *Emotionally Focused Therapy for Couples.* New York: Guilford, 1988.

Gurman, Alan S., ed. *Clinical Handbook of Couple Therapy.* 4th ed. New York: Guilford, 2008.

Hahn, Scott W. *Kinship by Covenant: A Canonical Approach to the Fulfillment of God's Saving Promises.* New Haven: Yale University Press, 2009.

Hallo, William W., and K. Lawson Younger, Jr., eds. *Monumental Inscriptions from the Biblical World.* Vol. 2 of *The Context of Scripture.* Leiden: Brill, 2000.

Hart, David Bentley. *The Doors of the Sea: Where Was God in the Tsunami?* Grand Rapids: Eerdmans, 2005.

―――. "No Shadow of Turning: On Divine Impassibility." *Pro Ecclesia* 11 (2002): 184-206.

Hauerwas, Stanley. *A Community of Character: Toward a Constructive Christian Social Ethic.* Notre Dame: University of Notre Dame Press, 1981.

―――. *The Hauerwas Reader.* Edited by J. Berkman and M. Cartwright. Durham: Duke University Press, 2001.

Hayes, Katherine M. *The Earth Mourns: Prophetic Metaphor and Oral Aesthetic.* Boston: Brill, 2002.

Heclo, Hugh. *On Thinking Institutionally.* Boulder: Paradigm, 2008.

Hector, Kevin W. *Theology without Metaphysics: God, Language, and the Spirit of Recognition.* Cambridge: Cambridge University Press, 2011.

Hengel, Martin. *The Septuagint as Christian Scripture: Its Prehistory and the Problem of Its Canon.* Translated by M. E. Biddle. London: T & T Clark, 2002.

Heschel, Abraham J. *The Prophets.* 2 vols. New York: HarperCollins, 1962.

Hill, Andrew E. *Malachi: A New Translation with Introduction and Commentary.* Anchor Bible 25C. New York: Doubleday, 1998.

Hillers, Delbert R. *Treaty-Curses and the Old Testament Prophets.* Biblica et Orientalia 16. Rome: Pontifical Biblical Institute, 1964.

Hoffman, Yair. "A North Israelite Typological Myth and a Judean Historical Tradition: The Exodus in Hosea and Amos." *Vetus Testamentum* 39 (1989): 169-82.

Hubbard, David Allan. *Hosea: An Introduction & Commentary.* Tyndale Old Testament Commentaries 22a. Downers Grove: InterVarsity, 1989.

Hugenberger, Gordon P. *Marriage as a Covenant: Biblical Law and Ethics as Developed from Malachi.* Supplements to Vetus Testamentum 52. Leiden: Brill, 1994.

Instone-Brewer, David. *Divorce and Remarriage in the Bible: The Social and Literary Context.* Grand Rapids: Eerdmans, 2002.

Irvine, Stuart A. "The Threat of Jezreel (Hosea 1:4-5)." *Catholic Biblical Quarterly* 57 (1995): 494-503.

Janzen, J. Gerald. "Metaphor and Reality in Hosea 11." *Semeia* 24 (1982): 7-44.

Jensen, David H. *God, Desire, and a Theology of Human Sexuality.* Louisville: Westminster John Knox, 2013.

Jewett, Robert, and John Shelton Lawrence. *Captain America and the Crusade against Evil: The Dilemma of Zealous Nationalism.* Grand Rapids: Eerdmans, 2003.

Kaminsky, Joel. *Yet I Loved Jacob: Reclaiming the Biblical Concept of Election.* Nashville: Abingdon, 2007.

Kant, Immanuel. *Religion and Rational Theology.* Cambridge Edition of the Works of Immanuel Kant. Translated and edited by Allen Wood and George Di Giovanni. Cambridge: Cambridge University Press, 1996.

Keating, James, and Thomas Joseph White, OP, eds. *Divine Impassibility and the Mystery of Human Suffering.* Grand Rapids: Eerdmans, 2009.

Kelle, Brad E. "Hosea 1-3 in Twentieth-Century Scholarship." *Currents in Biblical Research* 7 (2009): 179-216.

————. *Hosea 2: Metaphor and Rhetoric in Historical Perspective.* Academia Biblica 20. Atlanta: Society of Biblical Literature, 2005.

Kelle, Brad E., and Megan Bishop Moore, eds. *Israel's Prophets and Israel's Past: Essays on the Relationship of Prophetic Texts and Israelite History in Honor of John H. Hayes.* Library of Hebrew Bible/Old Testament Studies 446. New York: T & T Clark, 2006.

Kierkegaard, Søren. *Fear and Trembling/Repetition.* Kierkegaard's Writings VI. Edited and translated by Howard V. Hong and Edna H. Hong. Princeton: Princeton University Press, 1983.

King, Martin Luther, Jr. *A Testament of Hope: The Essential Writings of Martin Luther King, Jr.* Edited by James Melvin Washington. San Francisco: HarperCollins, 1986.

Kitamori, Kazoh. *Theology of the Pain of God.* Richmond: John Knox, 1958.

Knight, George A. F. *Hosea: Introduction and Commentary.* London: SCM Press, 1960.

Kutscher, Eduard Yechezkel. *The Language and Linguistic Background of the Isaiah Scroll.* Leiden: Brill, 1974.

Landy, Francis. "In the Wilderness of Speech: Problems of Metaphor in Hosea." *Biblical Interpretation* 3 (1995): 35-59.

LeCureux, Jason T. *The Thematic Unity of the Book of the Twelve.* Hebrew Bible Monographs 41. Sheffield: Sheffield Phoenix Press, 2012.

Legaspi, Michael C. *The Death of Scripture and the Rise of Biblical Studies.* Oxford Studies in Historical Theology. Oxford: Oxford University Press, 2010.

Levering, Matthew. *Participatory Biblical Exegesis: A Theology of Biblical Interpretation.* Notre Dame: University of Notre Dame Press, 2008.

Liang, Wang-Huei. "Is She Not My Wife, and Am I Not Her Husband?" *Horizons in Biblical Theology* 31 (2009): 1-11.

Lim, Bo H. "Which Version of the Twelve Prophets Should Christians Read? A Case for

Reading the LXX Twelve Prophets." *Journal of Theological Interpretation* 7 (2013): 21-36.

Linafelt, Tod, and Timothy K. Beal, eds. *God in the Fray: A Tribute to Walter Brueggemann.* Minneapolis: Fortress, 1998.

Lohfink, Norbert. "Hate and Love in Osee 9:15." *Catholic Biblical Quarterly* 25 (1963): 417.

Lundbom, Jack R. "Contentious Priests and Contentious People in Hosea 4:1-10." *Vetus Testamentum* 36 (1986): 52-70.

Macintosh, A. A. *A Critical and Exegetical Commentary on Hosea.* International Critical Commentary. Edinburgh: T & T Clark, 1997.

Mays, James L. *Hosea: A Commentary.* Old Testament Library. Louisville: Westminster John Knox, 1969.

———. "Response to Janzen: 'Metaphor and Reality in Hosea 11.'" *Semeia* 24 (1982): 45-51.

McCasland, S. Vernon. "Matthew Twists the Scriptures." *Journal of Biblical Literature* 80 (1961): 143-48.

McComiskey, Thomas Edward, ed. *The Minor Prophets.* Vol 1. Grand Rapids: Baker, 1992.

———. "Prophetic Irony in Hosea 1.4: A Study in the Collocation פקד על and Its Implications for the Fall of Jehu's Dynasty." *Journal for the Study of the Old Testament* 58 (1993): 93-101.

McConville, J. G. *God and Earthly Power: An Old Testament Political Theology, Genesis–Kings.* London: T & T Clark, 2006.

McDonald, L. M., ed. *The Biblical Canon: Its Origin, Transmission, and Authority.* Peabody: Hendrickson, 2007.

McKenzie, J. L. "Divine Passion in Osee." *Catholic Biblical Quarterly* 17 (1955): 287-89.

Menken, Maarten J. J., and Steve Moyise, eds. *The Minor Prophets in the New Testament.* Library of New Testament Studies 377. London: T & T Clark, 2009.

Miller, Vincent J. *Consuming Religion: Christian Faith and Practice in a Consumer Culture.* New York: Continuum, 2003.

Moberly, R. W. L. *The Bible, Theology, and Faith: A Study of Abraham and Jesus.* Cambridge: Cambridge University Press, 2000.

———. "'Interpret the Bible Like Any Other Book'?" *Journal of Theological Interpretation* 4 (2010): 91-110.

———. *The Old Testament of the Old Testament: Patriarchal Narratives and Mosaic Yahwism.* Overtures to Biblical Theology. Minneapolis: Fortress, 1992.

Moltmann, Jürgen. *The Crucified God: The Cross of Christ as the Foundation and Criticism of Christian Theology.* Translated by R. A. Wilson and John Bowden. Minneapolis: Fortress, 1993.

Mondin, Battista. *The Principle of Analogy in Protestant and Catholic Theology.* The Hague: Martinus Nijhoff, 1968.

Moran, William L. "The Ancient Near Eastern Background of the Love of God in Deuteronomy." *Catholic Biblical Quarterly* 25 (1963): 77-87.

Moughtin-Mumby, Sharon. *Sexual and Marital Metaphors in Hosea, Jeremiah, Isaiah and Ezekiel.* Oxford Theological Monographs. Oxford: Oxford University Press, 2008.

Newsom, Carol A. "Bakhtin, the Bible, and Dialogic Truth." *Journal of Religion* 76 (1996): 290-306.

Nicholson, Ernest W. *God and His People: Covenant and Theology in the Old Testament.* Oxford: Clarendon Press, 1986.

Nissinen, Martti. *Prophetie, Redaktion und Fortschreibung im Hoseabuch: Studien zum Werdegang eines Prophetenbuches im Lichte von Hos 4 und 11*. Alter Orient und Altes Testament 231. Neukirchen: Neukirchener Verlag, 1991.

Nissinen, Martti, C. L. Seow, and Robert K. Ritner. *Prophets and Prophecy in the Ancient Near East*. Atlanta: Society of Biblical Literature, 2003.

Nogalski, James D. *Literary Precursors to the Book of the Twelve*. Beihefte zur Zeitschrift für die alttestamentliche Wissenschaft 217. Berlin: Walter de Gruyter, 1993.

————. *Redactional Processes in the Book of the Twelve*. Beihefte zur Zeitschrift für die alttestamentliche Wissenschaft 218. Berlin: Walter de Gruyter, 1993.

Nogalski, James D., and Marvin A. Sweeney, eds. *Reading and Hearing the Book of the Twelve*. Society of Biblical Literature Symposium Series 15. Atlanta: Society of Biblical Literature, 2000.

Norton, Gerard J., and Stephen Pisano, eds. *Tradition of the Text: Studies Offered to Dominique Barthélemy in Celebration of His 70th Birthday*. Orbis Biblicus et Orientalis 109. Freiburg: Universitätsverlag Freiburg Schweiz, 1991.

Norton, Jonathan D. H. *Contours in the Text: Textual Variation in the Writings of Paul, Josephus and the Yaḥad*. Library of New Testament Studies 430. London: T & T Clark International, 2011.

O'Brien, Julia M. *Challenging Prophetic Metaphor: Theology and Ideology in the Prophets*. Louisville: Westminster John Knox, 2008.

Odell, Margaret S. "Who Were the Prophets in Hosea?" *Horizons in Biblical Theology* 18 (1996): 78-95.

Oden, Robert A., Jr. *The Bible Without Theology: The Theological Tradition and Alternatives to It*. San Francisco: Harper & Row, 1987.

Paris, Jenell Williams. *The End of Sexual Identity: Why Sex Is Too Important to Define Who We Are*. Downers Grove: InterVarsity, 2011.

Parpola, Simo. *Assyrian Prophecies*. State Archives of Assyria 9. Helsinki: Helsinki University Press, 1997.

Parpola, Simo, and Kazuko Watanabe. *Neo-Assyrian Treaties and Loyalty Oaths*. Helsinki: Helsinki University Press, 1988.

Paul, Shalom M. "The Image of the Oven and the Cake in Hosea 7:4-10." *Vetus Testamentum* 18 (1968): 114-20.

Pentiuc, Eugen J. *Long-Suffering Love: A Commentary on Hosea with Patristic Annotations*. Brookline: Holy Cross Orthodox Press, 2002.

Perdue, Leo G., Brandon Scott, and William Johnston Wiseman, eds. *In Search of Wisdom: Essays in Memory of John G. Gammie*. Louisville: Westminster John Knox, 1993.

Petersen, David L. *Zechariah 9–14 and Malachi: A Commentary*. Old Testament Library. Louisville: Westminster John Knox, 1995.

Phelan, Gerald B. *Saint Thomas and Analogy*. Milwaukee: Marquette University Press, 1941.

Philo. *The Works of Philo*. Translated by C. D. Yonge. Peabody: Hendrickson, 1993.

Pietersma, Albert, and Benjamin G. Wright, eds. *A New English Translation of the Septuagint*. New York: Oxford University Press, 2007.

Pinnock, Clark H. *Most Moved Mover: A Theology of God's Openness*. Grand Rapids: Baker Academic, 2001.

Placher, William C. *Narratives of a Vulnerable God: Christ, Theology, and Scripture*. Louisville: Westminster John Knox, 1994.

Pseudo-Dionysius. *The Mystical Theology and The Divine Names.* Translated by C. E. Rolt. Mineola: Dover, 2004.

Rad, Gerhard von. *Genesis.* Rev. ed. Translated by John Marks. Philadelphia: Westminster, 1972.

Redditt, Paul L., and Aaron Schart, eds. *Thematic Threads in the Book of the Twelve.* Beihefte zur Zeitschrift für die alttestamentliche Wissenschaft 325. Berlin: Walter de Gruyter, 2003.

Rendtorff, Rolf. *The Covenant Formula: An Exegetical and Theological Investigation.* Translated by M. Kohl. Old Testament Studies. Edinburgh: T & T Clark, 1998.

Renzetti, Claire M., and Raquel Kennedy Bergen, eds. *Violence against Women.* Boulder: Rowman and Littlefield, 2005.

Rivers, Francine. *Redeeming Love.* Chicago: Alabaster, 1997.

Rodd, Cyril S. *Glimpses of a Strange Land: Studies in Old Testament Ethics.* Edinburgh: T & T Clark, 2001.

Rossing, Barbara R. *The Choice between Two Cities: Whore, Bride, and Empire in the Apocalypse.* Harvard Theological Studies 48. Harrisburg: Trinity, 1999.

Rowley, H. H. *Men of God: Studies in Old Testament History and Prophecy.* London: Nelson, 1963.

Russell, Letty M., ed. *Feminist Interpretation of the Bible.* Philadelphia: Westminster, 1985.

Sandoval, Timothy J., and Carleen Mandolfo, eds. *Relating to the Text: Interdisciplinary and Form-Critical Insights on the Bible.* Journal for the Study of the Old Testament: Supplement Series 384. London: T & T Clark, 2003.

Schart, Aaron. *Die Entstehung des Zwölfprophetenbuchs: Neubearbeitungen von Amos im Rahmen schriftenübergreifender Redaktionsprozesse.* Beihefte zur Zeitschrift für die alttestamentliche Wissenschaft 260. Berlin: Walter de Gruyter, 1998.

———. "The First Section of the Book of the Twelve Prophets: Hosea-Joel-Amos." *Interpretation* 61 (2007): 138-52.

Scherer, Klaus R., and Paul Ekman, eds. *Approaches to Emotion.* Hillsdale: Lawrence Erlbaum, 1984.

Schmitt, John J. "The Gender of Ancient Israel." *Journal for the Study of the Old Testament* 26 (1983): 115-25.

———. "The Wife of God in Hosea 2." *Biblical Research* 34 (1989): 5-18.

Searle, John R. *The Construction of Social Reality.* New York: Free Press, 1995.

Seitz, Christopher R. *The Character of Christian Scripture: The Significance of a Two-Testament Bible.* Studies in Theological Interpretation. Grand Rapids: Baker Academic, 2011.

Seow, C. L. "Hosea 14:10 and the Foolish People Motif." *Catholic Biblical Quarterly* 44 (1982): 212-24.

Sheehan, Jonathan. *The Enlightenment Bible: Translation, Scholarship, Culture.* Princeton: Princeton University Press, 2005.

Sheppard, Gerald T. *Wisdom as a Hermeneutical Construct: A Study in the Sapientializing of the Old Testament.* Beihefte zur Zeitschrift für die alttestamentliche Wissenschaft 151. Berlin: Walter de Gruyter, 1980.

Sherwood, Yvonne. *The Prostitute and the Prophet: Hosea's Marriage in Literary-Theoretical Perspective.* Journal for the Study of the Old Testament: Supplement Series 212. Sheffield: Sheffield Academic Press, 1996.

Smith, Christian, and Melinda Lundquist Denton. *Soul Searching: The Religious and Spiritual Lives of American Teenagers*. Oxford: Oxford University Press, 2005.

Smith, James K. A. *Desiring the Kingdom: Worship, Worldview, and Cultural Formation*. Grand Rapids: Baker Academic, 2009.

———. *The Fall of Interpretation: Philosophical Foundations for a Creational Hermeneutic*. 2d ed. Grand Rapids: Baker Academic, 2012.

———. *Thinking in Tongues: Pentecostal Contributions to Christian Philosophy*. Grand Rapids: Eerdmans, 2010.

Soulen, R. Kendall. *The Divine Name(s) and the Holy Trinity: Distinguishing the Voices*. Louisville: Westminster John Knox, 2011.

———. "Theses on YHWH the Triune God." *Modern Theology* 15 (1999): 25-54.

Stienstra, Nelly. *YHWH Is the Husband of His People: Analysis of a Biblical Metaphor with Special Reference to Translation*. Kampen: Kok Pharos, 1993.

Strauss, Richard L. *Living in Love: Secrets from Bible Marriages*. Wheaton: Tyndale, 1978.

Stuart, Douglas K. *Hosea-Jonah*. Word Biblical Commentary 31. Dallas: Word, 1989.

Sweeney, Marvin A. *Isaiah 1–39 with an Introduction to Prophetic Literature*. Forms of the Old Testament Literature 16. Grand Rapids: Eerdmans, 1996.

———. *The Twelve Prophets*. 2 vols. Berit Olam. Collegeville: Liturgical Press, 2000.

Sweeney, Marvin A., and Ehud Ben Zvi, eds. *The Changing Face of Form Criticism for the Twenty-First Century*. Grand Rapids: Eerdmans, 2003.

Tomkins, Silvan S. *Affect Imagery Consciousness*. Vol. 1 of *The Positive Affects*. New York: Springer, 1962.

Torre, Miguel De La. *Reading the Bible from the Margins*. Maryknoll: Orbis, 2002.

Treier, Daniel J. *Introducing Theological Interpretation of Scripture: Recovering a Christian Practice*. Grand Rapids: Baker Academic, 2008.

Trible, Phyllis. *Texts of Terror*. Overtures to Biblical Theology. Philadelphia: Fortress, 1984.

Trotter, James M. *Reading Hosea in Achaemenid Yehud*. Journal for the Study of the Old Testament: Supplement Series 328. Sheffield: Sheffield Academic Press, 2001.

Tucker, Gene M., David L. Petersen, and Robert R. Wilson, eds. *Canon, Theology, and Old Testament Interpretation: Essays in Honor of Brevard S. Childs*. Philadelphia: Fortress, 1988.

Ulrich, Eugene, John W. Wright, Robert P. Carroll and Philip R. Davies, eds. *Priests, Prophets and Scribes: Essays on the Formation and Heritage of Second Temple Judaism in Honour of Joseph Blenkinsopp*. Journal for the Study of the Old Testament: Supplement Series 149. Sheffield: JSOT Press, 1992.

van der Toorn, Karel. *Family Religion in Babylonia, Syria, and Israel: Continuity and Changes in the Forms of Religious Life*. Studies in the History and Culture of the Ancient Near East 7. Leiden: Brill, 1996.

Vanhoozer, Kevin J., ed. *Dictionary for Theological Interpretation of the Bible*. Grand Rapids: Baker Academic, 2005.

———, ed. *Nothing Greater, Nothing Better: Theological Essays on the Love of God*. Grand Rapids: Eerdmans, 2001.

———. *Remythologizing Theology: Divine Action, Passion, and Authorship*. Cambridge: Cambridge University Press, 2010.

Wald, Glen H. Von. *Hosea and Gomer: A Love Story*. Baltimore: PublishAmerica, 2012.

Waltke, Bruce K., and M. O'Connor. *An Introduction to Biblical Hebrew Syntax.* Winona Lake: Eisenbrauns, 1990.

Watts, James W., and Paul R. House, eds., *Forming Prophetic Literature: Essays on Isaiah and the Twelve in Honor of John D. W. Watts.* Journal for the Study of the Old Testament: Supplement Series 235. Sheffield: JSOT Press, 1996.

Webster, John B. *The Domain of the Word: Scripture and Theological Reason.* London: T & T Clark, 2012.

Webster, John B., Kathryn Tanner, and Iain Torrance, eds. *The Oxford Handbook of Systematic Theology.* Oxford: Oxford University Press, 2007.

Wellhausen, Julius. *Prolegomena to the History of Ancient Israel.* Translated by M. Menzies. New York: Meridian, 1957.

Westphal, Merold. *Whose Community? Which Interpretation?* Grand Rapids: Baker Academic, 2009.

White, Douglas. *Forgiveness and Suffering: A Study of Christian Belief.* Cambridge: Cambridge University Press, 1913.

Wijngaards, J. "Death and Resurrection in Covenantal Context (Hos. 6:2)." *Vetus Testamentum* 17 (1967): 226-39.

Wilken, Robert Louis. *The Spirit of Early Christian Thought: Seeking the Face of God.* New Haven: Yale University Press, 2003.

Williams, Lee, Todd M. Edwards, JoEllen Patterson, and Larry Chamow, eds. *Essential Assessment Skills for Couple and Family Therapists.* New York: Guilford, 2011.

Williamson, H. G. M. "Jezreel in the Biblical Texts." *Tel Aviv* 18 (1991): 72-92.

Williamson, Paul R. *Abraham, Israel and the Nations: The Patriarchal Promise and Its Covenantal Development in Genesis.* Sheffield: Sheffield Academic Press, 2000.

———. *Sealed with an Oath: Covenant in God's Unfolding Purpose.* Downers Grove: InterVarsity Press, 2007.

Witte, John, Jr., and Eliza Ellison, eds. *Covenant Marriage in Comparative Perspective.* Grand Rapids: Eerdmans, 2005.

Wöhrle, Jakob. "'No Future for the Proud Exultant Ones': The Exilic Book of the Four Prophets (Hos., Am., Mic., Zeph.) as a Concept Opposed to the Deuteronomistic History." *Vetus Testamentum* 58 (2008): 608-27.

Wolff, Hans Walter. *Hosea.* Translated by G. Stansell. Hermeneia. Philadelphia: Fortress, 1974.

Wolterstorff, Nicholas. *Divine Discourse: Philosophical Reflections on the Claim that God Speaks.* Cambridge: Cambridge University Press, 1995.

Wright, N. T. *The New Testament and the People of God: Christian Origins and the Question of God.* Vol. 1. Minneapolis: Fortress, 1992.

Yee, Gale A. "The Book of Hosea: Introduction, Commentary, and Reflections." Pages 195-297 in vol. 7 of *The New Interpreter's Bible.* Edited by L. E. Keck. Nashville: Abingdon, 1996.

———. *Composition and Tradition in the Book of Hosea: A Redactional Critical Investigation.* Society of Biblical Literature Dissertation Series 102. Atlanta: Scholars Press, 1987.

Yoo, Yoon Jong. "Israelian Hebrew in the Book of Hosea." PhD diss., Cornell University, 1999.

General Index

Scripture Index